THE DIVINE ROMANCE

PARAMAHANSA YOGANANDA
(January 5, 1893—March 7, 1952)

THE DIVINE ROMANCE

by

Paramahansa Yogananda

SELF-REALIZATION FELLOWSHIP
Founded by Paramahansa Yogananda

Copyright © 1986 Self-Realization Fellowship

Material previously published
Copyright © 1972, 1973, 1974, 1975,
1976, 1977, 1978, 1979, 1980, 1981, 1982
1983, 1984, 1985, 1986 Self-Realization Fellowship

First printing, 1986

All rights in this book are reserved. Except for quotations in book reviews, no part of *The Divine Romance* may be reproduced in any form without written permission from the publisher: Self-Realization
Fellowship, 3880 San Rafael Avenue, Los Angeles,
California 90065, U.S.A.

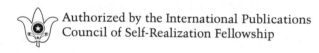 Authorized by the International Publications
Council of Self-Realization Fellowship

Self-Realization Fellowship was founded in 1920 by
Paramahansa Yogananda as the instrument for the
worldwide dissemination of his teachings. The
reader can be certain of the authenticity of writings
and recordings by or about Paramahansa Yogananda
and his teachings if the registered Self-Realization
emblem, and/or the statement of authorization
(shown together above), appears on that work.

Library of Congress Catalog Number: 86-063172
ISBN 0-87612-240-3

Printed in the United States of America

10631–54321

Dedicated by Self-Realization Fellowship
to our beloved president,
SRI DAYA MATA
whose faithful devotion to recording the
words of her guru for posterity has
preserved for us and for the ages the
liberating wisdom and God-love
of Paramahansa Yogananda

PUBLISHER'S NOTE

Since Paramahansa Yogananda's *Autobiography of a Yogi* was first published in 1946, his writings have received recognition in all parts of the world—from the literary and general public as well as from his followers. It is therefore not surprising that there are now a number of other publishers, organizations, and individuals claiming to represent his teachings. Some are borrowing the name of this beloved world teacher to further their own societies or interests, or to gain recognition for themselves. Others are presenting what is purported to be his "original" teachings, but what is in fact material taken from publications that had been poorly edited by temporary helpers or compiled from incomplete notes taken during Paramahansa Yogananda's classes. The Guru was very dissatisfied with the presentation of this material, and later did much work on it and gave specific instructions for its correction and clarification.

Readers sometimes inquire how they can be sure that a publication accurately presents the life and teachings of Sri Yogananda. In response to these inquiries, we would like to explain that Paramahansa Yogananda founded Self-Realization Fellowship in 1920 to be the instrument for worldwide dissemination of his teachings. He personally chose and trained those close disciples who constitute the Self-Realization Fellowship Publications Council, giving them specific guidelines for the publishing of his writings, lectures, and *Self-Realization Lessons*. The presence in a publication of the emblem shown above, or the statement, "Authorized by the International Publications Council of Self-Realization Fellowship," assures the reader of the authenticity of that work.

SELF-REALIZATION FELLOWSHIP

CONTENTS

ILLUSTRATIONS

Cover: Paramahansa Yogananda in Encinitas, 1938

PREFACE

The following was written by Sri Daya Mata, spiritual head and president of Self-Realization Fellowship/Yogoda Satsanga Society of India, to introduce the first published volume of lectures and informal talks by Paramahansa Yogananda, Man's Eternal Quest.

The first time I beheld Paramahansa Yogananda, he was speaking before a vast, enraptured audience in Salt Lake City. The year was 1931. As I stood at the back of the crowded auditorium, I became transfixed, unaware of anything around me except the speaker and his words. My whole being was absorbed in the wisdom and divine love that were pouring into my soul and flooding my heart and mind. I could only think, "This man loves God as I have always longed to love Him. He *knows* God. Him I shall follow." And from that moment, I did.

As I felt the transfiguring power of his words on my own life during those early days with Paramahansaji, there arose within me a feeling of the urgent need to preserve his words for all the world, for all time. It became my sacred and joyous privilege, during the many years I was with Paramahansa Yogananda, to record his lectures and classes, and also many informal talks and words of personal counsel — truly a vast treasurehouse of wondrous wisdom and God-love. As Gurudeva spoke, the rush of his inspiration was often reflected in the swiftness of his speech; he might speak without pause for minutes at a time, and continue for an hour. While his hearers sat enthralled, my pen was flying! As I took down his words in shorthand, it was as though a special grace had descended, instantly translating the Guru's voice into the shorthand characters on the page. Their transcription has been a blessed task that continues to this day. Even after such a long time — some of my notes are more than forty years old — when I start to transcribe them, they are miraculously fresh in my mind, as though they had been recorded yesterday. I can even hear inwardly the inflections of Gurudeva's voice in each particular phrase.

The Master seldom made even the slightest preparation for his lectures; if he prepared anything at all, it might consist of a factual note or two, hastily jotted down. Very often, while riding in the car on the way to the temple, he would casually ask one of us: "What is my subject today?" He would put his mind on it, and then give the lecture extemporaneously from an inner reservoir of divine inspiration.

The subjects for Gurudeva's sermons at the temples were set and announced in advance. But sometimes his mind was working in an entirely different vein when he began to speak. Regardless of the "subject for today," the Master would voice the truths engrossing his consciousness at that moment, pouring forth priceless wisdom in a steady stream from the abundance of his own spiritual experience and intuitive perception. Nearly always, at the close of such a service, a number of people would come forward to thank him for having enlightened them on a problem that had been troubling them, or perhaps for having explained some philosophical concept in which they were particularly interested.

Sometimes, while he was lecturing, the Guru's consciousness would be so uplifted that he would momentarily forget the audience and converse directly with God; his whole being would be overflowing with divine joy and intoxicating love. In these high states of consciousness, his mind completely at one with the Divine Consciousness, he inwardly perceived Truth, and described what he saw. On occasion, God appeared to him as the Divine Mother, or in some other aspect; or one of our great Gurus, or other saints, would manifest in vision before him. At such times, even the audience would feel deeply the special blessing bestowed on all present. During such a visitation of Saint Francis of Assisi, whom Gurudeva deeply loved, the Master was inspired to compose the beautiful poem, "God! God! God!"

The Bhagavad Gita describes an enlightened master in these words: "The Self shines forth like a sun in those who have banished ignorance by wisdom" (V:16). One might have been overawed by Paramahansa Yogananda's spiritual radiance, were it not for his warmth and naturalness, and a quiet humility, which put everyone instantly at ease. Each person in the audience felt that Gurudeva's talk was addressed to him personally. Not the least of the Master's endearing qualities was his understanding sense of humor. By some choice phrase, gesture, or facial expression he would bring forth an appreciative response of hearty laughter at just the right moment to drive home a point, or to relax his listeners after long and intense concentration on a particularly deep subject.

One cannot convey in the pages of a book the uniqueness and universality of Paramahansa Yogananda's vivid, loving personality. But it is my humble hope, in giving this brief background, to afford a personal glimpse that will enrich the reader's enjoyment and appreciation of the talks presented in this book.

To have seen my Gurudeva in divine communion; to have heard the profound truths and devotional outpourings of his soul; to have recorded them for the ages; and now to share them with all—what joy is mine! May the Master's sublime words open wider the doors to unshakable faith in God, to deeper love for that One who is our beloved Father, Mother, and Eternal Friend.

DAYA MATA

Los Angeles, California
May 1975

For a blessed half-century and more I have been humbly privileged to participate in and witness the growth of the *Kriya Yoga* mission of Paramahansa Yogananda. I have seen the fire of love for God that emanated from his being and ignited my heart similarly kindle divine love in countless other hearts, bestowing the blessing of its transforming light. So it is with deep satisfaction and joy that Self-Realization Fellowship presents *The Divine Romance,* a long-awaited companion volume to *Man's Eternal Quest.*

"The romance with God is perfect and everlasting," Guru-

deva once said. In Paramahansaji the glory and sweetness of
that eternal relationship with the Divine was fully expressed.
These years of endeavoring to follow his example—living by
the ideals and practicing the precepts he taught—have brought
an answer to every longing of my heart. The promise of that
first thrill of divine love that spread through my soul has been
fulfilled beyond all possible expectation.

Paramahansaji's one desire was to help others experience
God as a conscious reality in their lives. Often he wept tears of
compassion for all of God's children, praying to the Lord from
the depths of his soul, "May I be able to awaken Thy love in all
hearts." Divine love is the answer—the only answer—that can
permanently remove the ache of emptiness from every heart,
and cauterize and heal all wounds of division, hatred, and
nonunderstanding that have sundered the peace and unity of
this beautiful world created by God. May the flame of that
divine love reach out from the pages of this volume in fulfillment of Paramahansaji's fervent prayer, awakening the love of
God in every heart it touches.

Daya Mata

Los Angeles, California
November 19, 1986

INTRODUCTION

*The greatest romance you can have is the romance
with God....He is the Lover and our souls are the beloved,
and when the soul meets the greatest lover of the universe,
then the eternal romance begins.*

—Paramahansa Yogananda

The Divine Romance is a volume of talks by Paramahansa
Yogananda, one whose life was a continual romance with the
Divine. It is thus a book about God's love for each soul created
by Him, and how we as incarnate souls can experience God's
loving presence in our lives.

The author's message holds universal appeal, for what
human being has never yearned for perfect love—a love that
does not fade with time, old age, or death? Certainly everyone
has longed to experience the lasting satisfaction and perfection
of such a relationship, but the question has always been, "Is it
really possible?" Paramahansa Yogananda boldly declares that
it *is* possible. Through the example of his life and teaching, he
proves that the inner fulfillment and love we seek *does* exist
and *can* be attained — in God. "The greatest love you can
experience is in communion with God," he states, in the opening lecture of *The Divine Romance*. "The love between the soul
and Spirit is the perfect love, the love you are all seeking."

Paramahansaji does not speak from mere theory or theology; his words flow from experience of the love and wisdom of
God, providing an inspirational and pragmatic approach, that
"those who have ears to hear" may also discover this all-
fulfilling Divine Presence in their own lives. His wisdom is not
the studied learning of a scholar; it is the empirical testimony
of a dynamic spiritual personage whose life was filled with
inner joy and outer accomplishment, a world teacher who lived
what he taught, a *Premavatar* (incarnation of love) whose sole
desire was to share God's wisdom and love with all.

Paramahansa Yogananda was born in Gorakhpur, India, on January 5, 1893. He had a remarkable childhood that clearly indicated his life was marked for a divine destiny. His mother recognized this and encouraged his noble ideals and spiritual aspirations. When he was only eleven, the loss of his mother, whom he loved above all else in this world, made firm his inherent resolve to find God and to receive from the Creator Himself the divine love yearned for in every human heart.

Yoganandaji soon became a disciple of one of a line of exalted gurus with whom he had been linked from birth: the great *Jnanavatar* (incarnation of wisdom) Swami Sri Yukteswar Giri. Sri Yogananda's parents were disciples of Lahiri Mahasaya, guru of Sri Yukteswar. When Paramahansaji was an infant in his mother's arms, Lahiri Mahasaya had blessed him and foretold: "Little mother, thy son will be a yogi. As a spiritual engine, he will carry many souls to God's kingdom." Lahiri Mahasaya was a disciple of Mahavatar Babaji, the deathless master who revived in this age the ancient science of *Kriya Yoga*. Praised by Krishna in the Bhagavad Gita, and by Patanjali in the *Yoga Sutras, Kriya Yoga* is both a transcendent technique of meditation and an art of living that leads to union of the soul with God. Mahavatar Babaji revealed the sacred *Kriya* to Lahiri Mahasaya, who handed it down to Sri Yukteswar, who taught it to Paramahansa Yogananda.

When in 1920 Paramahansa Yogananda was deemed ready to begin his world mission of disseminating the soul-liberating science of Yoga, Mahavatar Babaji told him of the sacred responsibility that was to be his: "You are the one I have chosen to spread the message of *Kriya Yoga* in the West. Long ago I met your guru Yukteswar at a *Kumbha Mela;* I told him then I would send you to him for training. *Kriya Yoga*, the scientific technique of God-realization, will ultimately spread in all lands, and aid in harmonizing the nations through man's personal, transcendental perception of the Infinite Father."

Paramahansa Yogananda began his mission in America as a delegate to the International Congress of Religious Liberals in Boston in 1920. For more than a decade he traveled the length and breadth of America, speaking almost daily to capacity audiences in all the major cities. On January 23, 1924, the *Los*

THE DIVINE ROMANCE

How to Cultivate Divine Love

Self-Realization Fellowship Temple, Hollywood, California,
October 10, 1943

The world as a whole has forgotten the real meaning of the word *love*. Love has been so abused and crucified by man that very few people know what true love is. Just as oil is present in every part of the olive, so love permeates every part of creation. But to define love is very difficult, for the same reason that words cannot fully describe the flavor of an orange. You have to taste the fruit to know its flavor. So with love. All of you have tasted love in some form in your hearts; therefore you know a little about what it is. But you have not understood how to develop love, how to purify and expand it into divine love. A spark of this divine love exists in most hearts in the beginning of life, but is usually lost, because man does not know how to cultivate it.

Many people wouldn't think it even necessary to analyze what love is. They recognize love as the feeling they have for their relatives, friends, and others to whom they are strongly attracted. But there is much more to it than that. The only way I can describe real love to you is to tell you its effect. If you could feel even a particle of divine love, so great would be your joy—so overpowering—you could not contain it.

Think deeply about what I am telling you. The satisfaction of love is not in the feeling itself, but in the joy that feeling brings. Love gives joy. We love love because it gives us such intoxicating happiness. So love is not the ultimate; the ultimate is bliss. God is *Sat-Chit-Ananda*, ever-existing, ever-conscious, ever-new Bliss. We, as soul, are individualized *Sat-Chit-Ananda*. "From Joy we have come, in Joy we live and have our being, and in that sacred Joy we will one day melt again."* All the divine emotions—love, compassion, courage, self-sacrifice, humility—

---

* Taittiriya Upanishad 3–6–1.

would be meaningless without joy. Joy means exhilaration, an expression of the ultimate Bliss.

Man's experience of joy originates in the brain, in the subtle center of God-consciousness that the yogis call the *sahasrara*, or thousand-petaled lotus. Yet the actual feeling of joy is experienced not in the head but in the heart. From the divine seat of God-consciousness in the brain, joy descends into the heart center,* and manifests there. That joy comes from God's bliss— the essential and ultimate attribute of Spirit.

Though joy may be born in conjunction with certain outer conditions, it is not subject to conditions; it often manifests without any material cause. Sometimes you wake up in the morning "walking on air" with joy, and you don't know why. And when you sit in the silence of deep meditation, joy bubbles up from within, roused by no outer stimulus. The joy of meditation is overwhelming. Those who have not gone into the silence of true meditation do not know what real joy is.

We feel much happiness in the satisfaction of a desire; but in youth we often feel in the heart a sudden happiness that comes as if from nowhere. Joy expresses itself under certain conditions, but it is not created by those conditions. Thus, when someone receives a thousand dollars and exclaims, "Oh, how happy I am!" the condition of having received a thousand dollars has merely served as a pickax, releasing a fountain of joy from the hidden reservoir of bliss within. So, in human experience, certain events are usually required to bring forth joy, but the joy itself is the perennial native state of the soul. Love also is native to the soul, but love is secondary to joy; there could be no love without joy. Can you think of love without joy? No. Joy attends

---

* The *anahata chakra*, the subtle dorsal center; the seat of feeling; center of control of *vayu*, the vibratory air element, a manifestation of the creative *Aum* vibration. Man's life and consciousness are perpetuated by the power and activity within the "tree of life," the trunk of which is seven subtle centers located in the spine and brain. From these centers comes the power for all man's physiological and psychological functions and abilities. Owing to their common center of origin, some spiritual and psychological experiences are intertwined with physiological processes. For example, there is a definite connection between the physiological function of the heart and the subtle spiritual center of feeling in the heart. Working together, they express the great emotion of love, both human and divine. (See *chakras* in glossary.)

love. When we speak of the misery of unrequited love, we are talking of an unfulfilled longing. The actual experience of love is always accompanied by joy.

The Universal Nature of Love

In the universal sense, love is the divine power of attraction in creation that harmonizes, unites, binds together. It is opposed by the force of repulsion, which is the outgoing cosmic energy that materializes creation from the cosmic consciousness of God. Repulsion keeps all forms in the manifested state through *maya*, the power of delusion that divides, differentiates, and disharmonizes. The attractive force of love counteracts cosmic repulsion to harmonize all creation and ultimately draw it back to God. Those who live in tune with the attractive force of love achieve harmony with nature and their fellow beings, and are attracted to blissful reunion with God.

In this world, love presupposes duality; it springs from a mutual exchange or suggestion of feeling between two or more forms. Even animals express a certain type of love for one another and for their offspring. In many species, when one mate dies, the other usually succumbs soon after. But this love in animals is instinctive; they are not responsible for their love. Human beings, however, have a great deal of conscious self-determination in their exchange of love with others.

In man, love expresses itself in various ways. We find love between man and wife, parent and child, brother and sister, friend and friend, master and servant, guru and disciple — as with Jesus and his disciples and the great masters of India and their *chelas* — and between the devotee and God, soul and Spirit.

Love is a universal emotion; its expressions are distinguished by the nature of the thought through which it moves. Hence, when love passes through the heart of the father, fatherly consciousness translates it into fatherly love. When it passes through the heart of the mother, motherly consciousness translates it into motherly love. When it passes through the heart of the lover, the consciousness of the lover gives that universal love still another quality. It is not the physical instrument, but the consciousness through which the love moves that determines the quality of love expressed. Thus a father may express motherly love, a mother may express friendly love, a lover may express divine love.

Every reflection of love comes from the one Cosmic Love, but when expressed as human love in its various forms, there is always some taint in it. The mother doesn't know why she loves the child; the child knows not why he loves the mother. They do not know whence comes this love they feel for one another. It is the manifestation in them of God's love; and when it is pure and unselfish, it reflects His divine love. Thus, by investigating human love, we can learn something of divine love, for in human love we have glimpses of that love of God's.

Fatherly Love Is Based on Reason

Fatherly love is wisdom-born, and based on reason. Uppermost in the father's consciousness is the thought, "This is my child to take care of and protect." He does this unselfishly, expressing his love by doing things to please and instruct the child as well as providing for its needs. But fatherly love is partly instinctive, as are all forms of familial love; the father cannot help but love the child.

Motherly Love Is Based on Feeling and Is Unconditional

Motherly love is broader. It is based on feeling, rather than on reason. True mother love is unconditional. We can say that in many ways it is more spiritual and therefore greater than most human expressions of love. God implanted in the heart of the mother a love for the child that is unconditional, regardless of the child's merit or behavior. Even if the child in later life becomes a murderer, the mother's love remains steady, unchanged; whereas the father may be more impatient and less inclined to forgive. The unconditional love of the mother is perhaps the human love closest to the perfection of God's love. The true mother forgives her son even when no one else will. That kind of love exemplifies God's love; He forgives His children no matter what sins they have committed. Now who could have placed this love in the mother's heart, save God? In true maternal love God gives us distinct proof that He loves us unconditionally, no matter how wicked we are, or how many times we have sinned.

The Divine Spirit is not a tyrant. He knows He has put us in a world of delusion. He knows we are in trouble; He knows of our struggles. Man only increases the inner darkness of his spiritual ignorance when he thinks of himself as a sinner. It is better for him to try to correct himself, appealing to the Divine Mother for help, beholding in Her the reflection of God's infinite love and forgiveness.

While I was meditating last night, I sang this love song to the Divine:

O Divine Mother, I am Thy little babe, Thy helpless babe, secretly sitting on Thy lap of immortality. I shall steal my way to heaven secreted on Thy lap. In the shelter of Thy lap I shall steal my way to heaven. No karma can touch me, for I am Thy babe, Thy little babe, Thy helpless babe. Secretly on Thy lap I shall steal my way to heaven.

That is the relationship to have with God, for the love of the Mother is the all-forgiving love of the Divine.

Conjugal Love

At its most idealistic, conjugal love can be one of the greatest expressions of human love. Jesus implied this when he said: "For this cause shall a man leave father and mother, and shall cleave to his wife."* When man and woman genuinely and purely love one another, there is complete harmony between them in body, mind, and soul. When their love is expressed in its highest form, it results in a perfect unity. But this love, too, has its flaw; it can be tainted by the abuse of sex, which eclipses divine love. Nature has made the sex impulse very strong so that creation might go on; therefore, sex has its place in the marital relationship between man and woman. But if it becomes the supreme factor in that relationship, love flies out the door and disappears completely; in its place come possessiveness, over-familiarity, and the abuse and loss of friendship and understanding. Though sexual attraction is one of the conditions under which love is born, sex in itself is not love. Sex and love are as far apart as the moon and the sun. It is only when the transmuting quality of true love is uppermost in the relationship that sex

* Matthew 19:5.

becomes a means of expressing love. Those who live too much on the sex plane lose their way and fail to find a satisfying marital relationship. It is by self-control, in which sex is not the ruling emotion, but only incidental to love, that husband and wife can know what real love is. In this modern world, unfortunately, love is too often destroyed by overemphasis on sex experience.

Those who practice a natural—not forced—moderation in their sex life develop other enduring qualities in the husband-wife relationship: friendship, companionship, understanding, mutual love. For example, Madame Amelita Galli-Curci* and her husband, Homer Samuels, are the greatest lovers I have met in the West. Their love is beautiful because they practice these ideals of which I speak. When parted even for a short time, they eagerly look forward to seeing each other again, to being in each other's company, to sharing their thoughts and love. They live for each other.

The relationship between Ella Wheeler Wilcox† and her husband is another beautiful example of conjugal love. Mr. John Larkin, a student of mine who knew them, told me that he had never seen anything like their love. He said, "Each time they met, it was as if they experienced again the joy of the first time. They were utterly devoted to each other. For three years after his death, her constant thought was of reunion with him; then she passed on, his name on her lips."

I met a man of similarly unselfish devotion in this country. He deeply loved his wife, so much so that his love for her became transmuted into divine love. After she died, he wandered for years, seeking a way to find her again. At last he did succeed. In the end, he found God through his love for her. This is the story as he told it to me: In his wanderings after her death, he sought out a great saint in the Himalayas. He persuaded the holy man to promise to give spiritual initiation to him and his wife together. After assuring him of his promise, the saint asked, "Where is

---

* World-renowned soprano (1889-1963) who met Paramahansa Yogananda during his early years in the United States. She and her husband became devoted members of Self-Realization Fellowship. She wrote the foreword to Paramahansaji's book *Whispers from Eternity*. (See page 57.)

† American poet (1850-1919).

your wife?" The husband then told him that she was dead. The saint nevertheless kept his promise to give initiation to the two together. He instructed the man to sit in meditation, and began to invoke the presence of the wife. Suddenly she appeared. For a long time she talked with her husband. Then the two sat together and received initiation from the saint. Afterward, the holy one blessed them, and the wife departed. From that moment, the husband realized that the beloved form he had known as his wife was in reality an individualized manifestation of the consciousness of God—as is every human being. The true meaning of divine love, which is behind and responsible for every ideal human relationship, was revealed to him. His was a unique and true experience.

But conjugal love is tricky, and most people leave this world with an unsatisfied heart. They have not sought marital love in the right way. Attracted mostly by pleasing appearance, they look for their soul mate in a graveyard of beautiful, nicely dressed forms, unmindful that a devil may be housed within. I am not condemning man and woman for responding to the God-created law of attraction; I am condemning the perversion of that attraction through lustfulness. Every man who looks upon a woman as an object of lust, and who abuses woman to satisfy his lust, commits self-destruction: Continued sex-abuse impairs the nervous system and affects the heart, eventually destroying peace and happiness. Mankind must realize that the basic nature of the soul is spiritual. For man and woman to look upon each other only as a means to satisfy lust is to court the destruction of happiness. Slowly, bit by bit, peace of mind will go.

The abuse of sex is comparable to running a car without oil; the body cannot stand it. Each drop of vital essence lost is equivalent to the loss of eight drops of blood. But the important point to remember is to learn self-control. This comes with control and purification of the mind, and is far superior to abstaining outwardly from sex when the mind is yet dwelling on it. Mere suppression can be harmful.

Man and woman should look upon one another as reflections of the Divine. I find it very sweet when a husband calls the wife "Mother," or when she calls him "Father." Every woman should look upon man as a father. My attitude toward woman is as toward a mother. In my eyes she is not merely a woman, but an expression of the Divine Mother. It is Divine Mother I behold speaking to me through woman.

Women should not strive to attract men with "it."* One should always look neat, and it is not wrong to make oneself attractive, if it is done with good taste. But it is wrong to strive purposely to attract the opposite sex through sex appeal. Attraction between man and woman should come from the soul. Those who have sex control and do not flaunt themselves as sex symbols have a much better chance of attracting the right kind of mate. So many young girls have come to me and complained that the boys want sex first or they won't take them out. Sex experience is ruinous to youthful lives. In India, young people never touch or kiss until they are married. Love comes first. That must be the ideal. When two people feel an unconditional attraction for each other, and are ready to sacrifice for one another, they are truly in love. Then only are they ready for an intimate relationship in marriage. Mere possessiveness won't do. When one marriage partner tries to control the other, it shows a lack of real love. But when they express their love in continual thoughtfulness for the true happiness of the other, it becomes divine love. In such a relationship we have a glimpse of the Divine.

Many wives come to me and say, "My husband doesn't want me to become interested in spiritual matters." This is extremely selfish. If the wife is trying to make herself more spiritual, the husband should cooperate with her. He won't lose her; on the contrary, he will receive a part of her virtue. This same principle applies to a woman's attitude toward her husband. The greatest thing a husband or wife can wish for the spouse is spirituality; for soul unfoldment brings out the divine qualities of understanding, patience, thoughtfulness, love. But each should remember that the desire for spiritual growth cannot be forced on the other. Live love yourself, and your goodness will inspire all your loved ones.

After a few years of marriage, thousands of husbands and wives ask themselves, "Where has our love gone?" It has been

---

* At the time, a well-known catchword for sex appeal.

burned on the altar of sex abuse, selfishness, and lack of respect. When these qualities enter the relationship, love turns to ashes. Woman nags man when he strives to enslave her, or when she feels he has neglected her. However, tongue lashing is one of the worst treatments one can inflict on another. It is said that a woman's three-inch tongue can kill a man six feet tall. When man and woman mistreat each other, they destroy forever their happiness together. Man should strive to see the God in woman, and to help her realize her spiritual nature. He should make her feel that she is with him not merely to satisfy his sensual appetite, but as a companion whom he respects and regards as an expression of the Divine. And woman should look upon man in the same way.

Another wrong attitude is fear of the opposite sex; abnormal aversion, like abnormal attraction, is an unhealthy attitude. From my master, Swami Sri Yukteswarji,* I learned to regard woman, not as an instrument created for the entrapment and moral destruction of man, but as a representative of the Divine Mother of the Universe. If and when man begins to look upon woman as a mother symbol, he will find in her a loving protection he has never seen before. Through God's grace, I have been able to change the consciousness of many men and women with this spiritual thought: Every man should look upon woman as a symbol of the Mother of the Universe, and every woman should look upon man as a symbol of the Father of the Universe. When those persons left my presence, they felt that the Divine Mother and the Heavenly Father had spoken through me, because I addressed them from that divine consciousness.

I wonder if there would be any conjugal love at all, if there were no such thing as sex attraction. Ordinary persons would not have the capacity to feel such love, but those who are spiritually developed would, because they are not attracted on the basis of sex. Those who have cultivated their soul qualities know that sex has nothing to do with true love. If you develop the perfect love of your soul, you will begin to get a glimpse of the Divine. Jesus Christ manifested that love, which is pure and grand and wonderful. This love found expression also in the lives of many great saints.

* Paramahansa Yogananda's guru. (See glossary.)

Love Between Master and Servant

The tie of love between master and servant is based on mutual benefit. The more money and kindness given by the master, the more the servant loves him. The greater the service rendered by the servant, the more warmly the master regards him. This can be a relationship of love, but its basic motivation is the security each gives to the other.

Friendship—Grandest Relationship of Human Loves

The relationship that exists between friends is the grandest of human loves. Friendly love is pure, because it is without compulsion. One freely chooses to love his friends; he is not bound by instinct. The love that manifests in friendship can exist between man and woman, woman and woman, man and man. But in the love of friendship, there is no sexual attraction. One must practice celibacy and absolutely forget sex if one wants to know divine love through friendship; then friendship nurtures the cultivation of divine love. Such pure friendship has existed between saints and between others who truly love God. If you once know divine love, you will never part with it, for there is nothing else like it in the whole universe.

Love gives without expecting anything in return. I never think of anyone in terms of what he can do for me. And I never profess love to someone because he has done something for me. If I didn't actually feel love, I wouldn't pretend to give it; and since I feel it, I give it. I learned that sincerity from my Master. There may be some who do not feel friendly toward me, but I am a friend to all, including my enemies; for in my heart I have no enemies.

Love cannot be had for the asking; it comes only as a gift from the heart of another. Be certain of your feeling before you say to anyone, "I love you." Once you give your love, it must be forever. Not because you want to be near that person, but because you want perfection for that soul. To wish for perfection for the loved one, and to feel pure joy in thinking of that soul, is divine love; and that is the love of true friendship.

The Unconditional Divine Friendship of Guru and Disciple

The relationship between guru and disciple is the greatest expression of love in friendship; it is unconditional divine

Paramahansa Yogananda with California's Lt. Governor and Mrs. Goodwin J. Knight, who assisted him at dedication of Self-Realization Fellowship Lake Shrine and Mahatma Gandhi World Peace Memorial, Pacific Palisades, California, August 20, 1950. A portion of the Mahatma's ashes were enshrined in the stone sarcophagus behind the group. The memorial attracts thousands of visitors each year. *(See page 127.)*

During the first fifteen years of his work in America, Paramahansa Yogananda traveled almost ceaselessly in every region of the United States, conducting the largest yoga classes in the world for capacity audiences in dozens of cities. He personally initiated 100,000 students in the unique science of Kriya Yoga, with its definite techniques of God-communion. To ensure the perpetuation of his lifework—the worldwide dissemination of Kriya Yoga—Paramahansaji devoted succeeding years to writing books and preparing lessons for home study, establishing organizational guidelines for his SRF/YSS Society, and developing a monastic order for training those who would carry on his work and preserve its purity.

friendship, based on a shared, singular goal: the desire to love God above all else. The disciple bares his soul to the master, and the master bares his heart to the disciple. There is nothing hidden between them. Even in other noble forms of friendship there is sometimes diplomacy. But the friendship of the guru-disciple relationship is taintless.

I can think of no relationship in this world greater than that which I had with my Master. The guru-disciple relationship is love in its supreme form. I once left his ashram, thinking I could more successfully seek God in the Himalayas. I was mistaken; and I soon knew I had done wrong. Yet when I came back, he treated me as if I had never left. His greeting was so casual; instead of rebuking me, he calmly remarked, "Let us see what we have to eat this morning."

"But Master," I said, "aren't you angry with me for leaving?"

"Why should I be?" he replied. "I do not expect anything from others, so their actions cannot be in opposition to wishes of mine. I would not use you for my own ends; I am happy only in your own true happiness."

When he said that, I fell at his feet and cried, "For the first time there is someone who truly loves me!"

If I had been looking after the business of my earthly father and had run away, Father would have been very angry with me. When I had refused to accept a lucrative position offered to me, he wouldn't speak to me for seven days. He gave me the most sincere fatherly love, but still it was blind. He thought money would make me happy; money would have been the grave of my happiness. Only later, after I had started my school at Ranchi, did Father relent and say, "I am glad you didn't take that job."

But look at my Master's attitude; even though I ran away from the ashram to seek God, his love for me remained unchanged. He didn't even rebuke me. Yet at other times he always told me clearly when I was wrong. He said, "If my love can be bribed to compromise itself, then it is not love. If I have to alter my behavior toward you for fear of your reaction, then my feeling for you is not true love. I must be able to speak to you honestly. You can walk out anytime, but so long as you are with me I will remind you, for your own highest good, when you are going wrong." I had never imagined anyone could be so interested in me. He loved me for myself. He wanted perfection for me. He wanted me to be supremely happy. That was his happiness. He wanted me to know God; to be with the Divine Mother for whom my heart longed.

Was that not divine love he expressed? to wish constantly to guide me in the path of goodness and love? When that love is developed between the guru and disciple, the disciple has no desire to manipulate the master, nor does the master seek control of the disciple. Supreme reason and judgment govern their relationship; there is no love like this. And I tasted of that love from my Master.

God's Love Sublimely Manifest in Bhagavan Krishna

Lord Krishna expressed in his life pure love in its highest form. He has shown to the world that a love without any impurity can exist between man and woman. It is impossible to describe adequately his life for the general public, because it was unique and transcended mundane laws and standards. Someday I hope to put in print the true significance of Krishna's life, for it has been much misunderstood and misinterpreted. His expression of divine love was unique in this world.

Krishna had many women disciples, but one favorite, Radha. Each disciple said to herself, "Krishna loves me more than anyone else." Still, because Krishna often talked of Radha, the others were envious of her. Noticing their jealousy, he wanted to teach them a lesson. So one day Krishna feigned a terrible headache. The anxious disciples expressed their great concern over the Master's distress. At last Krishna said, "The headache will go away if one of you will stand on my head and massage it with your feet." The horrified devotees exclaimed, "We cannot do this. You are God, the Lord of the Universe. It would be highest sacrilege to dare to desecrate your form by touching your sacred head with our feet!"

The Master was pretending an increase of his pain when Radha came on the scene. She ran to her Lord, saying, "What can I do for you?" Krishna made the same request of her that he had made of the other devotees. Radha immediately stood on his head; the Master's "pain" disappeared, and he fell asleep. The other disciples angrily dragged Radha away from the sleeping form.

"We will kill you," they threatened.

"But why?"

"You dare to step on the head of the Master?"

"What of it?" Radha protested. "Did it not free him from his pain?"

"For such a sacrilegious act you will go to the lowest stratum of Hades."

"Oh, is that what you are worrying about?" Radha smiled. "I would gladly live there forever if it would make him happy for a second."

Then they all bowed down to Radha. They understood why Krishna favored her; for Radha alone had no thought for herself, but only for her Lord's comfort.

Nevertheless, because she received much special attention, Radha became filled with pride. So one day the Lord Krishna said to her, "Let us steal away together." He played on her vanity, making her think he wanted to be alone with her. She was feeling very happy and favored. They walked some distance, and Krishna wasn't at all inclined to stop for rest. Finally the weary Radha suggested, "Here is a nice place to sit for a while." Krishna looked disinterested and replied, "Let us find a better spot." They walked and walked. At last the exhausted Radha complained, "I cannot walk any further." Krishna said, "All right, do you want me to carry you?" This very much pleased Radha's vanity. But even as she sprang to his back, lo! Krishna was gone; she fell in a heap on the ground. Her pride shattered, on her knees she humbly cried, "My beloved Lord, I was wrong in wanting to possess and control you. Please forgive me." Krishna reappeared and blessed her. Radha had learned a great lesson that day. It was a grievous error to look upon the Master as an ordinary man, to be ensnared and controlled by feminine wiles. She realized that the Master was interested not in her form, but in her soul.

The Perfect Love Between Soul and Spirit

The greatest love you can experience is in communion with God in meditation. The love between the soul and Spirit is the perfect love, the love you are all seeking. When you meditate, love grows. Millions of thrills pass through your heart. If you learn to control sex attraction and attachment to human beings;

and if you strive to love all and to meditate more deeply, there will come into your life such love as you never dreamed possible. That is the love that Krishna gave, and that Jesus Christ expressed for all of his disciples. It is the love Jesus had for Mary. Martha worked hard for the Master, but her mind was on the chores, not on him; Mary thought more of the Master himself than of her work. Because of Mary's greater love, Jesus said of her, "Mary hath chosen that good part, which shall not be taken away from her."* And on another occasion, when Mary had brought ointment to anoint the feet of Jesus, and Judas said, "Why was not this ointment sold for three hundred pence, and given to the poor?" Christ answered, "The poor always ye have with you; but me ye have not always."† He accepted Mary's devotion, not for himself personally, but for the Spirit within him. And Mary, by anointing Jesus' feet, was expressing her love for God. That Mary thought first to offer her love to Him who is Master of the Universe, and then to others, shows her good judgment. There is no one to whom we owe love more than to God. And there is no love sweeter than the love He gives to those who seek Him.

So why spend all your time pursuing temporary human love? Conjugal, familial, fraternal—all forms of human love have blind alleys. Divine love is the only perfect love. It is God who is playing hide-and-seek in the corridors of hearts, that perchance behind lesser human loves you may find His all-satisfying love.

Therefore love God, not for His gifts, but because He is your own, and because He made you in His image; and you will find Him. If you meditate deeply, a love will come over you such as no human tongue can describe; you will know His divine love, and you will be able to give that pure love to others.

That divine love of God came over me last night. I had only a wink of sleep, so overwhelming it was. In that great flame of love I am beholding you all. Such is the love I feel for you! In your faces I see what is in your hearts.

In the consciousness of one who is immersed in the divine love of God, there is no deception, no narrowness of caste or

* Luke 10:38-42.   † John 12:2-8.

creed, no boundaries of any kind. When you experience that divine love, you will see no difference between flower and beast, between one human being and another. You will commune with all nature, and you will love equally all mankind. Beholding but one race—the children of God, your brothers and sisters in Him —you will say to yourself: "God is my Father. I am part of His vast family of human beings. I love them, for they are all mine. I love, too, my brother sun and my sister moon, and all creatures my Father has created and in whom His life flows."

True love is divine, and divine love is joy. The more you meditate, seeking God with a burning desire, the more you will feel that love in your heart. Then you will know that love is joy, and joy is God.

A New Look at the Origin and Nature of Cosmic Creation

First Self-Realization Fellowship Temple,
Encinitas, California, September 29, 1940*

Today I shall explain the origin and nature of cosmic creation in a new light. The picture I shall give will be different from any you have had from textbooks. It is coming to me from the Infinite as I speak.

All the knowledge there is to be known in every branch of science and art, including the mystery of the atoms and the history of the universe and of human beings, is already existing in the ether as vibrations of truth. These vibrations are all around us, and there is a way to contact them directly. That way is through the all-knowing intuitive power of the soul. To discover any truth, we have only to turn our consciousness inward to the soul, whose omniscience is one with God. When those who are receptive hear someone speak truth, it seems so familiar. Their first reaction is "I thought so!" The mind has simply recognized a truth already known intuitively by the soul.

From that source come all the lectures I give. If I had to read in order to gather facts and ideas for my talks to you, I don't know what I would do! I read very little, because it is not necessary. By the time I get through a few pages of a book, I know from its vibrations whatever truth it contains.†

---

* The first Self-Realization Fellowship temple, built in 1938 on the grounds of the SRF Hermitage in Encinitas, was on a bluff overlooking the Pacific Ocean. It was called the Golden Lotus Temple. Gradual erosion of the shoreline ultimately caused the structure to slip into the sea. Encinitas is still the site of a Self-Realization Ashram Center, the Hermitage, a retreat, and a temple where devotional religious services are held regularly. (See *Encinitas* in glossary.)

† "To the knower of Brahman, all the Vedas are of no more utility than is a reservoir when there is a flood in all directions" (Bhagavad Gita II:46).

Great souls who reveal to mankind deep spiritual truths receive their knowledge through direct attunement with the vibrations of those truths. Also vibrating in the ether are the concepts for every invention man has created, or will create in the future. When an inventor's concentration is right, he is attuned to receive intuitively the idea vibration for the creation of his invention. The discoverers of these ideas may say that they have invented this or that, but they haven't really invented anything. They have only uncovered what was already there: the vibratory blueprint hidden in the ether.[*]

The Beginning of the Cosmic Dream

To create a mental picture of how it was when God caused the universe to come into being, imagine that you are asleep and calmly dreaming of a vast space. Wherever you look, you behold endless space; naught else. You feel it as an infinite, blissful peace, permeated by an omniscient Intelligence. So it was, when that supreme Intelligence began to muse: "Long have I remained thus; alone, very peaceful, absorbed in My own bliss, consciousness, and wisdom. But now I am going to dream a cosmos."

Then this divine Intelligence, which is Spirit, began to create, consciously willing His ideas into being as dream manifestations. He divided His consciousness, differentiating His power from His absolute nature. His consciousness thus became separated into His unmanifest nature as vibrationless Spirit and

---

[*] A well-known example of this phenomenon, recounted in the book *Prodigal Genius*, by John J. O'Neill, is the manner in which the great scientist and inventor Nikola Tesla (1856-1943) "discovered" the principle of the rotating magnetic field—a discovery that made possible his many alternating-current devices and subsequent inventions that form the foundation of today's power and industrial systems. In 1882, while walking with a companion and reciting poetry in a Budapest park at sunset, Tesla suddenly froze into a rigid trance-like state. To his friend's dismay, Tesla soon began to speak of an inner vision: "Watch me. Watch me reverse it," he said, over and over again, in a voice bubbling with enthusiasm. The friend thought he was ill; but the great inventor later explained that he was actually "seeing" an alternating-current motor in operation: "I have solved the problem. Can't you see it right here in front of me, running almost silently?...No more will men be slaves to hard tasks. My motor will set them free, it will do the work of the world." Over the next few months, he continued to elaborate upon the detailed blueprints in his mind, where they remained stored for six years until he was able to put them into practical application.

His manifest nature as cosmic energy, consisting of infinite numbers of different vibratory perceptions or processes of His thought.

We know how thought works. When we think of a horse, we do not see the object of our thought; but if we dream about a horse, we behold its image, because our thought is more condensed. And when we see a horse with our physical eyes, our thought is still more condensed, attuned to the grossest vibrations of God's thought, those which manifest in forms tangible to the senses.

As soon as Spirit started His conscious dream, dividing His intelligence, His power of thought, into many things, the law of duality or *maya* came into being. When by the creation of duality the consciousness of Spirit separated Itself, a portion of that consciousness went out from Spirit as an active intelligent force, restless to express its power. We have many illustrations of this in nature. When a maple seed is put into fertile soil, it begins to germinate, growing and spreading until it assumes the form of a mighty tree. So when the seed of God's consciousness was planted in the soil of activity by His will, it sprouted into a vast creation.

But it must be remembered that God is dreaming it all; that this cosmic creation is nothing more than a dream condensation of God's thoughts. The first differentiation of Spirit was the manifestation of pure thought. Then, projected out of the thought seed of His consciousness, came light, cosmic light. Consciousness and light are the same, except that light is of greater density. The thought of light is finer than the dream of light, in the same way that the thought of fire is purely a mental concept, but the dream of fire is a perceptible image.

After God had willed light into dream existence, He contemplated what He had created. "Well," He thought, "this is not exactly what I want, just light spread all over cosmic space. There should be something more tangible." So He empowered that dream cosmic light to become definite forms. Now here again, do not forget the word *dream* in connection with creation. If you take away the dream concept, you will find this creation hopelessly mystifying.

So God's dream light began to play over the spatial territory of the universe. This light is the tissue of all creation, which God began to think or will into a specific system: the finer light of life force, which I call lifetrons, and a condensation of lifetrons into the grosser atomic light of protons and electrons. God gave these protons and electrons a further strength by which they arranged themselves into atoms and molecules. With a still stronger thought, He caused the atoms and molecules to condense into gases, heat, liquids, and solids—all creations of His thought. The nebulas, or gases, came first. Then He began to dream into those nebulas a very strong force, and He willed: "Let these gases be condensed to produce heat, liquids, and solids." And according to His dream idea, it was so. God had worked out a process of *maya* or delusion by which air, fire, water, and earth would appear to be different, though no difference really existed except in the thoughts of His dreaming consciousness. Then He said: "Let us now begin to enjoy this dream creation of Mine."

The Evolution of Intelligence

God didn't want matter to become something different from Himself, so He had imbued it with a dreaming intelligence which, by a process of evolution, would gradually awaken and realize that matter and mind (the idea vibrations of God) are one. The first expression of this innate intelligence in material creation is the first door through which matter passes to escape from this delusion or *maya* into the freedom of God-consciousness again. Locked in the elements and minerals, intelligence sleeps; so plant life came into being to provide freer expression. Out of scum that formed on the sea, living creatures appeared in the water, and some gradually evolved the capability to live on land. What had looked like inert matter began to take living form.

The weaker forms of life were helpless before aggressive stronger ones, and out of the struggle to survive came the process of evolution to higher, more efficient forms. "Survival of the fittest" seems to us a terrible law, but in the final analysis it is not. The animals that are killing each other are only different manifestations of God's thought. While encased in those forms they do not understand that they are images of mind. But when the little fish has been killed by the big fish, its dream form dissolves back into God's consciousness, and the individualized spark of God within it incarnates in another form of life of higher evolutionary value than that of its previous existence as a fish, giving the soul a greater potential for expression.

So death is the means by which dream matter changes back into the consciousness of God, releasing the soul within it for the next step in its progressive return journey to God. Thus death is a part of the process of salvation. The upward cycle of evolving intelligence in potentially more efficient instruments of expression continues until it reaches the ultimate form in man. Only a human being has the ability to express his innate divinity and to consciously realize God and transcend His *maya* dream.*

Reincarnation Is a Series of Dreams Within a Dream

When you reflect that this world is filled with death, and that your body, too, has to be relinquished, God's plan seems very cruel. You can't imagine that He is merciful. But when you look at the process of death with the eye of wisdom, you see that after all it is merely a thought of God passing through a nightmare of change into blissful freedom in Him again. Saint and sinner alike are given freedom at death, to a greater or lesser degree according to merit. In the Lord's dream astral world†— the land to which souls go at death—they enjoy a freedom such as they never knew during their earthly life. So don't pity the person who is passing through the delusion of death, for in a little while he will be free. Once he gets out of that delusion, he sees that death was not so bad after all. He realizes his mortality was only a dream and rejoices that now no fire can burn him, no water can drown him; he is free and safe.‡

But such is the delusion of desire for material things that,

---

* The human body, with its unique occult centers in the spine and brain (see *chakras* in glossary), was a special creation by God to equip the soul with a vehicle capable of expressing its divine potential.

† The astral world is the subtle sphere or "heaven" behind the gross physical world. (See glossary.)

‡ "No weapon can pierce the soul; no fire can burn it; no water can moisten it; nor can any wind wither it....The soul is immutable, all-permeating, ever calm, and immovable — eternally the same. The soul is said to be imponderable, unmanifested, and unchangeable. Therefore, knowing it to be such, thou shouldst not lament" (Bhagavad Gita II:23-25).

after a time of freedom from the body, he wants to come back to earth. Even though the soul knows that the body is subject to disease and troubles, these delusive desires for earthly experience veil that knowledge and deceive his consciousness. So after a karmically predetermined time in the astral world, he is reborn on earth. When death comes, he goes forth once more from the gross dream of this earth experience to the finer dream of the astral plane, only to be drawn back to this world. And again and again he returns, until he is no longer desirous of an earthly life.

Birth and death are doors through which you pass from one dream to another. All you are doing is going back and forth between this gross dream world and the finer astral dream world; between these two chambers of dream nightmares and dream pleasures.

Thus reincarnation is a series of dreams within a dream: man's individual dreams within the greater dream of God.

Someone is born on earth in France as a powerful king, rules for a time, then dies. He may be reborn in India, and travel in a bullock cart into the forest to meditate. He may next find rebirth in America as a successful businessman; and when he dreams death again, reincarnate perhaps in Tibet as a devotee of Buddha and spend his life in a lamasery. Therefore hate none and be attached to no nationality, for sometimes you are a Hindu, sometimes a Frenchman, sometimes an Englishman, or an American, or a Tibetan. What is the difference? Each existence is a dream within a dream, is it not? Will you continue helplessly to go through all these delusions and the difficulties they create? Each nation thinks its ways are justified, its customs the best. Are you going to go on with this delusion? I am not. For unless wisdom is supreme, reincarnation is a very troublesome experience. One should avoid forced reincarnation because it is a painful continuation of this dream delusion. For how long will you pass through these changes called life and death? Until you realize fully the dream nature of creation, and awaken in God from its nightmares.

Life Is a Dream Unworthy of Our Tears

The more I see of life, the more I realize it is a dream. I have found the greatest assurance in this philosophy I am giving to you now. Realize that you live solely by the grace of God. If He were to withdraw His thought, the physical manifestation would cease to exist. This world is a dream place, and we are all dreaming here. This life is not real; you are laughing and crying in the greatest delusion, and it is not worth shedding tears over. To give reality to our earth experiences is to invite untold misery. By identification of our consciousness with this world we see it as a place of suffering. What is going to free us from suffering? Will money do so? Nothing material can. Knowledge of God, and realization that we are forever one with Him, is the only way to freedom. Remember this always. God would be very cruel indeed if this world were real. But He knows that when we have gone through the furnace of suffering and death enough times, we shall awaken and overcome delusion: we shall realize this earth as His dream, and reincarnate no more. In the Bhagavad Gita God speaks through Krishna, giving this promise: "My noble devotees, attaining the highest success (in the tests of earthly life) by having discovered Me (Spirit), undergo no further rebirths in this abode of grief and transitoriness."*

Suppose a man is struck by a bomb and killed instantly. On the battlefield he was filled with fear; but after death he joyously realizes he is free from fear and from the tomb of the body. One need not go through some ordeal to attain this knowledge. It is better to acquire wisdom through conscious spiritual effort. And if we have to endure trials it should be with the right attitude. Think what Jesus went through as an example to us: He was nailed to the cross and had to pass through that dream of suffering. Yet before his crucifixion he had said: "Destroy this temple, and in three days I will raise it up."† He knew that the body, and the nails with which it was to be held to the cross, and even the process of death were but dreams. Because he realized this, he knew he could recreate life in his dream body again. Isn't that a wonderful way to view the delusion of life and death? It is the only way. Krishna began his revelatory discourse to Arjuna in the Bhagavad Gita with an exhortation to remember the transitory nature of matter and the eternal nature of That which dwells within it.

* VIII:15.   † John 2:19.

We Dream Our Own Limitations

Life teaches you to believe that it is real. You feel you must have your food and sleep every day, that you will die without them. Your habits compel you to eat all kinds of foods that are harmful to you, such as meat, and to smoke and drink, and to think you can't do without these things. We are all crazily dreaming different limitations on our consciousness, and when we slip into the rut of a bad dream of wrong behavior, we have a hard time to pull ourselves out of it. Think how much time and effort you spend catering to the body. And what does it get you? Do you know that the more solicitous you are of your body, the more suffering you will have? If you are too much identified with this dream form, you become hopelessly immersed in delusion.

As soon as you ascribe reality to the dream thoughts out of which God created all things, that dream reality begins to punish you with dream suffering. But when you realize that God is everything in this universe, nothing hurts you anymore. If you realize that both water and the body are dreams of God, you can walk on the water as did Jesus — one dream form can walk on another dream form. There is no longer a barrier of difference between solids and liquids, or any other form of matter. But you have to *realize* this; such power does not come to you by mere imagining.

There are cases in India where people have walked on fire without a single blister. Some of the foremost scientists of England observed one young boy as he walked through twenty-seven feet of fire. A newspaperman who was present thought the fire a fake; he tried the same experiment and was badly burned. The young boy, by certain processes of thought, had convinced his mind of the truth that the fire was nothing but consciousness, and therefore could not harm the body, which was also consciousness.

When you believe that cold weather won't hurt you, you won't be affected by it. But if you feel you are going to catch a cold from the chill, you will. The thing is this: you don't practice mind control. By controlling your mind you can experience the truth that this universe is a delusion. This is why the saints require their disciples to discipline the body and not give it too much attention. The purpose is not to torture the body, but to save the disciple from all the troubles that will beset him if he believes that comfort comes from material things. Comfort comes from the mind. Change your mental attitude and you will not feel discomfort.

It is best to simplify life. I have seen saints in India who eat hardly anything and live under the most rigorous conditions; yet they have wonderfully strong bodies, far better than those of the average well-fed, well-cared-for American. They have trained their minds not to be dependent on externals for health and contentment.

The world trains our minds in a different way. It gets us accustomed to too many things, and then we think we can't be happy without them. Make your life more simple. And simplify the lives of your children as well. If you don't do it, life's experiences will teach them through bitter disillusionment.

Self-Realization is a philosophy of living: right meditation, right thinking, and right living. Bring up your children in this philosophy. Don't pamper them, or teach them by wrong example to cater to their bodies and harmful desires; give them good training. Why enslave them in delusion? Give them true freedom by keeping their lives simple and cultivating in them inner peace and happiness. Do the same with your own life. Don't be bound by anything. That philosophy will save you. If I am sitting in a chair and it breaks, I am not going to be distressed about the broken chair. I will sit in another chair. It makes no difference.

Whenever you are attached to something, that possessiveness deepens your delusion. You will be rudely awakened one day to find that nothing belongs to you. Isn't it silly, therefore, to be attached to things that were never yours in the first place? Your attitude should be that you are looking after these things only for the time being, like a housekeeper who lives in her employer's home and devotedly, loyally, faithfully looks after it, but knows that her own home is elsewhere.

Don't Take Life So Seriously

This world is a terrible place; there is no safety here. But what are we to do? We must stop taking life so seriously. Delusion can be overcome by holding steadfast to one philosophy: Everything here is nothing more than God's motion picture. We are the players. We must play our parts well, but we must not identify ourselves too intensely with the drama. Meditation shows us the way to this inner freedom. It is the only way by which we can realize that this world is a dream, that the Lord has created the entire cosmos out of His thought. So, though He created this dream earth, He has also shown the way to get out of it.

Nothing terrible could happen in this world that we could not duplicate in a nightmare. You have had such experiences. If in a dream you feel your leg crushed under a car, your suffering seems just as real as if your limb were actually injured. But when you wake up, you laugh and say, "Oh, how silly. It was only a nightmare." This is exactly what will happen when you wake up in God. He will shake you out of this nightmare, saying: "What is the matter? You were only dreaming suffering and death." And He will show you reality. That experience He gives ultimately to all mankind. It is wonderful!

God's dream creation was not meant to frighten you, but to prod you to realize finally that it has no reality. So why be afraid of anything? Jesus said: "Is it not written in your law, I said, Ye are gods?"* Yet even Jesus for a little while forgot his immutable divine nature and cried out, "My God, my God, why hast thou forsaken me?"† But quickly he realized again that he was a son of God and could never be destroyed, which he proved by his resurrection. His whole life showed he had risen truly from the sepulcher of delusion.

If you know intellectually that life is a dream, but still have not realized it completely, and still haven't found God either, you are neither in this world nor out of it. That is a sad state. Don't remain trapped in that delusion. Make a supreme effort to get to God. I am speaking practical truth to you, practical sense; and giving you a philosophy that will take away all of your consciousness of hurt. Be afraid of nothing. If death comes, all right. What is going to happen, will happen. Refuse to be intimidated by this dream. Affirm: "I will not be frightened by ill

* John 10:34.   †Mark 15:34.

health, poverty, and accidents. Bless me, O Lord, that when You put me through trials, I realize their delusive nature and become victorious over them by positive action and by remaining inwardly united to You."

In Meditation Delusive Dreams Vanish

Meditation is the effort to realize and express that pure consciousness which is the reflection, or image, of God within you. Do away with the delusion of body consciousness, and the concomitant demands of body and mind for "unnecessary necessities." Be as simple as you can be; you will be astonished to see how uncomplicated and happy your life can become. So free yourself. Otherwise, death will surprise you and you will painfully learn how attached you are, how unprepared for your departure from this world. But if by right living, right thinking, and meditation you can race to the Infinite, the dreams of life and death will vanish in the ever new joy of His eternal Being. Therefore meditation is a dying to the world without dying. This is a new explanation the Lord has given me.

In meditation you do consciously what you do unconsciously every night in sleep. When you look at the body and think of its pains and sorrows, you say, "What is this? Surely I shall wake up and find this is all a bad dream?" The answer comes every night when you sleep: this dream world and this dream body with its pains and aches disappear from the screen of your consciousness. If life were not a dream, you couldn't get away from it even in sleep. Every night your consciousness leaves the body to remind you that you are not the body. And what you experience unconsciously at night in sleep, you can experience consciously in meditation.

Without falling asleep or losing consciousness, keep your mind calm and peaceful in deep meditation—just as it is in dreamless subconscious sleep—and enter the finer world of the superconscious. There the body is forgotten and you enjoy the peace and bliss of your soul, your true Self, and of the soul's oneness with God. In *samadhi* meditation I experience this joyous freedom. And meditation is the way by which you also must strive to rise above delusion and know your true nature. If you can hold on to that consciousness in activity as well as in meditation, remaining undisturbed by delusive experiences, then you will be above this dream world of God's. The dream will be over for you. This is why Lord Krishna stressed that if you want freedom in Spirit, you must be of even mind under all circumstances: "The man who is calm and even-minded during pain and pleasure, the one whom these cannot ruffle, he alone is fit to attain everlastingness."*

Never Become Mentally Ruffled

My master Sri Yukteswar's training in this was wonderful. No matter what happened, he accepted no excuse for my becoming mentally ruffled. I used to go to the ashram and sit at his feet, to meditate and listen to his wisdom. When the time drew near for me to go to catch my train, he would be aware of my mental restlessness, and would just smile at me and say nothing that gave me leave to depart. At first I thought he was very unreasonable. But after a somewhat strained period of this discipline, he explained: "I am not grudging your preparing timely to go to the train; but I say there is no need for you to be restless. Why allow nervous excitement to ruffle the mind? You should be naturally calm when you are with me; and when train time comes, calmly get ready to go." He made me miss several trains until I learned how to be calmly active as well as actively calm.

This you must learn, likewise. Instead of hurrying in a state of emotional excitement to get some place, and then not enjoying it once you arrive because you are restless, try to be more calm. There is no excuse for being restless within. If you are always calm, you will also be more efficient. And if you want to wake up from this cosmic dream world, you *must* practice calmness, no matter what happens. As soon as your mind becomes restless, give it a whack with your will and order it to be calm. Don't make a fuss about anything. Whenever you worry, remember, you are deepening the cosmic delusion within you.

It Is Your Own Dreams That Frighten You

In every form of sense experience you must remind yourself, "It is a dream." There are three dreams that God made

* Bhagavad Gita II:15.

strongest in man: the pleasures of sex, gold, and wine. Don't give too much importance to them. Learn to live moderately, and you will be free. The more you give strength to any one of these, the more it will become a demon to keep you away from God. But nothing can keep you away from God, not even the greatest weakness you have, if you want to be free. Remember that habits are nothing but dreams you have nurtured to enslave you. You think you can't do without drink, but it is the mind that is holding you to the thought of drink. Cut out that thought, and that dream will be over; you will be free. No one keeps you deluded but yourself, and no one but yourself can free you. You have no enemy greater than yourself, and no greater friend. God has given you free choice to keep yourself in delusion or to extricate yourself from it. It is your own dreams that are frightening you.

A man came to Lahiri Mahasaya,* greatly troubled. "I keep seeing the hand of a ghost trying to choke me."

Lahiri Mahasaya said, "You are frightened by your own dream."

"But it is not a dream," the man said. "I see it."

Lahiri Mahasaya said, "Still, it is not real; everything is a dream."

The man believed the Guru's words, and was healed. So should you use your mind to change yourself, to heal yourself. Always affirm: "Nothing can hurt me. Nothing can ruffle me." Realize that you are as good as the best man, as powerful as the strongest man. You must have more faith in yourself. If you make your mind strong, you will be rid of your nightmare.

The Power of the Mind Is Limitless

Miracles performed by great saints may be miracles to us, but not to them. When you know that mind is the power that creates this universe, there is nothing you cannot do. But don't try in the beginning to do "miraculous" things. The mind is everything; but until you have learned how to use its power, it is foolish to reason, "Since all is mind, I will jump off this cliff and

---

* Guru of Paramahansa Yogananda's Guru and great disciple of Babaji, through whom the Mahavatar made known the science of *Kriya Yoga* for the benefit of God-seekers in this age. (See glossary.)

be all right." But whatever you can truly convince the mind you can do, you can do. Since everything is made out of mind, it can be controlled by mind. As you develop more and more mental strength, ultimately you will be able to do anything. The great ones have demonstrated this. Jesus could heal the sick, awaken the dead, turn water into wine. Krishna lifted a whole mountain and suspended it over his devotees to protect them from a destructive storm. These *avatars* proved that all is mind. They didn't merely imagine this, they *knew*, and could say: "I and my Father are one."* And as the Father created all things out of His dream, so can those who are one with Him. That is how the divine ones perform their miracles.

"Know ye not that ye are the temple of God, and that the Spirit of God dwelleth in you?"† If you can clarify and expand your mind through meditation, and receive God in your consciousness, you too will be free from the delusion of disease, limitations, and death. This world was not meant to be a haven of peace, but a place of dreams — nightmares with occasional good dreams — from which we would ultimately awaken and return to our mansion in God.

Only in God Are You Safe From Delusion

So don't be attached to the passing dreams of life. Live for God and God alone. This is the only way to have freedom and safety in this world. Outside of God there is no security; no matter where you go, delusion can attack you. Be free right now. Be a son of God now; realize you are His child, so that you may be rid of this dream of delusion forever. Meditate deeply and faithfully, and one day you will wake up in ecstasy with God and see how foolish it is that people think they are suffering. You and I and they are all pure Spirit. Krishna said: "Of the unreal, there is no existence. Of the real, there is no nonexistence. The final truth of both of these is known by men of wisdom."‡

I could have meetings here with you every day, but that won't necessarily help you, unless you put into practice what you hear. In these Sunday meetings I have perhaps told you more than you would ever learn elsewhere in a lifetime. By coming to these services you will know how the cords of delusion can be

---

* John 10:30.   †I Corinthians 3:16.   ‡ Bhagavad Gita II:16.

broken. Study your *Self-Realization Lessons** at home and practice them faithfully. Each human being has to apply his own
individual effort to get back to God. Anyone who tells you
otherwise is not speaking the truth. God can help you, guru can
help you, but only if you yourself are making the effort to find
God. You can't get money by watching someone else work. You
have to work for it yourself. And only your working at finding
God will take you to God. So make your mightiest effort now.
Reserve your nights for meditation. Meditate with undivided
attention. Let there be no mockery of mechanical prayer. Give
your soul to God. Then you will see that your life — every
minute of it—becomes a magic existence.

* See glossary.

Practicing Religion Scientifically

First Self-Realization Fellowship Temple,
Encinitas, California, February 18, 1940

It is often said that there is a great conflict between science and religion. It is true that scientists look doubtfully at the scriptural statement that 'the heaven and the earth" were created in a matter of days. From their practical studies of the earth and the heavens, they have proved that creation came into being through a slow evolutionary process; and that the progression of earth alone, from gases to matter, plants, animal life, and man, required millions of years. So there is a great deal of difference between the findings of the scientists and a literal interpretation of the scriptural texts.

One of the virtues of the true scientist is that he is open-minded. Working from a little data, he experiments until he uncovers verifiable principles of nature and how they work; then he gives to the world the result of his investigations. And he is willing to consider and to research further any new evidence that comes to light. It is the efforts of such scientists that have resulted in the discovery of all the natural laws that have been harnessed for the benefit of the world today. Gradually we are learning to use these laws in an ever-widening range of practical ways; as for example in the numerous conveniences in our homes.

Scientists Work in Cooperation with God

Scientists are often branded as materially minded because of their questioning of unproved religious beliefs. But God does not condemn them for that. His universal laws operate with impartial justice regardless of man's beliefs. In this sense God is not a respecter of persons but a respecter of law. He has given us free will, and whether we worship Him or not, if we respect His laws, we shall receive the beneficial results of such regard. A doubting scientist might explain his position in this way: "Even if I don't believe in God, I do try to do what is right. If there is a God, He will reward or punish me according to my respect for His laws. And if there is no God, since I am obeying the laws I find to be true, surely I shall receive any benefit therefrom."

So, whether or not they are godless, or making their efforts for material gain, those scientists whose researches are uncovering more and more of God's laws are nonetheless working in cooperation with Him to do some good for the world.

Belief Is Only the First Step

Law governs everything in the universe; yet most people have never tried to apply the scientific law of experimentation and research to test religious doctrines. They simply believe, thinking it impossible to investigate and prove the scriptural texts. "'We have only to believe," they assure themselves and others; and that is to be accepted as all there is to religion. But the Bible tells us that "Faith is the *substance* of things hoped for, the *evidence* of things not seen."* Faith is different from belief, which is only the first step. If I were to tell you that behind this building there is a huge lion, you would probably say, "We don't see how it could be possible!" But if I insisted, "Yes, there is a lion there," you would believe me to the extent that you would go out and investigate. Belief was necessary in order to make you look into it—and if you didn't see the lion, you would say that I had told you a story! Similarly, if I want to persuade you to make a spiritual experiment, you have to believe me before you will carry it out. You can believe, at least, until you prove differently.

Faith, however, cannot be contradicted: it is intuitive conviction of truth, and it cannot be shaken even by contrary evidence. Faith can heal the sick, raise the dead, create new universes. Jesus said, "If ye have faith as a grain of mustard seed, ye shall say unto this mountain, Remove hence to yonder place; and it shall remove; and nothing shall be impossible unto you."†

Science is reasonable, willing to alter its views in the light of new facts. It is skeptical about religion only because it has not experimented in that field; although it is now beginning such research at Harvard. Experimental psychology has greatly ad-

---

* Hebrews 11:1.   † Matthew 17:20.

vanced, and is doing its utmost to understand the inner man. Machines have been invented that can record the different kinds of emotion man experiences; it is said that if one lies while being tested on a polygraph, he usually cannot conceal the fact, no matter how hard he tries.

Self-realization Is Necessary to Experience God

Scientific knowledge is built upon facts. The medical side is fairly well developed, though the causes and cures of certain ailments are yet to be discovered. But what science does know, it is more or less sure about, because the various factors concerned have been tested: theories have been tried and proven. In religion it is different. People are given certain facts or truths and told to believe them. After a little while, when their belief is not fulfilled, doubt creeps in; and then they go from religion to religion trying to find proof. You hear about God in churches and temples; you can read about Him in books; but you can *experience* God only through Self-realization attained by practicing definite scientifc techniques. In India, religion is based upon such scientific methods. Realization is what India specialized in, and those who want to know God should learn her methods; they are not India's sole property. Just as electricity was discovered in the West, and we in India benefit from it; so India has discovered the ways by which God can be known, and the West should profit by them. By experimentation, India has proved the truths in religion. In the future, religion everywhere will be a matter of experimentation; it will not be based solely upon belief.

Millions of people are changing from one church to another without truly believing in their hearts what they have heard about God. They say, "Well, I pray, but most of the time He does not respond." Nevertheless, God is always aware of us. He knows all about us, yet we remain absolutely ignorant of Him. This is the cause of the various kinds of doubts that play upon our minds. If God is, we must be able to know Him. Why should we merely read and hear discussions about Him, and yet know nothing from personal experience?

Yet there is a definite way to experience God. And what is that way? It is scientific experimentation with religious truths.

And put into practice what you believe! It is possible to put religion into practice, to use it as a science that you can prove by experimenting on yourself. The search for Truth is the most marvelous search in the world. Instead of being merely a matter of attending a Sunday service or performing one's *puja*,* religion must have a practical side. Learn how to build your life around spiritual ideals. Without practical application, religion is of little value.

A man who used to own a ranch near here was quite materialistic. I urged him to come to Encinitas from time to time, and he did so. After the first few visits, he said, with tears in his eyes, "I never realized there was a place whose very atmosphere could speak so much of God's presence." You see, religion must be practical. It must create some change in you — in your consciousness, and in your behavior. All those who have been coming here regularly have changed their life-style for the better. They have been spiritually influenced by this environment.

So religion must be experimented with, to prove it and make it practical. Many churches do great social good, but they do not show you how you can actually prove God to yourself, and how you can be in tune with Him.

The First Experiment Is Silence

The first experiment with religion must begin with silence. Most people never take time to be silent or to sit quietly in meditation. Hours and hours I remain in inner silence. When I am with people, I enjoy them immensely; I am with them fully and wholeheartedly. But when I am away from people, I am entirely alone in that supreme joy of life—the bliss of God. No matter where I am, that joy of God is always with me. Why don't you experiment with silence, so that you can live in this same way? Most of you can't sit still for even ten minutes without your thoughts running away in all directions. You have not learned to be at peace in your home within, because you are always restlessly chasing about in your mind. My master, Sri Yukteswar, used to say: "Locking the door of the storehouse of happiness, man runs everywhere else, begging for that happiness. How foolish, when he has the whole store of joy lying

* Ritual worship performed by Hindus.

within himself!" From my childhood I sought God, and communion with Him has given me happiness that no fulfilled material desires could ever give. You have nothing if you have not God. You have everything if you have God; for He is the Master of the universe.

If you haven't felt any results from religion, experiment in meditation. Shake God out of His silence. You must insist: "Lord, speak to me!" If you make a supreme effort in the silence of the night and in the early morning, after a little while you will see a glimmer of God's light or feel a ripple of His joy coming over your consciousness. Experimenting to know God in meditation, in silence, brings the most real, most remarkable results.

Scientists once thought that water was a single element. But experiments later proved that two invisible elements, hydrogen and oxygen, come together in a certain combination to make up water. Similarly, by religious experiment, wonderful spiritual truths are realized. When you sit quietly in meditation, and your mind is withdrawn within, you will have proof of God and of your own true nature. Experimentation with religious laws is marvelous because the result doesn't take place outside yourself; it is right within you.

The End Result of Truth Is Always Good

Only the application of religious methods can bring lasting happiness. One of the most important spiritual principles to apply is truthfulness. The meaning of truth is not clearly understood by most people. Truth is exact correspondence with Reality; hence its end result is always good. Those who develop the habit of telling little lies all the time will find it hard ever to be wholly truthful in any statement. Such chronic liars never think of the importance of speaking truth; they don't even realize they are lying. Their own imagination becomes truth to them, and they can no longer see the real truth in any situation.

Many who do not understand the importance of speaking truth rationalize their deceptions by saying, "Well, if I always tell the truth I am sure to be gypped, because the rest of the world doesn't work that way. A little lie now and then enables me to get along beautifully." How sad!

To be always truthful we must understand the difference

between fact and truth. If you see a crippled man and, reasoning that his lameness is an obvious fact, you greet him, "How do you do, Mr. Lame Man!" you will offend him. Your truthfully pointing out his defect only hurt; it did no good. Therefore, one should not speak unpleasant *facts* unnecessarily, even though they be true.

There Are No Harmless Lies

However, if for good reason you don't want to speak the truth, at least don't tell a lie! Suppose you are meditating in a corner, believing you are hidden from sight. Your desire is that nobody know what you are doing. But someone discovers you and calls out, "Hello! What are you doing?" And to hide the fact that you were meditating, you reply, "I was eating a banana." To tell such a lie is unnecessary. You could have replied, "I am busy now, and I don't want to be disturbed." This truthful statement is much better than even a little lie to shield from others' curiosity the fact of what you were doing. It is this type of lying that most people get into. Avoid it, because it encourages a habit pattern of being untruthful, even when there is no need to evade the truth.

It is also wrong to speak the truth when, by doing so, one betrays another person unnecessarily and to no good purpose. Suppose a man drinks, but tries to hide it from the rest of the world. You know about his weakness, and so in the name of truthfulness you announce to your friends, "You know that so and so drinks, don't you?" Such a remark is uncalled for; one should not be busy about other people's business. Be protective about others' personal faults, so long as they harm no one else. Speak privately to an offender about his failings, if you have an opportunity or responsibility to help him; but never, under pretext of helping someone, speak deliberately to hurt him. You will only "help" him to become your enemy. You may also extinguish any desire that he might have had to become better.

Truth is always wholesome; fact can sometimes be harmful. However true it may be, a fact that goes against good is only a fact; it is not truth. Never reveal unpleasant facts that cause meaningless suffering to someone else, such as speaking out unnecessarily against another's character. This is often done to well-known persons by sensation-seeking newspapers or magazines. The motive is to hurt the individual's reputation, or to reap personal gain at his expense. Do not bring upon yourself the bad karma that results from revealing harmful facts against others, when no true or noble purpose is served thereby. When you must evade revealing some unpleasant fact, be sure you also avoid implying what you are trying to hide. After all, God is forgiving; and we, His children, should be forgiving. Why should you be the medium of someone else's harm? Your hurtful action will rebound and harm you, too. We have to live through the results of every experience we put others through. There are men who live in peace, and there are men who live in worry and unhappiness. The latter have not had the wisdom to experiment and discover how it is possible to live in peace. Otherwise, they would have learned not to tell untruths and not to talk against others in a mean and harmful way.

The Importance to You of Others' Happiness

Learn also to be unselfish. To find happiness in making others happy is a true goal of one who loves God. Giving happiness to others is tremendously important to our own happiness, and a most satisfying experience. Some people think only of their own family: "Us four and no more." Others think only of self: "How am *I* going to be happy?" But these are the very persons who do not become happy!

It is not right to seek personal happiness regardless of others' well-being. If you unscrupulously take away others' dollars for yourself, you may become rich, but you will never be happy, because their thoughts of resentment against you will react upon you. The divine law is that whenever you try to make yourself happy at the cost of others' welfare, everyone will want to make you unhappy. But if you try to make others happy, even at the cost of your own contentment, everyone will think of your welfare. Whenever you think of your own necessities, remember the needs of others, too. As soon as you feel concerned for their well-being, you will want to make them happy. The unselfish person gets along beautifully with his family and with the rest of the world. The selfish person always gets into trouble and loses his peace of mind.

"Won't Power" Leads to Will Power

Religious experimentation will show you that an uncontrolled existence, also, is the way to misery. The individual who lives all the time in an undisciplined manner is constantly filled with restlessness and worries. But he who has learned self-control knows the way to real happiness.

Whenever you reason that you cannot do without something, you have become its slave. The secret of happiness is to be master of yourself. Many of the things you shouldn't do, you want to do. But when you have cultivated the power to control your desire to do something, even though you are tempted to do it, you have self-mastery. Most people need to develop "won't power"; it enables you to avoid doing things you shouldn't do. When you say, "I won't give in to this wrong habit," and you don't, that is self-mastery. "Won't power" develops strength of mind.

Man's outer behavior reflects his inner life. External luxuries cannot make the soul happy; it is only by control of one's life that the soul experiences happiness and peace. Every morning when I get up, I make certain resolutions, and then throughout the day I mentally whip myself to be sure that I fulfill them. This develops great will power; and when I see all my resolutions carried out, I feel I am a conqueror. So practice self-control. If you don't, you will find yourself constantly carried away on the waves of emotion.

A Practical Experiment in Religion

Practice religion every day of your life. On Sundays you learn about the divine law of forgiveness: if you are slapped on the left cheek, turn the right cheek also. But do you practice this in everyday life? or do you think it is foolish to do so? Experiment. When you retaliate by giving the other person a slap, you feel terrible; your action is just as bad as the other person's. Anger and bitterness react not only upon your mind, but upon your physical body. You feel a great heat in your brain, which upsets your nervous system. Why should you take on the contagion of the hatred of him who slaps you? Why should you disrupt your mental peace? Isn't it better to be able to say: "I am happy within myself because, in spite of your blows, I have done no harm to you and have wished you well." Though it is easier to slap in return for a slap, remember that the aftereffects of such a reaction—loss of mental peace, and physiological disturbance—are not worth the momentary satisfaction of revenge. When you refrain from retaliating, you will find that you have calmed down your enemy also; whereas if you hit back, you only rouse his emotions more.

So to be in control of your emotions is important to happiness. Then no one can get you angry, no one can make you jealous. You stand unchallenged in your own consciousness. You know what you are. You have experimented with your thoughts, and you know what treasure of peace you have within.

There Is Always a Way Out

Worry doesn't help you, either. Not only does it burn out your nerves, leaving you cranky and cross all the time; it puts an extra strain on the heart. When you leave your work for the day, forget it; do not pick it up mentally and carry it home with you. Worry only clouds your mind so that you cannot think clearly. You should learn to rely more on God. This is a science, a divine law. There is always a way out of your trouble; and if you take the time to think clearly, to think how to get rid of the cause of your anxiety instead of just worrying about it, you become a master.

Many people come to me to talk about their worries. I urge them to sit quietly, meditate, and pray; and after feeling calmness within, to think of the alternate ways by which the problem can be solved or eliminated. When the mind is calm in God, when the faith is strong in God, they find a solution to their problem. Merely ignoring problems won't solve them, but neither will worrying about them. Meditate until you become calm; then put your mind on your problem and pray deeply for God's help. Concentrate on the problem and you will find a solution without going through the terrible strain of worry.

No "If" About the Working of God's Laws

A prayer that is strong and deep will definitely receive God's answer. But if you do not make any real effort to pray to Him, naturally you will not feel any response. At one time or another, everyone has found some desire fulfilled through prayer. When your will is very strong it touches the Father, and the Father wills that your desire be fulfilled. When *He* wills, all nature takes notice. God does respond when you deeply pray to Him with faith and determination. Sometimes He answers by dropping a thought in the mind of another person who can fulfill your desire or need; that individual then serves as God's instrument to bring about the desired result.

You don't realize how wonderfully this great power works. It operates mathematically. There is no "if" about it. And that is what the Bible means by faith: it is *proof* of things unseen.

If you practice the presence of God, you will know that what I am saying is truth. Go to God; pray and cry to Him until He shows the workings of His laws to you and guides you. Remember, greater than a million reasonings of the mind is to sit and meditate upon God until you feel calmness within. Then say to the Lord, "I can't solve my problem alone, even if I thought a zillion different thoughts; but I can solve it by placing it in Your hands, asking first for Your guidance, and then following through by thinking out the various angles for a possible solution." God does help those who help themselves. When your mind is calm and filled with faith after praying to God in meditation, you are able to see various answers to your problems; and because your mind is calm, you are capable of picking out the best solution. Follow that solution, and you will meet with success. This is applying the science of religion in your daily life.

Seeing Is Believing—the Science of Religion

Everything that is visible is the result of the Invisible. Because you do not see God, you do not believe He is here. Yet every tree and every blade of grass is controlled by the power of God within it. That Power is not visible externally. What you see are merely the results coming from the Power in the seeds planted in the earth, which emerge as the tree and the blades of grass. You do not see what is going on within, in the factory of the Infinite. Every object in this universe, and every potential therein, has been produced first in the factory of the mind of God; and God sublets that power to the factory of the mind of man. From that little factory of man's mind comes everything he accomplishes—great books, intricate machines, outstanding achievements in any walk of life. Above all, in that mind-factory lies man's unique ability to find God.

The mind is a perfect instrument of knowledge when you have learned to base your life on truth. Then you see everything in a clear, undistorted way, exactly as it is. Therefore, learn to experiment with this mind. Learn to follow the science of religion and you can become the greatest kind of scientist, the greatest kind of inventor, the master of your own fate.

If you can just remember and apply the truths I have told you, there is nothing you cannot accomplish in life. And the greatest of all achievements is to find God. By the application of science in religion, your uncertain belief in spiritual possibilities can become realization of their highest fulfillment. Then you will be the most successful of all human beings, greater than all the scientists on earth. The great ones who have discovered Him never live in doubt; they experience the truth. "Ye shall know the truth, and the truth shall make you free."* You have everything when you have found God.

* John 8:32.

Finding the Joy in Life

Circa 1936

Have you ever tried to catch that will-o'-the-wisp of "something else" which still dances in the background of your feelings at the end of all accomplished desires? Analyze it: You hanker after something as long as you are not able to get it; but when it is secured, sooner or later you tire of it, and want something else.

Even if life gave you at one time everything you wanted—wealth, power, friends—after a while you would again become dissatisfied and need something more. But there is one thing that can never become stale to you—joy itself.

In all your seeking among different things, directly or indirectly, you are in reality seeking happiness through the fulfillment of your desires. You do not want those things that bring sorrow. Neither do you want those that provide a little pleasure in the beginning but sink you deep in remorse and suffering in the end. No matter what your goal, you seek it with eagerness, in expectation of fulfillment by possessing it, and you ought to feel joyous when you actually get it. Then why not seek joy directly? Why seek it through the intermediary of material pleasures and objects?

When you supplicate the favor of short-lasting material things, your happiness depends on their short-lasting pleasures. Material objects and the satisfaction of material desires are temporal; therefore all happiness deriving from them is temporal. Eating, smelling fragrances, listening to music, beholding beautiful objects, touching pleasing things—these are evanescent pleasures, lasting only as long as the sensations of tasting, smelling, hearing, seeing, and touching last, or until the mind becomes bored with a sensation and is tempted by a new stimulus.

You do not want a transitory joy that leaves sorrow in its trail when it vanishes. You crave joy that is not merely tantaliz-

Paramahansa Yogananda on ship en route to Alaska during transcontinental speaking tour, 1924

Paramahansa Yogananda and Luther Burbank, Santa Rosa, California, 1924. The world-famous plant scientist was a devoted follower of Paramahansaji's Kriya Yoga teachings.

Paramahansa Yogananda with Magistrate A.D. Brandon *(left)*, who had invited Paramahansaji to attend a session of the Pittsburgh Morals Court in 1926. Magistrate Brandon sought the Master's views on solving social and criminal problems. He later wrote to Paramahansaji: "If the people of this country would live up to the doctrines taught by you, there would be little or no use of the existence of the Morals Court."

ing, disappearing like the sudden flicker of gossamer wings beneath a flash of lightning. You should look for joy that will shine forever steadily, like the ever luminous radium.

Yet you do not want enjoyment that has too much sameness; you want a joy that changes and dances, enthralling your mind in many ways, keeping your attention perpetually occupied and interested. Happiness that comes by fits and starts is only tantalizing; pleasures that become monotonous are tiresome; mirth that lasts just a little while and brings sorrow in the end is undesirable; joy that comes momentarily and then flits away, sinking you in a state of deepening indifference by contrast, is torturing.

Joy that rhythmically changes all the time and yet in itself remains unchangeable, like an actor who entertains with different roles and poses, is what all of us are seeking. Such joy can be found only through regular, deep meditation. The inner fountain of unchangeable ever new joy alone can quench our thirst. By its very nature, this divine bliss is the only enchantment that can never tire the mind or make us want to exchange it for something else.

In the pursuit of evil or of good, it is happiness you are always seeking. The former promises happiness and gives sorrow; the latter may seem to offer sorrow by its requisite of discipline and will power, but will surely give lasting joy in the end. God is everlasting, ever new Joy, and when you have found Him, you need no longer pursue the eternally elusive will-o'-the-wisp "something else" that has always eluded you in all fulfilled desires. God is that "something else." Finding Him, you will need seek no further. In ever new Joy, you will have everything you ever sought.

Material objects that give pleasure remain outside the mind. They, and the gratification they give, gain entry into the mind only through imagination. Joy, by its very nature—being the blissful consciousness of Spirit in man's soul—lives closest to the mind, and is born in it when the mind is inwardly tuned. When external objects of sense pleasure are destroyed, the happiness they give is destroyed with them. But the ever new joy of God inherent in the soul is indestructible. So also, its expression in the mind can never be destroyed if one knows how to hold on to it, and if he does not deliberately change his mind and become sorrowful by nurturing moods.

So do not seek fulfillment through material mediums, or through desires born of such contact. Seek the unconditioned, indestructible pure Bliss within yourself, and you will have found the ever-existing, ever-conscious, ever-new Joy — God. Unlike material pleasures, this joy is not an abstract quality of mind; it is the conscious, self-born, self-expressing quality of Spirit. Seek it and be comforted forever.

When you have attained this ever new joy, you will never become a cynic, hating the world and condemning its human inhabitants. Rather, you will then be in a position to appreciate God's creation rightly. As His immortal child, you are supposed to enjoy the good and the beauty of His handiwork with the lasting blissful attitude of your eternal nature, which is per- petual joy. But people who delight in material things without knowing the superlative inner joy of God become material- istically minded. It is a disgrace to behave like a discontented mortal, chasing one desire after another, when you are made in God's immortal image of all-desire-quenching ever new joy.

When immortals behave like mortals, they experience the alternations of pleasure, sorrow, and indifference in their na- tures. That is why you must destroy this changeable nature grafted to your unchangeable, immortal nature. When you have found your true soul-nature of everlasting joy, that indestructi- ble bliss will remain with you throughout all experiences of life, whether they be pleasant or disagreeable. Your joy will stand unshaken amidst the crash of breaking earthly pleasures. You will enjoy everything with the Joy that is God. "Unattracted to the sensory world, the yogi experiences the ever new Joy of Being, His soul engaged in the union with Spirit, he attains indestructible Bliss."*

* Bhagavad Gita V:21.

What Is Fate?

Self-Realization Fellowship International Headquarters,
Los Angeles, California, November 16, 1939

Is fate a mysterious, implacable outside force that governs human destiny? This concept has influenced many to believe that what is to be will be, and nothing can be done about it.

Fate does mean something ordained—but it is ordained by you yourself, through the operation of the law of causation, or karma. God gave you the freedom to choose how you will act; but the law of causation governs the outcome according to the nature of the action. Thus every act becomes a cause that will produce a certain kind of effect. When you have set in motion a particular cause, the effect will inevitably correspond to that cause. Whether you do good or evil, you must reap the result of that action. So day by day you are creating the causes that determine your own fate.

Perhaps daily at the dinner table you say, "I will have a little bit more, please." After you have finished, you say, "I shouldn't have eaten so much." This is human nature. We are the funniest of all God's creatures. We call ourselves intelligent human beings, but we are slaves to our desires. Because you eat that "little bit" extra every day, you "suddenly" find you have heart trouble or stomach pains. Then sadly you ask, "Why did this have to happen to me? I must have been fated to be sick." But that is not so. You forgot about having eaten that "little bit" more, when you should have used self-control and taken a little bit less. If a motor is overloaded, and you add to that load, naturally it will be hard on the motor. It may give up. In the same way, you overworked your motor of digestion. That was the cause, and it was created by you; your stomach pains from ulcers or indigestion are merely the result.

Why We Are All Different From One Another

Behind the light in every little bulb is a great dynamic current; beneath every little wave is the vast ocean, which has become the many waves. So it is with human beings. God made every man in His image, and gave each one freedom. But you forget the Source of your being and the unequaled power of God that is an inherent part of you. The possibilities of this world are limitless; the potential progress of man is limitless. Yet it appears that each individual is born with definite limitations. These are the results of the operation of the law of karma. All the causes of ill health or sudden financial failure or other troubles that come upon you without warning, and without your knowing why, were created by you in the past, in this or in previous incarnations, and have been silently germinating in your consciousness.* If you had had the wisdom, you could have lessened the effects by right thinking and right living; but you lead a life that is generally unconscious of the possible results of your thoughts and actions, so when anything upsetting happens without apparent reason, you say, "Well, it was fate." Your failure or sickness or other troubles started with unwise actions in past lives, and the effects of those causes have been brewing within, waiting for the right time to bubble over.

Disease, health; failure, success; inequalities, equality; early death, long life—all these are outgrowths of the seeds of actions we have sown in the past. They cause us to come into this world with varying degrees of goodness or evil within us. So even though God made us in His image, no two people are alike; each has used his God-given free choice to make something different of himself. This is why some people suffer for the slightest reason. Others become angry at the least provocation. And there are those who eat endlessly without any self-control. Did God make them that way? No. Each person has made himself the way he is. There would be no justice in this world if God had arbitrarily made us the way we are. I sometimes think God must be watching in amazement this big zoo of human beings here, blaming Him because they have a headache or a stomachache, or are always getting into trouble. Don't blame God or anyone else if you are suffering from disease, financial problems, emotional upsets. You created the cause of the problem in the past and must make a greater determination to uproot it now.

---

* See *reincarnation* in glossary.

Three Ways to Deal With the Effects of Actions

Fate means that a cause has operated to produce an effect. You can change it, if you know the way. However, it is not always easy.

(1) You can minimize the effect of an action.

(2) You can resist the effect.

(3) You can completely stop it.

Why do people go to doctors? Because that is one way to *minimize* the effects of wrong actions. The physical way to lessen an illness or overcome it may be found in such remedies as proper diet, exercise, or medication. One Self-Realization student was recently healed of ulcers by a diet of bread and milk. But lessening or removing effects may not necessarily eliminate the cause. Under favorable circumstances the cause may send forth new effects in the same or a different form.

To *resist* the effects of karma is to use commonsense remedies, but rely more on the power of the mind. Refuse to accept any limiting condition. Affirm and believe in health, strength, success, even in the face of contradictory evidence. The effects of your actions have much less power to hurt you when you do not allow the mind to give in to them. Remember that. You can also resist by counteracting the bad effects of past wrong actions with good effects set in motion by present right actions, thus preventing the creation of an environment favorable to the fruition of your bad karma.

But how are you going to completely break the hold that fate has on you? The only way that you can permanently stop the undesirable effects of past wrong actions is by removing the cause of those effects. Harmful past-life seed-tendencies must be cauterized from the brain; then there will be no recurrence of any type of illness or other troubles arising from them. Roast them in the fire of wisdom. Man suffers because of his errors; and the root-cause of error is ignorance. Therefore seek the wisdom born of meditation, which removes forever from within you the darkness of ignorance. Krishna said: "As fire reduces to ashes all wood, even so, O Arjuna, does the flame of wisdom consume all karma."* When you meditate deeply, God's light of divine wisdom cauterizes the seeds of undesirable karma stored in the deep recesses of consciousness in the brain.

Even the Fate of Death Can Be Changed

Jesus demonstrated in a most dramatic way that there is no such thing as an unalterable fate. According to Lazarus' karma, he was destined to die on a certain day. The law was fulfilled, and Lazarus died. That was fated to be. But not even death is a fate irrevocable. Jesus satisfied the karmic law and brought Lazarus back to life again. How did he do it? He didn't just say, "Come forth." Jesus saw where the soul of Lazarus had gone, after it had left the physical form, and he first contacted that soul, encased in its astral (heavenly) body, in order to call it back again. But he didn't call Lazarus back to a body that had already begun to rot.† Jesus had to make that body whole again; he had to revive and restore the body of Lazarus before the soul and life could enter in. Only after the form had been made livable could he invoke Lazarus to come forth in it. So Jesus did two things: First, he put himself—his life and divine power—in the body of Lazarus. Thus he could work out Lazarus' karma: he took that karma on himself. Then, having freed the body of the cause of death, he renewed the bodily cells so that they would live again.‡ This is how Jesus could wake up Lazarus from the dead, even though there was no way of reviving him according to natural law.

If the bulb in a lamp is broken, the light will go out. Unless you replace the broken bulb with a new one, you cannot bring the light back again. Similarly, once the light of the soul leaves the body at death, it can't come back again except in a new body bulb in a new incarnation. But great sages of old knew, as did Jesus, that when a body is fated to be destroyed by death, that same body can be revived again by one who knows how to do it.

---

* Bhagavad Gita IV:37.   † John 11:39.

‡ "The law of miracles is operable by any man who has realized that the essence of creation is light. A master is able to employ his divine knowledge of light phenomena to project instantly into perceptible manifestation the ubiquitous light atoms. The actual form of the projection (whatever it be: a tree, a medicine, a human body) is determined by the yogi's wish and by his power of will and visualization."—*Autobiography of a Yogi*, chapter 30, "The Law of Miracles."

Of course, raising the dead is an extreme case of altering fate; but it does show that man potentially has power even over death— the so-called inevitable fate.

Mahavatar Babaji* also demonstrated the power of restoring life. A would-be disciple once sought out Babaji in the Himalayas, where this great master lives with a few highly advanced disciples. The stranger asked to be received into the sacred band, vowing to jump from the mountain if his plea were refused. Babaji said he could not accept him in his present state of development. The distraught devotee hurled himself over the cliff, while the other disciples looked on in horror. Babaji then told them to retrieve the body. The disciples obeyed, and laid the lifeless form at the Mahavatar's feet. He touched the broken body, healed it, and brought the devotee back to life. By his act of total faith and devotion, the disciple had worked out the last vestiges of bad karma that had made him theretofore unready to join Babaji's exalted company of devotees. The great Guru then accepted him as a disciple.

On another occasion, however, Babaji satisfied the karmic law by taking a devotee's karma on himself, thus mitigating the destined fate of death—which only a true guru has the power to do. The Mahavatar was sitting with Lahiri Mahasaya* and some other disciples. Before them a ceremonial fire was burning. Suddenly Babaji picked up a white-hot brand and hit the bare shoulder of one of the disciples. Lahiri Mahasaya spoke up in astonishment, questioning why the Guru had done such a terrible thing. Babaji looked at him and said: "Would you rather have seen him burned to ashes before your eyes? It was his karma to die a painful death by fire today. By hitting him with a burning ember and taking his karma, I have saved him."† Such are the blessings that can be bestowed on those who are in tune with a true guru, a God-realized master. Those who are with Godlike souls, in spirit and in truth, become Godlike themselves.

---

* See glossary.

†In both instances, the disciples were already highly advanced devotees, elevated souls passing a final test. It would be foolish for an ordinary man to conclude that he could, by similar means, wipe out his karma and gain divine grace. For a full account of these two stories about Mahavatar Babaji, see *Autobiography of a Yogi*, chapter 33, "Babaji, Yogi-Christ of Modern India."

Avoid Wrong Behavior to Prevent Unpleasant Results

Let us talk about preventable causes now. You should control all impulses to behave wrongly: overcome chronic greed, chronic jealousy, chronic anger, and other such tendencies that keep coming back all the time. All harmful emotions inside you must be brought under your control. These states are remediable. But you don't try to rid yourself of them.

Materialists concentrate on treating the symptoms and secondary causes. They don't believe in any deeper law or cause. They reason that when you start to break the laws of right behavior, there must be two causes: the influence of bad company or environment that affects you adversely; and lack of self-control. This is true.

But those who go deeper, seeing into the real causes of man's suffering, say in addition that the degree of your susceptibility to these present causes is in direct proportion to the real causes: the seed tendencies within you that have come from your past-life behavior. Even if a doctor heals you of an ailment, other diseases may come in its stead unless you have overcome the habit that caused it in the first place. If someone is healed of ulcers by the doctor, but continues to eat the wrong food, he will get ulcers again—or perhaps something worse. The metaphysician would see the cause, which in this case is greed—the habit from the past, and the present uncontrolled desire to eat what he likes rather than what is good for him. The metaphysician would then advise removal of the cause.

At the right time, and in the right environment, all good and bad actions of the past come to fruition, just as seeds sprout under the right conditions. This explains why it is important always to mix with good company. You don't know what kinds of seeds, whether of disease or other negative happenings, are dormant within you. Suppose you have in your consciousness from the past the seeds of craving for drink. You have never drunk in this life; but one day you take a drink at a party, and suddenly you are caught up in the desire for liquor. Eventually you become addicted to it again. The tendencies were already buried within you as a result of past living; your present actions provided the necessary conditions for their resurrection.

So it is very unwise to mix with people who encourage any

bad habit in you. You don't know what latent seeds of wrong action you carry within your consciousness. It is best not to give those seeds any chance to grow.

Do you see how deep these principles are? This subject of overcoming fate or karma is the most wonderful philosophy. It proves that man can fully govern his own life. And that life is a beautiful experience when you are not its slave, but its master.

Your greatest enemies are your bad habits. They will follow you from one incarnation to another until you overcome them. In order to free yourself from fate, you must cure yourself of bad habits. How? Good company is one of the best medicines. If you have a tendency to drink, mix with people who do not. If you are suffering from ill health, be with people who have positive minds, who don't think about sickness. If you have the consciousness of failure, associate with those who have the consciousness of success. Then you will begin to change.

Each of your habits creates a specific "groove," or pathway, in the brain. These patterns make you behave in a certain way, often against your wish. Your life follows those grooves that you yourself have created in the brain. In that sense you are not a free person; you are more or less a victim of the habits you have formed. Depending on how set those patterns are, to that degree you are a puppet. But you can *neutralize* the dictates of those bad habits. How? By creating brain patterns of opposite good habits. And you can completely *erase* the grooves of bad habits by meditation. There is no other way. However, you can't cultivate good habits without good company and good environment. And you can't free yourself from bad habits without good company and meditation.

Even if you were to flee to the jungle, your old habits would be with you still. You can't run away from them, so you may as well strive to overcome them. Clear out the jungle of your wrong habits. Then you will be free. A quarrelsome family says, "Oh, if only we had a nice home in the country, we would be so happy." Eventually they move into such a place, but having never learned how to get along with one another, they continue their disagreeable habit of quarreling, and make life in that home a nightmare too.

So don't wait! Change yourself by yourself. It can be the easiest thing to do, or the hardest thing to do: easy if you meditate and keep good company; difficult if you don't meditate and if you mix with people who wrongly influence you.

Never Give Up Your Good Efforts

Let nobody say that you are finished, all washed up. Why should you give up? Why should you think, "I can't change, I am old, I am finished"? You can change every day, any time you want to. I have noticed that some people remain the same year after year. I call them psychological antiques. And I have seen others who, no matter what comes, are always filled with ambition, doing something to improve themselves. That is the right kind of living.

I used to know the elderly wife of a senator. She was a fanatic about liquor; and when her husband died, she threw it all out of the house. This woman was a live wire. She exercised regularly, took up dancing, and was very active in useful projects. According to her view, being old was no reason for her to give up all her interests and prepare for death. She kept on this way for quite a few years, and remained enthusiastic, healthy, and happy. She was no ordinary person, and I very much admired her spirit.

Many people grow old before their time. You don't have to give up just because you are seventy-five or eighty. Never tell your age; nor let anyone pity you that you are getting old. Keep yourself youthfully erect and alert. Feel young. It is the spirit within that keeps you young. Be enthusiastic. There are lots of young people who are already psychologically old and as good as dead. They have no ambition, no enthusiasm. They don't try to change. You are finished only when you say or think you are. No matter how others judge you, your own decree of defeat is the worst of all. You give up.

The moment you say, "I have tried, but I can't contact God," you are through. You won't get to Him. Some teachers say that if one doesn't start his search for God before he is thirty years old, he cannot find Him. This is not true. God will come to you any time you are willing to make the effort. It *is* true, however, that the earlier one starts to seek God or Truth earnestly, the easier it is, because habits have not yet become thoroughly formed. But Krishna taught that in spite of negative habits, one can find God if he earnestly seeks Him: "Even an evildoer who turns away from all else to worship Me exclusively may be counted among the good, because of his righteous resolve. He will fast become a virtuous man and obtain unending peace. Tell all, O Arjuna, that My devotee never perishes!"* So if you make the determination, "I will keep on seeking God, even if I drop dead while trying," then know that you will feel God's presence; you will find that He responds.

Angels Are Made on Earth, Not in Heaven

Don't depend on death to liberate you from your imperfections. You are exactly the same after death as you were before. Nothing changes; you only give up the body. If you are a thief or a liar or a cheater before death, you don't become an angel merely by dying. If such were possible, then let us all go and jump in the ocean now and become angels at once! Whatever you have made of yourself thus far, so will you be hereafter. And when you reincarnate, you will bring that same nature with you. To change, you have to make the effort. This world is the place to do it. Man comes here for the sole purpose of learning to break the cords that bind his soul. Disease, failure, negation, greed, jealousy—break these bonds now. You are in a cocoon of your own bad habits, and you must get out of it by self-effort. The butterfly of the soul must be freed to spread its wings of beautiful divine qualities. If the silkworm is still in its cocoon when the silkman comes, it gets caught in a trap of its own making, and dies there. So do you weave silken threads of bad habits about you, and you die still bound in them.

To the last day of your life, be positive; try to be cheerful. Even at the very end, don't think, "I am finished." Instead of pitying yourself, you should be thinking, "O ye who are left on this desolate shore still to mourn and deplore, it is I who pity you." Death will not give you any trouble if you have a clear conscience; and if you go with this thought: "Lord, I am in Thy hands."

* Bhagavad Gita IX:30-31.

How Meditation Changes Your Fate

If you really want to rid yourself of present bad habits and to escape those decrees of fate that have caused you suffering, you have no greater recourse than meditation. Every time you meditate deeply on God, beneficial changes take place in the patterns of your brain.

Suppose you are a financial failure or a moral failure or a spiritual failure. Through deep meditation, affirming, "I and my Father are one," you will know that you are the child of God. Hold on to that ideal. Meditate until you feel a great joy. When joy strikes your heart, God has answered your broadcast to Him; He is responding to your prayers and positive thinking. This is a distinct and definite method:

First, meditate upon the thought, "I and my Father are one," trying to feel a great peace, and then a great joy in your heart. When that joy comes, say, "Father, Thou art with me. I command Thy power within me to cauterize my brain cells of wrong habits and past seed tendencies." The power of God in meditation will do it. Rid yourself of the limiting consciousness that you are a man or a woman; *know* that you are the child of God. Then mentally affirm and pray to God: "I command my brain cells to change, to destroy the grooves of bad habits that have made a puppet out of me. Lord, burn them up in Thy divine light." And when you will practice the Self-Realization techniques of meditation, especially *Kriya Yoga,* you will actually see that light of God baptizing you.

But you must concentrate; you must deeply commune with God. Night is the best time for this. How wonderful it is to try to commune with God then—when the world around you is quiet. I have received my greatest experiences with God at night before I go to sleep. I never even think of sleep if I don't want to. I want to be with the Lord at night, and He takes care of me.

The Most Important Consideration Is to Be With God

I never worry about the future or the past. I just live each day for God, that is all. I will do my best, whatever I can; but I don't worry about anything. I am working only for God in this world, and I don't care what happens to me. What can happen that I will not still be with the Lord? When I was in India, I wrote to those at Mt. Washington: "I never miss you all because I am with you evermore. And when this wave shall be gone from the surface of the ocean of life, somewhere else I will be; but whether here or there, we will all be in the same ocean of life in God."

So when you shall know God, you will never grieve for your friends and loved ones when you are parted from them. Many friends that I knew in the past I have found again in this life. And many who know me now shall know me again hereafter.

When I first came to America, I saw the faces of some of you in vision. That is why I wrote, "Sleeping memories of friends once more to be did greet me, sailing o'er the sea."* I was feeling very sad as the ship came into the harbor of this strange land; I was apprehensive, and my India was hushed in the distant darkness of thousands of miles. But then I saw in vision the faces of many here whom I had known before in previous lives, and a great joy came over me.

I know that I knew Madame Galli-Curci† and her husband before. One day, a record was playing, and I asked, "Whose record is it? Play it again." The voice was Galli-Curci's. "I am going to meet her," I said. Later, one night in Chicago, a friend came and told me, "You know, Madame Galli-Curci is here in the city. I feel you should meet her." I was given a letter of introduction, and others tried to approach her on my behalf. But the tickets for all her concerts were sold out. At last the manager himself gave me his son's ticket. When Madame Galli-Curci and I met after the concert, she greeted me and said, "I scolded them for not making a ticket available to you sooner." We have been friends ever since, and she and her husband follow this path faithfully.

Be a Jailbreaker From the Prison of Fate

Although life seems capricious, uncertain and full of all kinds of troubles, still we are always under the guiding, loving protection of God. We are in a sort of jail, imprisoned by the consequences of our wrong actions. But we can break out of this

---

* From *Songs of the Soul*, a book of poetry by Paramahansa Yogananda, published by Self-Realization Fellowship.

† See footnote on page 8.

prison and be one with God again. Though we are surrounded by the bars of fate — evil, moral troubles, weaknesses, sickness, financial difficulties — we have the power within us to sunder them.

In your youth you feel you have the power to conquer the world, but as you get older you feel you have lost it. Day after day, you prove that you are a slave to your environment and habits. Instead, day after day you should affirm: "I am the conqueror of all. I may die, but I will die free in the bosom of God. I will not remain behind the bars of bad habits, the bars of fate." This freedom will come if you meditate every day and strengthen your will power. Not God, but you created the jail. You forged those bars, and so you must break them. You must be jailbreakers — breaking out of this prison of flesh. Escape from every jail cell of bad habits, attachment, emotion, desires, life, and death. The bars of this jail in which your soul is imprisoned can be severed with the saw of wisdom. The more you will saw at them in meditation, the freer you will become through the power of God. In Him you will know that this life is like a dream; it is just a drama.

Dear ones, I very much enjoy these meetings with you, because I don't come here to give a lecture; I talk to you only with the consciousness of Spirit, and not in a mechanical way. I speak to you what comes from my soul. I seek only those who are deeply interested in finding God. Such lovely souls I meet here, and such wonderful souls live here in our Mt. Washington ashram. Years and years, one peace and harmony. I give thanks to the Lord, for all is His glory.

It is not always easy to do good. But the greatest thing in life is to live in the castle of your own clear conscience, knowing you are pleasing God. He is the only answer; for in God lies the greatest happiness. "By always performing right actions, by taking shelter in Me, and by My pleasure, he [the devotee] obtains the eternal, unchangeable state."* You should love and bless all, and try to see God in everyone, even the error-stricken. And no matter how hard it seems at times, you must follow the path of Truth; then you will break the bars of fate.

* Bhagavad Gita XVIII:56.

The End of the World

First Self-Realization Fellowship Temple,
Encinitas, California, May 26, 1940

Considering present world conditions, you can well appreciate why I have taken for my subject, "the end of the world." My talk today will help you to understand many things that are yet to come.

When we study current events, or those that have passed, our view of these happenings is determined by how clearly or distortedly they are reflected in our consciousness. People judge what happens according to the way they live, and by the measure of their own mind and intelligence. Self-interest, prejudices, hatred, and anger prevent true understanding of the events and mysteries of life. Only by communion with God can we comprehend His divine laws, which are working everywhere. In spite of all the ruthless, desecrating ways in which man has wrought destruction in God's creation, still we will find that evil destroys itself, and that the power of God marches on in the face of every opposition.

The end of the world has various connotations, as I shall show you. First of all, there is the literal meaning. In this sense, the end of the world is of two kinds: partial dissolution and complete dissolution. It will be a long, long time before we can expect complete dissolution. Yet periodically some fanatical group predicts that the world is coming to an end. A few years ago we read in the papers about a sect in New York whose leader, misguided by mental phobia, or imagination, had frightened many of his followers by such a prediction. Those who seek to hold their followers by instilling fear in them are not true teachers. We should always be actuated by wisdom, never by fear.

To get back to my story: The members of this sect made ready for the coming holocaust. They gave their property away and went with their teacher to a mountaintop to await the end of the world. They waited and waited. Several days passed, and their hunger pangs were increasing. Still nothing happened, and they finally gave up. Eventually, they had to institute lawsuits in order to get back their property.

This is just one instance in which people have been alarmed by predictions of war or some other major disaster. More often than not, these proved to be false predictions. But in any case, we need not be frightened. After all, what is life? It is a temporary dream. Death is nothing but a sleep and another dream. When the dream is over, it is gone. Viewing it from that consciousness, I am not sorry for those who die on the battlefields, because for them the dream of torture is over. But I grieve for the wounded, because pain is a dreadful nightmare. Much of the time my mind is not here; I am roaming on the battlefields of Europe.* You might think as I tell you this, or if I were to tell you of other unusual experiences, that I am suffering from an overwrought imagination; but that is not so. Naturally, it is hard to believe that others can have realizations that we ourselves do not. But if you live for years in the mental world, whence God is sending forth these dreams of creation, and if you continuously work with the divine powers of the mind, you can see, as I do, all the mysteries of God's creation unfold before you.

The Good and Evil Actions of Man
Affect the Harmonious Balance of the Earth

Partial dissolution of the world is brought on by the evil activities of people in general. If we all begin to fight with explosives, by this direct action we can reduce drastically the extent of civilization. And maybe if we work hard enough, we can dissolve this world, too! God has given man the power of destruction as well as the power of creation. We have made the world beautiful, and we have the power to destroy it. When we desecrate the world, the environment undergoes a violent change, which is called partial dissolution. Such upheavals have occurred many times — one example is Noah's flood. These partial dissolutions are due to the wrong actions and ignorant errors of mankind. Don't think the happenings of this world are

* This talk was given during World War II.

going on automatically without God's knowledge. And don't think that man's actions have no effect on the operation of His cosmic laws. Everything that has happened throughout the ages is recorded in the ether. The vibrations of evil that mankind leaves in the ether upset the normal harmonious balance of the earth. When the earth becomes very heavy with disease and evil, these etheric disturbances cause the world to give way to earthquakes, floods, and other natural disasters.

It is the same as when you live wrongly for a long time; various inharmonies begin to manifest in your body, as well as certain diseases. Disease is not a punishment. It is a poison that you yourself create in the body, and the Lord wants you to get rid of it. But all too often, by the time you try to throw it off, the body has become completely deranged, and you die. So, just like the human body, the earth suffers from inharmonies and disease. And it is because the combined actions of all people all over the world affect the planet on which we live. There is no question about that. The good and bad karmic conditions created by man determine and influence the climate; they affect the wind and the ocean, even the very structure of the earth, sometimes causing earthquakes. All the hatred, the anger, the evil we send out into the world, and the agony and rebellion they cause—all these are disturbing the magnetic force of the earth, like static in the ether. In the destruction caused by this war we are seeing a partial dissolution of the world—dissolution of lives, money, homes. In many ways it is worse than Noah's flood; it is a flood of fire and bloodshed. But one thing is encouraging: the good karma of mankind is greater than the evil karma. If this were not so, the earth would explode from the negative vibrations. Contrary to appearances, the earth is in an ascending cycle, and good will triumph.

The Life Cycles of the Earth

The world is a sort of living being, with a predetermined age. We are the children of this great mother earth. We suckle her breast to partake of the food she produces. She also nurtures us through the circulating currents of oxygen, the sunshine, and the water of her atmosphere. Just as we go through youth, middle age, old age, death, and reincarnation, so also does the mother earth. There is the young mother earth, the middle-aged mother earth, and the old-aged mother earth. The earth "dies" through partial dissolution, then reincarnates again to give human beings new life, new strength, a new habitat in which to work out their karma. Many times the earth has undergone partial dissolution and reincarnation. But complete death will come to the earth only when it dissolves back again into God.

I will explain briefly about the life cycles of the earth.* These cycles consist of 24,000 years, divided into four *yugas* or ages—12,000 years of ascending through these *yugas* to increasing enlightenment, and then 12,000 years of descending through the *yugas* to increasing ignorance and materialism. Each of these half-cycles is called a *Daiva Yuga*. The earth has already passed through many complete cycles since the dawn of creation. The four ages of each *Daiva Yuga* are *Kali Yuga*, the dark or materialistic age; *Dwapara Yuga*, the electrical or atomic age; *Treta Yuga*, the mental age; and *Satya Yuga*, the age of truth or enlightenment.

Dwapara Yuga, the Present Cycle

The earth has already passed through *Kali Yuga*, the materialistic age of 1,200 years' duration. According to the calculations of my guru, Swami Sri Yukteswar, we are about 240 years into *Dwapara Yuga*, the second age, which consists of 2,400 years. Now in its ascendancy, this is the electrical age, even though it may yet seem very materialistic. If you think about it, you will see how man has progressed from comprehending only gross matter to understanding and harnessing the energy in matter. In this age, man will make great headway in the electrical or electromagnetic field of science.

As *Dwapara Yuga* progresses, diseases will be treated and healed more and more by rays. Vibratory energy can reach the electronic factors of the atoms, the building blocks of matter, where gross chemicals cannot penetrate. After this war, you will see a great surge of development in electrical science. Aviation will develop tremendously also. Travel will be much, much more by air. Planes are still viewed with doubt by many today, just as trains were once looked upon with fear; but planes are

---

* See *yuga* in glossary.

already taking over, and trains have become almost a thing of the past. Gradually, automobiles will come to be considered as carts.

The trouble in this second age is that there is not enough security, because science plays the part of Dr. Jekyll and Mr. Hyde. Man uses science not only to create and do good, but to destroy as well. Therefore scientific development is not yet safe. The present World War shows how the technology of science is being used to destroy mankind. Out of the conflict we will learn how to employ more scientific devices for human comfort. But unless we develop spiritual forces, we will also continue to use scientific knowledge to destroy.

People will learn from this war the devastating consequences of the misuse of technology. In the First World War, and in earlier times, it was considered chivalrous to fight. But the idea of chivalry has gone. In this war, no one wants to fight. After it is over, there will be so much fear of world devastation that if anybody tries to start a war, the rest of the world will fall upon that nation. I am telling you things far ahead of my time.

Armament is necessary now. A defensive plan is good, but it will not bring ultimate peace. So long as anyone will use brute force, there will always be someone else who will be more brutal. As Christ said truly, if you use the sword you will perish by the sword. Brute force will be subdued only by making mankind understand the eternal message of Christ and the Great Ones: only by spiritual force will wars be stopped.

Ultimate peace will come when by mutual agreement *all* nations of the earth will have continued peace conferences, and will scrap their weapons and instead help to destroy the earth's slums. Think how much better it would have been if all the nations and their leaders had gotten together to use the money they are spending in war to do away with the poverty of the world. Instead, even when war is over and one nation surrenders to the other, people will continue to live in fear, and there will still be poverty. These present armaments will be junked, and billions of dollars will be wasted. By believing in brute force, man is engaging in great folly. How long will it go on? How can this be changed? Only when nations have had their brains battered by war will they begin to realize their shortsightedness.

But I tell you, though it may not seem so, this war is being fought for the freedom of all downtrodden nations. The karmic forces are at work to give India and other foreign-dominated countries their independence.

Spirituality Must Be Kept Strong in All Nations

What is to be dreaded even more than this present war is the godlessness of bolshevism, the greatest enemy. There is a story that when a lion and a bear fought over the carcass of a stag, the bear was killed, and the lion had a broken back and couldn't get to the deer. A fox, who had been watching and waiting on the sidelines, came forth and claimed the prey. Godless communism is waiting to spread. We must, above all, strive to keep spirituality strong in all lands.

What prevents people from taking from others? the sharing of others with them, so that they too have what they need; and the knowledge that God is our Father and we are all His children, brothers of one universal family. National patriotism is not enough. If the ideal of God and brotherhood is taken away, there will be no reason to live any more. Who created this world? Who created us? We know that there is a God. Let nothing take away that idea. The doctrine of belief in God is the only one that will ultimately bring peace on earth. No other ideology will be able to do so.

Loyalty to One's Country

So long as you live in any country, you must be loyal to it. We must not allow subversive elements in this country. Treachery, I think, is the most terrible of all crimes, the most dreadful of all evils in this world. Never be treacherous to your family, your neighbors, or your friends. And never be treacherous to your country; those who cannot be faithful to their country cannot be faithful to God. Remember the story of the bat. When the birds and the beasts were fighting, the bat sided first with one and then the other, depending on who was winning at the time. After a truce was signed by the birds and the beasts, both made a resolution: "Let us destroy the bat."

So remember, it is of utmost importance to be loyal to your country. If you don't like its ideals, give it your blessing and go somewhere else. There is too much lack of patriotism in this country. I don't mean that you should love America with the kind of patriotism that tries to destroy other nations; rather, love America and her ideals so that you may in turn love the whole world. Remember, you are living in America for just a little while; in other incarnations you may live in other countries. If everyone first loves his own country and then expands that love to include all other countries as his own, there will be no more wars.

So never tolerate anyone who is not a true patriot. No one has a right to live in this country who doesn't love it. It is wrong to bite the hand that feeds you. I would rather that people beat me up or kill me than be treacherous to me. Treachery I abhor; I have never betrayed anyone. The love I have given to all, I have given sincerely. There is no one who can stand before me and truthfully say I have been treacherous. When I give my love, I give it wholeheartedly. That doesn't mean I am not aware of those who are insincere with me; before the searchlight of divine love, everything is revealed. So, dear ones, never be treacherous to anyone; and whenever you see treachery, correct that person and refuse him cooperation or support in his wrong-doing.

God knows who is wrong and who is right. Let us all be united in everything that is noble. Uphold the ideals of this country. If ever aggressive war came to destroy this country and America needed my help, I would give it—for the love of the people, and to defend the nation on whose land I live. We should do our part to help protect America and all those we love, but at the same time we must not allow ourselves to be filled with hatred. Never has the world needed love so much as now. Love will be a potent factor in eradicating war. Let us all resolve that no matter what happens, we will make God the polestar of our love, and that we will send that love to all. Mentally pray with me: "Heavenly Father, Thou art love; I am made in Thine image. I am a sphere of love. I expand this sphere to include all mankind in the kingdom of my love."

This war will not be the war to end all wars. Whoever wins and then uses that power to penalize other nations, those nations will try to strike back with greater force some day. Man's destructive potential has grown much greater than his constructive power. There will be no safety in the electrical age. Methods of war on a greater and greater scale will come. So thank God that *Dwapara Yuga*, the electrical age, is only 2,400 years.

Treta Yuga

Next we will come to *Treta Yuga*, the third era or age, of 3,600 years' duration. That is the mental age, when most people will use mind power. The power of the mind will be much more highly developed than it is now. To a great extent, everything will be accomplished by that power. There will be an increase of wisdom, and therefore more safety in that age; people will make a stronger effort to use peaceful means for settling their problems. There will be less use of electricity, and growing use of the power of the mind. This is not to say that everyone will be able to know others' minds. But just as there are powerful radios that can tune in even weak stations, and weak radios that can pick up only strong stations, so some people will have stronger mental powers than others in the age of the mind.

In that mental age, by the power of the mind we will be able to know our fellow beings better, so that it will be difficult for anyone to be wicked. There will be very little hypocrisy, because people are hypocritical only when they think others do not know their real feelings. As a result of greater understanding, humanity will learn to live more peacefully with one another. Mind power will be used for healing and as food for the body.

Satya Yuga

After the third age will come *Satya Yuga*, or the age of truth, when the mind of man will be able to comprehend all mysteries of creation, and to live in communion with God. People of this age will find no barrier between the material world and the astral heaven — they will be able to enter the astral world and commune with those souls who have gone on to that sphere. The ascending *Satya Yuga* will last for 4,800 years. Many fully evolved souls will find liberation in that *yuga*, more than in any of the other ages.*

But even the end of *Satya Yuga* will not signal the end of the

---

* "Most anthropologists, believing that 10,000 years ago humanity was living in a barbarous Stone Age, summarily dismiss as 'myths' the widespread traditions of very ancient civilizations in Lemuria, Atlantis, India, China, Japan, Egypt, Mexico, and many other lands." *Autobiography of a Yogi.*

world. The cycle will be continuous, descending and reascending through all four ages again and again. Intermittently, cataclysms will occur, in which the world will die and then begin anew its continuous cycle. The earth was created to bring souls to their divine destiny; it is carrying a heavy burden. Until all our work is done—until our souls evolve back to God—this earth will never totally dissolve. It is only when God no longer needs it for the evolution of souls that the world will be no more. Then will come the real end of the world. So don't be afraid that our earth will tumble into the oven of the sun, which is so hot that all things would melt and vaporize in just a few seconds. The ultimate end of the world is far off. It has a lot of work to do yet.

Rise Above the Age in Which You Are Born

You do not have to wait for the end of the world in order to be free. There is another way: rise above the age in which you are born. In the material age, the majority of mankind is materially minded. But you will also find those who are living ahead of their times, Christlike souls. In the mental and electrical ages, you will find predominant the mentalities characteristic of those *yugas*. At the same time, there are other mentalities— some that are more highly evolved, and others not yet as highly evolved. Thus in this electrical age you can find people who are still living in the stone age. There is always a balance: some who are living ahead and some who are living behind the age of civilization in which they are born.

Through repeated incarnations, those of lesser development will gradually advance until they express the mentality of the age in which they reincarnate, and eventually, the qualities characteristic of the higher ages yet to come. The cycles of this world are like a see-saw going up and down. But when we hasten our evolution through right living and a spiritual technique such as *Kriya Yoga*, * we live ahead of our time and can find freedom in God within this or only a few lifetimes.

The World Ends for Us When Our Minds Are Detached

Another way in which we experience the end of the world is in the detachment that is felt in sleep, in dreams, in losing one's

---

* See glossary and *Autobiography of a Yogi*, chapter 26.

mind, and in death. These conditions are forced on us; so it seems that the experience of the end of the world is necessary to us. Its purpose is to teach us the delusive nature of the world and the true nature of our Self, the soul. The soul comes on earth and becomes entangled in the mesh of delusion. Through the suffering that comes to us then, the Lord wants us to see that the world is not perfect. In this way He helps us to break our attachment to it. God is trying to make us realize, through nonidentification with it, how delusive our existence here is. The more I saw of the world and its defects, the greater became my determination to know God.

The World Ends for Us When We Are Free From Desires

In a metaphysical sense, the end of all earthly desires is the end of the world. For your own happiness, you must strive to live free of worldly desires. If there is anything you can't do without, you still have a terrible lesson to learn. Imagine yourself taken away from this earth with all of your desires unfulfilled. They are like cankers in your soul. You would have to return here many times, enduring heartaches and disappointments again and again, to cure yourself of those desires.

It is far better to say to God, "Lord, I didn't ask You to create me. I am here because You put me here. I will do the best I can, but I have no desires except to do Your will. I don't want to be sent back here to suffer any more. I don't want to go on endlessly returning, sometimes as a rich man, sometimes as a poor man; sometimes with ill health and disease; sometimes with sorrows, sometimes with snatches of happiness. I am not a mortal being. I am the immortal soul."

Don't worry that by freeing yourself of desires you will become petrified, like a stone. Desirelessness is a most marvelous state of consciousness. I enjoy everything, but I have no desire for anything, so there is never any pain or disappointment from unfulfillment. Whatever I do, wherever I go, I enjoy myself.

So the way to true happiness is to do your best in the role in which God has placed you, without creating further desires. Then you can be a king within, no matter what your outer conditions. You can be happier than a millionaire—in fact, if you knew the troubles of millionaires, you wouldn't want to be one.

The fear of losing all that money; the fear of disease; the feeling of insecurity, never knowing who one's real friends are; these are some of the struggles and sufferings of those who have too much. I wouldn't want anyone to like me just because I had money. What kind of love is that?

To me, true friendship is the greatest of all treasures. I love friendship that is given without any demand, friendship for the sake of friendship, without expectation of anything in return. That is one thing that you can never buy—not with money, show, fear, or power. It must be given freely. If sometimes you fail to receive that kind of friendship, don't be discouraged. If you are sincere, you will find those true souls who will appreciate you.

Live without being attached. Wherever you are, carry within your bosom a portable heaven of joy. Remember that you are here in this world to be entertained. When you go to a movie, whether you see a tragedy, or a comedy, or a drama, you say afterward, "Oh, it was a good movie!" So must you look upon life. Have no fear. If you live in fear, health will go. Rise above disease and troubles. While you try to remedy your condition, inwardly be untouched by it. Be strong inside, with full faith in God. Then you will conquer all the limitations of the world; you will be a king of peace and happiness. That is what I want you to be.

The Lord gives you that freedom every night, in sleep. When you retire, say to Him, "Lord, the world has ended for me. I am resting in Thine arms. Thou hast put me here to watch Thy movies of life: tragedy and laughter, health and disease, life and death, wealth and poverty, war and peace—these are naught but dreams to entertain me. Untouched, I rest in the thought of Thee, the only Reality."

The End of the World Is Realized in *Samadhi*

Last of all, the end of the world is realized in *samadhi,* or divine ecstasy. There are two kinds of *samadhi.* When at first you try to sit and meditate, your mind runs away in all directions. You think it is impossible to go deep. But if you sit still and persist long enough, you will begin to feel that wonderful silence of God. When your mind is withdrawn, centered in Him, the world is forgotten and you find in that silence a happiness greater than any worldly pleasure. That state, when you are totally absorbed in inner awareness of God, no longer conscious of the world, is called *sabikalpa samadhi*. It is "partial dissolution of the world" because, when you return to ordinary consciousness, the delusions of the world will again somewhat affect you, unless you are highly evolved and free of all desires and attachments.

The second and highest state of *samadhi* is when you are in the world but not of it — carrying on your duties, but every moment conscious of God. That is *nirbikalpa samadhi*. It is the end of all limiting desires and attachments. Delusion is vanquished, and that is the true end of the world.

I would urge you to commit to memory my poem, "Samadhi,"* because that state of soul freedom is the goal of every human life roaming this earth. Many people fear that if they go off into *samadhi* they may not return to consciousness of this world. Yet they do not fear dropping off to sleep at night, when identification with the body and the world is forgotten in subconsciousness. It is nonsense to think this way about *samadhi*. It is not cessation of consciousness, but expansion of consciousness.

End Your Dream Delusions in God

End the world for yourself now, by being with God. Don't desecrate the temple of your soul with restless desires and boisterous worldly pleasures. Stand immaculate in the light of your conscience, and in the light of love for God. Reach that stage now. Then, perhaps during war in this electrical age, or in the mental age, or in the truth age, you will come like a Christ to give peace on earth and to say to mankind: "I learned the lessons God wanted me to learn. Troubles, diseases, and death mean nothing to me. I am one with the Eternal Light. The world has ended for me. Come, my brothers and sisters who are still suffering from the nightmare of this world of life and death and endless rounds of incarnations — come with me! I will show you that the end of the world means the end of your dream delusions

* The poem appears in *Autobiography of a Yogi,* chapter 14, "An Experience in Cosmic Consciousness," and also in *Songs of the Soul*.

of this earth. Learn this lesson so that your soul may shine forever—an eternal star—in the bosom of the great Lord."

Remember, you are here on earth for only a little while, but you are God's child for eternity. Don't rally with the forces of ignorance. First get to know God. Whatever He tells you to do then is all right, whether it is fighting for your country, or being a businessman, an artist, or a spiritual teacher. When you will truly know Him, you will be guided aright in life. That is why the Scripture says, "Seek ye the kingdom of God first...."

If you can live by even a few of the truths I have given, you will be a different person. You will know God if you follow the teachings of Self-Realization. When I am with you, I don't want to give you just intellectual satisfaction about truth; I want you to perceive God for yourself. I have told you how to end your imperfections so that you can go beyond—to *Him*.

The Why and How of Religion

A Sunday afternoon class on the Yoga Sutras *of Patanjali,* *
Self-Realization Fellowship Temple, Hollywood, California,
January 17, 1943

Aphorisms are tabloids, summarizing in concise statements some law or principle. The Yoga Sutras or aphorisms of the sage Patanjali are tabloids of truth. He begins by saying: "Now I speak of the discipline of Yoga," which sets the theme for his exposition of the Eightfold Path of Yoga.

Of the six principal systems of Hindu philosophy,† Sankhya expounds the *why* of religion, Vedanta describes the end to be attained, and Yoga provides the method for that attainment. Together, these concepts constitute true religion, whose twofold purpose is to show man how to avoid suffering and how to contact the bliss of the Supreme One: that lasting happiness which is not conditioned by either painful or pleasant experiences.‡ Thus religion has two phases.

Sankhya philosophy has to do with the first phase, pointing out that the primary goal of everyone is the avoidance of spiritual, mental, and physical suffering. However, we can live in a painless state and still not be happy. There are a lot of people who are suffering, and a few who are not, but it doesn't necessarily follow that those who are for the moment unafflicted are happy. The state of painlessness is agreeable, but is not itself happiness-producing. To attain true and lasting happiness, which Vedanta describes as the end or second phase of religion, a full understanding and application of the principles of religion are necessary. This is Yoga.

---

* The oldest text extant on the sacred science of Yoga is Patanjali's *Yoga Sutras* (also known as *Patanjali's Aphorisms*), which outlines the principles of the yogic path. (See *Yoga* and *Patanjali* in glossary.)

† Yoga, Vedanta, Sankhya, Mimamsa, Laya, Vaisesika.

‡ See *Sanatan Dharma* in glossary.

People who are not suffering often take the attitude, "Well, I am perfectly happy without religion." By such rationalization, many are convinced that religion is a course which those who are thus inclined may follow, and others need not. But you don't know what is coming tomorrow. The possibility of suffering is there. The ordinary human being is not free from that possibility. This is why Sankhya says that you should follow those divine laws by which you will be freed permanently from the *causes* of physical, mental, and spiritual suffering, so there is no possibility of their recurrence.

But Vedanta philosophy explains that this is not enough; this is not the whole end of religion. If you experience only the peace of mere absence of pain, sorrow, or excitement, you will eventually say, "Knock me on the head to relieve this boredom." You don't want to be merely peaceful. A person who has had too much of peace, without positive happiness, is willing to accept even sorrow in order to have a little change in his life. Beyond peace is the state of divine consciousness, ever new bliss that will never grow stale. Religion not only frees you from all suffering, but binds you to this eternal happiness, to cosmic happiness in God. Religion kills the germs of sorrow, so they can't infect your happiness. It destroys the roots of suffering, and ensures attainment of positive Bliss.

Yoga Fulfills the Purpose of Religion

How to reach that state? Patanjali says that after studying Sankhya, you should study Yoga. That is, once you understand *why* you should be religious, you must learn *how*. You have to know the way to remove whatever suffering is already present in your body, mind, and soul, and to avoid that which might arise in the future.

So long as you are still in the domain of suffering, so long you cannot be free from sorrow. You may be thinking, "Is that freedom possible?" Well, it was possible for Jesus, wasn't it? What was the purpose of Jesus' life unless to demonstrate what you too can do? That purpose is not fulfilled in just worshiping Jesus. His life was meant to inspire every one of us to be like him. Salvation is for all. Freedom from this jail of life is for all. Babaji is free. Lahiri Mahasaya and my great master, Swami Sri

Yukteswar, are free. St. Francis is free. Patanjali is free. Free souls! That is what this teaching of Self-Realization is for: to free your soul from all possibility of suffering.

So Yoga shows you the way and gives the method. And Vedanta describes the end — that after freeing yourself from suffering by finding God, you will have eternal happiness, eternal joy, eternal wisdom, eternal existence. That state is so desirable! You will be conscious of your blissful existence, and you will know that you are immortal. This experience is indescribable.

If you tell people that you are following a Hindu religion—or for that matter, any religion other than their own—prejudice immediately arises in their minds. But Patanjali goes beyond all personalities and dogmas. He states that Yoga is the heart of all religions; it is the science of religion, by which the true principles of religion can be proven with exact and known results. Yoga fulfills the purpose of religion: achievement of oneness, or union, with God—the ultimate necessity of every soul.

The Universal Science of Religion

India's *rishis*, her great sages, regarded religion as a science, the practice of which severs the bonds of human suffering and reunites the consciousness with the cosmic joy of God, in whose image we are made. Yet many people hesitate: "Oh, I am not ready for spirituality." This is the greatest untruth one can speak. Why? Because the soul is like a round peg that will not fit into the square hole of delusion. The one thing that everyone is seeking—unalloyed happiness—the world cannot give. Hence there are thousands of unhappy people throughout the world.

Some whom I have met have everything I once thought I wanted; yet they have not found happiness in the fulfillment of those desires. I sought God first, and I found that His joy is all-satisfying, ever new, more tempting than any temptation.

Since everyone's ultimate desire is to be happy and to have the joy of making others happy, and since God is the source of all happiness, there is no way you can avoid Him. And why should you? All else will betray you with lies and false promises; for naught but God can give you true and lasting joy.

In the beginning of life, in the middle of life, at the end of life, seek the happiness of God, because that alone will free you forever from all sorrows. If you think money will give you happiness, you are wasting your time; it will never do so. If you are seeking human love, you will find in God a love that is a multimillion times greater. To find God is to receive everything the heart craves. And whatever you think you need you will find fulfilled in God. To be spiritual is to open doors to health, happiness, and success. Therefore a study of the scientific conduct of life is really important. To learn how to banish suffering and attain the joy that cannot be taken away is something practical. If I had not had this study from my childhood, I would have made a horrible failure of my life.

The Age of Logic Is Here

Man lives in the grip of limitation. How does he know that in the next instant he is not going to be hurt, or that someone is not going to break his heart? The only true security is that which the great ones such as Jesus found. To have that security, and to be able to give it to every other human being, is the only real freedom, and the highest wisdom.

The age of commandments has passed. The age of logic is here. You must look in the face of every experience with intelligent discrimination until you understand it; then you will not be deluded anymore. There is a reason for everything. And in this age of analysis, you must seek that understanding. The little boy who is forced to go to Sunday school doesn't get much out of that discipline, because he hasn't been properly trained to understand why it will be helpful to him. I remember observing the Sunday schools in a Christian community in India. Instead of devotional study, there was a lot of noise and restlessness. The children had no idea how much they could have gotten out of that class.

Modern religion has divorced itself from life. It has become a Sunday morning habit, with a little prayer and singing and a message; then it is all over with for the rest of the week. On other days, it is all right to fight with one's wife; to abuse the senses; to kill one's enemies. The very foundation of religion has been forgotten.

Religion must be felt as a practical personal necessity.

When the scriptures or the saints advise you not to do a thing, use your logic and you will see that it is in your highest interest not to do it. For instance, "Thou shalt not commit adultery." Why? Because a host of troubles comes from misuse of the powerful creative force. Abuse of this sacred power is destructive to the nervous system and general health. Secondly, the emotional complications upset the heart, which is the center of feeling. One should never toy with the heart of another.

It is unwise and unkind to marry unless you are absolutely sure that the person you have chosen is someone you will want to live with the rest of your life. Never marry with the idea that if it doesn't work out you can always separate. When two people marry and want to get out of it after a few months or a few years, there was no real bond of love holding them; only sex, which quickly palls without love. If marriage is based only on sensual satisfaction, rather than on love and higher principles, then even that relationship is adultery, and the end result will be misery. If love is absent in the sexual experience between husband and wife, gradually they will seek other sex relationships. Such mistakes can and should be avoided by using discrimination before marriage.

Find Joyous Fulfillment in Divine Love

Loyalty and love between husband and wife gradually free the mind from limitation to the sex plane and uplift it to the plane of divine love. When divine love grows out of sex, that supreme love sublimates the sexual appetite into a beautiful human relationship. Sexual gratification alone does not satisfy the heart; without real love, the heart will remain hollow. But if man and woman sincerely share in the marital state the love that rests in the soul, they will find a joyous fulfillment.

One can find this fulfillment in the perfect love of God as well, and to a greater degree. Jesus didn't marry. Many of the greatest saints didn't marry, because they found a higher bliss in communion with God. He who realizes that happiness is the highest goal, and who seeks happiness in God, follows the path of wisdom.

Human beings are the cause of thousands of evils in this world, yet I don't like to refer to man as evil. To say he is in error is better. It is the senses that lead one astray into bad habits.

Don't be bound by your senses. What is the use of abusing them until your health and peace are gone? To help you prevent this, religion teaches the eternal principles of self-control and moderation, by which you can master sensual instincts. Take the sense of taste, for example. Why should you not give in to greed? Because overeating will harm your system. Some people eat any time they are near food; but all kinds of diseases arise from overeating and wrong habits of eating.

Evil Is a Boomerang

I am speaking now of the philosophy of Sankhya, which explains the *whys*. I am showing you the necessity of following the laws of religion in your daily life, and not just on Sundays.

Why should you not bear false witness against another? Because it develops an insincere attitude. Treachery is the highest sin before God. To lie about someone for personal gain or retaliation is to perjure one's soul. If everyone were insincere with everyone else, what pandemonium there would be! Suppose you tell someone that you are going to meditate, but instead your intention is to slip off to do some wrong against him; that is treachery, insincerity in its worst form. Also, to bear false witness against another in support of a wrongdoer is to participate in his wrong conduct. It will cause serious emotional and mental conflict within. Even if temporarily rationalized, it will eventually boomerang and create great distress in the consciousness.

To covet another's property is also to draw suffering to oneself, for what you give forth you will attract to yourself again. Give love and unselfishness, and you will receive love and unselfishness. But express greed, selfishness, jealousy, and you will attract in kind.

And why shouldn't you steal? Think what the world would be like if everyone lived by robbery. The greatest crimes would be perpetrated. There would be vicious fighting and killing to protect property and to regain stolen articles. Stealing is an anti-social action that deprives another of his rights. It is against the very laws of existence. And society hasn't the proper facilities and know-how to deal with wrongdoers. When thieves are put in jail they may be strengthened in their bad habits, and also acquire new ones, by association with other criminals. If this happens, they are worse than ever when they come out.

Errors in Judgment Make Us Do Wrong

There was a young man, the son of one of my students, who was imprisoned for stealing. When I went to see him, he said scornfully, "Oh, another preacher. Go on, preach to me."

"Don't be too sure," I said. "Why can't we just have a heart-to-heart talk?"

"All right," he agreed. "I will tell you my side of the story. My father was quite wealthy. But by clever manipulation, another man got all his money away from him. I went to that man and asked him to help me so I could help my family. He knew he really "stole" that money from my father; but even so, he wouldn't help me or give me a job. So I decided I didn't want to be a part of that kind of "honest" society. In two weeks I had accomplished seventeen holdups. But every robbery was committed with the intention that I would pay it back. Because of that, I figured there was no real wrong in what I was doing."

"Well," I said, "if there are twenty people in a room, and if one person says, 'I will meditate'; the second says, 'I will play music'; the third says, 'I will recite poetry'; another says, 'I will write'; another says, 'I will sleep'; and so on, everyone would be hindered by everyone else. Would any one of them be successful in doing what he wanted?"

"No," the boy admitted.

"There are many cases like yours," I continued, "but if everyone who is in need started robbing in order to get his necessities, how would it be? From the viewpoint of your reasoning, your actions do not seem wrong. But they are certainly wrong from the broader perspective of fundamental laws of existence." That struck him. I went on:

"Your desire to help your family was worthy. But instead of doing good, you have caused them much unhappiness. You failed in your effort because you used the wrong methods."

He began to weep. Later, fortunately, he was able to get a parole.

So you see, it is error in judgment that makes us do wrong.

This is why wisdom is so important. There is nothing more pure, and more purifying, than wisdom.

A Reason for Every Law

There is a reason behind every spiritual injunction. And the exposition of these reasons is the purpose of Sankhya.

"Honor thy father and mother." Why? Father and mother are representatives of God. They are but masks for the Divine Parent. Never insult the Divine Parent behind those father and mother forms. Honor them because God is in them. He gave them to look after you. But if father and mother urge the child to forsake God and righteous ways, then another law comes into play. No parent has the right to dissuade a child from seeking God and following truth. That is the one time the father and mother may be disobeyed; for our loyalty is to God, who loves us through our parents.

"Thou shalt not kill." Why? Some interpret this to mean we should not kill animals. Others say it means we should not kill human beings. And if you take the position that we should not kill anything, then we will not be able to eat at all; because eating vegetables is also taking life. Wanton destruction of any form of life is wrong—and especially so in the case of its higher expressions in animals and man. Life is a manifestation of God and rightfully commands our reverence. "Thou shalt not kill" was intended mainly as a commandment against killing one's own kind, humankind. It is wrong to take the life of another human being, because you have no right to deprive someone else of the same privilege of existence that you enjoy. You shouldn't take from anyone else something you yourself don't want to part with. The greatest love man has is for himself; so killing is wrong, because you wrest from another the very thing that you love most. A second reason is that every individual is created by God, in His image. Since you are not the maker of life, since you cannot create life, it is not your prerogative to destroy it. And a third reason is that God has built this school of life on earth where souls can come and learn; you do wrong if you deprive a soul of his schooling here. When you kill, you transgress the laws of society and the laws of God.

War is killing. It is against the principles of God. It is also against the principles of Christianity and other religions. Yet see how many wars have been fought in the name of religion, as well as of politics. War never settles anything. The First World War was said to be the war to end all wars. But that war was nothing compared to this one.* This war will be a crusade. The world has evolved, and you will see a better world. This war means the beginning of freedom for all downtrodden nations. But this could have been accomplished without war.

In the earlier days of history, kings and leaders went to the battlefield with their men; but today, those who determine that a nation will go to war remain safely behind. The next time leaders talk of warring, all the people should get together and send those leaders to the front lines. Give them a big arena with wonderfully effective ammunition, and the war will be finished in a day.

What man would want to take arms against his brother? Yet he fights and kills men living in other nations because he doesn't know that they are his brothers. Every human being should be taught from his earliest years that we are all children of the one Father. And that if we learn to love others they will learn to love us too. If everyone were educated to think this way, there could not be any wars.

When a man arms himself with a sword, his neighbor will arm himself with a gun. And if the first man gets a gun, his neighbor will get a machine gun, and so on. Man is developing bigger and more violent ways of killing. Militaristic nations will destroy themselves by fighting, but there is a justice—a divine justice — that will settle these differences. There are those mysterious laws of God that will mete out justice as it should be, and not necessarily as man wants it to be.

The Real Armament: Peace and Love

There is, of course, a difference between righteous war and aggressive war, but it would have been much better if all nations had put up their swords and said, "Let us get together and unselfishly work out our problems." In unselfish sharing and cooperation, every nation would have everything it needs. Jesus spoke of

* World War II.

the real armament: peace and love. This kind of armament will have to come. No matter how far man goes astray in wrong behavior, one day he will have to return to the immortal truths.

Sadly, the world is not yet schooled in the eternal verities and their absolute necessity in life. Patanjali's aphorisms show that these laws of righteousness are not for the church only. Politics, social life, moral life, spiritual life — all should be governed by the divine laws. I have analyzed each of the eternal commandments of religion. They are the supreme laws of happiness.

The principles of right behavior, and the *whys* of right conduct should be taught in the home, in the schools, and in Sunday schools, to guide children's lives from the very beginning. Our saints in India say that children should be started on the path of religion, the path of yoga, from the age of three, because habits begin to form then.

Obedience to a True Guru
Is the Surest Way of Wisdom

Ignorance is the archenemy of man. Therefore, to guide yourself and others by wisdom is the greatest wisdom. To all those who are around me, I speak without weighing my words. If I see error in their ways, I tell them so. But I never try in any way to muffle anyone's reason.

Obedience to the guru is the surest way when one is seeking God. Master [Swami Sri Yukteswar] first told me what to do, and afterwards he gave the reasons. I found him unerring in his wisdom. By listening to him, I saved myself many incarnations of roaming and trying to find out truth by myself. Guru is he who has experienced Truth. He serves as a guide in the dark forest of life. If you follow him, he will lead you out of the darkness. If you try to find the way alone, you may needlessly lose yourself in the forest for many incarnations. So follow the guru, and he will take you through safely.

Forms and dogma should not control religion. Religion must be based upon reason, and that reason is supplied by Sankhya philosophy. As prodigal children we have run away from God, and we must reunite our souls with Him. Uniting the soul with Spirit is Yoga — reunion with that great Happiness everyone is seeking. Isn't this a wonderful definition? In the ever new Bliss of Spirit you are convinced that the joy you feel is greater than any other happiness, and nothing can get you down.

If you are posing as religious and are not living the life as stressed by God, you should wake up. It is wrong to be insincere. The best time to begin a religious life is when you are youthful and well. If you have a short time to live, you must work harder at it. And if you have a long time to live, you should not waste that precious opportunity.

You are all alone here on earth. You owe no one but the Divine Spirit. All human relations are real only because the love of the Divine Father is in them. He is more concerned about you than are all those you think of as your loved ones. But remember, there is one thing the Master of the Universe doesn't have, and that is your love. He has been waiting throughout incarnations for each one to return home safely and say, "Father, I went a little bit astray. I made a few mistakes; but I found at last that every stream of desire leads to Thy great ocean of bliss."

What joy I felt when this realization came to me: "When I was little I thought it was my father who looked after me, my mother who caressed me, my sister who warned me, my brother who protected me; but I woke from my dream to sweetly hear 'tis Thou alone who didst tend me here. It is Thou, O God, whom I am seeking."

Dear ones, have no illusions that your dream, your goal, your aim, is any different than mine. We are all seeking that eternal, divine happiness, which is God.

The Spectrum of
Spiritual Consciousness

*Self-Realization Fellowship International Headquarters,
Los Angeles, California, August 1 and 3, 1934*

Spiritual consciousness is a vast subject; it comprises the entire scope of this human consciousness we possess.

Consciousness in its essence is ever pure. It engages in all actions, both good and evil, yet remains unaffected and untarnished. A sword may cut a leaf and become stained by it, yet the sword itself is not changed. Such is consciousness. A sword that has been used to kill an innocent man is condemned as evil. A sword that has been used to destroy a wicked enemy is honored as virtuous. Similarly, when consciousness is used to do good things, it is called spiritual consciousness, and when it is used to do wrong, it is called evil consciousness.

Just as a river has a source, so the river of consciousness has a source. It descends from Cosmic Consciousness, the consciousness of God that is beyond all creation. When Cosmic Consciousness comes into the realm of matter—into each of the atoms that make up the planets and island universes, and the different forms of plant, animal, and human life—that Consciousness is called Christ Consciousness. When Christ Consciousness descends into the soul and pure mind of man, it is called superconsciousness. When superconsciousness descends into the realm of imagination, it is called subconsciousness. When subconsciousness descends into the muscular and sensory phase of human life, it is called human or waking consciousness. When waking consciousness becomes attached to the senses and material things, it is called worldly consciousness, and when it is used to harm oneself or others, it is evil consciousness. But when it is used to do good things and to produce attunement with God, then it is called spiritual consciousness.

These are the steps by which Cosmic Consciousness makes its entry into human consciousness, descending from Spirit into the body and into our material and spiritual desires. In this way, Cosmic Consciousness becomes material consciousness as it flows downward and outward. Our souls are like derelicts floating on this river of consciousness, going farther and farther away from their source in Spirit toward the rocks of misery. The only way to stop this evolutional floating downward in the stream of consciousness is to swim against that current, back to the source in Spirit. Those who are carried on and on with the downward flowing stream of consciousness, toward finite proclivities, are spoken of as having material consciousness; and those who are going upstream, toward the source, the Spirit, are spoken of as possessing spiritual consciousness.

From time to time, the trend of human thought and consciousness may change, being either predominantly upward toward good, or downward toward matter. The trend can be predominant in these ways in a family, in a nation, or in the world in general, as well as in an individual. For just as individual human beings go through different states of consciousness, so, collectively, do families, nations, and the world. India, in her golden age, had the highest material intelligence and spirituality. America has the highest material efficiency now, and is passing into spiritual development.

India is more advanced in the science of spirituality than any other nation on the globe. Her spiritual development is seen in her saints of Self-realization. Look at Mahatma Gandhi: this one little man is dictating to the mighty British Empire. You must know that there has to be a great spiritual power behind one who can rule millions, not by a sword, but by the word of Truth, by living Truth.

Real spiritual truth in a nation or an individual is distinguishable as scientific knowledge of life and of the art of living in attunement with cosmic laws; and as greater contact and divine communion with God as Spirit. Such spiritual development does not come from swallowing theological ideas, but from assimilating the truth behind theology. One must be able to shave the husk of dogma and theory from the kernels of truth.

What Is Truth?

The outstanding feature of Self-Realization Fellowship is that it teaches you how to know the truth through actual experience. Truths are not truths to you unless you realize them within yourself. Without realization, they are just ideas. This is why, before spiritual development comes, individuals, and nations too, go through ruts of spiritual suspicion: what is spirituality? why is it necessary? will it really make me happier? what is truth? Doubt is removed only by realization. So the best laboratory in which to test truth is your own Self-realization; for spiritual perception, spiritual consciousness, lies not in vague theological ideas, but in the acquisition of Self-realization. Individual knowledge and the knowledge of nations should be tested by this criterion.

The word "truth" has been so abused that it has come to mean most anything one wants it to, especially when used to connote spiritual ideas. In everyday living, truth is a consciousness that is guided by spiritual wisdom, which propels us to do certain things, not because anybody says to, but because they are right.

Truth cannot be monopolized by any group or individual. Every human being has a right to express truth within his own life. Its expressions may be various, but its substance will ever be one and the same. This is what makes it so interesting. Truth cannot be circumscribed. It is eternal. It will keep on manifesting eternally, through cosmic law and through enlightened human beings, whether or not the majority of the world accepts it. Fortunately, the cosmic absolutes are not dependent on man's belief and sanction.

Spiritual Consciousness Obeys All the Rules That Make Life Complete

Spiritual consciousness means the use of superwisdom, truth, to do the things that supremely benefit yourself and others. Dwell on that thought. It includes selfless service to others, right behavior, adherence to hygienic and all other laws of life, and a harmonious performance of all your duties, material and spiritual, without allowing one duty to contradict another. Spiritual consciousness is a perfect internal expression of truth that manifests as a balanced, harmonious life, giving you true happiness, which you in turn share with others.

A consciousness that does not obey all the rules that make life complete is not spiritual consciousness. Some people become artists, for example, and in the pursuit of art they forget other practical and spiritual duties. Certainly, art is a beautiful expression, and may well convey spiritual ideas; yet the man who produces it may not be spiritual. To live a contradictory life — to do one duty and use it as an excuse to neglect other duties — is to live unspiritually. When you perform all duties cheerfully, without letting any duty upset your inner calm and happiness, and when you avoid any contradiction of duties that makes your life unbalanced, you will have true spiritual happiness. The trend of all your mind and consciousness will be turned back toward the source, toward God. Spiritual consciousness is the supreme consciousness you must attain in order to have a harmonious and peaceful existence. Without that spiritual balance in life, happiness is impossible. To live a contradictory life is to be unbalanced, and to lead an unbalanced life is a sure way to unhappiness.

The Inner Versus the Outer World

The senses are at the root of material consciousness. The ordinary individual is more inclined toward the world and material things than toward spiritual things, because the searchlights of his senses are directed outward. He is playing the five searchlights — of sight, hearing, smell, taste, and touch — on material objects and pleasures. This is why everything outside seems beautiful and enjoyable. You never behold the "inner world" unless these searchlights are reversed and concentrated within. Only if you learn not to be carried away by the operation of the senses will you be able to enjoy spiritual consciousness.

When you withdraw your mind inward, you will begin to perceive that there are many more wonderful things within than outside. If you think the music of this world is beautiful, you will find the astral music far more enticing. As you enjoy the touch of the cool breeze and the warm sunshine and all other wholesome sensations, so inside, as you interiorize your consciousness, you will feel the supremely enjoyable subtle perceptions of the forces in the spiritual cerebrospinal centers in the body. Everything beautiful in this world is but a gross copy of the radiant grandeur of the astral world. Nothing material can compare with those wondrous visions of the inner world. Spiritual consciousness brings astral perception of the wisdom and beauty that is behind all material phenomena.

The beauty of nature is like a fountain. You see the beauty of the spray, but you do not see the wonders inside the droplets. The astral light and color behind each atom are indescribably beautiful. In this fountain of beauty in nature, you see only the gross external, not the subtle inner beauty, nor the Power that gives that beauty to nature.

"O Lord, all things are beautiful because they have borrowed their beauty from Thee. The moon smiles and the stars twinkle because Thou art sparkling there. Because Thou art beautiful, all things are beautiful; without Thee, nothing is beautiful. O Infinite Beauty, Thou art more beautiful than all things beautiful that come from Thee. The beauties of nature are but waves of Thy beauty, dancing in Thee, O Invisible Spirit of Beauty!"

Spirituality Embraces a Wide Field of Controlled Activity

To be spiritual is not to be an angel with wings, but something infinitely greater — one who is in touch with God. You must live differently than the ordinary man, who is in touch only with sense consciousness. Spiritual consciousness lies in absolute victory over human consciousness. Now, spirituality does not mean only to meditate; it embraces a very wide field of controlled existence. However, meditation is the best foundation. It is the greatest way to be spiritual, the simplest way to spiritualize the consciousness. It will bring into your life all the good you have ever dreamed of acquiring. But to meditate, on the one side, and be angry or lead a desultory life on the other, is like putting your feet in two boats going in opposite directions. You must not only meditate, but also learn to behave. To have spiritual consciousness is to be able to do those things that are in your highest interest. And I can bet that ninety-nine percent of the people do not know in what lies their own good.

A practical way to understand right from wrong behavior is to introspect and criticize ourselves. Every person should keep a mental diary. Mental diaries are much better than material ones, which are objects of curiosity to others. Many people write down nice thoughts and resolutions in their diaries, and then promptly forget about them. It is better to keep a mental diary in which you constantly watch your thoughts and actions. At certain times during the day have a check-up on your physical, mental, and spiritual machines, to see how they are behaving. This will help develop your spiritual consciousness.

God alone will look into your mental diary. If you fill it with right thoughts and behavior, it is your passport to heaven. So put into your mental diary only the things that are good. Do not listen to negative things, do not talk negatively, do not think negative thoughts. Let no action of yours cause anything negative in others; harm to others acts as a boomerang and hurts you most of all. Sin is not like dynamite, which you can explode from a distance without harm to yourself. It has to be defused within your own soul.

Never be mean. Have resentment toward none. I prefer some sinners with good hearts to some so-called good people who are bigoted and uncompassionate. To be spiritual is to be broad, to understand and forgive, and to be a friend to all.

If you say you are a friend to all, it should be true. If you proffer friendship, you must mean it. You must not show kindness or cooperation outside, and inside feel the opposite. Spiritual law is very powerful. Don't go against spiritual principles. Never deceive or be treacherous. As a friend, know when to mind your own business; understand your place; know when you should have the willingness to cooperate, and when you should have the will to noncooperate.

If you make people feel you are their friend, if they know you are a friend ready to help, that is a wonderful power to live by. I have always been trusted. My guru, Sri Yukteswar, said to me, "If ever I do wrong, take my head on your lap and bless me." Such was his humility and perfect expression of what divine friendship means.

I remember a boy in my school in India; he had been a problem child, and his parents brought him to me. We used to take only children under twelve, and he was much older. I had a heart-to-heart talk with him. I told him that there were no bars on the school doors, that he could walk out any time. I said he could stay only if he were willing to be good. I reasoned with him: "You have made up your mind to smoke, and your parents do not want you to. You have succeeded in defeating your parents, but you have not succeeded in defeating your unhappiness. You are the one who is the most miserable as a result of your misbehavior."

My arrow struck home. He began to weep, saying, "They are always beating me."

I went on: "Think of what you have done to yourself. Come on, I will take you on condition that I will be your friend but not your detective. As long as you are willing to mend your mistakes, I will be your helper. But if you lie to me, I will do nothing for you. Lying destroys friendship." I added, "Any time you want to smoke, don't do it behind my back; rather, tell me, and I will get you the cigarettes."

One day he came to me and said, "I feel a terrible desire to smoke." I gave him money and told him to go and buy the cigarettes. He could not believe his eyes.

"Take back the money," he said.

I was pushing him to go, but he would not go. At last, after this tug-of-war, he said, "You will not believe me, but I do not want cigarettes anymore." He became a saintly person. I had roused the spiritual consciousness in him.

Sincerity and Intensity of Effort Is What Counts

Spiritual consciousness lies in the sincere internal effort to go upstream toward real lasting happiness. Many people say they are following a righteous course, but very few are really making a sincere effort. It isn't demanded of you that you be an angel all at once. Since only the Absolute is perfect, we can say that before God even the best angel is a sinner. But saints are sinners who did not give up. No matter what your difficulties, if you do not give up, you are making progress in your struggle against the stream. To struggle is to win the favor of God. You must make that supreme effort. Do not idly let life float you down the stream.

You can't fool God, because He sees your thoughts. He won't measure how long you have worked for spiritual attainment; it is your intensity that counts. No matter how many incarnations of bad karma you might have, if your devotion and sincerity are deep enough to bring into your consciousness the light of God, all darkness of the evil of incarnations will be burned away.

So no matter if your sins are as deep as the Atlantic Ocean, make constant mental effort to become good. For a few incarnations you have been a human being, but throughout eternity you have been a child of God. Never think of yourself as a sinner, because sin and ignorance are only mortal nightmares. When we will awaken in God, we will find that we—the soul, the pure consciousness—never did anything wrong. Untainted by mortal experiences, we are and ever have been the sons of God. We are like gold in the mud: when the mud of ignorance is cleansed away, the shining gold of the soul, made in God's image, is seen within.

Spiritual consciousness comes from a firm mental resolve. No matter how others are behaving around you or toward you, you yourself have to be good. The greatest enemy of yourself is yourself. You procrastinate about being good. I used to get into mental ruts, and many months would pass when I couldn't meditate deeply. Yet I continued to make the mental effort. Progress came fast when I suddenly realized that I had to be more determined to control all my habits and exercise my spirituality. Similarly, you have to take control of your behavior and consciousness. Do the things you know you should do, and don't do anything that is contrary to spiritual consciousness.

The Opposite Modes of Material and Spiritual Consciousness

Spiritual and material consciousness are opposite in their modes of operation. You can test yourself as to whether you are filled with material or spiritual consciousness. Spiritual consciousness tells you that you must include in your happiness and prosperity the happiness and well-being of others. Material consciousness tells you that you should make a dollar any way you can, and keep it for yourself. The depression in the thirties began out of material consciousness. Material consciousness says to eat your apple and cookies yourself. Spiritual consciousness says to divide and share with someone else.

If somebody angers you, know you are in material consciousness. Even if you have been maltreated, still you should be ready to forgive. When you forgive, you are in spiritual consciousness. Forgiving means to give your enemy a chance to gain better understanding. If you become vengeful or angry, you only make your enemy more blind and angry. You may even make more enemies, for an angry person is the target of all. In addition, as soon as you get angry, you also begin to misunderstand. You back up your wrong feelings with the comforting warmth of your anger and false reasoning. Never let anger control you. If you have this tendency, cut it off. It is one of the worst traits that destroy spirituality. Know that it is for your own good that you should not get angry. Anger is destructive to your happiness. Never let your mental thermometer go up. Be calm inside. Control anger from within. Never give it a place in your heart.

Material consciousness is quarrelsome; spiritual consciousness gets along with everybody. Make the effort to be good yourself, and you will see that you influence others to be good automatically. That is spiritual consciousness. Be kind in speech and thought. From my childhood I have never knowingly been unkind. Don't be critical, cither. When people complain about others, they usually have a grudge. Jesus said, "Judge not, that ye not be judged."* If you want to judge someone, judge yourself. If you want to talk about others' faults, talk about your own. Have only love in your heart for others. The more you see the good in them, the more you will establish good in yourself. Hold the consciousness of good. The way to make people good is to see the good in them. Do not nag them. Remain calm, serene, always in command of yourself. You will then find out how easy it is to get along.

I am an optimist where people are concerned, because I love them. When you love everyone, you see God in all. If you know that everybody is an expression of God, then to be angry or unkind with anyone is to be angry or unkind with God. When you are angry or mean or uncompassionate, you put a blind between your soul and the souls of others.

Arrogance and insolence are also unspiritual traits. They are

* Matthew 7:1.

born out of an inferiority complex. Suppose I am the cook in this ashram, and when somebody gives me a little suggestion about my work, I say that I already know it all—that is insolence. The insolent person advertises the limitation of his knowledge, and also his lack of breeding. If you want to favorably impress others, why advertise your inferiority by a display of insolence and arrogance? It shows nothing more than a lack of manners and intelligence, and an uncontrolled temperament. Insolence and arrogance are forms of ignorance—unspiritual habits in their primitive state.

Your Highest Good Lies in Spiritual Consciousness

Understand in what lies your highest good. Wherever you are, whatever your responsibilities, your greatest happiness lies in living in harmony with the ideas you are taking from these teachings of Self-Realization. Good and evil are not the creations of man, but virtue and sin are. They result from your acceptance of either good or evil. In spiritual consciousness your whole consciousness, no matter what your faults are, is turned toward good—toward God. Remember these simple guidelines:

Control the senses. Turn those five searchlights inward in meditation. In that inner silence, you will know the Beauty and Bliss—beyond material imagination—that is God. The senses do not keep their promises of happiness. If you have everything in this world, you will find you still want something else; and your happiness will be a slave to your possessions. To be supremely happy and free, you must be a man of renunciation— one who is master of the senses and is nonattached to possessions. True renunciation means to renounce material consciousness for spiritual consciousness. It is not exclusive, but inclusive, for to have spiritual consciousness is to possess everything that will make you truly and lastingly happy.

Control your habits and behavior. A life of spiritual harmony — whether lived in the context of the individual, the ashram, the family, the nation, or the world—requires willing cooperation with the rules of right behavior, and a loving understanding and cooperation with others. The standards and rules of spiritual harmony are higher than those of material harmony. Follow them strictly. Be your own judge, and court-martial yourself. If the verdict is that you have done wrong, correct yourself. Otherwise, your bad habits and wrong behavior will act against you like a boomerang. Better still, guide all your actions by the inner voice of spiritual consciousness, so that you will do no wrong.

Live a balanced life. That is, live in harmony with the divine laws governing material and spiritual duty (let not one responsibility contradict other important duties); health (millions need a greater consciousness of health, for diseases are not created by God but by man's breaking God's laws); prosperity (include others in your own well-being); and human relationships. Do not leave anybody out of your love. Keep everyone in your heart, and they will keep you in theirs. You will be a king on the throne of all hearts, commanding their love and influencing them to goodness, not by force, but by your love.

The Mind:
Repository of Infinite Power

*Self-Realization Fellowship International Headquarters,
Los Angeles, California, October 12, 1939*

The Western point of view is that knowledge of God can be received through book learning. But one defect in this approach is that every study should have a practical as well as a theoretical side. You can acquire a mental concept from a story you read in a book, but its practical value in daily life remains to be seen. All too often the intellect becomes satisfied with just a theory about God. Great and glorious is the story of God's presence; but greater and more glorious is the actual perception of the Infinite. I speak only of what I have experienced, for personal experience is the practical aspect of religion.

If you practice one millionth of the things that I tell you in these Thursday night meetings, you will reach God. Success doesn't lie in listening to my sermons, but in practicing what I have told you. Today you will learn how to develop the seeds of your innate God-given faculties of the mind.

Our Little Minds Are Part of God's Omnipotent Mind

The mind of God created the stars and all the worlds. Mind is the supreme factor that is working throughout creation, that is keeping the cells of our bodies together. And this wonderful consciousness in every particle of matter is all the work of that divine mind—the mind that needs no instrument to accomplish its object.

Our little minds are part of the omnipotent mind of God. Beneath the wave of our consciousness is the infinite ocean of His consciousness. It is because the wave forgets it is a part of the Ocean that it becomes isolated from that oceanic power. As a result, our minds have become weakened by our trials and material limitations. The mind has stopped its work. You will be surprised how much it can do if you cast off the limitations you have put on it.

The pure mind of the child, which is open and imaginative, free of prejudices and habits, is more attuned to the mind of God. But when the child grows up and experiences the trammels of material life, his mind takes on the limitations of that existence and becomes restricted in its scope. You become your worst enemy when you limit your mental power. To work with your mind is tremendously worthwhile. You haven't tried its powers at all. To break through mental limitations is what you should strive for. I have always done that, because I wanted to be different. And when I met my guru, Swami Sri Yukteswar, I realized how supernally different he was. Most people are copies of someone else, imitating what others do. They have no independent thinking. You should be a different individual, expressing the very best of your own unique nature.

Why shouldn't you develop your mind power and use it for any attainment you desire? All around are storms of difficulties, and everyone is after his own; nobody is thinking of you. And in this clash of individualities you are a little mind about to be crushed and swept away. But if you reason this way—"God loves me even as he loved Jesus, Krishna, and Buddha. He cannot be partial; He has given me this mind, which contains the germ of infinite power, and I am going to cultivate this power"—you will win.

The Seeds of Success Are Within You

Success doesn't come from outside; it is in your brain. As soon as you think a right thought, work it. Some people have a good idea but they haven't the tenacity to think it through and work it out. You must have courage and perseverance, and think, "I am going to see my idea through. It may be that I won't win out in this life, but I will make the effort." Think and act, think and act. That is how to develop your mind power. Every idea is a little seed, but you have to grow it.

Suppose you have determined that you are going to make a thousand dollars. You continuously flow that thought through your brain, and you take certain actions; and you earn the thousand dollars. Essentially, it is the mind that did it. If there had been no thought in the mind that you wanted a thousand dollars, you wouldn't have made it.

Seeds look so small, yet in a tiny seed may be a huge tree, with towering trunk and heavy branches. But the potential alone doesn't make the tree. You have to put the seed in the ground, give it water and look after it. Then, when the tree is full-grown, you can say that the little seed has produced that mighty tree. So with success: it is a little seed-thought and you have to develop it. It won't grow without your help, just as seeds will not grow without your giving them care. All kinds of seeds of power are within you, waiting for you to develop them.

Thought Can Be Materialized

Truth is more real than mere thought or imagination, but whatever we think or imagine may sometime come to be true. Years ago, Jules Verne wrote several scientific adventure novels which at the time were regarded merely as fiction; but since then, many of his concepts have become realities.* Imagination is a very important factor in creative thought. But imagination has to be ripened into conviction. You can't do that without a strong will. But if you imagine something with all the power of your will, your imagination will be converted into conviction. And when you can hold that conviction against all odds, it will come true. Master [Swami Sri Yukteswar] used to say that if your will is strong, whatever you imagine will be created for you. It is a fact.

You can develop that kind of imagination. You could conceive of a mansion floating in the ether, and if your imagination is strong enough, you might see it; and if your imagination becomes hardened into conviction, you might be able to materialize that building or be the cause of its creation through natural means. This is not a dream; it is possible. In Kashmir, and on several other occasions long before I came to America, I saw in vision this building that is now our Mt. Washington international headquarters.† I found and chose this place my-

---

* Jules Verne (1828–1905) forecast with remarkable accuracy many later technological developments, such as the submarine, television, and space travel.

† See *Autobiography of a Yogi,* chapter 21.

self, without anyone else's guidance. It was built for this purpose, because that thought was in the ether.

Thought works! It is a marvelous force. Believe in the power of thought, which comes from God, and use all the strength of your heart, your will, to try to materialize that thought. Remember, God is with you. You are exercising His power, which you have borrowed from Him, and when you do that He will be nearer to you to help you.

Many things that I have thought have come into being. A long time ago I was thinking of our need for a place where we could have a temple closer to Hollywood than is Mt. Washington. I applied my will to that thought and we got our second temple.* I had also wanted a temple by the Ganges in India. It is through the wish and the blessing of Lahiri Mahasaya and Babaji that I have been able to acquire a most beautiful place right on the banks of the Ganges at Dakshineswar, our Yogoda Math.† It is about twenty minutes from Calcutta, and is a great asset to our work. I am very happy about it.

"Whatsoever ye shall ask in prayer, believing, ye shall receive."‡ You must *believe* that. When devotees go to the Tarakeswar Temple in India — famed for miraculous healings effected there — and think and strongly imagine that God will heal them, He does. Instantaneous cures are the result. When your prayers or wishes are not successful, it is because you have no will, and you have no faith. If with a doubting mind you ask

* Self-Realization Fellowship services were held at this temple, at 711 Seventeenth Street in Los Angeles, from December 1934 to September 1939. The temple property was later taken over by the city of Los Angeles for a freeway right-of-way.

† Dedicated in 1939. "Yogoda" is a word coined by Paramahansa Yogananda in 1916, and is derived from *yoga,* union, harmony, equilibrium; and *da,* that which imparts. A *math* is, strictly speaking, a monastery, but the term is often applied to an *ashram* or hermitage.

The Yogoda Math at Dakshineswar is the headquarters of Yogoda Satsanga Society of India, the name by which Paramahansa Yogananda's organization is known in India. In the West, Yoganandaji rendered the name of his society in English, incorporating his work there as Self-Realization Fellowship. Sri Daya Mata has been president since 1955 of both Yogoda Satsanga Society of India and Self-Realization Fellowship. (See glossary.)

‡ Matthew 21:22.

God to heal you, you won't be healed. Or if you meekly ask, "Lord, shall I have a hermitage by the Ganges? I know it is impossible, but I would like to have it," God says, "You can't have it." But if you say, "I am going to have it; I shall be just like a bulldog that won't let go," and then use your will to work toward that goal, you will succeed.

To Achieve Something Is to Please God

Everyone here has some ideals; that is what I like about America. The American spirit is to try to create something new and better. In Washington, D.C., millions of patents have been registered. Your creative ability is wonderful to see. No one should live without creative effort. If you haven't exercised your will power to accomplish something difficult in life, you haven't lived up to the standard of a child of God. You have insulted the image of God within. You must exercise your divine gift of creativity in some way. It is never too late. Do you know what old age is? It is when your mind becomes "hardboiled"—accepting the limitations imposed by body-consciousness and closing its doors to creative thinking. I have had people of all ages, some of them ready to step into the grave, telling me all the things they intend to accomplish, and how much money they are going to make!

It is better to try to achieve or to create something worthwhile, for to live idly is to do yourself the worst possible harm. What you don't realize is that in life you cannot stand still. You go either backward or forward. And most of you go backward, because your will is stationary, inert. So you must be watchful not to be physically or mentally lazy, not to imitate others rather than be creative.

If you have not achieved anything in life, you may as well consider yourself dead, because like a zombie you are moving toward the valley of death. But every time you make use of your will power, God says, "This person has done rightly; he has used his God-given power." Everything you do is recorded within yourself. The effect of each positive action is locked up in your brain, and that mental tabloid tendency becomes a powerful potential to bring about any achievement you are seeking. And to achieve something, whether mental or physical, is to be favored by God.

How much better it is to use that power of mind than to let it ossify and become like a fossil: for millions of years it lies in the sunshine and doesn't change. A person with a mind like that is done for. He cannot make a success of life. So don't be a mental fossil; be a living tree, constantly spreading out new growth. The strong-hearted soul says, "There is sunshine in my life, and I have every chance to throw out shoots and branches of accomplishment. One day I will be a success: the Lord of the universe shall come to bless and praise the fruits that I have created." So develop your mind, be creative.

Work on Your Progress With God

If you are not accomplishing anything in life, make a start: Watch your health—change your diet, if necessary; give up bad eating habits. Change your thinking — give up negative, dark thoughts, and be more positive, so that you can acquire something materially when you wish to. Above all, work on your progress with God. This is the most important of all creative thinking. If your will is being broken in spite of your spiritual resolve, do something about it. Everything will come to tempt you as soon as you want God. You are made to feel that in worldly diversions you will find happiness, but that diversion takes you away from your spiritual pursuits and destroys your will power. When I started on this path, never did I go to movies or seek other such distractions. I meant business with God—and now, after finding Him, whatever I do is like child's play. He has given me everything; but there is nothing more interesting to me than that constant communion within myself with the Beloved of my universe.

Complete surrender to God is the only goal in life I could conceive of. It is only through God, and in God, that I can see the perfection I had sought, and so it is to Him alone that I can give my complete allegiance; for everything else disillusions us. When you watch people with the eyes of wisdom, everyone falls short. Only God satisfies. He gave to me more than I ever expected in life. I had refused to think as others were thinking, to act as others were acting, to be like others. I knew there was something more to be sought in life. It is all right to have material things, in their place; but I have no need or desire of my own for these things. For me there is only One, the Lord. The joy of His being is always there.

I want you to know that whenever I have told of personal experiences, it is not to extol myself, but to tell the joy of the accomplishment to encourage you, that you might try also. It is because you think you are licked that you are licked; but no matter how many times you are bowed by the bludgeons of circumstances, lift up your head again! Tell yourself, "My body may be beaten, but my spirit is not conquered." That is the way to have success. Power of mind, the power of creation, is necessary. Then you know the joy of accomplishment.

Make the Best of Circumstances

Nineteen years have gone by since I came here to America. When I see what I have been able to achieve I have no complaint, I have no regrets. But every bit of it has been hard work! This spirit cannot be had by weaklings. It is possessed only by the valiant. So be powerful. Before disease and poverty strike you down, make the most of the opportunity you have now. I am always thinking of what I can create—not that I want to be noticed by the world, but to please God. Each one of you can be like that. You can do good in hundreds of thousands of ways. God doesn't expect you to do spectacular things, but he does want you not to be a lazybones. He wants you to use all the power you have. Otherwise, as His child, you desecrate His name. Whatever your present circumstance, make the best of it. No matter how many times you fall down, get up with the determination to be victorious. Whatever I wanted to accomplish, I made up my mind it was going to be, and it was! Try it. You will see how much power you have. You will see this power work. You will have a lot of fun with it.

We get what we merit in life. So if you want to be a success, you must create that success now. There are no limits to your mind. In every kind of work, whether religious or commercial, there are those who have done their utmost to bring a certain status to their lives. When such a person has worked his way up to become the head of a business or spiritual organization, he highly respects those under him who can help in attaining the goals of the organization. But those less successful tend to wonder why that person should hold such a big position, and why they couldn't have had it instead. They forget that he was creative and worked hard. Some may feel that he got the job through "pull," but the truth is that a successful individual has created that vibration of success during this life or previous lives. Otherwise, he couldn't have attained his present position.

Wherever there is money, the vultures of envy and greed will come. So no matter how unselfish you are, there will be those who will be jealous of your accomplishment. Some people want to live lazily on the efforts of others. Be honorable enough never to hang on anyone else. You are a child of God. You have all the power necessary to take yourself where you want to go. Various ways I have had to try in order to support this work of Self-Realization on my own initiative. Never beg; I have never done so. Don't think that somebody else should give you a lift. The pleasure is in making a success of your life, not in getting things easily.

Never Accept Failure

You are living in a world of competition. Competition doesn't throttle you if you have determination. It makes you stronger. You have to do your best every day under all circumstances, and then you can be a success. But most people don't apply themselves. Or they are always thinking that everything goes wrong for them — that they always have bad luck. Why shouldn't things go wrong? They don't give time to growing the seeds of success that are within their minds; they are too busy with useless things. Many of you think you don't even have any seeds of success in you, but you *do* have. You can succeed. You can make it. But if you think, "I am done for," you are finished right then; you have already given yourself the decree that you have failed. But if you remain positive and think, "All right, I will succeed," and go on trying, you will succeed.

Don't brood over past failures. People who do always say that everything they touch ends in failure. Why do they fail? Because their minds have been convinced that they will fail. More than once I have become completely penniless in trying to support this work, but I have always regained the necessary resources. It requires courage, because the mind will say, "After all these years, you are right back where you started." But I say to the mind, "Keep quiet. I will make you work. We will see who is boss." You have to work; you have to make the effort to accomplish. Every failure gives you the privilege of learning something new: you see how to avoid those things that were wrong before. It is only when your mind becomes weak that your body becomes weak and you refuse to work. Then you are done for—you are dead. So never give up.

This life is a great game. Make the effort to win it. Thousands of people in this world are suffering—some have no hands, or no feet to walk with. How can you, with all your faculties at your disposal, admit failure? You must not do so. When you go backward your mental outlook is so dim that you think the whole world is going backward. But you will always advance if you are accomplishing something. Develop your mind power. Let the whole world be at your command.

Seek Divine Guidance

Schedule your life. Don't waste time. If you socialize with people all the time, you can't amount to anything. Be by yourself. Get away from people and dive deep within yourself. Ask, "How am I going to succeed?" Whatever you want to do, think about it until you are lost in that idea. Think, think, think, and make plans. Then take a little time; don't jump into anything at once. Take a step, and then think more. Something within tells you what to do. Do it, and think some more. Some further guidance will come. By learning to go deep within, you will connect your consciousness with the superconsciousness of the soul, so that with infinite will power, patience, and intuition you can grow those idea-seeds of success.

While you try to create what you have in mind, always ask the Father to guide you. If your ego is blind and has a strong voice, it may drown out intuition and mislead you. But if you seek only to please God by your efforts to do something worthwhile, He will guide your footsteps from error to good. The right way to work toward success is to try to please God, do your best, and then don't worry about it.

In this world, you have to play your part in God's drama; but if you get lost in the drama, you will make a mess of your life. You will know too late that you have wasted your time. Why shouldn't you turn the wheel of life instead of being run over by it?

You Create Your Own Helplessness or Strength

Whatever you make up your mind to do, you must be able to carry out. So many people make themselves helpless by wrong habits. Get away from those persons who influence you to do evil. The helplessness you feel is caused by no one but yourself. Your weak mind is being pulled backward by the very cords that you have tied to bad habits. Most people are self-hypnotized by their environment and wrong habits, and by strong tendencies and moods brought with them from past lives. It is an insult to your mind and to the image of God within to allow yourself to be hypnotized by these limitations. You must break your bad habits and develop the power of mind by which you can command your own life.

Begin to live rightly. Exercise, eat wisely, and so on. Don't think you can get away with eating and living wrongly, even though you are not suffering now. All too soon the devastating effects will catch up with you. I remember a student who weighed two hundred pounds and looked rather homely and aged. She asked me if she could do anything about her health. "Of course you can," I said, "provided you have will power. You have been thinking that you can't do anything with yourself; you have hypnotized your will to accept that thought." I told her to exercise by walking, to eat plenty of fruits, vegetables, and nuts, and to cut out all starchy foods and sweets. I reminded her that in the beginning her mind would urge her to take a little something sweet, and she would be tempted to give in. "But you must make up your mind that you are going to lose weight, and then follow through, with will power," I said. Several months later I saw this woman again and I asked, "Is this you?" "Yes," she answered; "it is so wonderful." She had lost her heaviness and looked so much younger and happier.

Have you looked in your mental account book to find out whether your income of good experiences has been greater than the cost of your wrong actions? No. You would see that, for the most part, expensive bad habits have eaten up the profits of happiness. I used to introspect like that so that I could make my life the way I wanted it to be.

Analyze your own life. In the morning you get up and quickly say a short prayer. Then you eat and go to work. Next comes lunchtime, more work, and then dinnertime and some useless diversion; and before long you are off to bed. The same old thing, every day! And every day your will is being broken by the dictates of your habits and environment. Why do you allow this? You excuse yourself and say, "Someday I will try to do those things I know I should do." But that day may never come. Why limit your capability to the adage, "Don't bite off more than you can chew"? I believe you should bite off more than you can chew, and then chew it! Don't be useless. Make your life worthwhile.

Material Success Becomes Empty Without God

Everything moves so fast in America. You are always busy doing something. And it is better to reap the harvest of the world than to be a lazy man. But you must also reap the richest harvest of life — God. The only way to attain true happiness is to accomplish something in this world *and* to achieve success with the Lord. Your most worthwhile activity is daily communion with God. The demands of the world are constantly breaking your will power to seek Him. But no matter what the world gives you, your heart will still wish for God. You know that when you die, not all the power on earth can do anything for you. Who can help you then? God. And this is why you must always reason that this world is only a stopping place. Your home is with Him.

After all you have done, this earth life becomes empty because you are going to have to leave everything eventually. One day you will have to part with all your material possessions. You envy the power and wealth of a Henry Ford, but he too will have to leave everything behind, except that great will power and success consciousness which he has attained. He will be able to use those in another incarnation to find God more quickly when he begins his search divine.

You may say that life is ebbing away and you are going to die anyway, so why try for success? I would answer as the Gita says,* that at the moment of death, even one second before, if you can leave the body with the conviction that you are victori-

---
* Bhagavad Gita II:72 and VIII:6.

ous in life, so shall it be. If you go with the conviction that you will be with the Lord, so shall it be. But if you go with the consciousness that you are done for, so shall it be. Whatever thoughts predominate as a result of the way you have lived your life, those thoughts determine your after-death state and the pattern of your next life. Can you remember that? There is no excuse to say that you are too old or otherwise unable to succeed materially and spiritually.

Jesus demonstrated the ultimate in success. He did what a million businessmen would not be able to do. Why? Because he had God. So, let your greatest ambition be to find God, to be with God, to commune with Him, and to use your will power to do the things in life that you ought to do—for Him. If you see that you are not pleasing God, ask yourself how you can better please Him: how you can be nicer to everyone; how you can meditate deeper. Think, and then act. This is the way to develop.

Make God Break His Vow of Silence

No matter what happens, if you are more and more with God, you will find that He is with you always. But will you make that effort? Every day, in the beginning, my mind used to say, "You can't know God. Only great ones like Krishna, Jesus, and Buddha could." Then I would reason, "If God favored them, He is partial; but I know He is not—He does not favor anyone. Even they had to go through great trials. But they were divinely successful, so I too can realize God."

Make the effort to find God by trying to convince Him that you want Him, and by trying to bend His will to speak to you. You have to make God break His vow of silence; then He will speak. That is what makes it difficult to know Him. It requires devotional perseverance. How many years I secretly cried for God! But I know that I can never lose Him now, because He is not apart from me. He is ever with me. When the wave melts into the ocean and becomes one with it, the wave cannot feel lost from the ocean anymore. So are we: when we become one with Spirit, we cannot feel separated from God again.

Above all, then, find time for God. No matter how tired you are at the end of the day, as soon as everyone else retires, you get up and throw yourself at His feet. Don't sleep until you have communed with Him. Pray to Him in the language of your heart:

"My Lord, You come first. I have made up my mind that in the temple of night I shall give myself to loving You. You are my everything: You are my sleep. You are my life. You are my death, if necessary. I want You alone. You are sufficient. I offer all my power, all my inner thought, all my love, to feel You, to be with You, to love You."

"Lord, Don't Make Me a Spiritual Clown"

Much of the time now I remain secluded from people. I don't mix with those who just waste my time. I found it was the only way I could be with God. As soon as you are too much with people on the social plane, you are not with God anymore. I used to accept all kinds of invitations, but I gave that up. The kings of Europe used to keep a clown in the court to amuse them. "Lord," I prayed, "don't make me a spiritual clown in this cause of Self-Realization. I would rather eat dirt than have to bow to some person who would give me money for Your work and tell me that I have to do this or that in return. I would prefer to be with the yogis in the jungle, who have renounced everything, and who quietly bless the world with their God-communion." Unlike the minister who bows to the rich in order to make his church prosperous, these saints are real kings—great spiritual men—rulers of themselves. You see their joy—such contentment, peace, and bliss. That comes not from material gain, but by using the will power to develop cosmic consciousness—that consciousness that is one with God. Be inwardly free like those yogis. Be with God, so that you can laugh at life when it tries to strike you down.

My life is finished. I have accomplished what I wanted to do. But one thing is never finished—my love for the Lord. It will be an eternal enjoyment within the sanctum of my soul. I couldn't work for myself, but I love to do for God and to help others. It is a lot of fun making success for God. Just think how a little thought in your brain, when put to work, can do something wonderful to make others happy and to leave "footprints in the sands of time."* Meditate and draw others to this path of Self-

---

* "Lives of great men all remind us / We can make our lives sublime, /And, departing, leave behind us / Footprints in the sands of time."—*A Psalm of Life*, by Henry Wadsworth Longfellow.

Realization. That is the highest service you can perform.

The Joy of Pleasing God

These are my happiest days. I am happy for two reasons: I have been able to please God, and I have been able to fulfill the pledge that I gave to my guru, Swami Sri Yukteswar, to build this work of Yogoda Satsanga/Self-Realization to spread the message of Kriya Yoga. The forces of evil have always battled me, but God has destroyed them all. On and on this work is marching!

Every day I say, "Lord, my dreams are all finished. The only thing I know now is my love for You." Such is the joy of God. There is nothing else to live for. In India, hundreds of young men are crazy for God, as hundreds here are crazy for money and power. It is better to play at hide-and-seek with God than to play with the will-o'-the-wisp of materialism that leads to death. "Death" means disillusionment. It is the point when you accept defeat and give up. You have to come out of this ignorance of your divine potential. The Lord says, "Come *now*. Resurrect yourself from the tomb of ignorance." Finally, when you refuse to be laid beneath the slabs of your weaknesses, you become free.

All who have heard this message, make the effort to find God now. Meditate every day and prune out all the weeds of weaknesses, that the garden of your life may be beautiful. The world wants to make a slave of you. You must snatch time away from the world to be alone with God. Suppose you are resting with eyes closed: someone comes and places flowers before you, but you are too sleepy to open your eyes. When you do, those flowers are gone. So it is with people who seek God halfheartedly. He comes to them, but their eyes are closed in dreams of this world; and when they open them again, He is gone. Seek Him sincerely, day and night, in meditation and in all your activities. When the dreams of your desires die away, you will find Him everywhere.

Pray with me: "Heavenly Father, bless me that I develop all the seeds of spiritual power and success that are within me, and that I use them to please Thee, whom I love more than all Thy gifts. Be Thou mine evermore."

Why Evil Is a Part of God's Creation

Self-Realization Fellowship Temple, San Diego, California, November 17, 1946

Some say that God doesn't know evil, because they can't explain why a God who is good allows robberies, murders, disease, poverty, and other terrible happenings that are going on constantly on this earth. These misfortunes are certainly evil to us; but are they evil to God? If they are, why would God permit such evil? And if the evil did not come from Him who is the Supreme Creator of all things, where did it come from? Who created greed? Who created hate? Who created jealousy and anger? Who created harmful bacteria? Who created sex temptation, and the temptation of greed? These were not the invention of human beings. Man could never have experienced them if they had not first been created.

Some people try to explain that evil does not exist, or that it is merely a psychological factor. But this is not so. The evidence of evil is here in the world. You cannot deny it. If there is no evil, why would Jesus pray, "Lead us not into temptation, but deliver us from evil"?* He is saying plainly that evil does exist.

So the truth is, we do find evil in the world. And where did it come from? God.† Evil provides the contrast that enables us to recognize and experience goodness. Evil had to be, if there was to be any creation. If you wrote a message with white chalk on a white board, no one would see it. So without the blackboard of evil, the good things in the world could not be magnified at all. For instance, Judas was Jesus' best publicity agent. By his evil act, Judas made Christ eternally famous. Jesus knew the role he

---

* Matthew 6:13.
† "I am the Lord, and there is none else. I form the light, and create darkness: I make peace, and create evil: I the Lord do all these things."—Isaiah 45:6-7.

had to play, and all that was going to happen to him in order that he might demonstrate the love and greatness of God; and a villain was necessary to this enactment. But it was not good for Judas that he chose to be the one whose dark deed, by contrast, extolled the glories of Christ's triumph over evil.

Perfection Is Not to Be Found in This World

It is hard to know where the dividing line is between good and evil. Certainly it is terrible that bacteria kill two billion people every hundred years. But think of the chaos of overpopulation if there were no death! And if everything here were good and perfect, no one would leave this earth of his own accord; no one would want to go back to God. So in a sense misery is your best friend, because it starts you seeking God. When you begin to see clearly the imperfection of the world, you will begin to seek the perfection of God. The truth is that God is using evil, not to destroy us, but to make us disillusioned with His toys, with the playthings of this world, so that we might seek Him.

This is why the Lord Himself permits injustices and evil. But I have said to Him, "Lord, You have never suffered. You have always been perfect. How do You know what suffering is? Yet you have put us through these tests; and You had no business doing it. We didn't ask to be born as mortals and to suffer." (He doesn't mind that I argue with Him. He is very patient.) The Lord answers, "You don't have to go on suffering; I have given everyone the free will to choose good instead of evil, and thus come back to Me."

So evil is the test of God to see if we will choose Him or His gifts. He created us in His image and gave us the power to free ourselves. But we don't use that power. At night, when we cease to be active, we all become godlike. But in the daytime we become devils—not all of us, but most of us. Why not live in tune with God in the daytime, for then we shall know no fear, we shall know no evil. It is easy to say this, but hard to practice it.

While evil in itself is something we don't want, yet it is like poisoned honey—it is palatable. At the table, we are tempted to eat too much and to eat the wrong things. Then we begin to get fat here and there, just where we don't want it. In response to our wrong actions, Nature takes revenge and seems to be poking fun at us all the time. It is indeed a funny world. But the results of our wrong actions don't seem very funny to us! That is why I quarrel with God and scold Him, "Why have You created all of these terrible temptations that your children succumb to? Why have You made them so pleasurable?" Well, that is the trick of God—if you are going to act like an idiot, you deserve to suffer.

The Lord says, "I made you in My image, and you ought to behave like Me."

I say, "But, Lord, they don't know they are made in Your image."

His response is, "Well, My saints are trying to tell them. I am not going to force them to be good."

"But why did You put us in this mess? You have never been in this quagmire of delusion; why did You put us here?"

This is where the Lord smiles and answers, "That is how it is; and that is the way it is to be."

So the thing is this: There is no perfection in this world. Why seek it here? You may find a little short-lived pleasure, but mostly you will find suffering and injustice. Pain was given to make you know when something is wrong with the body. But when the pain of cancer comes, there is no reason in it. The sufferer has no relief from his pain, and he doesn't know why he has to suffer. And there are those who need money and can't get it; and those who don't need it who easily acquire more. Those who have much want still more; and those who have nothing want just a little, but can't get even that. Isn't this true? Why these injustices? Some people are as healthy as can be, and some are always sick. But health or ill health doesn't necessarily determine whether or not you are happy. It is the state of your mind that makes you happy or unhappy. St. Francis suffered much of the time, and yet he was healing the sick and was filled with the joy of God. Suffering has a different meaning for you when you have attained the freedom of God. But you have to attain that freedom first.

You must learn to work without desire, and to live in this world without attachment. As soon as you are caught by desires or attachment, you will have all the evil that is coming to you. This is why the Gita says: "O Arjuna! no (compelling) duty have

I to perform; there is naught that I have not acquired; nothing in the three worlds remains for Me to gain! Yet I am consciously present in the performance of all actions."* Those who want to be liberated must do likewise, engaging in serviceful, joyful, nonattached activity. Most people willingly work hard for money, but they won't make even a little effort for their salvation. We must work for God. The way to do this is to noncooperate with evil and to behave as God would have us behave.

The Greatest Conquering Force Is Love

Imagine, as a weapon of war they are speaking of releasing vapors filled with germs that will infect whole populations, causing the people to suffer a lingering death. Such are the deadly instruments of destruction they are creating, instead of developing the weapon of love, which can destroy all the hatred, meanness, and selfishness in men's hearts. In war, each side always blames the other's actions as the cause of conflict. But remember, you can't clap with just one hand; you have to have two hands. True, some people or nations are more evil at times than others; but those who are good should conquer evil, not by evil, but by good.

You must love people. Sometimes it is hard, I know. I have loved my enemies, and I know that I shall never be an enemy to anyone. By a thought I could destroy them; but I have never done it, and I shall never do it. Jesus had that power. When his enemies taunted him to save himself from the cross, he said, "Thinkest thou that I cannot now pray to my Father, and he shall presently give me more than twelve legions of angels? But how then shall the scriptures be fulfilled, that thus it must be?"† He conquered by love. If the ordinary man is slapped, the great desire is to slap back. Therefore, God does not give His divine power to those who are spiritually weak, because they would misuse it. The desire and the strength to forgive come from attunement with God.

Someone once asked me, "Why do you go through the struggle of supporting so many people‡ and having to deal with

---

* Bhagavad Gita III:22.   † Matthew 26:53-54.

‡ The monastics in the Self-Realization Fellowship/Yogoda Satsanga Society Ashrams in America and India.

all their problems, when you are free and don't have to?"

I responded, "Why does God do it? He is supporting every creature on the whole earth when He could be free from all of this bothersome creation. I do it because I know His will. And because I also find much pleasure in seeing the progress of those who respond, and in being able to build His temple in their hearts."

How few you find in this world who are sincere and who want to be your friend for your sake, and not for something they can take from you. Those sincere souls are most enjoyable. Greater than all riches is true friendship. If you can be a true friend to people, you will find God. If you sincerely love people, you can know them; just as when you look through a clear glass, you can see what is in the glass. But your perception of people is unclear unless you love God, and unless you love others with the love of God.

"I Can Give My Life for a Sincere Soul"

I can give my life for a sincere soul, but insincere souls I stay away from. I am never insincere with anyone, and that is the way we all should live in this world. We must be fearless, sincere, surrounded not only with those whom we can inspire, but with those who can inspire us as well. When we are strong, then we can help those who are evil. But don't try to help them until you yourself are stronger. Otherwise their company may weaken you instead. So many who try to reform others become infected with their evil.

If you have a mind that absorbs everything like blotting paper, you must keep that mind free from evil influences. Just as a blotting paper that has become soaked with spilt oil will no longer absorb water, so must your mind first be saturated with good until it becomes impervious to evil.

Be strong in your own goodness, and try to be helpful to others. The man who only looks out for himself and his own family won't find much happiness. If he doesn't think of anyone else who might be suffering, he denies himself the joy of helping another, so his own cup of satisfaction will remain small. Money means to me just one thing: that I can use it to do good and help others.

The Cosmic Motion Picture

There is another angle about duality, or good and evil, that I want to explain to you. If a movie producer made motion pictures only of angels, and showed them in the film houses morning, noon, and night every day, he would soon have to close up his business. He has to produce variety in order to attract people's attention. The bad man makes the hero look so much better! And we like plots that are filled with action. We don't mind looking at exciting movies about danger and disaster because we know they are only pictures. I remember one time when I was taken to see a movie in which the hero died; it was such a tragedy! So I stayed and watched the next showing of the picture until I saw the hero alive again; then I left the theater.

If you could see what is going on behind the screen of this life, you wouldn't suffer at all. It is a cosmic motion picture show. This movie that God is projecting on the screen of this earth has no value to me. I look at the beam of God's light, which is projecting these scenes on the screen of life. I see the pictures of the whole universe coming from this beam.

Another time I was sitting in a movie house watching an exciting drama on the screen. And then I looked into the projection booth. I saw that the projectionist was not interested in the picture, because he had seen it over and over again. Instead, he was reading a book. The projection machine was doing its job: there was the sound, and the beam of light was casting the realistic pictures on the screen. And there was the audience, caught up in the drama. I thought, "Lord, You are like this man sitting here in the booth, absorbed in Your own nature of bliss and love and wisdom. Your machine of cosmic law is throwing on the screen of the universe the scenes of jealousy, of love, of hatred, of wisdom, but You remain uninvolved in Your plays." From age to age, from civilization to civilization, the same old pictures are shown over and over again, only with different characters playing the parts. I think God gets a little bit bored with it all. He is tired of it. It is a wonder that He doesn't just pull the plug and stop the show!

When I took my gaze from the beam of light that was casting the scenes of action on the screen, I looked at the audience in the motion picture house and I saw that they were going through all the emotions of the actors in the movie. They were suffering with the hero and reacting to the evil of the villain. To the audience it was a tragic experience. To the operator in the projection booth, it was only a picture. And so it is with God. He has created pictures of light and shadows, the hero and the villain, good and evil, and we are the audience and the actors. It is only because we are too much identified with the play that we are in trouble.

Without shadows as well as light there could be no picture. Evil is the shadow that converts the one beam of God's light into pictures or forms. Therefore, evil is the shadow of God that makes this play possible. The dark shadows of evil are interspersed with the pure white beam of the virtues of God. He wants you not to take these pictures so seriously. The director of a movie sees the murders and the suffering and the comedy and the drama as means to create interest for the audience. He stands apart from the play and directs and observes it. God wants us to behave with detachment, realizing we are only actors or observers in His cosmic show.

Though God has everything, we can still say that He has some desire: He wants to see who will remain unintimidated by this picture, and who will play his part well and come back to Him. You can't run away from this universe, but if you act in this play with your thought fixed on God, you will be free.

I often say to Him, "Lord, this is a motion picture to You, but it is terrible to us." And the Lord replies, "I make you realize it is a dream every night when you go to sleep. Why don't you remember this in the daytime?"

One day as I was entering my room, I saw my body lying on the bed, dead. And the Lord said to me, "How do you like that?" For a moment I was shaken; then I replied, "My Lord, it is all right, for I am aware of You; I am talking to You." And I felt completely all right about it.

For Him Who Realizes God, There Is No Evil

The way to supreme happiness will not be found by the scientist nor by material-minded people, but by those who follow the masters who say: "Go back to the booth of the Infinite from which you can see the projection of all these cosmic motion pictures. Then you won't be troubled about God's creation, God's play."

My only interest in people is to help them. And as long as breath shall flow in these lungs, so long shall I try to help others and tell them to get away from this motion picture of delusion. Because you are a part of it now, you suffer. You must stand aside and watch it, and then you cannot suffer. When you are an observer, then you can enjoy this play. This is what you must learn. To God, this is only a movie, and when you turn to Him, it will also be a picture show to you.

I will tell you a little story. A king fell asleep and dreamed that he was poor. He was crying out in his sleep for just a penny for some food. Finally, the queen woke him and said, "What is the matter with you? Your treasury is full of gold, and yet you are crying for a penny."

Then the king said, "Oh, how silly of me. I thought I was a beggar and was starving for lack of that penny."

Such is the delusion of every soul who is dreaming he is a mortal, subject to the nightmarish evils of all kinds of disease, suffering, troubles, heartbreaks. The only way to escape this nightmare is by becoming more attached to God and less attached to the dream images of this world. It is because you have put your attention on the wrong things that you suffer. If you give your heart to man, or drink, or greed, or drugs, you will suffer. Your heart will be broken. You must place your heart with God. The more you seek peace in Him, the more that peace will devour your worries and sufferings.

You suffer because you have allowed yourself to become so susceptible to the evils of this world. You must learn to be spiritually tough, spiritually strong. Do all the things you have to do, and enjoy what you do, but inwardly say, "Lord, I am Thy child, made in Thine image. I don't want anything but You." The devotee who follows this principle, and who attains this realization, will find that for him there is no evil in this world.

The Mystery of Mahatma Gandhi

This talk was given in 1932. In 1935, Paramahansaji visited Mahatma Gandhi at his hermitage in Wardha, India. At that time, the Mahatma requested initiation into Kriya Yoga. Ten years earlier, Gandhiji had paid a visit to Paramahansaji's Yogoda Satsanga school for boys in Ranchi. Expressing keen interest in the balanced curriculum of the Yogoda program, he inscribed in the guest book a gracious tribute.

Toward the end of the medieval era, during which the church had come to rule politics, the state had to divorce itself from religion. From then on, governments have made a tremendous blunder by trying to get along without the guiding principles of religion.

Once separated from spiritual principles, which govern all phases of human action, politics began to wander away from truth itself. The word "politics" has ever since had a connotation of graft or other unscrupulous methods sometimes used by politicians or others to gain their ends. The end does not always justify the means, for all good things should be attained by good methods as well. When evil is employed in the hope of gaining a good end, that evil will remain indelibly associated with the good, even if that end is attained.

The belief that religion should stand aloof from all other human activities is impractical. Sermons calculated only to inspire imagination and to give orthodox views do no real good in changing the depraved moral, social, and political aspects of society. Such isolated spirituality can do little practical good to mankind. On the other hand, some religious leaders harangue their friends and followers with misconceived ideas of politics, devoid of real spirituality.

Religious Principles Are the Foundation of the Art of Living

True religion consists of ultimate religious principles that govern all phases of the social, political, and spiritual man. Religious principles are the foundation of the art of living and of every true standard of the best human conduct in all races and nationalities.

Jesus said: "Render, therefore, unto Caesar the things that are Caesar's, and unto God, the things that are God's."* Lord Krishna, the great prophet of India, was a supreme example of this principle; he was both a king and a savior of mankind. We can picture a saint in the solitude of the woods, but his saintliness is better proven when his spiritual attainments are consciously tested by applying them to helping depraved human "beasts" that infest the jungle of civilization.

Krishna was not only a prophet, but a saint, with kingly responsibilities to test his saintliness. He was one of the greatest successes as a man of nonattachment, even though he was a king. A man of renunciation harboring secret material desires is a spiritual failure; whereas Krishna, though he had the riches of a king, was a man of the greatest renunciation at heart.

Jesus would not have commanded as much attention as he did, if he had lacked the courage to battle prelate and political power with the calm influence of his spiritual realization. By his silence before the prelate, Jesus spoke loudly about the errors of mankind and the evil principles of politics. With the sword of his love and the all-conquering utterance: "Father, forgive them, for they know not what they do," Jesus not only conquered his contemporary political foes, but stands second to none in showing to people of all times how spirituality can conquer the most formidable enemies. The political power, with vast armies, that condemned an unarmed, innocent Jesus to the cross, and expected thereby to crush his heretic philosophy, found its crowning defeat in its most ignorant act. Jesus willingly gave up his body for his cause, knowing that the temple of spiritual aspirations and divine progress is imperishable. Jesus said: "My kingdom is not of this world." The kingdom of God governed by true principles of spiritual learning must come to reform the malpolitic-laden atmosphere of this earth.

Politics must be reformed by application of true religious principles. In the Bhagavad Gita, Sri Krishna teaches that whenever there is decline of virtue and predominance of sin, man

* Mark 12:17.

should salvage the sunken religious principles and free the virtuous. God comes on earth using the vehicles of prophetic minds to drive darkness from the souls of men.

Mahatma Gandhi: A Political Savior of All Politic-Ridden Nations

Before Jesus came Krishna, Buddha, and others. After Jesus came Swami Shankara, Babaji, Lahiri Mahasaya, Swami Sri Yukteswar Giriji, and many others. Now comes the great Mahatma Gandhi.* He is not only the savior of a few devotees and religious followers, but a political savior of all politic-ridden nations.

All great religious leaders and saints have had large followings in their own particular religious sects. Gandhi has not only influenced millions of religious followers, but also thousands of politicians, and almost all races and countries inhabiting this strife-stricken earthly home. Unlike his predecessors, Gandhi left religious leadership to enter the field of politics.

Gandhi is in the world but not of the world. The Bhagavad Gita says it does not matter whether you are a family man earning a living, or a politician, or a business man. You must perform action in the world, not for your own material ends, but to please God. Gandhi is a family man, with children, and had been a lawyer and a rich man. He renounced all his riches, for he believed that to own more than his fellowman was a sin. He eats very little because the people of India are poor, and millions cannot have even one square starch-laden meal a day.

Gandhi does not wear the loincloth for publicity or effect, but because millions in India cannot afford to wear more. King George VI and his queen had to break their traditional rule of court attire and receive him in his loincloth. The "mountain" of a king went to the "Muhammad" of a Gandhi.

A Living Embodiment of Scriptural Truths

We hear of scriptural rules, but we see them lived and manifested in few people. Mahatma Gandhi lives and practices

---

* His family name was Mohandas Karamchand Gandhi. He never referred to himself as "Mahatma" ("great soul"), the title accorded him by his millions of followers.

scriptural truths in all their details.

The words of no other prophet or savior have had such an effect on a powerful nation as have those of Gandhi on England. No other prophet ever was invited to join a round-table conference. It is customary for maharajas to stand and not to speak until the viceroy of India, Lord Irwin, has spoken; but when Mahatma Gandhi met Lord Irwin, the latter remained standing while the Mahatma spoke to him in a sitting posture.

When Gandhi was unconditionally set free from prison the last time, he was heard to say: "I am coming back," which prophecy was fulfilled by his present internment. Gandhi's first thought was not of his own beloved little family and children, but to return to prison to help the sixty thousand political prisoners who were still there. He did not want to be free unless they were free. Think of it.

When he first met Lord Irwin, after being imprisoned by him, the Mahatma had not the slightest enmity in his heart. Lord Irwin addressed him: "How are you, dear friend?" and presented him with goat's milk and dates. Newspapermen marveled and wrote that Mahatma did not show any trace of anger when he met Lord Irwin.

In South Africa Gandhi was stabbed by a man. When urged to take legal proceedings against him, Gandhi refused, saying, "I will send him my love." Later, when this would-be assassin heard of Gandhi's attitude, he became his follower. The attitude of so many people is, "Yes, we read in the Bible that we should turn the right cheek if the left one is slapped, but that is nonsense. If you slap me I will give you in return twelve slaps, a kick, and maybe a bullet; but I still call myself a good Christian." When Gandhi, although so seriously wounded as to be at death's door, kept blessing this man, he gave not only forgiveness but deep love, and won over his adversary.

A Perfect Example to Politicians

With all his manifold political activities, Gandhi is a perfect example to all biased, one-sided politicians who use their God-given intelligence for selfish material gain, but have no time for God. He shows that duty to God must be observed first by keeping the Sabbath, or day of silence for communion with God.

One day a week he remains in silence. Nothing can make him speak. Whenever the time for his silence came, Mahatma cut off conferences about the most vital problems of India and left it to Lord Irwin to continue the talks the next day. When Gandhi was arrested the last time, in the middle of the night, his wife and followers were all crying, but he was unmoved. He blessed them; and since it was his day of silence, he wrote instructions before his departure, but he did not speak. Mahatma has never broken his day of silence. He does not forget that duties cannot be performed intelligently and efficiently without first receiving the power from God. His first duty of all duties is in meditating upon God regularly for a time every day and in communing with God one whole day a week in silence.

Gandhi is a strict moralist, a man of self-control, a master of his senses.

I deem that the greatest of all Gandhi's political and spiritual victories was the conversion of his own wife to his principles. A modern husband cannot fail to appreciate and understand the depth of my statement. In South Africa Mrs. Gandhi suffered and fasted for weeks in the jail along with Mahatma, fighting for the cause of freedom.

No man has been able to collect money from poor India for spiritual and philanthropic causes as has the Mahatma. He has raised millions of rupees by his own personal appeal. He could do this because people trusted him absolutely. A princess gave him a costly silver chair for his own personal use. He put it up for auction instantly and gave the money to the public cause. He is so versatile that he can reply to letters through secretaries, attend to politics, and keep strict account of all public money spent.

"Each for All and All for Each"

Mahatma Gandhi believes in the one God and in the universal brotherhood of man. He makes no distinction between Christians and Hindus and outcasts. He says that whoever follows truth and loves India is an Indian. He calls his Christian, Hindu, and Moslem followers Indians. He says: "Down with patriotism that disregards the patriotic love of other nations and the freedom of other nationalities!"

Patriotism must include international well-being. Gandhi believes in the doctrine, "Each for all and all for each." His doctrine is fundamentally different from communist principles in that the latter political methods are based on force, whereas Gandhi teaches conquest of inferior powerful brute force by superior spiritual force. He says that hatred increases hatred—it never conquers it. A strong man may tyrannize over his weak victims, but cannot conquer his own hidden hatred. If the weak victim were suddenly to receive help, he would quickly take double revenge on the strong man; but if the spirit of hatred in the weak enemy were destroyed by the fires of love, then that victory would be more permanent, grand, and free from all germs of possible outbursts of hidden hatred and trouble.

Gandhi says that if you have a revolver and your powerful enemy has another, and if you are afraid and flee, saying, "I forgive you," then you are a coward. He says that it is better to use the gun than to be a coward, but he advises the use of a superior weapon rather than running away or shooting when confronted by an armed enemy bent on doing wrong. This superior weapon is "resistance by love, and noncooperation with the enemy's evil ways." Practice of this will make you a really victorious, spiritual man.

If there are ten brothers and the youngest becomes crazy with anger and takes a sword to kill the others, but the eldest takes another sword and beheads the youngest brother, and then goes to their mother and says: "Mother, I have killed my youngest brother to save the rest of your children," the mother would cry out, "Oh, my son, how could you slay my youngest boy, your dear brother?" and she would sob in frenzy.

How much better it would have been if instead the eldest son had come to her and said, "Mother, my youngest brother ran amok and raised a sword to kill all my other brothers, and I stepped in front of him unarmed and said: 'I resist you with my love and implore you not to kill; but if kill you must, kill me first.' Mother, my youngest brother did not realize what he was doing, until he was convinced of my harmless love, which did not retaliate or get angry although his sword plunged into my arm. After the first stroke, conquered by my love, he broke his own sword, bandaged my wound, and asked forgiveness."

If God, with all His power, punished man, where would man be? God does not use material force to influence us; He uses the self-reforming power of love to convert us. By His love God makes Himself our Father, the dearest object of all our aspirations.

What Gandhi's Ideals Have Done for India

Gandhi has succeeded in stopping about eighty percent of the liquor traffic and the opium trade in India. No nation should derive revenue by degrading people through encouraging the use of drugs and intoxicants.

The people of India need thin, finely woven clothes because of the warm climate. The government passed a law forbidding the making of fine thread by the Indians, so that cotton grown in India had to be sent to Lancaster to be manufactured into cloth and then shipped back to India. In this way the Indian people were deprived of their own trade and became dependent on clothing imported from England. Gandhi advised the people of India to make their own clothing with the coarse thread spun on their own cheap spinning wheels. Owing to his example, the importation of cotton goods manufactured in England has fallen off about eighty percent. This has revived home industries [in India]. Instead of depending upon making a living in the cities and factories, people have become self-reliant and are now growing their own food, and are making their own clothes from cotton grown in their own fields.

Gandhi uses trains and automobiles to go from place to place. By no means is he a man who does not recognize the usefulness of modern machinery; but he warns against the enslaving effects of being used by the machine—involved in the worry of creating and acquiring more material things.

Reestablishing the Christian Doctrine

By preaching, Gandhi has accomplished what no emperor of India, nor the British government, has been able to accomplish by legislation. Hindus have preached in Moslem mosques and Moslem priests have preached in Hindu temples. In many instances Hindus and Moslems have eaten from the same plate.

As there has long existed the Negro problem in America, so the Hindus have had their problem of prejudice against the dark-skinned aborigines, and pariahs and outcasts. The caste and clan systems are almost as strong in America as in India. The Negroes and American Indians are almost outcasts here, and the dark-skinned Sontals, Kohls, Vheels, and low castes are outcasts in India. India segregates them, calling them "untouchables." In the South in America, Negroes have separate waiting rooms in railroad stations, and they have to ride in different sections of the trolley cars and trains. As Negroes for the most part perform menial labor and are social untouchables in America, so the outcasts in India are servants and social untouchables there. In Washington, D.C., the national capital, I had to conduct separate classes for my Negro and my Caucasian brethren. This surprised me very much.

Mahatma Gandhi is reestablishing the Christian doctrine. All men—white, brown, yellow, and black—are the descendants of Adam and Eve, our common grandparents, and as such have one blood flowing in their veins. Thus Gandhi has helped the outcasts, who are now coming to claim their rights.

Gandhi also believes in freeing young widows from the compulsion of remaining single and dependent.

Gandhi believes in equal rights for women; he teaches equality of the sexes. Why condemn women, and say that wine, women, and wealth are delusions? Women have just as much right to say that wine, men, and wealth are temptations that lead to destruction.

Gandhi teaches freedom for women. Hence, Saint Gandhi has such women as Madeleine Slade, daughter of an English admiral, and Sarojini Naidu* as his followers. He freed Indian women from household seclusion, and they are the foremost soldiers in his great spiritual army, battling against political evil. Madeleine Slade said, "For all the world I would not go back to my old ways and forget what Mahatma Gandhi has taught me."

Gandhi's compassion includes kindness and love for all animals. He does not believe in hurting anything, yet he is not a fanatic on this subject, for he ordered a cow to be killed to relieve it from the suffering of disease.

---

* Well-known Indian poet and writer, and the first Indian woman to be president of the Indian National Congress and governor of a state of India.

Gandhi has said that Jesus Christ, the Bhagavad Gita, and Tolstoy have been the greatest influences in molding his life. Jesus did not live to see much of the results of his work and suffering. Gandhi has been more fortunate. By his ideal conduct, Gandhi is growing in popularity and will go down through history as a great savior who has changed the destinies not only of individuals and of India, but of other nations. Instead of criticizing him, even his deadliest enemies admit that Gandhi is sincere and that he cannot be bribed by money, flattery, concessions, or political fame. He never compromises his principles.

Resisting Evil by Love

Gandhi's doctrine of resisting evil by the force of love has already proven to be practical. In this machine age when man's destructive power has grown to far exceed his powers of construction, Gandhi has given a universal panacea for the ills of our social system. To conquer all social and political evils, we must use the most formidable spiritual weapon, namely, "resistance by love." War breeds war, and it can be prevented only by noncooperation and the overcoming power of love.

When Gandhi went to South Africa as a lawyer, he started his first noncooperation movement by initiating a period of fasting until redress measures were effected. He, his wife, and about three hundred followers, after twenty-one days of fasting, were released; Generals Smuts and Bothas were brought to their knees and the Hindus won their cause. That was Gandhi's first victory.

During the Boer and Zulu Wars in Africa, Gandhi was a loyalist and won two gold medals for raising an ambulance corps and bravely picking up the wounded amidst flying bullets.

Later, in India, General Dyer ordered his soldiers to shoot into a harmless, unarmed crowd of two thousand people until ammunition ran short. The only offense of the people was that they had gathered to protest, which was against the order of the police. This occasion turned Gandhi against the British government and ever since he has said: "I love the British people, but henceforth I am the deadliest enemy of any wrong form of government that the English may impose upon India." Many chivalrous English newspapers severely condemned the action of General Dyer and he was recalled to England.

Gandhi stopped the noncooperation movement when it broke into violence on one occasion. But this last time he was put in prison, he said: "The movement must go on," and ever since, thousands of India's most renowned men have courted jail [through nonviolent noncooperation] in the cause of freedom. Gandhi has also visited jail many times, not as a prisoner but as a saint who has converted prison into a temple of liberty. This will remain in the minds of men forever. Gandhi in prison is dangerous. Gandhi dead in prison will be alive evermore to preach his gospel of liberty and equality.

True Equality Is Achieved Through Love

Gandhi does not believe in creating equality by force, by wresting acquired power from the rich. He believes in spontaneous renunciation and selfless giving from the heart. He tries to unite people by cultivating brotherhood in their hearts. He is preaching love, so that all nations may help one another even as loving, prosperous brothers help a distressed brother.

Gandhi's greatest triumphs came when his weaponless army, his spiritual battalion, resisted government orders not to make salt and not to assemble. Eyewitnesses have described how the police, armed with sticks and machine guns, charged the people; how brave men fell with shattered skulls and wounded bodies, and how they stood up again saying, "Kill us, but we will not move." On many occasions the police fled, leaving their instruments of war, tired of killing their unarmed brothers. Gandhi has gained the armistice, and a promise of self-government has been urged upon England. By resisting with spiritual force, Gandhi has accomplished more for India in three years than Ireland was able to accomplish in seven hundred years by using violence.

I believe that the way to end war will be demonstrated when India attains her goal without beating or killing English people. Then a politically crucified India will be victorious and will be the savior of nations. As Bishop Fisher said: "Mahatma Gandhi is the most outstanding figure in all Christendom and is teaching the nations of the world a new way to combat war."

If ever there have been practical contributions to the cause of world peace, they are those of Woodrow Wilson and Mahatma Gandhi. President Wilson, by the mere utterance of the plan for the League of Nations, gave the world an ideal of freedom toward which it can work. It does not matter that Mr. Wilson did not live to see the fulfillment of his dreams. His work will go on.*

Destroy Hatred, and Peace Will Come to Stay

Mahatma Gandhi has given to the world an intensely practical method, not only to crush war, but to make war impossible. Why must people blow their brains out trying to settle disputes in a manner that has never yet settled anything?

No politician except Gandhi has included the interests of the whole world when considering the welfare of his own country. Gandhi wants freedom for India and for all subject nations in order that the world may be a safer and happier place for people of all nations to live in. The secret dynamite of hatred causes war. Destroy hatred, and peace will come to stay on earth. Gandhi is the spokesman of the age, a world reformer, a great political savior who has come on earth to conquer the world with the invincible weapon of love and understanding, and to establish a United States of the World with Truth as its president. By his suffering, renunciation, and universal love he is making nations feel that they are brothers and as such they must make up their differences.

Politics as spiritualized by Gandhi, and the consecrated altars of the hearts of men God-illumined through meditation, can establish the heaven of peace within and without in the family, social, political, and spiritual life of man.

Gandhi is bringing a paradise of peace and brotherhood into the hearts of the people of all nations; and in all nations, Yogoda Satsanga [Self-Realization Fellowship] is bringing the everlasting bliss of God into the souls of men.

Let the Western brothers continue to win the Orient with material efficiency, and let the Eastern brothers continue to win the souls of their Western brothers with love. This will make the people of East and West uniformly developed, both materially and spiritually.

Mahatma Gandhi is the modern spiritual mystery. His life

---

* The concept of cooperation among nations to promote peace and the betterment of the world later evolved into the establishment of the United Nations.

will show the way to solve the complicated problems of the East and West.

[*Mahatma Gandhi was assassinated on January 30, 1948. On February 1, Paramahansa Yogananda conducted a memorial service in honor of the martyred saint. Dr. V. M. Nawle, a publisher and journalist from Poona, India, an old friend of Paramahansa Yogananda who knew of the spiritual bond between Gandhi and Sri Yogananda, subsequently sent a portion of the Mahatma's ashes to him. After receiving the ashes, Paramahansaji conducted a second memorial service on February 27, 1949.* In closing, he prayed:*]

"Bless the soul of Gandhi, and bless us all, that we may remember his spirit—that we may remember how to fight evil, not by evil means and destroying the world, but by constructive goodness and love, as Christ taught and as Gandhi taught. May Gandhi live forever in our hearts, in God, and in India, and in the hearts of all nations."

---

* Paramahansaji conducted the dedication of the Gandhi World Peace Memorial at the SRF Lake Shrine in Pacific Palisades, California, on August 20, 1950. On October 24, 1951, Dr. Nawle wrote Paramahansaji:

"Regarding Gandhi ashes, I may say that [they] are scattered and thrown in almost all the important rivers and seas, and nothing is given outside India except the remains which I have sent to you after a great ordeal....You make India and the whole world shy, as you are the first in erecting a Gandhi Memorial. You are the only one in the whole world who received Gandhi ashes outside India."

Magnetism: The Inherent Power of the Soul

First Self-Realization Fellowship Temple,
Encinitas, California, July 29, 1939

Why is it that when some people speak, everyone is enthralled, while others can talk about the same thing and no one is interested? Even with all their obvious faults, dictators are able to wield tremendous influence. What is the secret of this power? It is called magnetism.

Everyone is divinely endowed with personal magnetism. Then why do some obviously possess it and others seem not to? It is because very few know how to develop that magnetism; it lies dormant in most people. Many of the faculties the Lord has given us remain dormant within for lack of use. Some of you have gone through life without cultivating your health potential through proper exercise. And what is the result? premature old age and disease. When you think of physical development, you don't mean strengthening one arm and ignoring the rest of the body. Someone with a peanut-size head and a large body would appear disproportionate. Your development will likewise be disproportionate if you cultivate only some of your God-given mental faculties and not the others.

What is magnetism? Hypnotism has been called animal magnetism; it is a sort of mental chloroform administered through the suggestions of the hypnotist. But spiritual magnetism is something different. It is the power of the soul to attract or create whatever it needs for all-round happiness and well-being. The magnetism of most people is not so highly evolved; it is predominantly on the plane of animal or physical magnetism—subject to the cosmic hypnosis of *maya* or world delusion—and functions primarily on the level of materialism.

The Effect of Dietary Habits on Magnetism

There are many factors that affect the development of magnetism. First, consider the kind and quantity of food you eat. Overeating and wrong eating are dangerous to the development of magnetism because of their adverse effects on the vital forces in the body. Those who overload their systems with meat, for example, diminish their magnetism. This is also true of other foods not suited to the body. On the other hand, pure foods such as fresh fruits increase magnetism. As to the quantity of food ingested, it should be just enough that when you leave the table you are still a little hungry. Don't fill yourself to the gills. Overloading the stomach drains the inner life force and causes a loss of magnetism. Those who consistently overeat are not magnetic, whereas those who fast regularly increase their magnetism.

Your body should be always under your control; it shouldn't control you. Those who don't fast usually fear that if they go without food for even one day they are surely going to die. Yet when you are on a long fast, you find after a time that your hunger is gone and you lose all desire for food. Unless you know how, it is dangerous to fast for a long period; but when you know what you are doing, it is all right.* The body's vital forces are enslaved by overeating, but by regular fasting, for one to three days at a time, they become revitalized, increasing the body's magnetism.

You, the soul, are far more than the perishable body of flesh. In fasting you discover that it is the cosmic energy, or *prana*, in the body that actually sustains you. This intelligent energy, which has become dependent on food, learns to depend more on itself. By fasting, you train the body to rely more on cosmic energy. Jesus pointed this out when he said: "Man shall not live by bread alone, but by every word that proceedeth out of the mouth of God."† The "mouth of God" is the subtle center in the medulla through which divine life energy, the "word," flows into the body from its cosmic source.

* Those who are inexperienced should seek medical guidance before undertaking a long fast.
† Matthew 4:4.

During a fast, hold to the consciousness that you are not starving yourself, that cosmic energy is sustaining you. You will be astonished to see how this energy flows into your body directly, not through the agency of food. You haven't known about this power, the real sustainer of life, and that is why you are enslaved by food.

Suppose you stuff food into the stomach of a dead man's body. Will it digest the meal and become full of energy again? No. It will remain lifeless. But if you put food in the stomach of a living man, what happens? It will be digested. This shows that it is not the food that gives life. It is the *prana* or intelligent life force in the body that changes the food into energy. That life force has become so enslaved by identification with the body that it thinks it cannot sustain the body without food. But Jesus reminded us otherwise. *Prana* enters the body with the soul at the time of conception, and throughout one's life it is constantly replenished, through the "mouth of God." Fasting is one way you can develop the self-sustaining power of that inner energy.

Fasting cleanses your blood and gives rest to your organs; a revitalized energy begins to flow through your eyes and hands and feet. Thus, when you are fasting, you can transmit more healing energy to others when praying for them and practicing the Self-Realization healing technique.* As soon as you begin to realize you are living on cosmic energy and not on gross substances, your body becomes magnetic. A different quality of magnetism comes into you. These are the great things you learn.

The Vibrations of the Whole World
Pass Through Your Body

There is a constant exchange of magnetism between you and your surroundings and the people with whom you come in

---

* Prayers for healing of physical disease, mental inharmony, and spiritual ignorance are offered daily by the Self-Realization Fellowship Prayer Council, composed of renunciants of the SRF Order. Prayers for oneself or one's loved ones may be requested by writing or telephoning Self-Realization Fellowship, Los Angeles. This mission of prayer is supported by the Self-Realization Fellowship Worldwide Prayer Circle, consisting of SRF members and friends around the world, which regularly offers prayers for world peace and the well-being of all mankind. A booklet describing the work of the Worldwide Prayer Circle is available on request.

contact. For example, on meeting someone, you may become aware that something is happening to you; you are actually receiving a current from that person. In order to receive another's magnetism, you must be near him.

When you shake hands with someone, a magnet is created, and you exchange magnetism. If you are the more powerful or positive one, you will give the other person your vibrations; but if you are the weaker, you will receive his vibrations. This explains why people unconsciously like to shake the hands of famous men and women.

All actions, both positive and negative, create vibrations in the ether. These vibrations are everywhere present. When you are in the environment of these vibrations, they pass through your body, just like radio waves. If you live or associate with people who are doing wrong, you will feel the magnetic vibration of their wrongdoing, no matter how you try to avoid it. Weak-minded individuals should by all means shun the company of those with bad habits. Only the strong-minded can mingle with such persons and help them to change without being adversely affected themselves. That is the law. If somebody drinks and the magnetism of his habit is more powerful than your will to refrain from drinking, don't associate with him. When you mix with persons of poor habits, you must be sure that your magnetism for good is greater than their negative magnetism. Self-styled teachers and reformers who don't protect themselves by first developing strong spiritual magnetism are apt to fall victim to the bad vibrations of those they try to help.

When I shake hands with anyone, or am with others, I give magnetism; and sometimes when I want to receive their vibrations, I receive. But when I don't want to receive, I don't tune in. I keep myself out of range. Because I have developed a strong magnetism, my current is more powerful, and I can shut out all unwanted vibrations. These mysteries of existence I see all the time. And people think they are just so many pounds of flesh!

Calmness Protects You From Negative Vibrations

It has been shown that six years of man's life are cut off because he lives in the midst of noisy vibrations, of too much noise. When you are nervous, you are more receptive to disturbing vibrations of all kinds, which further affect the nervous system. When you are calm, irritating vibrations cannot disturb you. They get at you when you are cranky and nervous; but the minute you become calm and strong in mind again, they cannot touch you.

Change and strengthen your own vibrations by thinking, "I am peaceful," or "I am happy." Day after day, affirm that thought, and you will develop that peaceful or happy magnetism. If you find that your environment isn't suited to your goals, find another that will aid you. By changing to the right environment, you help to develop your magnetism and to change yourself for the better. Mix with those people who are models of what you would like to be. If you want business magnetism, mix with businessmen. Keep your clothes and body clean and neat, and wherever you go, conduct yourself with the consciousness that you are the master of yourself. If you want to be a writer, seek those who have a literary vibration. If you want to be saintly, mix with holy people.

How to "Steal" Magnetism From the Saints

Great saints don't waste their time. You have to convince them of the urgency of your heart. Then they will be attracted to you, and you can "steal" magnetism from them. Automatically you will get their vibration if you are near them. But you can also feel their magnetism thousands of miles away, because their spiritual vibrations are limitless.

I receive the vibrations of my guru Sri Yukteswar all the time, even though he is now reborn on another plane. When he was still living in India, I used to feel his vibration. In this way I came to know intuitively that he was going to leave his body; and then he wrote to me, telling me he was just waiting for my return to India. I told Mr. Lynn* that I must go to my Gurudeva; he had waited fifteen years for me, and I knew if I didn't go then, he would be gone. Three months after my arrival in India, Master left his body.

So it is true that you can receive the magnetism of saints

---

* Later known as Rajarsi Janakananda, first spiritual successor to Paramahansa Yogananda. (See glossary.)

even from a great distance, because it is so powerful. If you want to be an artist, you have to mix with artists, to live among them. But you can receive magnetism from spiritual persons at any distance. Of course, they have to be spiritually developed in order to give that magnetism, and you have to be receptive in order to feel it.

To receive magnetism from spiritual people, you should feel that they are with you as you meditate and pray. That thought brings their magnetism to you immediately. The vibrations of my prayers for others are very strong between the hours of seven and eleven in the morning.* Those vibrations are going on all the time, but they may be especially felt if you tune in during this period. While you are praying, visualize that I am praying with you, and you will feel a great reinforcement of power.

Also, if you go to a place where masters have lived, the vibrations there will quicken your realization. That is the value of pilgrimages to holy places. When I went to the Holy Land I felt great inspiration and realization. Jesus incarnated in that troubled land in a time of great difficulties to show that his magnetism could outride every evil. His divine vibrations are still there, just as strong as when he was physically present. Those who are in tune when they go there will feel that presence. But first, one has to meditate and prepare himself.

Use Your Time Wisely

Most people spend their time on useless things. Try each day to do something worthwhile, so that you feel you have made a contribution, that your life has some meaning. Great magnetism is developed by accomplishing something every day that you thought you couldn't do.

Watch your thoughts. All your experiences come percolating through your thoughts. It is the company of your thoughts that uplifts or degrades you. You see, your body is a carriage drawn by five horses, the senses. You, the soul, are the owner and driver of this carriage. Unless you use the reins of the mind to control these horses, the carriage will go out of control and run

* During these hours it was the Guru's practice to offer special prayers on behalf of those who sought his divine intercession.

into the ditch of disease, suffering, and ignorance. If you want the carriage to carry you successfully through life, and to take you to God's kingdom — which is your true destination — you must control these five sense-horses. Through such control you will attain self-mastery, and thus real happiness.

Why waste time? Use your time to meditate and to study magazines such as *Inner Culture,* * which inspire you with right thoughts. You can so easily kill time. A whole life can be wasted. You are the master of the moments of your life. Use them wisely, so that they will give you your salvation. Why spend time in cards and useless things? I have seen that people sit and play cards for hours on end in smoke-filled rooms. Such a waste of life is the most vicious thing you can do to your soul. So much time is consumed, and it gives you nothing in return. For relaxation, it is better to get out and walk and have some healthful exercise.

Don't Be a Chatterbox

And if you would have magnetism, don't talk too much. Don't be a chatterbox—talk, talk, talk. Idle talk dissipates your magnetism. It is also dangerous, because those who talk too much always end up saying the wrong thing. These little words that come out of the cannon of the mouth have the power to explode empires; or, if they come from a man of wisdom, to bring peace. The person who talks too much is a shallow thinker and has very little magnetism. But when a silent man of wisdom talks, people listen. That is how my guru was. When he spoke, his words were full of meaning and power; otherwise he was silent.

As soon as two or more people get together, each one wants to be heard and no one wants to listen. Learn to listen more, to sit quietly and enjoy the company of others. Edison and one of his friends used to sit together and say hardly a word; and when they parted company, they said, "Good-by, we have had a wonderful visit."

When you do talk, give your whole attention to the person you are talking to, and talk sense. When you speak with your soul, everyone will want to listen. The power of the whole world

* In 1948 Paramahansaji changed the name of the magazine to *Self-Realization.*

and the truth of God will be behind your words. You will change others with your words. That is magnetism.

If you would develop magnetism, you must also learn to introspect, and keep a daily mental diary of what you have done. You will be surprised at the amount of time wasted in doing nothing. Whoever would be great should analyze himself in this way. Every night, sit still and ask yourself, "What have I done today?" This will help you to see clearly how you can use your time more wisely. If you remember just this one key, you will become a different person. As soon as you take control of your life and start doing what you should do, your will power is developing, and so is your magnetism.

Our only savior is our will power. Will is the switch that controls everything in this universe. If you don't exercise your will power, you will be a weakling, easily influenced by your environment. Development of the will is the secret of magnetism. Men of success are men of great will power. When you develop will, no matter how you are pounded down by life, you rise again and say, "I am successful. I can win."

Suppose you tell yourself, "Now today I will find time to meditate." *Do* it; sit for at least a few minutes. The next day, resolve to stay a little longer in meditation. And the next day, in spite of obstacles, make a little more effort. Accomplish something by your will. That is how to develop magnetism.

The Magnetism of Unselfish Love

Cultivate within yourself that spiritual magnetism which is in Christ and Krishna and the masters. In order to do this, you have to become unselfish; you must express selfless love for all. Try always to be helpful. Develop your usefulness to your family, to your community, to your friends. Be willing to help wherever you are. That makes you a magnetic person.

If you want friends, you must learn to love all unselfishly. To use anyone for selfish ends is wrong. Very few persons love you for your own sake; but if you can love others without any motive, then you can have divine magnetism. Remember that truth. The husband should love the wife out of friendship, not because of her physical beauty. You should think of your friends, not because of their riches, attractiveness, or power, but because you love them. The magnetism of unselfish love for all evolves when you are always ready to help others without any motive but to be a friend.

Let God Flow Through You

Among the people who have come to me there have been some that I immediately told, "Your motive is not right. Change your motive." A few have not liked it, but others have changed. Nothing is gained from being a hypocrite. The smartest person can't hide what is in his eyes. The whole story of one's life is written there. If you know how to recognize another's nature by his eyes, and you always pray, "Lord, I want to know the truth about this person; I don't want to be deceived," you will feel, right in your heart, what his nature is. You will never make a mistake.

When you are talking to others, hold the eyes of the one you are talking to, and speak with all the force of truth and the love of God behind your words. And when you shake hands, do so consciously, so that you give the magnetism of your sincere friendship. Try to help that person. Be positive and develop your own spiritual magnetism, and you will have the power to change others. With the eyes you can convey that magnetism. Just look at the one you want to help, and think, "God's blessing is flowing through me." Never feel *you* are the doer.

Let God flow through you continuously. Then wherever you go, you will be a magnet. Even at a distance you can change an enemy. Just send him your love. One of my students told me how he had practiced this after hearing one of my lectures. An associate had maligned him and ruined his business; but still, whenever he thought of this man, he kept on giving him love. One day the student met him, and treated him as if nothing had happened. They were coming down in an elevator together, and when they reached the outside the student offered him a lift in his car. All the time he was mentally giving him love.

A few weeks later the man came to the student and said, "I must talk with you. I haven't been able to get you out of my mind. I wronged you. Now I must go from person to person to right the wrong I have done." And that he did.

So if someone makes himself your enemy, go on trying to be

kind to him. Be friendly from your heart, and do something by which he will know you want to be friendly. If that doesn't work, just silently give him love. He will change. Love is powerful. It absolutely will conquer. But it is wrong if your motive is to control that person. Never misuse the power of love, but continuously increase it to help others.

It Is the Ego That Keeps God Away

From childhood I noticed that people always seemed drawn to me. In this connection I remember one great lesson that my Guru taught me. In his ashram there was a boy named Kumar, who was very jealous of me because the others sought me out, and because Master had placed me in charge of the ashram duties. One day Master said to me, without explanation, "You go back to the sweeping from today. I am placing Kumar in charge." I said, "All right, Master." I didn't get angry. I accepted it, for I had faith in Master's great wisdom.

This boy then began to tyrannize over me, among other things, asking me to shine his shoes! I did so. But even though he was in charge, the other boys still kept coming to me and not to him. One day I overheard Kumar complain to Master that I was undermining his authority because the ashram devotees still came to me and not to him. Master replied with firmness: "That is what I wanted you to learn. He does his work without complaining and with the right attitude. Even though he was put in the lowest position, his servicefulness and right behavior make him a natural leader; and you see, because you have not learned how to behave, you cannot lead others, even though you were placed in charge." Master relieved him of his position and gave it back to me.

Don't be filled with ego. Take the back seat. That will make you magnetic. So long as the ego will be bobbing inside you, God will never be there. He stays away. To the egotist He says, "You are but a little spark and yet you extol yourself so much. I own the whole universe, but I remain silent, in the background."

When you are with God, you have everything. The millionaire, the billionaire, cannot make you bow down. My elder brother, Ananta, used to say how hopeless I was, because I would fly school and spend my time in meditation instead. He often told me that my life would be worthless, like dry leaves that fall. But I replied, "Dry leaves can make wonderful fertilizer, Brother!" Ananta acquired a good position and money, but he lost his life early to illness.

The Love of God Is All-Consuming

When I entered this path, everyone thought I was crazy. I used to sing my songs of devotion to God, and some in my family lamented that I had gone wrong. Whenever I sang, they used to hide themselves in sorrow for me. But in time I convinced them that they were mistaken. Then they also began singing my songs of love for God and trying to meditate. They became my students, right in my own home. That is very unusual; for as it is said, a prophet is without honor in his own country.

The love of God, the love of the Spirit, is an all-consuming love. Once you have experienced it, it shall lead you on and on in the eternal realms. That love will never be taken away from your heart. It shall burn there, and in its fire you shall find the great magnetism of Spirit that draws others unto you, and attracts whatsoever you truly need or desire.

I tell you truthfully that all my questions have been answered, not through man but through God. He *is*. He *is*. It is His spirit that talks to you through me. It is His love that I speak of. Thrill after thrill! Like gentle zephyrs His love comes over the soul. Day and night, week after week, year after year, it goes on increasing—you don't know where the end is. And that is what you are seeking, every one of you. You think you want human love and prosperity, but behind these it is your Father who is calling you. If you realize He is greater than all His gifts, you will find Him.

In the science of yoga meditation India has given the answer to how to find Him. I traveled through that land. I sat at the feet of a true master. I am not only convinced that God is, but I give you my testimony of His presence. If you heed my words, from your own realization you too shall someday say that God is. You shall know I tell you the truth.

Every blade of grass, every spark of fire, every thought you think testifies to His presence, His intelligence. He is the Source whence all things come, but you are not conscious of Him. India specialized in the science of going to that Source.

God is not partial. Whoever has asked for Him and sought Him has received Him. Everything you have desired in your heart, in this and all former lives, is fulfilled in Him. Concentrate on the Source of all power. India has shown you the technique by which you can do so: meditation. When you read a wonderful book on science, or study about the body or the mind, you realize how many things you didn't know before about yourself and the world you live in. But if you use that time to meditate, to become attuned to God—He who has created you and all things—you will gain so much more.

Scientists do not make discoveries by prayer alone, but by application of the laws of nature. Similarly, God comes to him who follows the law, who applies the science of meditation. People have wandered in the forest of theology and have lost themselves. In vain I went from temple to temple seeking God; but when I found the soul temples in great lovers of God, I saw that He was there. He is not bribed by beautiful edifices. He comes to the tear-washed altar of the heart that is continuously calling unto Him. God is real. The masters who have devoted themselves to meditation for years and years have found Him.

Listen to What the Spirit of God Has to Tell You

It is from my own experience of Truth that I talk to you. You don't want to listen to a spiritual victrola; you want to hear what the spirit of God has to tell you. Whatever I say to you is from Him, and for your highest welfare. I am not for sale; I cannot be bribed. I came here to serve. When the Lord calls me, I will walk out. I am here only to give you the truth. And those who shall receive, with them I shall be pleased. I have spoken before thousands, but I want you to know that it is for such as this temple and this environment, and for you who are sincere in your wish to seek God, that I stay. I know those who are marching toward God. Great shall be their reward.

It is my duty and privilege to be here with you in this garden of souls and to speak to you of God. When you enter these grounds, speak no evil, hear no evil, see nothing negative, and you will feel the sacred vibrations that are always present. I have never talked of anything negative here. That is why the vibrations are so pure. I want you to observe this also—to be only positive and pure-minded, for in such temples of the mind God loves to come and to stay.

By study and meditation, each one of you can charge your soul with His power, so that you also will speak with the voice of God. That is the kind of magnetism you want to have. Meditate deeper and deeper every day, and you will acquire tremendous magnetism.

I have seen some who come to the ashram and from the beginning try to teach us, when it is they who need to change themselves. Such persons do not belong in the ashram. We look for those who are harmonious and humble, who will cooperate one hundred percent with the work of our line of Masters through Self-Realization.

My greatest wish is to change souls, to turn them toward God. For this purpose I used to concentrate on healing; but I found that when the body was made well, the student was satisfied and left. My interest is in those who seek to be healed of ignorance—man's greatest sickness. Those who want God and come to me with receptive hearts shall never be the same again. They shall realize a great truth: "When this 'I' shall die, then will I know who am I." In this body it is not Yogananda anymore, but He.

Now pray with me: "Heavenly Father, charge my body and my mind with Thy magnetism. And be Thou established in my soul, that I may be spiritually magnetic. By my love for Thee I shall attract Thee unto me; and in Thee I shall have all things whatsoever I truly need. *Aum...Amen.*"

Psychological Furniture

Self-Realization Fellowship International Headquarters,
Los Angeles, California, May 30, 1940

My talk today is based on extensive observation of human behavior. From what I have discerned, you will understand why humanity can be called "psychological furniture." This concept came to me years ago in India, as a result of my experience with a very learned professor who was head of a scientific association. The professor's flaw was that he loved flattery—so much so, that he wanted others always to agree with him, regardless of their own opinion. The first thing he expected was that we bow down to him and touch his feet. I did it sincerely, however, because I had a high regard for his learning. Studying with the professor were two young men who were trying to get a scholarship to a university in Japan through his recommendation. One of them had very high qualifications, but he would not bow down to the professor. As a result, the professor denied him the scholarship, but approved it for the other, less-qualified student, who had prudently flattered him. So the scholarship was won not so much on merit as on that student's awareness of the set characteristics of the professor, and of how to make use of that particular type of psychological furniture to serve his own purpose.

First, we should understand the significance of the expression, "psychological furniture." When we think of the different furnishings in a home—rocking chairs, tables, cabinets, and so forth—we see them as distinctive objects, solid and unchanging, each with its own definite uses and typical characteristics. The wood for each one was gathered, cut, chiseled, and polished in order to create that particular piece. Furniture comes in various styles—Spanish, early American, French, and so on. We have antique furniture. There is also today's ultra-modern style (and in some homes it looks good). The design of a piece of furniture expresses a certain personality. When you go into a home, you can tell a lot about the owners by their furniture. You can recog-

141

nize people of good taste by the way they furnish their houses. It isn't necessarily the money they have put into it, but the taste with which they have selected and arranged everything, that makes their places attractive. The right furnishings can make a home inviting, beautiful, and comfortable. So furniture is more than inert objects. It is "living" in the sense that each piece has its distinctive purpose and personality.

We human beings are a lot like furniture, as I will show you. Even as a wide variety of furniture is made from one material, wood, so are all humans made of the same stuff. When we were first conceived in the mother's body, we were just one little cell. But in four days a complete design of what we were to become was present in that embryo. Some intelligent force composed a definite individual pattern—different from all others—of what we were destined to be.

Most newborn babies look very much alike. Of course, you can tell a Chinese or an Indian baby from an American baby, but for the most part there is very little difference in their appearance at birth. However, as the baby begins to grow, the unique pattern of what he is to become slowly unfolds.

When the furniture-maker begins his work, he has a particular pattern in his mind, a chair, for example, which gradually takes shape as he carves the wood. In the same way, out of the first tiny cell of a baby's body a predetermined pattern starts to emerge. That form continues to develop after birth until each individual, each soul, shows the distinctive physical and mental characteristics that uniquely identify that human being—just as the chair was shaped in a certain way from a formless log.

What Instruments Mold Us Into Psychological Furniture?

What are the instruments that create this bewildering variety of human psychological furniture? There is the influence of heredity and of the family; and more importantly, the influence of our karma, the effects of our actions of past lives. God made us in His image, but we chose to make ourselves into these individualistic pieces of psychological furniture. We fashioned our present bodies and minds by our thoughts, actions, and desires in past lives. It makes no difference whether we believe in karma and reincarnation or not. The law of cause and effect operates with or without our sanction. You have probably wondered why the same parents can give birth to one child of keen intelligence and another who is mentally deficient. If both infants were created in the image of God, and God is just, how could this be? Such enigmas are explained by the karmic law of cause and effect at work in each human life. It is not the chisel of heredity alone that shapes an individual into a particular piece of psychological furniture; his past-life actions create their own good or bad effects in this life. It is karma that sets the pattern from which the instruments of present-life influences work and shape us as we are today.

So, heredity and family, the effects and influences of our environment, climatic conditions, our free-will responses to karmic conditions brought on from the past, and the civilization or era in which we are born — all of these serve to mold our bodies and our mentalities. For instance, the intense sunlight and heat peculiar to India and Africa have caused the evolution of a race of people with darker skins than those who dwell in the moderate climate of America or the extremely cold climate of Russia.

Babies are "raw material." If they are fashioned in the factory of a Chinese family in China, they come out with slanting eyes and flat noses, and will adopt the mannerisms and dress of Chinese culture. A piece of American psychological furniture will be different. You can easily spot him: He says, "Okay," and "Go ahead," and is definitely American in his dress and behavior.

Every kind of furniture has a use, unless it is ready to crumble. Even then it has value if some worthwhile memory or ideal is associated with it, as with the chair on which Lincoln sat. Similarly, the different kinds of psychological furniture produced by different nations all have their own special value and usefulness.

Human Peculiarities

This concept of human beings as different types of furniture is very amusing, isn't it? Why do women wear skirts and men trousers? See how we are molded into psychological furniture — every piece different and interesting! The Hindu furniture says, "Look at the American furniture. He wears funny trousers and eats with forks and knives." And the American furniture says, "Look at the Hindu furniture. He goes about with just a little cloth draped over his body, and eats with his fingers."

The Hindu furniture, the English furniture, the American furniture, the Chinese, French, Russian, German — we should learn from and appreciate the distinctive qualities of them all. Observe their different characteristics. Every nation has some predominant ones. There is some good to be learned or enjoyed from each nationality. Take for instance the difference in foods; they characterize a nation. When I came to this country, I heard so much about apple pie, I was eager to try it. The first time I ate it, I liked it. Most Americans like apple pie. Hindus like curries and mangoes. Italians like spaghetti. Chinese like their dried meats and rice. Eskimos like raw fish. So you see, in every nationality, there are some particular characteristics that may seem very strange to others, yet are natural to those people; they are molded, like furniture, to exhibit those traits.

What we should do is seek out from different nationalities those qualities we ought to follow or adopt in our own behavior. For example, I like the American's "go ahead" temperament. In spite of difficulties, he has the enthusiasm and the spirit of marching on. And I like the English tenacity, and the freedom from race consciousness of the French. I like the exactness of the German mentality; the scientific mind comes primarily from Germany. I like the Chinese morality and the Hindu spirituality. The Hindu mentality is able to chisel or mold the soul so beautifully that it produces saints who make this earth a better place in which to live. We are meant to learn from all different nationalities, to select their best qualities and adopt them in our own behavior. When we combine those ideals with the best that is in our own unique nature, we become psychological furniture of exceptional quality and value. Just think! if people would stop hating each other and learn to appreciate and adopt what is good in every nation, a millennium would come on earth.

Never deride or ridicule anyone of any nationality. That person may have cause to think the same way about you. Remember, some of your traits seem just as funny to those of another culture as theirs may seem to you. One can even laugh at his own kind from times past. For instance, you laugh at the huge skirts, the long mustaches, and checkered trousers of the Gay Nineties. But people of that era would laugh at the way you dress today. Your modern styles would appear equally outlandish to them. Even though we consider ourselves an advanced civilization, we have lots of peculiarities!

And, speaking of peculiarities, have you ever noticed the hats that some ladies wear?* Each style reveals a certain kind of mentality. There are women who wear attractive, conservative hats; and others who wear incredibly flamboyant styles. Those who buy such hats have a conscious or unconscious desire to attract attention. And it works!

I have also seen some unbelievably crazy modernistic paintings. Yet those who admire them expect everyone else as well to think they are wonderful. And there are monstrosities in furniture, too. The idea is, there are certain things that are unattractive to the majority, and certain things that are attractive to the majority. We reveal something of our mentality by what we are drawn to, by our tastes. Some mentalities make themselves ridiculous or repulsive to people of all nations, even their own. If the majority find you an unattractive personality, analyze yourself. There may be some traits in your make-up that are repugnant to others. Perhaps you talk too much, or you make it a practice to put your finger into everyone else's pie, or you have the habit of telling others what is wrong with them and how they should lead their lives, and you won't accept any suggestions for improving yourself. These are examples of psychological characteristics that make us unattractive to others.

Dangerous Psychological Furniture

Now, just as there is unattractive psychological furniture, there is also dangerous psychological furniture. There are certain behavioral traits that make one a danger to society or to himself. You wouldn't want any furniture in your home that is unsafe to use or have around; similarly, dangerous psychological

---

* At the time this lecture was given, a lady would not consider herself well dressed without a hat. Since women in India do not wear hats, these "creations" that American women put on their heads were a real curiosity to Paramahansaji. He often made some good-humored comments about them, to the delight of his audiences.

furniture is to be feared and avoided by all. Such furniture should be mended before it can harm anyone.

One dangerous trait that all should avoid is treachery. He who is treacherous psychological furniture will betray friends, family, everyone. He does not know the meaning of the word "loyalty." I say to you that treachery is the greatest punishable crime before the tribunal of God. Jesus prayed for his crucifiers, "Father, forgive them, for they know not what they do." In other words, he urged God to forgive those whose psychologically misguided mentalities made them misunderstand him and what he stood for. He also forgave Mary Magdalene, who was accused of adultery. But what did he say about Judas and men like him? "Woe to that man by whom the Son of man is betrayed! good were it for that man if he had never been born."* Treachery is the highest sin, because it is a deliberate act intended to harm those who trusted the betrayer. It is a deliberate stabbing of the soul.

Suppose someone professes great friendship for you, and trustingly you confide your troubles to him. If he takes advantage of this, and for his own ends, or out of spite, tells your problems and faults to others, that is a sin of treachery against God in man. One who accepts a guru, and then breaks his vows to the guru and betrays him, is guilty of the deepest treachery. There is no greater sin before God than for one to turn against the messenger sent to him by God Himself. So never profess loyalty or friendship for anyone unless you mean it. It would be better to tell him what you truly think. Never talk against a friend behind his back. If you have something to say about a friend, say it with kindness in front of him, or to his face; or else don't say it at all.

The knife of treachery reaches the soul, and anyone who uses that knife will be forsaken by God and by man. Never allow yourself to become treacherous psychological furniture. There is no necessity or excuse for treachery at any time. Shun those persons who are traitors. You can speak up and try to show them the error of their ways, but if that only makes matters worse, then just remain away from their company. Though a treacher-

---

* Mark 14:21.

ous person may hurt you a little bit, he hurts himself far more. He is like a valuable piece of antique furniture that is infested with termites. It is hard to restore rotten psychological furniture that gives evil for good and returns hate for love. If ever you encounter a treacherous person, you will remember this definition.

Friendship should be unconditional. If you give that kind of friendship to others, and are never in speech or action disloyal to them, you will be surprised to see how God comes to you through true friends.

Conversation Pieces

There are some furnishings you call conversation pieces. They don't serve much purpose other than to be the butt of jokes. Similarly, there is a type of psychological furniture that no one takes seriously. No matter what such persons are saying, others don't really listen to them because they have a reputation for being comical and light-minded. No one really wants to be thought of as funny all the time. He wants to be taken seriously by his friends. Furthermore, to be always joking and light takes away his inner peace.

Make Constant Effort to Increase in Value

Don't be a stationary piece of furniture, either. I have seen some people again after ten or twenty years, and they are still just the same — going on in the same old rut year after year, never any change for the better. Always strive to be better. Quality furniture that receives proper care becomes more valuable as it gets older. Psychological furniture should also improve with age. Habit-bound people are stationary psychological furniture. The selfish ones hold on to their miserliness to the last day of their lives. Others are greedy, and no matter what you say to them, they will continue to eat themselves into the grave. Some are oversensual, dwelling so much on the plane of the senses that whenever they are with the opposite sex they want to make love. They go on drowning themselves in sensual pleasures until the end. Why lead a life of slavery like that?

We should keep on striving to improve ourselves. Businessmen and other creative people are progressive psychological furniture. They shape themselves according to the ideals that will enable them to realize their ambitions. That is good. But I feel very sorry for a person who doesn't change through the years. Such people are like valueless antiques; they just get older, but never better. To remain bound to habits is to remain in slavery. Of course, it is beneficial to adopt good spiritual, emotional, physical, and mental habits, and to be constant in them. But never allow yourself to be a slave to any bad habit. No matter what you have been or done in the past, don't worry about it or brood over it. Just continue to strive to be better in every way.

Those who never change, but grow old in their same fixed habits, I call "psychological antiques." Among them there are some spiritual antiques, such as grandma and grandpa, who lead an idealistic, peaceful life, but fail to grow in understanding, and therefore remain set in their ways. They cannot appreciate the needs, the enthusiasm, and the interests of the younger generation. That is all right to a certain point. But when they blindly condemn the younger generation, it merely shows they have become antiques mentally. On the other hand, many young people fall needlessly into error because they don't respect these spiritual antiques. They think that grandma's and grandpa's ideals are old-fashioned, and therefore won't listen to what they have to say. In their zeal to be modern, they break every "old" rule they can. But they should remember that antiques do have their value. They have been around a long time, and have seen and learned much. The younger and older generations should make more effort to learn from one another, for antiques and modern furniture both have their uses.

Strive to Understand the Intrinsic Characteristics of Others

In your relationships with others, it is extremely necessary to recognize and appreciate the characteristics that they have chiseled out in themselves. If you study people with an open mind, you will better understand them and be able to get along with them. You will instantly be able to tell what kind of person you are dealing with and know how to deal with him. Don't talk to a philosopher about horse racing, or to a scientist about housekeeping. Find out what interests an individual, and then talk with him about that subject, not necessarily what interests you.

Always avoid being critical or sitting in judgment while striving to understand or deal with other people. But do be critical of yourself. Every day look at yourself in the mirror of introspection. That is a much clearer mirror than the one before which you groom yourself every morning. Not a day passes that I don't look in my own mental mirror. And I don't spare myself. If there is anything reflected there that I have done which is not up to my standard, I admonish myself severely. That is the way you can become flawless in the spiritual mirror of your soul, a living asset in the kingdom of God.

Wisdom Is a Chisel, Love Is the Sandpaper

The best instruments you can use to fashion your life into a beautiful quality piece of psychological furniture are the chisel of wisdom and the sandpaper of love. Man needs intellectuality, but intellect must be tempered with love. When carving a piece of furniture, you have to smooth it with sandpaper or it will remain rough. Love is the sandpaper that takes away the harshness of intelligence, and smoothes your intellectuality. With both wisdom and love, you become a useful, practical piece of furniture that is admired by all, and loved by God—and that is what you are seeking to make of yourself.

You must not shape yourself into a valueless psychological antique. Instead, every time you look in the mirror, and especially in the mirror of introspection, ask yourself: "Am I developing better habits? Am I being more positive? Am I smiling more sincerely from my heart? Am I improving every day?" You must strive to be spiritual psychological furniture that will be used for decorating the kingdom of God. Wouldn't you like that? Some pieces of furniture are so beautiful that they don't require any more work on them. So be thou that perfect piece of psychological furniture that needs no further change. That time will come when you are one with God. All great saints who have come on earth have chiseled their lives with wisdom and love and meditation into perfect spiritual psychological furniture that will forever serve mankind and decorate eternally the kingdom of God.

The Unknown Potential of Memory

*Self-Realization Fellowship Temple, Hollywood, California,
September 12, 1943*

Memory is an important human faculty. Just imagine what it would be like if we could not recall anything! We would not remember the results, good or bad, of any of our actions. We could not remember names, or how to walk, or how to do the simplest task. Throughout life, each act, each bit of information would have to be learned as though for the first time every time we needed to do or know it. Without memory we would remain like children.

The word "remember" comes from *re*, "again," and *memorari*, "to be mindful of." Memory is the original mental note made of every thought, act, or experience when it first occurs. Each memory is recorded in the brain as a particular thought pattern. To remember is to recall to conscious awareness any one of these countless records.

All our experiences of past incarnations, as well as those since birth in this life, are present in our subconscious mind. Yet most people do not remember past lives—who they were and where, and what they did—or much from the early years of this life. But you can easily recall even minute details of your immediate past, such as what food you had yesterday, and where you ate it. A similar total recall of all your myriad experiences in this life and in previous lives would so crowd your conscious mind that you would have no peace. Fortunately, memory is selective, enabling you to remember the salient features of your experiences without having to relive them in complete detail whenever you think of them. Recollection of past lives comes only as you develop a very strong memory.

The memory of a spiritually enlightened person operates in an entirely different way from that of the average human being. To illustrate: You are aware of every part of your body without "remembering" or reproducing that awareness in your consciousness. You do not have to recall the fact that you have a body; you know it, because your consciousness is awake throughout your body. Similarly, on a grand scale, God is in everything, and everything is in Him. He has no memory; He has no need for memory, because He is omnipresent in all past, present, and future experiences. In His eternal conscious awareness He has nothing "past" to remember. In my own experience, I find mortal memory fading away; the divine consciousness of my eternal omnipresent soul-nature has become predominant. In this consciousness all knowledge and perception comes to me, not through mental processes or memory, but as intuitive experiences.

Memory reproduces in the consciousness those experiences that are past and forgotten. We do not need memory for that which is happening in the now. Here in this temple, as we consciously look around us, we are aware of the windows and drapes and other details of the room. But to "see" similarly any other part of the temple, we must turn to memory to reproduce whatever we have previously observed there.

Limiting Effect of Man's Mortal Nature

Because of the predominance of his mortal nature, man is cut off from the universal consciousness and the full potential of his human brain.* He remains unaware of his divine intuitive consciousness and has to rely on his all-too-poorly developed faculty of memory, which cannot even recall all the early experiences of this life, much less past ones. He may remember his childhood home and a few outstanding experiences of that time, but most of what happened then has been forgotten. Of course, some persons remember more than others, because they have developed a greater ability to retain the facts of their experiences.

---

* "It is conservatively estimated that the human brain can store an amount of information equivalent to an astounding 100 trillion different words. This would mean acquiring one word per second continuously for a million years. Of course, no one ever uses more than a fraction of this storage space. In a lifetime of 70 years a human being may store information roughly equivalent to a mere trillion words" (Gordon Graff, "Chemical Memory for Instant Learning," *Science Digest*, September 1973).

A minister who had lived and preached in Boston for many years had a sudden loss of memory. Oblivious of his name and profession, he moved elsewhere and remained for three years in his new environment, working as a grocery clerk. Then one day he suffered a blow on his head; the shock revived his consciousness in that tract of his brain which was connected with the past, and he remembered his real identity.

Memories of Past Lives

The memory of your past lives has vanished similarly from your mind. If all the brain cells were awakened, you would be able to remember everything. I recall many of my past incarnations. It is not mere belief; one can test such memories of the past, and I have verified these recollections. Quite a few people have heard me mention a previous life in which I lived for many years in England. Experiences of that life come clearly to my mind. There were certain details about the Tower of London that I remembered very well, and when I went there in 1935 I saw that those places were exactly as I had seen them within. From childhood I knew also that in one incarnation I had lived by the ocean. As a little boy I used to see in my mind's eye many places and events of that incarnation. When I spoke of these things some laughed at me, but they don't laugh now. I was able to prove to them that those past-life experiences I had seen inwardly as a child were factual. If you are calm, and concentrate deeply enough to attain the state of cosmic consciousness, you can recall the very faint etchings of all past experiences, for every one has been recorded in your brain.

The habits you cultivated in past lives have substantially created your physical, mental, and emotional makeup in this life. You have forgotten those habits, but they have not forgotten you. Out of the crowded centuries of your experiences, your karma follows you. And whenever you are reborn, that karma, consisting of all your past thoughts and actions and habits, creates the kind of physical form you will have—not only your appearance, but your personality traits. It is these individually created past-life patterns that make one person different from another, and account for the great variety of human faces and characteristics. The very fact that you are a woman or a man was determined by your self-chosen tendencies in previous lives.

Most people do not analyze themselves, and so never realize how bound they are by influences of past actions. Day in and day out, they remain in the same physical and mental ruts. When you say, "I like this," and "I don't like that," it is because certain experiences in the past helped to create an affinity for the one and a distaste for the other. In the ashram of my Guru* in India, Master taught us to be guided by wisdom, not by likes and dislikes. Begin to analyze yourselves more, to understand why you are as you are. You may have noticed that some children are born with certain moods and habits. They brought these tendencies from the past; for in this life they have not yet had time to form such patterns of behavior.

From childhood I was interested in creating buildings. My first attempt at construction in this life was the renovation of a little mud hut in Calcutta when I was a young boy. This interest was prominent because I had done much building during my incarnation in England. So many experiences I recall from other times! Although I had never learned anything about music in this life, I have played many Indian instruments and have been told I would make a fine musician. This aptitude is a result of knowledge carried over from the past. If you analyze yourself, you also will recall tendencies of early childhood that are indicative of a previous life.

Select Only the Good Habits of Past Lives

Habits can be differentiated between those created in this life, and those brought from past lives. Most habits created in this life are results of the influence of past-life habits. In this incarnation I nurtured only those habits that were good. By constantly watching and correcting myself from early childhood, I was able to throw off bad habits from the past and become free.

Through the right use of memory we can reproduce those experiences of our past lives that are beneficial for the increase of knowledge in this life. Remembering the good and bad effects of past experiences, we are better able to discriminate and get rid of habits that are causing us pain and sorrow in this life. We should all be able to do this.

Side by side in man's memory are the good and bad habits he

* Swami Sri Yukteswar.

has created. They are all present in his brain, whether he remembers them or not. Every time you do good to someone, the
memory of it is stored in your brain. And every time you
do harm to someone, this likewise is added to your mental
storehouse. Anything you have consciously done to others, good
or bad, will be "remembered." Your present actions are unconsciously influenced by these past actions. When a good person
with good habits from the past performs a good act, the influence of his past goodness causes that action immediately to
become a good habit. Similarly, when a wicked person performs
a wrong act, the reinforcing influence of his past evil habits
causes that action immediately to become a bad habit. Make up
your mind to rid yourself of bad tendencies brought from the
past, as well as those created in this life. Try to remember only
your good deeds. Even a little bit of goodness, no matter in what
incarnation performed, is never lost to you. Use those good
memories to influence your present actions. Remind others,
also, of their potential goodness.

Forget Past Errors

Avoid dwelling on all the wrong things you have done. They
do not belong to you now. Let them be forgotten. It is attention
that creates habit and memory. As soon as you put the needle on
a phonograph record, it begins to play. Attention is the needle
that plays the record of past actions. So you should not put your
attention on bad ones. Why go on suffering over the unwise
actions of your past? Cast their memory from your mind, and
take care not to repeat those actions again.

Reflection on negative things is not the purpose of man's
God-given memory. Some people go on remembering all the
suffering they passed through, and how terrible the pain was,
from an operation that took place twenty years ago! Over and
over again they relive the consciousness of that sickness. Why
repeat such experiences? To deliberately recall painful or evil
experiences is a misuse of memory and a sin against your soul.
By nurturing unpleasant memories you will carry them into the
future, and this is not good for you. If you feel a deep resentment
toward some person, and every day you recall that feeling and
retaliate by mentally striking him, it will take you incarnations

to erase the remembrance of that hatred. To become the victim of a memory filled with ugly recollections is dangerous. Cultivate forgetfulness of past wrongs and vengeful feelings, and encourage only the remembrance of good.

Few people in this world try consciously to develop the potentials of body, mind, and soul. The rest are victims of circumstances of the past. They plod on and on, pushed by past wrong habits, helplessly going down under their influence, remembering only: "I am a nervous man," or "I am a weakling," or "I am a sinner," and so on.

It lies with each one of us to cut with the sword of wisdom the cords of our bondage, or to remain bound.

God has given everyone freedom to act as he will. Never impose your will on anyone else, but if you would persuade someone to do what you humbly believe to be best for him, influence him by love. When Mahatma Gandhi was in South Africa, he was stabbed and lay near death. The officials naturally wanted to prosecute his assailant, but Gandhi refused. "No," he said. "If I put him in prison, he will be a greater enemy. I will win him by love." When the attacker learned of Gandhi's forgiveness, he became his disciple.

Concentrate on the True and the Good

Nearly everyone is familiar with those three little monkey-figures that depict the maxim, "See no evil, hear no evil, speak no evil." I emphasize the positive approach: "See that which is good, hear that which is good, speak that which is good." And smell, taste, and feel that which is good; think that which is good; love that which is good. Be enthroned in the castle of goodness, and your memories will be like beautiful flowers in a garden of noble dreams. If you continuously add to the good things you can remember, you will in time remember the greatest good, which you have forgotten; and that is God. In the awakened memory of Him lies the key to freedom.

Use your memory to recall what you are—an immortal soul—and forget the evil memory of mortality. This is why Self-Realization teaches you to constantly remember the truth: you are Spirit. Every morning, repeat to yourself: "I am not the body of flesh; I want to remember my real soul-nature, invisible and formless Spirit." In the daytime your habits perpetuate the false memory of your limited physical being; but at night the heavenly angel of sleep reminds you of your formless divine being. God gives you sleep, in which you blissfully lose all consciousness of body and form, to remind you that you are Spirit, and your nature is Bliss.

Ways to Improve Memory

It is true that man's mental capacities are inherited according to his past karma, but memory can be cultivated. Various practices help to improve this faculty:

Diet plays an important role. Fresh milk and milk curd (yogurt) are conducive to keen memory. Overeating adversely affects it. An excess of fat in the diet impairs digestion and ultimately affects memory. Fried and fatty foods may be eaten once in a while, but only in moderation. Strictly avoid pork or pork products. Memory can be ruined by their excessive use. Perhaps you are thinking, "I eat pork products, but I still have a good memory." My response is that you have brought that good memory from the past. Continued regular consumption of pork will undo it.

Cold showers are beneficial to the memory and to the nerves. Cooling the nerves helps to promote mental calmness. A calm mind becomes an instrument for reproducing experiences clearly.

To be overactive sexually is detrimental to memory, draining its power more than any other factor. Those who have self-control can develop tremendous power of memory, tremendous power of mind. An example of this was the extraordinary memory of Sir Isaac Newton, who lived as a celibate.

Memory can also be developed by making a conscious effort to recall things you have learned or known. Try to recollect details of past experiences. It is helpful, also, to add and subtract figures mentally. Unfortunately, many people never exercise their memory in these ways.

Another method for developing the power of memory is to gently tap the top of the head with the knuckles.

Learn to do everything with deep attention and concentration, but do not be like those people who apply such concentration that they become overly fastidious, nagging and fussing about unimportant details. Most people perform their duties absentmindedly; they do not always know what they are doing!

Writing poetry or prose develops memory. As a rule, you are able to recall quickly what you have written, because you have put much feeling and attention into it.

The stimulation of feeling that accompanies some experiences helps you to remember them. Whatever you have done or experienced with deep emotion you easily recollect. Even a man of poor memory recalls his sorrows.

Last of all, make it a point to recall only good things of the past; never misuse your memory to bring evil thoughts into the temple of your consciousness. Keep that temple holy with the remembrance of God. Allow not the robbers of evil memories to enter this inner sanctuary. Open it only to angels of goodness. There is happiness in the divine soul-temple within you. There is goodness there; and loyalty, hope, courage, peace, and joy. All these qualities you can garner in your temple within, by re-membering only the good.

Remember Your Oneness With Spirit

If you keep your brain, your mind, your body filled with happy memories, the greatest good of all, God, will come and remain with you. Remembering only the good experiences of the past, you shall eventually remember your oneness with Spirit. You will remember that you have come down from Spirit into this flesh, into this little cage of bones which is a prison of disease and trouble. Get away from mortal consciousness. Remember in meditation that you are one with the vast Spirit. Go on remembering, and expanding that remembrance. There is no end to your consciousness; all things are glittering like stars in the firmament of your being. Suddenly you will find that your memory has subtly become intuition, the infallible insight of the soul. You no longer have to make the effort to remember anything, because memory has metamorphosed into all-knowing, omnipresent intuition. In that omniscient light of divine recollection, you shall not only remember — you shall realize that you are the Infinite Spirit.

Harmonizing Physical, Mental, and Spiritual Methods of Healing

Self-Realization Fellowship International Headquarters, Los Angeles, California, January 4, 1940

This evening I want to talk to you about healing, as the inspiration is coming through me now. Those who are suffering from some physical trouble feel that the pain will never end, while those who are not ailing think they are fine and never expect to be unwell. If you are in good health, be grateful; and whenever you see someone in trouble, mentally say to yourself, "But for the grace of God, there go I." The human machine is most imperfect, and therefore unreliable. Yet see how it lasts for so many years. Have you seen any car run as long as the human body does? Nevertheless, this wonderful machine that God has created is anything but perfect.

We must know the characteristics of the human machine. Just as a car needs water, gas, and electricity, so does the body. Your gas and water supply come from the solids, liquids, and oxygen you take into your body. To utilize them, the energy of life—*prana*—must be present. That is the electricity. Without this life-electricity you couldn't digest your food or assimilate oxygen. You can liken the body to an automobile battery; both require inner electricity to produce "electricity" or energy. A battery is better, because when it dies you can recharge it from an outside source. But when your physical body is dead, you cannot revitalize it.

The stomach is the weakest part of the human machine, and often the most abused. When digestion malfunctions, owing to overeating or wrong eating, it causes all kinds of troubles in the body. Ordinarily, when you see yourself in your mirror in the morning, you think you are quite all right. You don't realize that you are carrying many poisons in your system. The body is full of them. If you don't know how to get rid of these poisons, and the system can no longer handle them, disease results. In the American diet, protein poisoning, from the toxins in undigested protein, is usually the most at fault. In the East, the diet is often lacking in protein, but in the West it is overstocked with protein, because you eat too much meat. One of the effects of undigested protein — in addition to serious consequences such as heart disease and cancer — is that the toxins work on your nasal membrane and make you susceptible to catching colds.

Bad colds affect the whole body adversely, and even obstruct the mind so that you cannot think clearly. Colds are extremely disruptive to the yogi's meditation, preventing correct practice of *pranayama* * techniques. Therefore Satan seems to delight in getting into the nose and throat area. All those who need their voices, such as singers and lecturers, are usually susceptible to throat troubles because they are more or less sensitive about the throat, and this mental fear makes it easy for Satan to establish himself there. So when a cold first starts in the nose, you should arrest it immediately. If you don't, it gradually settles in the throat and lungs. Do you know why? The heat of the body becomes unbalanced.†

Speaking of colds, let me give you some practical suggestions: Gargling daily with a glass of warm salt water is a very good preventative for colds, as are right diet and exercise, and daily sunbaths for ten to thirty minutes (depending on the intensity of the sun and the sensitivity of the skin). If you do get a cold, it is best to stop it while it is only in the nose, before it goes down into the throat and chest. The best way to quickly bring the cold under control is to fast.‡ It will arrest the condi-

---

* See glossary.

† *Prana*, or subtle life energy (see glossary), is the true sustainer of life and health in the body. Its specialized functions are referred to in Yoga treatises as the "vital airs," the subtle powers behind all bodily functions. When these pranic currents are disturbed or unbalanced by unnatural living, the corresponding physiological processes are upset and various disorders and diseases result.

‡ Occasional fasting for two or three days on unsweetened fruit juices, while taking a natural laxative to ensure regular elimination, has a definite cleansing effect on the body. During a cold, it is best not to fast on citrus juices—such as orange juice — as this produces excessive mucus, which aggravates the symptoms of a cold. Fasting for longer than three days at a time should be done under the supervision of somone well trained in the science of fasting. Persons suffering from a chronic ailment or an organic defect should fast only upon the advice of a physician experienced in fasting procedures.

tion. There is nothing that kills a cold as quickly as fasting. If you can fast twenty-four hours, the cold usually goes away. But if the condition is chronic, you must eat plenty of fruits and vegetables, and also have plenty of fresh air and sunshine, and exercise. Many people believe in drinking lots of water when they have a cold. This is good if they have a fever, or congestion with thick mucus. Otherwise, excess water may make the mucous membrane very active. One of the worst things you can do when you have a cold is to drink hot beverages. Cold contracts, and heat expands. The heat may feel good for a little while, but it expands the cells and disturbs their normal function. And don't take ice-cold drinks either.

If you get a chest cold, dip a turkish towel in very hot water, wring it out and rub the chest with it. Then wipe the chest area with a dry towel. Repeat this five times, two or three times a day. Keep the chest well covered after each treatment.

These are the physical ways of preventing or getting over a cold.

In spite of precautions and remedies, colds as well as other diseases sometimes linger, and sometimes they go away quickly. The reason for this may be karmic. That is, the state of the body as determined by the law of karma, cause and effect. The cure of a disease depends in great part on one's karmic condition—the sum total of the effects of his past actions—plus the antidote taken for that illness. Some people think that since our karma predestines us to suffer, we might as well give up and accept the inevitable. But it is not right to be fatalistic. To try to help yourself and then give up when you don't get immediate results is foolishness, because every effort you make will help to break down that karmic pattern. "God helps him who helps himself."

The Three Basic Methods of Healing

The physical, mental, and spiritual laws of healing are all God's laws. They are not separate, but different aspects of the same divine principle of healing. The division created by supporters of each method is caused by ignorance. Each of these laws gets results when practiced rightly. Why deny that doctors can cure? Or that mind can heal? Or that faith can restore health? Lahiri Mahasaya was so great because he was not one-sided. He was balanced. He never ridiculed doctors; in fact, he had many doctor disciples. Lahiri Mahasaya would sometimes give an herb to a sick disciple, and to others he would merely say, "You are all right."* Occasionally, he would recommend a doctor. It depended on the nature of the ailing person.

I have sometimes told people to go to a physician. God can work through them. One must have a sane view. After all, who created all the plants and chemicals from which medicine is made? It is God who is the sole creator of everything, and it is He who works through His physical, mental, and spiritual laws.

I also know of ways to use simple herbs that are very effective in healing the body. So there are various methods of healing in this world, and the quarrel between the mental and physical healers is unnecessary. Tremendous healings are being accomplished in the field of medical science. Its scientists do not claim to have found all the laws of healing, but they have developed antibiotics and vaccines and other treatments that are curing and eradicating many diseases. They are on the verge of discovering a ray that will destroy some types of cancer cells. We must give credit to medical science. Doctors understand the mechanism of the human body better than the ordinary layman does.

On the other hand, do not depend solely on pills, but learn to rely more on the power of the mind. It is ignorance to deny the effect of material things on the body; and it is false reasoning not to recognize and develop the power of the mind. If you depend too much on material methods, the mind will not work. It is better to learn how to use the superior power of the mind. But if you don't know how to operate that mind, the sane view is to use commonsense material methods while gradually developing the power of your mind.

Self-Realization followers do not deny any of the three methods of healing—physical, mental, or spiritual. We accept the truth as discovered by medical science and by mental science. We only say that in some cases medical science works better, and in others mental science works better—depending entirely on the individual.

* Many examples of how Lahiri Mahasaya healed people in this way are described in *Autobiography of a Yogi.*

The spiritual method of healing by God's power is the greatest, and it can be instantaneous. But if your karma is not good, and your faith is lacking, it will take time for the spiritual methods of God to work upon your body and mind. Even if you think you are receptive, that doesn't necessarily make it so. A farmer may think that his land is fertile. He sows seeds upon the land, but they do not bring forth plants, because the farmer didn't test and condition the soil first. Merely thinking that you have the receptivity to be healed may not be enough. Possibly there is some mental kink lodged in the subconscious mind. Only when the subconscious, the inner superconscious, and the outer conscious minds are convinced, do you have the sprouting of the healing plant of life.

Everything Is Thought Force

In the ultimate analysis we find that everything is thought force. Your body, the house you live in, the light of day, everything you behold, the glasses you are wearing to help you see better—all are nothing but condensed thought. Suppose you fall asleep right now and dream you are walking in a garden. Suddenly a snake darts out and bites you on the leg. You suffer great fear and terrible pain. You are taken to a doctor who gives you an antidote, and gradually you feel all right. There is no more pain. Now, what happened in that dreamland? You enjoyed the beautiful garden, you experienced fear and pain, you appreciated the sense of well-being after being treated by medicine, yet all of these experiences were nothing but the fruits of your thought in your dream. When you awaken, you say, "Oh, my goodness, there is no bite on my leg. There was no medicine. What happened to me? It was nothing but a dream!"

In the dreamland, the snake, the bite, the pain, the garden, the medicine, all seemed so real. In order to cure that dream bite you had to take some dream medicine. But in the dreamland, what was the difference between the bite, the pain, the medicine, and the garden? Nothing. They were only different thoughts. But your imagination gave them such strength that when you were bitten by a dream snake, you felt a dream pain. And when you took a dream medicine, you felt a dream relief from that pain.

Similarly, you are dreaming this finite world and this physical body, and you have to admit the relative reality of all things that are happening. You cannot say that everything is a delusion and be unaffected by that delusion while you are dreaming this cosmic dream. The body does exist in this dream of creation, and so long as you are in the body, you have to admit its existence. You cannot say that matter is not real. It is real, in the relative sense. If it were not so, one could drink poison and not be affected by it. But for the ordinary man who takes poison, the result is death. It is folly for him to believe that matter has no reality. He is in delusion to say so.

A man on the East Coast told me of a woman who boasted to him about her superior conviction of the unreality of matter. "This fire is a delusion," she said. "It can't hurt me." He said nothing. But one day he saw his opportunity. When she wasn't looking, he warmed the poker in the fireplace and touched it to her back. She cried out, "Ow! Why did you do that?" He answered calmly, "Well, fire is a delusion. Your body is a delusion. The pain is a delusion. So how could I hurt you with a hot poker?" She was very angry. But he proved his point, that so long as you are in the delusion, you cannot say that matter is not real.

When you have a pain in the body, it is very hard to realize that the body is a delusion. So we must not be fanatics. We must proceed moderately, and gradually develop our will power and the power of the mind until we come to that state where we actually perceive that everything in this world is the dream-thought of God.

Mind Works if You Know How to Control It

The mind is a very strange thing. When it is right, it is right, though all the world think otherwise. And when it is wrong, not all the power of world opinion behind it will make it right. If you want to see how the mind works, you must bring it under your control. Without a controlled mind, you can't realize anything of what I am telling you. This requires gradual development. Mind power is not a simple matter. It works very subtly. To understand its subtlety is to know its power. Mind works in everything. If you know the secret of the workings of the mind, you will find this to be true.

Once a student in my classes in Minneapolis asked for help. She had been in a car accident. Her hand was all crippled, with a growth on it, and the thumb was sticking straight out. She couldn't bend it. The doctors had not been able to help her. Right before the whole audience I took her hand and pulled the thumb. It became free; she could move it. Her hand was healed. The following day, in gratitude, she gave a large donation to this work to help carry it on. So you see, mind power does work; but there must also be faith—as she had faith.

It is not God's desire that the mental scientist and the physical scientist should fight. Both are dealing with laws of God. The body is nothing but mind in action. There is no difference between the body and the mind except in their manifestations. The body is a grosser manifestation and the mind is a finer manifestation. In its elemental form, H_2O is invisible. Condensed, these gases become water, a liquid. When water is frozen, it becomes ice, a solid. However, the invisible H_2O, the water, and the solid ice are essentially not different. And as H_2O can appear as water and ice, so mind can appear as life and body—electrical or "fluid" life, and the "solid" physical body. Mind* is the invisible man or soul; life or *prana* is "liquid" mind; and the body is gross or "solid" mind. A simple philosophy, but a realization very hard to attain.

With the power of your mind you can work changes in the life in the body as well as in the body itself. Who but your mind is giving strength to the body? By healthful stimulation of the body you can make the mind feel better. By stimulation of the life, you can make the mind and body feel better. They are all correlated. The physical affects the mental and the mental affects the physical because they are interrelated. Therefore, you can affect the body through the mind, or the mind through the body. Thus, many people think they have to have a drink in order to feel happy—again, interrelation between the body and the mind. But a thousand bottles of wine could not create the intoxicating joy that I can produce just by mind power—and without devastating side effects.

---

* In the context of this talk, the word "mind" is used in a broad sense, meaning the consciousness in man: the soul, and its inherent powers of intelligence, will, and feeling. When differentiated, the term "mind" (Sanskrit, *manas*) has a limited connotation of sense-consciousness—like a mirror, it receives and reflects the impressions from the senses, which are then interpreted by the intelligence, reacted to by the feeling, and responded to by the will.

Mind can enable you to do anything you want, but you must experiment first in little things until you fully develop that power. If you don't constantly work at developing mind power, don't try suddenly to depend wholly on it. Never discredit the effects of the mind on the body, but remember that you have to gradually train the mind until you *know* that its power works. People who take medicines all the time become dependent on medicine and doctors. And those who are fanatical and refuse medical help when they need it often do great injury to themselves. You will not be forgiven for your ignorance of God's laws; you will have to suffer the consequences. You must use common sense.

To know and use little remedies such as putting iodine on a finger when it is cut is all right. What is the sense of risking infection by saying that mind will heal it? When you break your finger, does your mind straighten it out? Common sense tells you to have it set properly so that it will grow straight again. In either case, it *is* the mind that ultimately heals; commonsense remedies merely cooperate with and support the laws that promote the healing process when mind power is not yet perfectly developed.

Mind Can Produce Negative as Well as Positive Results

Mind is very tricky; it can produce negative as well as positive results. I remember one time when my sister had a sore throat. I never saw such a terrible infection. She couldn't eat; she couldn't swallow anything. She cried to me, "Please do anything you want to help me."

I said, "It is your mind that is creating this sore throat." I brought some food and told her to eat. She was unaware of my hand on her throat as I sent the power of my thought there. But the first thing she knew, she was eating, and didn't feel any pain. She was so happy that her throat was healed.

After I left, she got up and looked at her throat in a mirror. When she saw the ulcers still there, the pain returned and she let out a shriek.

When I came again to the house and saw her suffering, I asked, "What did you do?"

"I looked at my throat," she answered.

I said, "I saw your throat perfect in the light of God, and that is why you were well. But you saw the disease, and that is why you are feeling pain." Then I told her, "Drink this water." Because her mind was receptive, she was able to swallow the water, and was quite all right once more. She didn't look at her throat again.

So you see, mind has a great deal to do with it. In nervous diseases—which are nurtured by wrong thoughts—the mind can promote healing very fast, when its power is correctly applied.

On another occasion, the wife of a very dear friend in Long Beach came to see me. Her throat was paralyzed, the result of an accident, and she was seeking my help. "I can't eat anything," she told me. "I have to be fed through a tube."

I asked, "Can you drink milk?"

"No," she replied. "As soon as I try to drink liquids there is a spasm in my throat, and I cannot swallow."

"But that is all in your mind," I said. "You cannot leave here today until you have drunk a glass of milk."

She smiled. I asked for some milk to be brought.

"Now drink it!" I said firmly.

Because of the limiting thoughts in her mind, put there by the doctors and her past experiences, she was convinced that she couldn't drink. But my thought was stronger. After all, the nerves and cells are all controlled by the mind. But hers was so poisoned with doubt that she firmly believed she couldn't swallow. So the first gulps of milk were expelled from her mouth. She was sure that I was wrong.

Then I said, "I mean it; you cannot leave this room until you have finished that glass of milk."

"It is impossible," she argued; but I used my stronger thoughts to counteract her negative thoughts. She tried again, and this time she was able to swallow. She was cured.

Man Is Kept Hypnotized With Delusion

You see, this world is a world of maya, delusion, and man is kept hypnotized with that delusion. Our mind has convinced us of so many limitations. Someone says, "I must have my coffee."

Another says, "I must have my juicy piece of steak," and so on. It is a crazy world. I see it so clearly. But I follow the rules — as much as I want to, and then I say, "Down with rules! It is the mind that rules." And it works.

Death was such a reality, life was such a reality, but they are no more real for me. Never was I born, though in my dreams of earth life I was born many times. And never have I died, though many times I dreamed the death of my body in this dream world. In this one incarnation I can sleep and dream that I am born in England as a powerful king. Then I die and dream I am born a devout man. And then I die again and am born as a successful lawyer. Again I die and am reborn as Yogananda. But they are all dreams. That is what I am saying. I used to find such pleasure in discovering my past incarnations. But that has lost its enchantment. They are just so many dreams. When I realized everything is mind stuff, and that it is God's thought which is creating all these things, all these dreams all the time, then it had a different meaning for me. God can dissolve these dreams any time and bring them back again in better forms. But nothing is erased from the Infinite Mind; every dream is eternally imprinted there.

Delusion is so strong that it is pretty hard to believe it is delusion when you have needs and no money to meet them. It is difficult to believe that this world is *maya* when you are sick and suffering. But when you constantly keep your mind in God, you will realize that this world is His dream.

This is why in India we don't pay as much attention to physical healing as to the healing of the soul's ignorance. To heal the soul of ignorance — that is, to remove the delusion that covers the soul — is the greatest of all healings, because that healing is lasting. And when you heal the soul, then you realize the body is nothing but a dream shell in which the soul resides.

Suffering Can Be for the Welfare of Others

Although St. Francis healed many others, he did not heal his own body, because it meant nothing to him. But that didn't mean his soul was suffering. He didn't care to wipe away the body's karmic conditions, because he willingly took that karma from others in order to heal them and create faith in God. He didn't ascribe that healing power or glory to himself. The more you want people to know how wonderful you are, the less great you will be. The more you try to demonstrate your powers of the mind and make a ballyhoo about it to show off, the less mind power you will have. Before your own conscience and the almighty Lord you must stand immaculate, free of egoity, and then He will give you wonderful power and experiences.

No one can escape suffering. Even Jesus suffered. Although he didn't have to endure a disease, he suffered greatly on the cross because he took on his own body the sins or karma of others.

The doctor who is dedicated to healing others of diseases does not fear for the welfare of his own body. For example, my body will be subject to physical troubles, not because I have transgressed, but because I have taken on the karma of many people. Just before Christmas, I twisted my leg and threw this knee joint out of action. On top of that, yesterday I stepped on a rock and wrenched it more, so that last night this leg was so painful I had to be carried on a chair to get from one room to another. Yet see, today I am with you, and there is no pain in this leg. How? Through mind power. My case, however, is different again. Not that I have used mind power to heal this leg. I have given my body to God, and whatever He wants to do with it, He is welcome. Though this leg has troubled me since Christmas, when it is time for me to come to these services, God has taken all pain away without my asking. The devotees urged me not to come down to speak tonight because my knee was so bad. But I scolded them for asking me not to come. Whatever is God's will is my will—suffering or no suffering. And you see, here I am this evening. Through God's grace I walked down three flights of stairs to be here with you tonight.

Awaken in God to Be Free From Delusion

So that is the best way — depend more on the Lord. The power of God is supreme. The greatest key to His healing power is to believe in that limitless power, and at the same time realize that your body is a dream and pay not too much attention to it. Why be overly solicitous about it? Take reasonable care of the body, and then forget it. That is what Christ meant when he said:

"Take no heed for the body...." And be constantly watchful of the Lord—keep your mind on Him—that He may show you that this world is His dream. Be reasonable and sane, not denying the body, but so living in the thought of the Lord that He will suddenly pull away the strands of delusion and you will see that this frail body that you are afraid of hurting is a mental concept of His, and you have nothing to fear. This is the state of perfection. This is why Jesus said: "Destroy this temple [the body] and in three days I will raise it up." He realized what I have been saying tonight, that everything is mind.

With most people, the suggestion of their karma is so strong that they cannot understand this divine principle. But think how many times you have been born on earth with a physical body, and have created and conquered bad habits, and have experienced joys and suffering, pleasures and disease, old age and death. How long will you continue to go through this self-hypnosis? Get out of it. Krishna taught: "Get away from this ocean of suffering, O Arjuna!" Be one with the Supreme Lord. Awaken in God. As soon as you wake up in Him, there will be no more fear.

The body that once used to be so real to me is nothing to me anymore. Sometimes I see my body lying still and lifeless; I am beholding one dream within another dream—the dream of this dead body within the dream of this world. But as soon as I look within and see the Spirit, there is no dream at all. These are actual experiences.

You can go on exercising mental power to get a little healing, only to find that another trouble has come. Wouldn't you prefer to make the supreme spiritual effort to be on the lap of God and see that the body is a dream, and that you are untouched by its experiences of health and sickness, life and death? When your soul is healed of delusion so that you actually realize the dream nature of the body, you will also find that God has healed the body. You will not suffer again unless, like St. Francis, you are willing to do so to help others.

This may be too deep for you to conceive of now. But you can understand this analogy: Two people are separately dreaming they are in the hospital. One is cured, and the other remains sick. The first thinks, "Oh, how happy I am! How well I feel!"

The other thinks, "I feel so sick; how miserable I am." But when they awaken from their dreams, both realize that they were neither ill nor healed. In reality there is no disease or ill health at all. Delusion causes these experiences. As soon as you *realize* that everything is the condensed thought of God, the condensed dream of God, then you don't mind this play of His. You have awakened from that dream of duality, that dream of sickness and health.

A Miraculous Healing

I used to do a great deal of healing in my early days, but I found that people wanted only physical healing. When they were cured, I never saw them again. Few people are interested in soul healing, which is everlasting. The joy of material existence comes and goes. The joy of spiritual existence never ends.

But I will tell you of one of the unique experiences in my life: While I was in India in 1935, the wife of one of my boyhood friends became very ill. He wanted me to come to his home to see her, but I said, "Please don't ask me. Do what I say, and she will be all right." He continued to insist that I go to see her. At last I said to him, "Please, do as I tell you, and see what happens."

He went home and followed my instructions, and her fever went away. But the next day at three o'clock in the afternoon it came back. And every day thereafter, around the same time, her fever returned. One day he came and said, "Master, her fever has not left. Please, please do something."

I replied, "God alone will heal her."

He pleaded, "If once you come, she will be well."

I relented. But when I went to the home, the fever raged in great violence.

A few days later, I was in the car, just leaving to go somewhere, when the husband arrived, crying, "My wife is dying!" I sat quietly in the car and prayed deeply. As soon as I prayed, I knew my prayer would be answered. I drove to his home. About twenty-five people were present. His wife was lying deathlike on the bed. Her husband cried as he told me, "I was shaking her, thinking it might bring the breath back into her body." It angered me that he didn't have faith in God.

I wish that all of you had been there that day, for you would surely believe in the power of God. I put my hand on her forehead. Then I gently touched her chest. It looked as though there were no life in her body at all. But in a little while, as I held my hand on her chest, her feet began to quiver. Her tongue, which had been hanging out of her mouth, receded, and she opened her eyes. She moved, and looked at me with a little smile on her face. It was one of the most wonderful things I have seen in my life. She was healed by God's power; and her fever never returned.

I speak of this only to show you the glory of God. When you know God, you never give the glory to yourself. Her husband had heard that I had the power to heal others, but I was trying to convince him to have faith in God's limitless power. It requires faith in order to be healed. Without the cooperation of the mind, and without faith, healing does not occur. When his wife didn't get better, his belief was shaken. I was glad, because I did not want him to believe in my power, but in God. When he saw that miraculous healing through God's blessing, he was convinced of God's power and understood how God was testing his faith.

Have More Mental Strength

Do you realize all I have told you tonight, that even life and death are dreams? Then what is the conclusion? Have more mental strength. Develop such mental power that you can stand unshaken, no matter what comes, bravely facing anything in life. If you love God you should have faith and be prepared to endure when trials come. Don't be afraid of suffering. Keep your mind positive and strong. It is your inner experience that is most important.

The Self-Realization view is that in simple things one should use commonsense remedies to take care of the body. Self-healing depends on good karma, proper diet, sunlight and exercise, and continuous faith that in the mind lies the omnipresent healing power of God. Gradually strengthen the mind so that you can depend more on its power, and you will be better and better every day. Think only positive thoughts, even in the face of contradictory circumstances. Practice even-mindedness in times of difficulties. Cater less to the demands of the body, realizing that you are not the body, but the soul. Learn to fast for one to three days at a time. The minute you think you should not eat something, desist. These are the ways to develop mind power. And above all, meditate deeply every day. Make actual contact with God, that you might in truth realize all I have said tonight, that delusion might be forever banished from your soul.

If you live with the Lord, you will be healed of the delusions of life and death, health and sickness. Be in the Lord. Feel His love. Fear nothing. Only in the castle of God can we find protection. There is no safer haven of joy than in His presence. When you are with Him, nothing can touch you.

Mind Power Can Help You Lose or Gain Weight

First Self-Realization Fellowship Temple,
Encinitas, California, June 2, 1940

I have chosen this particular subject because someone noticed that I have lost a lot of weight—I have taken off about forty pounds in less than four months—and asked if I had been sick.

There are causes for our physical condition that are not known to many doctors and food scientists, who ordinarily think of the body as governed only by biochemical laws. The long history of the nature of the body involves more than just physiology, anatomy, nutrition, and medicine. What I tell you is from my own personal experience; and if you remember these things, they will ultimately help you very much.

Don't think it is inevitable that someone who has a tendency to become heavy, or to remain too thin, is not healthy; or that the cause is necessarily or wholly physical. For instance, why is it that some thin people can eat five meals a day and still not get fat? In my early youth I wanted to gain weight, because in India, where so many people are thin from malnutrition, it is considered desirable to be heavy. I used to purposely eat everything that was fattening, but still I couldn't put on weight. Then the grace of my guru Sri Yukteswarji changed my thought, and from that day on my body took a different turn. I have been heavy ever since. Before Guruji's blessing, my body was so terribly thin that I looked like a bean pole with a coconut on top!

If you have a tendency to become fat, don't blame your eating habits alone. The mind has a lot to do with it. You must so train your mind that you will not have any tendency toward being either too fat or too thin. It is good to be flexible, so that you can put on weight or take it off at will.

173

Of course you shouldn't ignore dietary rules, unless you have a divinely strong mind. If you want to lose weight or avoid gaining it, there are a few important points to remember. One is: never drink water, milk, or other liquids with your meals. It is best to take fluids a half-hour before a meal or two hours afterward. When your body weight increases, the cells become very hungry for water. It is strange that sometimes the strongest urges we have are for those very things that hurt us. Drinking plenty of water and fruit juices helps to keep the body free from disease; just don't drink them with your meals.

Take a glass of milk in between meals; it will help to keep your body healthy, because milk supplies your body with all the elements that are necessary. But avoid the cream in it—take skim milk.

Another important point is to eat plenty of fresh fruits and vegetables, preferably raw. Cut out sugar and starches and fried foods. It is all right if you eat these once in a while, but it should not be an everyday habit. Remember, too much starch in the diet is very unhealthful, as well as fattening. When you are hungry for sweets or a snack, the best thing to eat is fruit. For extra nourishment, put on it a dressing of finely ground nuts mixed with fruit juice or some other base.

Your body needs protein, but too much protein is dangerous to your physical being. Don't make a habit of eating meat protein, because it will create poisons in your system. One more important rule is to avoid fats; however, a little olive oil every day will help keep the joints healthy.

In general, follow a moderate diet that contains all the elements the body requires, and eat only as much as the body actually needs. That is the way to stabilize the weight by proper eating. If you overeat, the sad fact is that ladies will get fat in back and gentlemen will get fat in front. So eat less, and get plenty of exercise to keep the muscles well toned. Never let the abdominal muscles get weak. It is always a good practice to hold the abdominal muscles in.

When trying to lose weight, don't be over-anxious. There is danger in using drastic means to get rid of fat in a hurry.

Excess weight is hard on the whole system—from the feet to the heart. For every pound of flesh there is a mile of blood vessels that have to be irrigated by the heart. Even so, you would be surprised how the mind can compensate for every condition of the body. Trailanga Swami of India weighed three hundred pounds, and yet he was reputed to have lived three hundred years.* He could do that because he lived by mind power.

Think Thin

Mind will do everything for you. Along with proper diet you must also *think* thin.† There was a time when I was trying to lose weight by following all the usual stringent methods of dieting — and still I saw that days went by and there was no change in my weight. Then I thought: "So, Mr. Body, you are playing tricks with me! Some people have a tendency toward thinness, and some have a tendency toward fatness. If I want to lose weight, why not adopt that tendency? Why should I have to think all the time about diet, diet, diet?" I really got impatient with myself. So I said, "Eat!" and I started taking regular meals. I relaxed my mind, but I instilled the thought: "You are losing weight." I held tenaciously to that thought. And it actually happened. I began to see that I was losing weight. Several times I even ate fattening foods, and still I found I was losing steadily. The thought was so strongly established in my mind that the whole body was working to throw off the weight that was not necessary to my well-being. After reaching a hundred and eighty pounds, I stabilized myself to maintain that weight all the time.

* Paramahansa Yogananda wrote in his *Autobiography of a Yogi*: "Trailanga's renown is so widespread that few Hindus would deny the possibility of truth in any story of his astounding miracles. If Christ returned to earth and walked the streets of New York, displaying his divine powers, it would cause the same awe among the people that Trailanga created decades ago as he passed through the crowded lanes of Banaras....Trailanga sought to teach men that human life need not depend...on certain conditions and precautions....He proved that he lived by divine consciousness: Death could not touch him."

† Within recent years, the capacity of the mind to change and control physiological processes has received increasing attention in medical and other scientific research. A study of "spontaneous" remission of cancer by Dr. O. Carl Simonton, a radiation oncologist in Ft. Worth, Texas, revealed that all such patients, regardless of what they considered the cause of healing, had consistently held a positive idea that it was taking, or had taken place. In his book, *Think Yourself Thin*, Frank J. Bruno advanced the premise, based on personal experience, that anyone, by use of his natural human ability to think and reflect about his behavior, can literally think himself thin.

I have been eating normally, and still I have not gone over that mark.

Until you can do it by mind power alone, losing weight is best accomplished by combining mind power, exercise, and proper eating. But do you know, after I had applied the power of the mind, I even stopped exercising, except for the Energization Exercises,* and ate what I wanted; but still the body absolutely did not take on any more flesh. It remained just the same. And although I lost so much weight, my skin is just as firm as ever. Ordinarily, if you take off forty pounds quickly, you find that your flesh becomes flabby. But when I used mind power, it stabilized the flesh. So mind has a great deal to do with gaining and losing weight. The important thing is that you must deeply instill the right thought in your mind.

There are some people who eat anything they want, and still they remain thin, without any conscious effort on their part. Why is this? It is because their bodies are stabilized in this life as a result of right eating habits in their past incarnations. Therefore, they neither get fat nor thin, no matter what they eat or don't eat. But this doesn't necessarily mean they have corresponding health and vitality, or that they can ignore the simple rules of good health. You may have built up a certain physical stability from right eating and proper exercise in your past life, but it is very important to continue to eat right and apply the principles of healthful living. If you neglect your body and ignore physiological laws now, you will have to pay for it sometime in the future.

My message to you is that I have proved, by every means, that mind power works. When I followed dietary laws alone, it didn't work. But when I applied mind power, then I began to lose weight. Now I have the ability to be thin or fat at will. That can only be done by applying mind power. You also must learn to regulate your weight at will: Obey the laws of right diet; eat more raw fruits and vegetables and less fats, starches, and sugars; drink plenty of water or other liquids (fruit and vegetable juices, milk, and so on), but not with meals; and, most impor-

* A unique system for recharging the body with vitality, discovered by Paramahansa Yogananda in 1916 and taught to students of the *Self-Realization Fellowship Lessons*. (See glossary.)

tant, strongly think that you have perfect control of the body. Every morning and night, affirm deeply: "I am the master of this body. It will obey my mind irrespective of any food I eat. Any tendency toward fatness or thinness must go!"

Don't Be a Diet Fanatic

The point is, balance your diet, and then forget it. Once in awhile it is even good to break your diet. If you have a craving for some food that isn't particularly good for you, don't be finicky; eat it. But don't make a practice of it, and thus let it become a habit. So many people are all the time fussing about their food. What is the use of having a body that you have to fuss about all the time? Your body should be your servant; don't allow yourself to become its slave. Think of the power of your mind; believe and know that it is the repairer of your body. Live by that mind power!

How do you think the cow remains strong and healthy by eating only grass? Out of that simple food it gets all the elements it needs. Of course, there are good elements in the grass to begin with, but the main thing is that the mind of the cow has been conditioned by evolution to that way of life, and its body responds accordingly. You have an advantage over the cow, because you can consciously command your mind according to your will. Then whatever your mind strongly tells your body to do, it will do.

Essentially, everything you think of as necessary to support the body is a delusion. I definitely know that mind is the supreme power; it will create everything the body requires. But until you actually have that realization, you must use your common sense. It is wisdom to obey the health laws of God, and believe without doubt that mind is the supreme force. You are the one who has created your present bodily condition, and you have the power in your mind to keep your body in good health. If iron is missing in my system, I suggest iron to my mind and the condition is corrected. When the body comes under your control, it will obey whatever you tell it through the powerful suggestion of your mind.

God's will was strong enough to create the whole universe. Your little body is a product of that divine will. Your mind is an expression of that same will, and whenever you make a strong suggestion to your mind about your body's well-being, or even about your destiny, it will come to pass. Remember, thought is the master of this machine of creation. By strengthening your thoughts, you can reach whatever goal you want to attain.

How To Work Without Fatigue

From a talk given on March 28, 1940

To work without fatigue is a universal desire of mankind. Some people can work hard with little fatigue; others tire easily. In the absence of any other cause, it is often assumed that persons who have abundant energy must have been born strong; and that those who suffer from fatigue must have been born weak. There is some truth in this theory, that our normal energy level is the result of hereditary or congenital causes that have trailed us since birth. But when we begin to understand the total being that is man, we realize that he is no simple physical organism. Within him are many powers whose potential he employs in greater or lesser degree in accommodating himself to the conditions of this world. Their potential is vastly greater than the average person thinks.

Man learns to work with whatever energy is at his command, usually without understanding whence it comes. He only knows that when he becomes fatigued he wants to rest or to have something to eat or drink, because these measures give him some relief. It is generally true that a tired person feels better after eating or resting; but as the body grows older, a time comes when no amount of food or rest restores strength. Clearly, something happens to the body that causes the material sources of life to fail us. Hence we should analyze and understand the physiology of the body, that we may know how it recuperates, and from what sources it derives energy and strength.

The most commonly thought of source of bodily energy is food, which consists of solids and liquids. When they are taken into the stomach, the bodily machine breaks them down into simpler chemical substances, and finally into energy. Solids can be converted into liquids, liquids into gas, and gas into energy. Therefore all food, whether solid or liquid, is essentially energy. Fatigue means that too much bodily energy has been spent; it must be restored, and nourishing food is one source of energy replacement.

God created in nature an abundant variety of edible vegetables, fruits, grains, and other foods, everything necessary for man. Man cannot bring forth even a grain of wheat, much less a new plant or fruit. Only God can do this. He has to originate the species first. Man can only modify what already exists, as Luther Burbank did.

Cultivated Tastes Versus Natural Hunger Instincts

God also gave man water, in the mountain spring; and milk to nourish him, in the cow and in the human mother. From the moment of birth man instinctively seeks these natural sources of sustenance. The impulse of hunger stirs the impulse to eat. Had God not given us the hunger-impulse, we would not eat at all.

Man unwisely perverts his natural hunger and sense of taste through misuse. The theory that hunger is the result of the habit of eating is true, at least, of the greedy person. Greed is a mental hunger. If one lives naturally, he has no desire to eat more than a normal diet, and his taste preferences are also normal. The abnormal appetite created by greed kills untold numbers of men and women. During the era of the Roman Empire great feasts were indulged in by the wealthy. A special room was provided where, after eating, they could go to vomit so that they could continue their feasting. Such is the debasement of greed!

We see all kinds of eccentricities in man whenever he becomes a criminal against his own welfare through misuse of the senses. When man forgets the purpose of an action and clings rather to the action by which the end is to be accomplished, he makes a grave mistake. Hunger and taste were given to man to help him select the proper quantity and right type of food to sustain his body in a healthful way; but wrong habits of living and eating have distorted this natural dietary instinct, creating preferences that are not always best for him. Something that tastes good and fills the stomach doesn't necessarily satisfy bodily needs. Since food is an important carrier of energy into the body, it is best to ensure a good supply of energy through proper eating. In a boiled dinner most of the vitamins have been destroyed; you will tire easily on such a diet. Fresh raw food is better because the vitamins are still present. Many vitamins are destroyed by the heat of the cooking and canning process. Hence a diet in which such foods predominate is not sufficiently nourishing to fill the needs of the body.

The stomach and digestive tract distill the chemicals from our food and distribute them to the proper types of cells throughout the system. The body is composed of various chemical elements, and you should see that your diet replenishes these elements every day. A good diet should contribute as many of the necessary elements as possible at every meal. Eat sufficient protein, many vitamins and minerals, some fats and oils, and some natural carbohydrates (but few refined starches and sugars).

Fresh Fruits and Vegetables Vital to Health

Meat protein is not the only vital source of energy. Some of the mineral salts that are found in fresh uncooked vegetables and fruits are important sources also. A large serving of steak will give plenty of energy, it is true, but a preponderance of meat in the diet, if continued for a long period of time, ceases to give strength. Overmuch heavy protein results in protein poisoning, a cause of fatigue and also disease. Too much protein is just as harmful as too little.

If you want to be rid of fatigue, then one remedy is to eat properly. Remember that meat may give strength temporarily, but it loads the body with poisons. By eating more raw foods you will have less cause for fatigue, and therefore an abundance of energy. Whenever the body feels tired, drink a glass of pineapple or orange juice; it will give you much energy. Whole fruits and vegetables are even more nutritious than their juices, but most people won't take the time to consume them this way. An excellent energy provider is orange juice with finely ground almonds mixed in. Nuts are more readily assimilated in combination with orange juice.

Remember, it is important to drink an abundance of liquids. When good water is unavailable, fresh fruit juices, coconut water, and watermelon provide an excellent supplement and partial substitute. In the future, more and more people will drink fruit and vegetable juices, to their benefit.

Do not forget to include some butter and milk in your diet. Milk should be taken separately from meals; best not to drink it with other food. Milk has helpful laxative properties, but its mucus-aggravating tendency is not good for those who have sinus trouble. Orange juice, also, can be an irritant for those who have sinus problems or frequent colds. In some cases, too much orange juice may even cause colds. Many persons afflicted with these troubles have found great improvement by omitting regular intake of orange juice from their diet, upon my advice. Although lemon has excellent disinfecting qualities, it similarly aggravates sinus irritation.

There is nothing more satisfying than bread made from freshly ground whole wheat. Although persons with a tendency toward phlegm should generally avoid starches, whole wheat bread may be taken, if thoroughly toasted.

Constipation is another cause of fatigue, which is related to the accumulation of poisons in the body as well as to the energy from food. If you are constipated, use some kind of laxative, preferably a natural one. If you keep your body free from poisons you will not be fatigued. It is the poisons in the body that make you feel tired.

Any kind of drug, also, will fatigue you, just as the narcotic opium saps the work initiative of its addicts. They don't want to do anything but sleep and dream.

A most important way to eliminate fatigue is to conserve the sex vitality. The single person should be fully self-controlled, and married couples should be moderate in their sexual relations. Tremendous vitality, both physical and mental, is lost through promiscuity or overindulgence.

Exercise Removes Fatigue

Exercise daily. Lack of exercise causes fatigue; regular exercise removes fatigue. When you exercise, you expend some energy, but you get back much more — if you don't overdo it. Proper exercise vitalizes the body; overexercise and violent exercise cause fatigue. The body should be charged with only as much energy as it can stand. For example, 2,000 volts of energy sent through an ordinary electric bulb will burn it out, but will not harm a bulb made to stand that much current. Similarly, the body absorbs a beneficial amount of energy from proper exercise, but overexercise causes fatigue because it creates toxins faster than they can be handled by the system.

After forty you should be careful not to undertake any form of exercise for which your system has not been kept properly conditioned. Walking is good, and swimming is excellent; but strenuous exercise should be avoided. It will only cause greater fatigue, because it overstrains the capacity of the body to handle the sudden expenditure of energy. By gradually strengthening your body you can enjoy strenuous exercise, but a person of lifelong sedentary habits should not try to be an acrobat at sixty; he will burn out his system.

Sufficient sleep helps to give energy. I think six or seven hours of sleep is enough. After that you don't actually sleep; you drug the body. It loses energy instead of accumulating it. Sleep ten hours and you will feel depleted of energy. You won't want to work the rest of the day; you will just drag yourself around.

Fatigue can also be removed by oxygenation. When you are tired, instead of heading for the kitchen for a snack, go out in the fresh air for ten to fifteen minutes and exhale and inhale deeply, off and on, several times. Don't breathe hurriedly, or with force, but in a relaxed way, very slowly and deeply. After this time spent in the fresh air, your fatigue will be gone.

If you were to fast a whole day, and every hour get out in the fresh air for about five minutes and do some deep breathing during that time—exhaling poisons, and inhaling oxygen—you would not miss food at all. Because of habit, it may seem in the beginning difficult to feel satisfied without food, but after you get used to it you will find that you have received from the oxygen all the energy you need.

Lahiri Mahasaya and other great masters knew how to operate the law that renders food totally unnecessary in sustaining the body. But he used to say that eating serves a good purpose, for God has created food in abundance and variety, and hunger is part of the plan that keeps the cosmic show going.

Avoid Wasting Energy

Energy is continually wasted in useless activities, unrestrained emotions, and improper living habits. When you are at peace you use little energy, but when you are angry or hateful or otherwise emotional, you use a great deal of energy. Proper care is necessary in operating a delicate machine; the same consideration ought to apply in using the body-machine.

When you work you employ your muscles, nervous system, mind, thoughts, feelings, and spiritual perceptions. Currents of energy are required in all these areas in any kind of work. When you are running you are using about four or five horsepower of energy. If by removal of gravity you no longer felt the weight of your body, you would use very little energy in running. The greater the body weight, the greater energy required to move it. A very practical reason to avoid overweight!

The battery of an electric wheelchair will move the weight of the chair and its occupant about fifteen miles before its energy is exhausted. Did you ever stop to think that your body-battery is wheeling this physical vehicle around all the time? Its energy powers not only the muscular motion of the limbs, but all other actions as well. When you are talking, for example, you are using thought force as well as muscular force, and thought requires energy. Without it you cannot think or transmit thoughts into speech. When you are thinking deeply you burn up a tremendous amount of energy, exhausting the brain's reserves. Let us suppose you have sixty thoughts per minute. In a month, allowing eighteen hours of wakefulness daily, you would have had nearly two million thoughts. In a lifetime of sixty years you would have produced more than a billion thoughts. After that many thoughts, most people would be dead; the brain's stored energy from food and cosmic sources would have been used up. When we ponder how much energy-current we are using all the time, the wonder is how we live as long as we do! Nevertheless, by adequate replacement of expended energy, we can live longer and more efficiently.

There are two sources from which man draws energy for his body: from food (which includes oxygen) and from the medulla or "mouth of God."* The energy thus imbibed is distributed to the body cells; any excess goes to the brain, to be stored there for use as needed.

* See *medulla* in glossary.

Food is only a secondary source of energy supply. The greatest flow of energy into the body comes from the intelligent cosmic energy that is all around the body and omnipresent in the universe. It is drawn into the brain storehouse through the medulla. This intelligent cosmic energy or vibration is the basic "substance" of all matter. Scientific experiments conducted by Dr. Crile* have shown that the brains of dead calves continue to emanate considerable current. In death the cosmic energy loses only the physiological channel of the nervous system.

The Secret of Vitality

It takes hours for the body to convert food into energy, but anything that stimulates your will generates energy instantly. Will draws vitality from the electroprotonic center of the bodily cells and from the reservoir of the brain, where energy that has already been distilled from food is stored. Will also draws new energy from the cosmic source into your system through the medulla.

The secret of vitality, therefore, is to conserve the energy you have and to bring new energy into the body by will power. How? First, you must act willingly. If a thing is worth doing, it is worth doing willingly. When you work willingly, you have more energy because you not only draw upon the reserves in the brain, but also attract a greater flow of cosmic energy into the body through the medulla. A woman preparing an elaborate dinner for her beloved is happy and filled with vitality; but if compelled to cook when she doesn't want to, she feels tired from the start. Remember: *will brings energy*.

The system of Energization Exercises† that Self-Realization Fellowship teaches is based on the principle of using will to draw energy from the cosmic source, and to distribute that energy by will to the trillions of cells in the body. We draw most of the

---

* Dr. George Washington Crile (1864-1943) was an army surgeon who devoted his career to discovering a better understanding of the phenomena of life. Unsatisfied by the conventional explanations then to be found in physiology and biochemistry, he established the Cleveland Clinic Foundation, where for twenty-two years he conducted biophysical research that led him to formulate in 1936 his "radio-electric" theory of the life processes.

† See glossary.

current for our actions from the physical supply of the body battery — energy distilled from food, oxygen, and sunshine. We don't draw enough energy from the invisible cosmic source, through the conscious use of will.

Will and Energy Go Hand-in-Hand

There is a difference between consciously applied will and imagination. Imagination is a conception of something that one desires to manifest. By imagining day and night that you are feeling more vitality, you will gain some strength, because imagination requires at least a small degree of will. By contrast, when one *wills* vitality, the energy is actually there at once. Suppose you are angered and strike at someone violently; the will, stimulated by emotion, draws energy for that action; but immediately afterwards the energy is cut off, and your vitality is depleted. But if in a positive way you continuously will energy into your body and apply the principle of the Self-Realization Energization Exercises, conscious life-force control, you can draw, by the use of will power, unlimited energy from the cosmic source. Since the body is simply a cluster of cells, if it lacks energy and you thus energize the whole body with will, those cells are recharged instantly and continuously. Will is the switch that lets more energy into the body from the divine source.

Will is thus a potent factor in maintaining youth and vigor. If you convince yourself you are old, the will becomes paralyzed and you do become old. Never say you are tired; it paralyzes the will and then you *are* tired. Say, "My body needs rest." The body must not be allowed to dictate its limitations to your soul. The soul must rule the body, because the soul is neither caused by nor dependent on the body. In the soul's will lies all power. God willed, and there was light — the cosmic creative energy that condensed into the heavens, into our bodies, and all other forms. Will is light, for light was the first manifestation of God's will. And He saw that this light, or electrical energy, was a satisfactory unit out of which life forms could be created.* The scientist ponders whether matter is light or whether light is matter. Light came first, and constitutes the essential structure of matter.

---

* "And God said, Let there be light: and there was light. And God saw the light, that it was good."—Genesis 1:3-4.

Therefore, we must realize that energy and will go together. It is a very simple formula. We have been so conditioned to the idea that energy comes only from material sources, that we fail to believe in and draw upon the cosmic source, which responds instantly to will.

If you learn the Self-Realization method by which you use your will to draw energy directly from the boundless cosmic source, you will not suffer from fatigue anymore. Those who know me know that I take only two or three hours' sleep at night; and even if I don't sleep at all, I don't miss it. I can remain awake for days without fatigue. While I was writing *Whispers from Eternity** I once went without sleep for five consecutive nights, and my body felt no weariness at all.

You must awaken your will. As you begin to draw energy from the Infinite, you will require less food as well as less sleep. You will begin to rise completely above the need for material methods of sustenance. You need not be limited by material laws. The magic method of working without fatigue lies in the use of your will power. When you can draw energy from the cosmic source, you can eat breakfast or go without, and it won't make any difference; you won't feel any lack. You will be above that consciousness.

Love Is One of the Greatest Stimulants to the Will

Whatever I do, I do with the greatest love that I have in me. Try this, and you will see that you do not become fatigued at all. Love is one of the greatest stimulants to the will. Under the influence of love the will can do almost anything. You can demonstrate this in your life if you depend more on will power. Your body will not need eight hours of rest; you will find that six hours of sleep will be plenty, along with one balanced meal a day, and perhaps fruit juice now and then. You will remain always well. Through God's grace I feel the same—and I think I look almost the same!   as I have throughout these nineteen years that I have been in this country. I obey nature's laws insofar as I can; I am not unswervingly orthodox or fanatic in anything. But I do believe strongly in will power. I have proven it works.

* A book of spiritual inspirations and answered prayers, published by Self-Realization Fellowship.

When I am with people, I am with them wholly, with the greatest joy; and when I am alone, I am alone with that joy. When I work, I work with the greatest will and happiness. No matter what your task, do it joyously and willingly. If you don't you only devitalize yourself. And remember to be always sincere. Through sincerity you can work more harmoniously with others. Develop sincerity along with will power.

Do some creative work every day. Writing is good for developing creative ability and will power. I have never cared to do merely mechanical work. I am always seeking to accomplish something new. Being creative is more difficult, of course, than following a mechanical existence, but when your will battles with new ideas it gains more strength. When it becomes stronger still, so that it can work changes not only in your body, but in the universe, your will has become divine will. That power of divine will is what Jesus referred to when he said, "If ye have faith, and doubt not, ye shall not only do this which is done to the fig tree, but also if ye shall say unto this mountain, Be thou removed, and be thou cast into the sea; it shall be done."* Why not? The Lord is whirling untold tons of universes through space by His will—divine will. Don't look on yourself as a weak mortal. Incredible amounts of energy are hidden in your brain; enough in a gram of flesh to run the city of Chicago for two days. And you say you are tired?

A revolving wheel generates electrical current. When your will power revolves around an idea, it too creates a current of energy that can be directed to heal, materialize objects in front of you, or make any other kind of change in the atomic structure of the universe.

When your will becomes strong, united with divine will, you can indeed, as Jesus said, lift mountains and cast them into the depths of the sea. Our will is part of the divine will; and when we develop the will that is within us, we can create universes, and we can demonstrate that there is no death, no decay, but that all matter is eternal energy. Then there can be no fatigue.

The purpose of life is to find God. Under no circumstances

* Matthew 21:21.

allow yourself to become buried in the debris of mortal habits and limitations and all the other humiliating experiences of delusion. Use your determination to wrench your will free, and attain mastery over your body and the universe. In the development of your will lies the ability to discover the hidden image of God within you.

Ridding the Consciousness of Worry

First Self-Realization Fellowship Temple,
Encinitas, California, May 12, 1940

Worry is a psychophysical state of consciousness in which you are caught in feelings of helplessness and apprehension about some trouble you don't know how to get rid of. Perhaps you are seriously concerned about your child, or your health, or a mortgage payment. Not finding an immediate solution, you start worrying about the situation. And what do you get? A headache, nervousness, heart trouble. Because you do not clearly analyze yourself and your problems, you do not know how to control your feelings or the condition that confronts you. Instead of wasting time worrying, think positively about how the cause of the problem can be removed. If you want to get rid of a trouble, calmly analyze your difficulty, setting down point-by-point the pros and cons of the matter; then determine what steps might be best to accomplish your goal.

If you have no money, you feel forsaken; the whole world seems to be going backward. But worry will not provide a solution. Get busy and make this determination: "I will shake the world to get my share. In order to keep me quiet, the world must satisfy my need." Each person who has performed some work, even clearing away weeds, has done something worthwhile on earth. Why shouldn't everyone receive his just share of the earth's bounty? No one need starve or be left out.

The present money standard will go; remember what I say. Money creates a desire for power, and too often it makes the possessor heartless to the sufferings of others. Accumulation of wealth is all right if the wealthy person also has the desire to help others in their need. Money is a boon in the possession of unselfish people, but it is a curse in the hands of the selfish. I used to know a man in Philadelphia who was worth ten million dollars, but it never gave him happiness; it brought him only misery. And he wouldn't even buy a ten-cent cup of coffee for anyone else. Gold has been given for our use, but it belongs to no one save the Divine Spirit. Each child of God has a right to use God's gold. You must not admit failure and give up your right.

Success or Failure Is Determined in Your Own Mind

God made you His son. You have made yourself a beggar. If you have convinced yourself that you are a helpless mortal, and you allow everyone else to convince you that you can't get a job, then you have passed the decree in your own mind that you are down and done for. No judgment from God or fate, but your own pronouncement on yourself, keeps you poor or worried. Success or failure is determined in your own mind. Even against the negative opinion of the rest of society, if you bring out by your all-conquering God-given will the conviction that you cannot be left to suffer in difficulties, you will feel a secret divine power coming upon you; and you will see that the magnetism of that conviction and power is opening up new ways for you. Do not grieve over your present state, and do not worry. If you refuse to worry, and if you make the right effort, you will remain calm and you will surely find a way of reaching your goal.

Remember that every time you worry, you put on a mental brake; and in struggling against that resistance, you place strain on your heart and mind. You wouldn't try to drive off in your car with the brake on, because you know it would severely damage the mechanism. Worry is the brake on the wheels of your efforts; it brings you to a dead stop. Nothing is impossible, unless you think it is. Worry can convince you that it is impossible to do what you want to do.

Worrying wastes time and energy. Use your mind instead to try to make some positive effort. It is even better to be a go-getting materialistic man and accomplish something, than to be lazy; the lazy man is forsaken by both man and God. Many fortunes have been made by enterprising people, but don't make money your criterion of success. Often it isn't the money, but the creative ability exercised in earning it, that brings satisfaction.

It is foolish to try to flee from your worries, for wherever you go, your worries go with you. You must learn to face your problems fearlessly and with a clear conscience, as I have done.

Now I have no more prayers for my soul or my body, for I have achieved eternal assurance from God. This is sufficient. For me, to pray would be to doubt. My conscience is free, for I have done no wrong to any human being. I know this to be truth. To be able to say to oneself, "I have wronged no one," is to be the happiest person on earth.

When I think of the many wonderful souls who have faith in me—not out of emotional blindness, but through intelligence and reason—I know I am very much blessed. Of all possessions, I love true friendship most. Be a friend to all. Even if your love and trust are betrayed by some, don't worry. Always be yourself; you are what you are. This is the only sincere way to live. Though all may not want to be your friend, you should befriend all, never expecting anything in return. I understand and love all, but I never expect of anyone that he should be my friend and understand me. On the strength of this principle, I am at peace with myself and the world, and never feel any cause for worry.

The Lesson We Have Come on Earth to Learn

The treasure of friendship is your richest possession, because it goes with you beyond this life. All the true friends you have made you will meet again in the home of the Father, for real love is never lost. On the other hand, hate is never lost, either. Whatever you hate, you also attract to yourself again and again until you overcome that intense dislike.

Love is short-lived unless it is divine love. What of all the lovers through the ages who have promised eternal fidelity to one another under the light of the silvery moon. Their skulls are strewn over the earth, and the moon laughs at most of them and says, "How they lied, for their love has not been forever." But if the love you feel in your heart is not of this earth, not worldly; if you have achieved love for all on a basis of divine friendship, and not carnal attraction; if you love others for themselves, and not for selfish ends, you have attained and expressed God's divine love. To develop pure and unconditional love between husband and wife, parent and child, friend and friend, self and all, is the lesson we have come on earth to learn.

You must not hate even your enemies. No one is all bad. If

you hear someone playing a piano that has a defective key, you are inclined to judge the whole piano as bad. But the fault lies in just one key. Fix it, and you will see that the piano is perfectly good. God lives within all His children. To hate anyone is to deny Him in yourself and in others. This earth is the laboratory of God. We burn ourselves in the fire of mortal experience so that our divine immortality, which is buried beneath the dross of our consciousness, may be once again revealed. Love all, keep your own counsel, and do not worry.

Give your troubles to God. When you worry, it is your funeral, all arranged by yourself. You don't want to be buried alive by your anxieties! Why suffer and die every day from worry? No matter what you are going through—poverty, sorrow, ill health—remember that somebody on this earth is suffering a hundred times more than you are. Do not consider yourself so unfortunate, for thus you defeat yourself, and close out the omnipotent light of God that is ever seeking to help you.

Just think what is happening in the lives of people in Europe today, and realize how much more fortunate you are. There is no excuse for this war. This is progress? This is civilization? Mother's Day should remind all mothers of their divine role to feel with a mother's heart for all mankind. I feel for those boys on the battlefield. If one is killed in action, he at least has freedom from this miserable world; but how cruel it is to have to live the rest of one's life in a mutilated body. Seeing an arm and a leg cut off in the viciousness of war, the mind has no desire to continue residing in that dismembered form. In my meditations I see souls groaning, some on the battlefield with their bodies torn open, others in hospitals, suffering from cancer, with just a little time to live. How tragic is this world! It is a place of uncertainty. But no matter what has happened to you, if you throw yourself at the feet of the Father and seek His mercy, He will lift you up and show you that life is but a dream. I have seen this truth. When I put my mind at the Christ center,* I don't feel the body at all. No sensation or mental torture can affect you if the mind is dissociated from it and anchored in the peace and joy of God.

* See glossary.

Practice Mental Neutrality

Even-minded endurance is called *titiksha* in Sanskrit. I have practiced this mental neutrality. I have sat and meditated all night long in icy water in bitterly cold weather. Similarly, I have sat from morning till evening on the burning hot sands in India. I gained great mental strength by doing so. When you have practiced such self-discipline, your mind becomes impervious to all disturbing circumstances. If you think you can't do something, your mind is a slave. Free yourself.

I don't mean that you should be rash. Try to rise above disturbances gradually. Endurance is what you must have. Whatever may be your trouble, make a supreme effort to remedy it without worry; and until it is resolved, practice *titiksha*. Isn't this practical wisdom? If you are young and strong, then as you gradually strengthen your will and mind you can practice more rigid methods of self-discipline as I did.

If you are thinking that the winter weather is coming, and you are bound to catch cold, you are not developing mental strength. You have already committed yourself to certain weakness. When you feel you are susceptible to catching a cold, mentally resist: "Get away! I am following commonsense precautions, but I will not allow worry about it to invite the illness by weakening my mind." This is the right mental attitude. In your heart, sincerely do your best at all times, but without anxiety. Worry only paralyzes your efforts. If you do your best, God will reach down His hand to help you.

Sleep is a blessing, because no matter what your troubles are, you are free from them when you are asleep. Learn to be free consciously, during your waking hours. If you haven't tasted sugar, you can't know its sweetness; if you haven't used the full potential of your mind, you do not realize its wondrous power.

In Washington, D. C., a young lady came to me and said, "I have chronic heart trouble. I have consulted a specialist, but I am getting no better. Is there any way you can help me?" I looked into her mind and felt what the trouble was. (You also can develop this intuitive power if you are calm and if you meditate deeply. There is no limit to what you can do with the innate power that God has given you.)

I said to the woman, "You have no heart disease. If ever I speak the truth, it is now. If you still have heart trouble tomorrow, you can say I was the greatest liar, and forget all about me. But I know that your ailment will be gone."

"How?" she asked. I replied with a question.

"Have you had a recent unhappy love affair, a very sad one?" She was surprised.

"Yes, how did you know?"

"Isn't it true," I went on, "that day and night you are thinking about that grievous experience?" She hung her head and admitted it was true. "You must give up your moping," I told her. "The milk has been spilt; why cry now? Find someone who will appreciate your love. There is no sense in giving loyalty to an individual who doesn't love you. Your former loved one is enjoying himself with someone else, and here you are hopelessly pining away for him." She said she would try to forget him. "Not just try," I insisted, "you must, this minute! Release this man from your mind."

The woman was receptive; a short time later she came and told me, "You were right. The moment I stopped thinking about that man and about my unhappiness, my heartbeat became normal."

If you counsel yourself in the way I have suggested to you today, if you do not acknowledge weakness in the face of troubles, and if you refuse to worry about your problems, you will find out how much more successful, peaceful, and happy you are. Through my own effort, I have realized this in my life. You should do the same. Daily, make this affirmation: "I will be neither lazy nor feverishly active. In every challenge of life I shall do my best without worrying about the future."

God Can Never Forsake You

Remember that the mind cannot suffer any pain unless it accepts the suggestion of pain. Mind cannot suffer from poverty or anything else unless it accepts the unpleasantness of the condition. Jesus was severely treated—his life was filled with problems, obstacles, and uncertainties—yet he had no worries. Remember, you also are a son of God. You may be forsaken by everyone else, but you cannot be forsaken by God, because He loves you. You should never worry, because God made you in His indomitable image.

Don't grieve for what you don't have. The most materially successful man may have the greatest worries and unhappiness. In contrast, I have seen in humble little huts and caves in India men who were true monarchs. The earthly "throne" of one such saint was a dried grass mat. If I could place him here before you, you would see a true king. He wore only a little loincloth and did not have even a begging bowl. Such are the real kings of the earth. Some of them I have seen in the Himalayas — no food, nothing at all; nor are they beggars. They are richer than the world's millionaires. Because they are the friends of all, people love them, and love to feed them. In bitingly cold weather, I saw one saint in the Himalayas who had nothing on. "Won't you catch cold?" I said. Sweetly he answered, "If I am warm with God's love, how can I feel the cold?" Saints like him are greater than any crowned king. If without food, without any visible means of security, such men can be like kings, peaceful and without worry, why can't you?

Realize that the infinite presence of the Heavenly Father is ever within you. Tell Him: "In life and death, health and sickness, I worry not, O Lord, for I am Thy child evermore."

If God Is Free From Karma, Why Aren't We?

Self-Realization Fellowship Temple, San Diego, California, November 18, 1945

Karma is the fruits—the good or evil effects—of action. If you swallow poison, your action produces the evil fruit of death. If you eat wholesome food, your action yields the good fruit of better health. Today I am speaking primarily of evil karma: that which brings pain and suffering. If we are made in God's image, as the scriptures tell us, and God is free from karmic suffering, why aren't we also free?

Evil karma is the result of misuse of our God-given power of free choice. Animals are free from individual karma. They can do no evil because they have no power of discrimination. Their lives are governed by instinct and by mass karma, the effects of their environment. Although sexually indiscriminate, they are not punished for it, since their behavior is not self-determined but instinct-bound. So animals don't suffer from the effects of their actions as human beings do. Man has the gift of reason by which to choose all his actions, and is thus accountable for them.

Then the question is, "Why is God eternally free from the fruits of actions, and we are not?" Let us go deep into the subject and you will understand it as never before.

God is spoken of as eternal existence, eternal consciousness, eternal bliss. As such, He has never suffered. Why then did He conceive suffering for us? Isn't that strange? I know the answer, but still I argue with Him: "Lord, if You wanted to create this little play world, why did You have to make suffering a part of it? What is play to You is death to us. Why didn't You create this earth with beautiful flowers and no weeds; with life and no death or pain or other sufferings of karma, and no mass karma to plunge us into the terrors of war? Why, Lord, didn't You create a world without delusion?" What can He say, except that we *are* free, only we don't know it.

The fact that God did create delusion should not make us pessimistic. I am the greatest optimist. Optimism doesn't mean being happy so long as everything goes well, but when pain comes, turning gloomy and saying, "God, You are terrible." God had nothing to do with our present state of misery. When He created us, He gave us freedom to suffer or to rise above it. Optimism means being able to laugh at both pleasure and pain—to mentally get away from the hurtful effects of duality.

Pain Has Three Causes

Pain is the greatest curse of the soul. For those who are suffering, it is dreadful. Even if you are all right now, how do you know that you won't some day be a victim? So long as there is any possibility of suffering, you must try to remove its causes by the roots.

There are three factors behind man's sufferings: first comes delusion; second, the effects of man's own wrong actions; and third, the effects of mass karma, such as the destruction of both good and evil individuals when Hiroshima was bombed.

Delusion causes identification with the flesh. From the beginning of life, the child thinks of his body as himself, that he and the body are one. This is why he cries if you pinch him, and why he likes it when you soothe his hand. The delusion of identification with the body came with the creation of man, and that identification increases by pampering the body.

In India our training is different than here in the West. We are taught to conquer the flesh, to mentally rise above body consciousness. If you love the body too much, you become unduly sensitive; you suffer whenever the body is uncomfortable. You have been taught to suffer, because you have been taught to depend too much on physical comfort for happiness. The desire for all sorts of comforts is a major source of pain. This is why the saints say we should not be attached to anything. If plain food is served, don't miss your favorite savory dishes. Never be so attached to anything that you become dissatisfied or unhappy or pained over the absence of it.

Human beings suffer because they relate to an ego: the

consciousness of self as a physical being. Animals suffer much less than man because they are not egoistically identified with the body. They cannot relate to an ego as humans do. We also relate to others according to the degree of our identification with them. Seeing a stranger with a broken leg, you say, "How unfortunate!" You feel sympathy for him, but you are detached from the pain of his injury. If you had broken your own leg, you would be suffering with the pain. In the same way, a mother who sees her neighbor's child killed doesn't feel as sorrowful as she would if it were her own child. In each case, identification is the cause of suffering. You identify yourself more closely with your own body than with someone else's; and you relate more readily to those persons or things that are nearest and dearest to you than to those that are not personally close to you.

The Connection Between You and Bodily Pain Is Only Mental

The fact is, if you learn to live in your body without thinking of it as yourself, you won't suffer so much. The connection between you and bodily pain is only mental. When you are asleep and unconscious of the body, you feel no pain. Likewise, when a doctor or a dentist gives you an anesthetic and performs surgery on your body, you don't feel any pain. The mind has been disconnected from the sensation. On the other hand, by strongly picturing in your mind the suffering of another person, you can experience his pain in yourself.

The best anesthesia against pain is your mental power. If your mind refuses to accept it, pain will be greatly lessened. I have seen, at times when this body got hurt and felt severe pain, that if I put my mind at the Christ center—that is, if I identify myself more with God and less with the body—there is no pain at all. So when pain comes, concentrate at the Christ center. Be mentally apart from pain; develop more strength of mind. Be tough within. When you are feeling pain, inwardly say to yourself, "It doesn't hurt me." When a hurt comes, recognize it as something to be cared for, but don't suffer over it. The more you concentrate on the power of the mind, the more your body consciousness drops away. And the more you love the body and are overly solicitous of it, the more limited the redeeming power of the mind will be.

You heighten suffering by imagination. Worrying or feeling sorry for yourself won't ease your pain, but rather increase it. For instance, someone wrongs you; you dwell on it, and your friends talk about it and sympathize with you. The more you think of it, the more you magnify the hurt — *and* your suffering. When someone wrongs you, it is far better to love him spiritually, give him your blessing, and forget it.

God is conscious of our suffering. Certainly He feels our aches and pains. Didn't Jesus say that not one sparrow falls without the feeling and knowledge of God?* When the sparrow is being killed by the hawk, the Lord knows the little bird's sensations. He also knows your pain. Do you think it makes Him happy to see you suffering? No. He is affected when you are in trouble. So He is not as happy as you think. When God dwells in His absolute state beyond all creation, He knows He is the happiest being there is. But as soon as He feels the desires and sorrows and troubles of His children, He is not so happy. You can sympathize with somebody else's sufferings without actually feeling the same sensation; but if you become completely identified with that person, you will feel his pain as your own. The idea is, God knows what is going on in His creation, but still He is free from the delusion of identification with it. So even though God feels your suffering, and mentally suffers for you, His suffering isn't the same as your delusion, because He is not identified with this universe of dualities in the same way you are. He wants you to become like Him. That is, you should live in this body, but not be affected by it. Then you will see that you are free from karma. It is not God alone who is free; you, as the soul, made in His image, are potentially free also. Be like God, who is carrying on all the work of creation without being identified with its delusive nature.

In Sleep You Are Free From Karma

How to know that state of nonidentification with your troubles? I will tell you. Even if there is a serious problem you can't solve, or your body is in trouble, when are you asleep you are free within, free from karma. Do you see? Even by just closing your eyes and shutting out the sight of the world and

* Matthew 10:29.

your body, it is possible to separate yourself to some degree from identification with the body. You begin to understand that you are consciousness; you are thought. Thought cannot be invaded by the sensations of the body unless you permit it. Close your eyes and you can feel this truth within. Try it out. It will work. When with closed eyes you remain fortified within yourself, and do not allow your mind to be excited by the sensations of the body, you become free from karma. Isn't that a marvelous thought?

See the compassion of God, that for eight hours every night, while you sleep, you experience no pain, no suffering, no knowledge that you have no money in the bank—no difficulties at all. In this way He shows you that when you free your mind, you are free from karma. Many drink or take drugs to forget their troubles, but that is not the way. Liquor and dope only add to your troubles. So when you have a problem, one way to help yourself is to sleep it off.

Death Is a Reward

Sleep is pleasant because you forget the worries of the day. So also the deeper sleep of death is very pleasant, when it comes. But don't wish for death in order to fly away from your hard lessons in this school of life. That would be wrong. Whatever your tests in this life, you must pass them bravely. When you conquer here, death comes as a reward. It is the end of suffering. When someone is in great agony, people think, "How dreadful." And if he dies, they feel very sorry that he had to go. His friends and loved ones collect about him and lament, "Oh, how sad." But they have the wrong idea. Death has rewarded him with freedom from all suffering. He is much better off than they are. He no longer has to endure pain and discomfort. He is happy; he is free. So when your time comes and you are told you are going to die, smile and reply, "Is that all? Fine. I will be free from all travails and responsibilities."

I once wrote about a vision I had of a dying youth, in which God showed me the right attitude toward death. The youth was lying in bed and was told by his doctors that he had just one day to live. He replied, "One day to reach my Beloved! when death shall open the gates of immortality and I shall be free from the prison bars of pain. Don't cry for me, ye who are left on this desolate shore, still to mourn and deplore; it is I who pity you."*

There is no reason to dread death; pain is what we are afraid of. The pain of death itself is very little. But why didn't the Lord give us the power to change our old worn-out body as we change our old clothes? Wouldn't you like to come out with a young body when this one grows old or weak, without having to die and be born again? This is what some yogis do. Once in India a very old yogi came to the cremation grounds. Upon a funeral pyre was a young man's body, ready to be cremated. The old man cried out, "Stop! I need that body." And even as he said it, the young man's form, enlivened by the spirit of the yogi, jumped up from the pyre and the saint's old body fell dead. Wearing his new physical habitat, the yogi ran off and soon disappeared in the crowd. The astonished mourners cremated his old body.

On a little island in the Bay of Bengal there lived a saint. One day his devotees found him sitting on a pile of wood. He spoke wonderful truths to them. After he had finished his discourse, they asked, "Why are you sitting on the wood?"

"To save you the trouble of cremating this body," he answered. "I have stayed here long enough, and have decided to give up this body now."

As he took a match and lit the pyre, he remarked, "Lest you think I am burning alive, please come and see for yourselves that this body is dead."

And he consciously left his body. The devotees rushed forward and found that his form was indeed lifeless.

Lahiri Mahasaya left his body in a similar manner: Announcing to a group of devotees assembled around him that he was going, he lifted up his eyes and was gone. The saints say this is how you must treat the body, as a temporary residence. Don't be attached to it or bound by it. Realize the infinite power of the light, the immortal consciousness of the soul, which is behind this corpse of sensation.

How glorious is life after death! No more will you have to lug about this old baggage of bones, with all its troubles. You will be free in the astral heaven, unhindered by physical limi-

* From "The Dying Youth's Divine Reply," in *Songs of the Soul.*

tations. The astral world is not off somewhere in the clouds; it is another dimension of infinite beauty and variety hiding just behind the grossness of this physical universe. On the inner side of my consciousness, I am in that astral world all the time, so I know. In comparison, this earth is a bedlam; in the astral world you can order things according to your wish. In your astral "car" you can travel any distance instantly. If you desire flowers, they are there immediately, just by willing them. And when you no longer want them, remove the thought and they are gone. You do these things subconsciously in dreams. You can do them even on this physical plane, but you have to develop much greater mental power in order to create as God does. In the miracles he performed, Jesus demonstrated he could do it. And he said: "He that believeth on me (the Christ Consciousness, or universal intelligence of God in all creation), the works that I do shall he do also; and greater works than these shall he do."*

So remember, death is nothing to fear. You are in the movie house of God, and when the show is over, don't cry about it. Once I saw a movie in which the hero was killed, and I felt so sad. Then I thought, "Well, he will come on the screen again in the next showing. I will wait until he comes back to life." Then, before he got killed once more, I left the theater! So it is with souls who die and awaken on the astral plane. They leave the physical movie screen and reappear on the astral movie screen; they never really die. Many, many devotees who have died I have seen again. This is why I don't sorrow. When you know God, He shows you everything; and you will no longer miss anyone. Sometimes the astral form of a person will be sitting right by your side. You won't see him, because you can't see an astral being with the two physical eyes; but I can see him. You need the "X-ray vision" of the third eye, the spiritual eye, to see souls in their astral forms. You have to develop that spiritual eye.

You are living here on earth in a dream. This is the Lord's world; only when you become one with Him will it be yours. Be like the maidservant living in the home of her employer, looking after the children. She is thinking, "This is my home, this is my family," but inwardly she knows it is not so, because her real

* John 14:12.

family is in another town. You have duties to fulfill in this world, but it is not your permanent home. When you die, you won't even be an American, or an Indian, or an Englishman any more. Live with the consciousness, "Lord, this is Your world; I am not attached to it, and I am not willing to be attached to this body or my other incarnations. I want first to know You, and why I am sent here. And I want to be free from karma *now!* Being made in Thine image, I am not affected by this world or by this body. I will perform my duties without being identified with them, even as Thou art not identified with Thy cosmic work. I am free."

Destroy Bad Karma With Right Action

Don't allow yourself to think you are forever bound by karma. Deny it. Whether your karma is good or bad, don't accept any karmic limitation. You have to have good karma to destroy bad karma. Then rise above them both.

Give your karma to God. He will help you if you ask Him to. It isn't that we should seek special privileges, but if we have faith in God, all things are possible. It is His grace that counts, and that grace comes when we do our part to behave like children of God. Whenever you see you are not able to control your pains and troubles, keep trying. If you don't try, you will never get anywhere. Never yield to pain and trouble. Every time something gets you down, get up again and say, "I am all right now." The minute you admit you can't do it, it is over. You have given the verdict that you are bound by karma. You are the judge. It doesn't matter what your troubles are. If you say, "I am all right," you can overcome. But if you say, "I can't do it," you remain jailed behind the prison bars of your karma. If you recognize a mistake and resolutely determine not to make it again, then even if you fall, that fall will be very much less than if you had never tried. You will see in time that you are a master of yourself, and free from karma, even as God is.

Why be forced to change by repeated deaths and rebirths? Why not change now? Why not give up moods when you know they are wrong? Why not rid yourself of anger? When you get mad, it is because somebody has put salt on your wounded ego. You will be a much better and happier person if you remain calm. Let others slap you or hate you, but never show anger in return. You will see then that nobody can touch you inwardly. Whenever anyone points out your mistakes quietly correct yourself. That is the way to self-mastery. That is how my guru Sri Yukteswar was, like a little child. Hate no one. Have no likes or dislikes. Have no attachments; a child plays with a toy, but if he breaks it, he soon forgets it. If you have a possessive love for anything, you will suffer.

The impulses of evil come not only through your own inclinations but are sometimes tests of God. Pray to Him:

"Lord, I know what virtue is, but I don't seem to practice it. I know what vice is, but I can't stay away from it. O Creator of all my senses, do Thou guide me! Thou hast created both good and evil, and yet Thou art free. I am made in Thine image. I am surrounded by good and evil, but being Thy child, I am free!"

The justice of God is that He has given us the sword of reason, which we can use to free ourselves from this world of delusion. But you have to apply that God-given power of discrimination to choose right action in preference to wrong action, and to be mentally above your troubles. Let nobody tell you your suffering or problems are your karma. You have no karma. Shankara said: "I am one with Spirit; I am He." If you *realize* this truth, you are a god. But if you keep mentally affirming, "I am a god," and in the background of your mind you are thinking, "But it seems I am a mortal being," you are a mortal being. If you *know* you are a god, you are free.

The Guru's Help

The guru will help you. God talks to you and guides you through a guru, one who loves God day and night. His one duty is to plant love for God in your consciousness. He seeks nothing from you but your own spiritual effort. Whether you curse him, or whether you praise him, he is not affected by it. But if you tune in with him, he will be able to help you remove the veil of ignorance from your consciousness.

When you follow the guru's advice, you will see you are free. Even when Master [Swami Sri Yukteswar] told me something that I felt certain could not be so, right away it came to pass. Many times he warned others of the consequences of their intended actions. Those who didn't listen found their lives shattered by disappointments. A true guru warns you only to help you avoid the pitfalls along your path. Some lesser teachers fly off the handle when their disciples are not obedient. But Master would only say, "Don't you think this is right?" I repeat a thing twice; Master used to say only once. And those who didn't take the advice would find out that they should have.

Three Ways to Rise Above Karma

If you want to rise above karma, try to realize these three truths: (1) *When the mind is strong and the heart is pure, you are free.* It is the mind that connects you with pain in the body. When you think pure thoughts and are mentally strong, you cannot suffer the painful effects of evil karma. This is something very cheerful I have found. (2) *In subconscious sleep, you are free.* (3) *When you are in ecstasy, identified with God, you have no karma.* This is why the saints say, "Pray unceasingly." When you continuously pray and meditate, you go into the land of superconsciousness, where no troubles can reach you.

You can be free from karma right now, by these methods. Whenever karmic troubles plague you, go to sleep. Or, think pure thoughts and make the mind like steel, saying to yourself: "I am above it all." Or, best of all, in deep meditation go into the divine state of superconsciousness. The bliss of that consciousness is the natural state of your soul, but you have forgotten your real nature by being so long identified with the body. That untroubled, blissful state of the soul has to be reacquired.

Ordinarily, you are free from consciousness of the body only eight hours of the day. During the other sixteen, you make yourself miserable through your bondage to body consciousness. By keeping your mind happy, and by not dwelling on your troubles, you will suffer much less. But if you can remain in ecstasy, you will see you are free from karma all the twenty-four hours of each day.

Kriya Yoga Sunders the Prison Bars of Karma

So, dear ones, get away from this world; not by flying away to a cave in the Himalayas, but to the cave of your mind, where you are free of the body and of the world. Practice *Kriya Yoga*, and you will surely succeed on the spiritual path. That is my own experience. The liberating power of *Kriya Yoga* sunders the prison bars of karma. I have never found in East or West such a great technique as this. Everyone who is a follower of *Kriya* and of this path of Self-Realization Fellowship will go far ahead. Meditate and see the results in yourself after a few years. Give yourself a little time. Don't expect results in a minute. You can't make health or money overnight. You must give time. It requires eight years to form a habit. If you meditate and practice *Kriya* deeply for eight years, you will see you are on the way to self-mastery.

As a part of your meditation each night, make this affirmation—repeat it over and over again to yourself: "Father, Thou art free from karma. I am Thy child. I am free from karma, now and forever." That is what I want you to feel.

What has been said today is one of the greatest messages I have given to you for the overcoming of all misery. I don't want you ever to forget it. Material remedies—medicines, physical comforts, human consolation—have their place in helping to remove pain, but the greatest remedy is the practice of *Kriya Yoga* and the affirmation that you are one with God. This is the cure-all for every trouble, pain, and bereavement—the way to freedom from all individual and mass karma.

This world is not our home; our home is on the other side, in the cosmic consciousness of God. There, behind the atoms, we are safe and sound in the kingdom of our Father. I pray for you all:

"Lord, it is Thy light I behold. I deeply pray for all souls on this path of Self-Realization, that soon You release them from the terrible delusion of their karma and mass karma. For all the errors of our conduct, for all our omissions and ignorance, still we are Thy children. Remind us of this evermore; that even behind the prison bars of karma, we are one with Thee. As soon as we close our eyes, as soon as we are in ecstasy, we know we are made in Thine image. We are free. O Lord, Thy love is overwhelming! We bow to Thee."

The Yoga Art of Overcoming Mortal Consciousness and Death

Written in 1923

Yoga is that science by which the soul gains mastery over the instruments of body and mind and uses them to attain Self-realization—the reawakened consciousness of its transcendent, immortal nature, one with Spirit. As an individualized self, the soul has descended from the universality of Spirit and become identified with the limitations of the body and its sense-consciousness. The Bhagavad Gita says: "The Supreme Spirit existing in the body is the detached Beholder, the Consenter, the Sustainer, the Experiencer, the Great Lord, and the Highest Self.... The Self, though seated everywhere in the body, is ever taintless."* The soul remains essentially untouched and unchanged by its confinement in the body. But, through *maya* or delusion, it becomes subjectively identified with change and mortality, until the consciousness evolves and, through Self-realization, reawakens to its immortal state.

Yoga is a complete science, encompassing the spiritualization of each aspect of man's threefold nature: body, mind, and soul.

The yogi sees the human organism as a gross condensation of subtle spiritual forces under the control of the soul.

He realizes that the body, and the life or consciousness within it, are distinct entities; and that man is not the mortal body, but the transcendent immortal consciousness.

He learns that the efferent and afferent nerves are the means of the soul's communication with matter; and by spiritualizing this communication the soul expresses through the body its divine potential.

* XIII:23, 33.

The yogi learns that by means of imagination or visualization, will, and *pranayama* (life-energy control) he can dim the lights of the senses—sight, hearing, touch, smell, and taste—whenever he doesn't wish to be disturbed by their messages.

He has full control over, and can enter at will, the waking state, the dream state, the deep-sleep state (i.e., the psychological, the subconscious, and the super-subconscious), and the superconscious state.

The yogi masters the art of mind control. He shuts off mental restlessness and imagination, and avoids absentmindedness by practice of the following:

(a) passivity, or even-mindedness under all conditions;

(b) positive concentration (keeping the mind on one particular thought at a time);

(c) negative concentration (using discrimination and will to eliminate unwanted thoughts);

(d) transferring consciousness from feeling to will or ideas;

(e) transferring consciousness from emotions, such as love or hatred, to self-control, or creative thinking, or pure feeling;

(f) holding the thought on one sensation (sight, sound, smell, taste, or touch) at a time;

(g) visualization of mental images, and creating and dissolving dreams at will;

(h) mental anesthesia (receiving sensations of pain as informative reports rather than experiences of suffering).

Physiological Methods of Self-Mastery

The physiological methods employed by the yogi to gain self-mastery include:

(a) outward relaxation and removal of physical restlessness by skeletal, nervous, and muscular discipline;

(b) relaxation of involuntary organs, such as the heart and lungs;

(c) fasting to cleanse the body and make it more dependent on *prana* or life force, the true sustainer of life and energy in the body;

(d) learning to sleep and wake at will.

When the yogi has mastered the processes of life, he is also a master over death.

Is Death a Misfortune or a Blessing in Disguise?

Death is a peculiar phenomenon, signifying cessation of all vital functions of the body without capability of resuscitation. It is cessation of the soul's residence in that bodily form.

The very word "death" strikes terror in the hearts of human beings because of the following associations:

(a) the predominant dread thought of excruciating corporeal pain, supposedly accompanying death;

(b) the psychological pain of facing separation from family and friends, and from the joys of earthly life and possessions;

(c) the fear of losing one's existence.

But natural death is nothing to fear. The indwelling soul is immortal. Natural death is a blessing, because it offers the soul an opportunity to exchange a dilapidated, tottering dwelling-place for a new and sturdy one. The soul requires the successive instrumentalities of new and better organisms in order to express itself fully. If the individualized soul, cloaked in delusion and sent out to evolve itself back to God, didn't have a chance to express itself — to assert its nature — through various changing bodies, it would have to remain in a nascent or latent disembodied state. And imagine, if the immortal soul had to live forever in an old bent body, pallid and shrunken! No greater punishment could be meted out to this great one, the soul, than to behold and express through the same decrepit organism forever. Instead, the inhabited organism undergoes the soul's discipline, as the soul experiments with it; and when the soul's work is finished on that particular form, it works on another.

Matter is wrought with change; and the spirit within it, though essentially unchangeable, superficially undergoes change by its subjective experience of that phenomenon. As subjective consciousness of sameness of identity is retained from early childhood to old age (except, perhaps, in the less perceptive earliest stages of infancy and the last stages of extreme old age), so also there is no reason why that subjective consciousness cannot be retained before birth and after death. With that continuity of consciousness, death is seen truly as the soul's best friend, giving it infinite opportunities to wrestle with matter and finally overcome it—even after a million defeats. This true friend teaches the soul to manifest its unchangeable nature by transcending the consciousness of change.

The human mind prefers change in environs, tastes, habits, and possessions, not because it cannot stick to one thing, but because it is constantly finding out that its attention has been misplaced and misdirected. Its craving for something unknown does not remain satisfied with the acquisition of possessions of the world of changing things. Through new opportunities afforded by death and changing conditions, the soul is seeking its innate changelessness, and so never feels satisfied until it acquires and becomes reestablished in its natural state of oneness with Spirit. Hence death, or change of the condition in which the soul temporarily resides, is conducive to the soul's growth and development.

The growth and education of life mean nothing more than that the manifesting consciousness in matter evolves to ultimately express its full potential; thereafter to be sifted from matter in order to know and free itself as an independent entity that can stay without the agency of matter. During the learning process, before the self-pushing diligent soul realizes its superiority and transcendental nature, it is strongly attached to the bodily instrument through the compelling sensory and egoistic ties created during its residence in the body. Hence the soul watches its new body in each new incarnation with the care and possessiveness of a man with a newly bought automobile. Consequently, death that is brought on prematurely by disease from unnatural living or bad karma, or by so-called accidents and other misfortunes, involves mental and bodily pain, because the manifesting soul becomes extremely worried when it sees its vehicle of expression being taken away before the expiry of the natural term.

The Spiritual Psychology of Pain

The pain produced on a human organism by a pinprick is beneficial; as a warning, it reports to the soul the punctured condition of the skin, needing repair. The sensation ought not to vex the soul, but should serve as a matter of academic information. It is possible to know each bodily or mental experience of ourselves and others without being moved or troubled by any of them. Vexation and suffering are born of strong imagination and the soul's bad habit of translating sensation into pain. If this bad habit and imagination, and the ensuing restless or excited state of feeling, were to disappear from human consciousness, man's bodily suffering would be cut down one hundred percent. He would not even require anesthesia during surgery. (But one should not venture to forego anesthetics if he is not sufficiently strong-minded. A sudden imagination of pain might cause such reaction as to produce death.)

In Indian ashrams in olden times, children were taught from an early age how to watch bodily changes with an academic interest. This doesn't mean indifference, or negligence in attending to a wound or treating disease; rather, it is denial of pain and refusal to suffer, recognizing that suffering is not endowed to man, either by nature or by divine fiat.

Bodily pain is merely a sensation intended to give an intimation or report to the brain of a certain bodily state requiring attention. It should not cause suffering. Attend to bodily pain, but do not worry or weep over it.

The Suffering of Death Is Self-inflicted

Ordinarily, to the animal-man (one living unnaturally, out of harmony with his soul nature), untimely death is a terrible thing; it does produce great agony. But this so-called suffering is brought on by the soul's bad habit of magnifying and changing an intellectual perception into feeling. For example, suffering that comes from belief in goblins and spooks, as in nightmares, or intense fears that produce traumas and convulsions, demonstrate that acute pain is experienced in the physical organism through mental agency only.

Natural death—that is, in old age, or whenever the soul is ready to change its mortal form—is just like the falling of ripe fruit from the tree, of its own accord, without the resistance that green fruit exhibits when being pulled down by a storm or other great force. But in premature death—through disease, accident, or other causes—the soul puts up strong resistance; hence acute agony is witnessed in the body.* In this tumult and struggle of consciousness, there is a great sorrow, a sense of helplessness; and the soul's deluded nature finally becomes unconscious as death occurs, like the onset of deep sleep.† This helplessness during death is mistakenly supposed by some to be a punishment from God. As a matter of fact, it is just a working out of the soul's persistent, self-created bad habit of being identified with change, instead of regarding bodily changes as a means of expressing itself.

Thus, the fear of death (acquired through social or hereditary agency) and the agony of untimely death (the result of identifying oneself with bodily changes instead of viewing them as a witness) are self-inflicted, which is despicable, terrible. Ordinary painful death is to be avoided by attaining Self-realization. In that consciousness, the yogi

(a) experiences no pain in natural death;

(b) retains consciousness and identity after death;

(c) lives in his soul nature, and knows that nature as all-powerful and immortal.

Why, After Death, the Ordinary Man Forgets His Former Life

Unnatural death, and death in a state of bodily attachment, are not only painful, they also obscure memory. Of course, unless one is spiritually advanced, it is not always desirable to remember one's former life. The after-death oblivion of one's previous identity allows him to forget his past consciousness of failure, pain, and attachments, and to begin life anew. The only disadvantage is that if he has not learned from past wrong actions, he may repeat those experiences, ignoring the warning of their consequences—just as the inveterate alcoholic continues

---

* The external symptoms are minimized today by modern drugs not available when these notes were written in 1923.

† After death, the soul, in an astral body of light, gradually awakens to a new existence in the astral world, or heaven—on a high or low plane corresponding to the merit of its actions on earth. The soul remains in the astral world for a karmically predetermined time; then it returns to earth in a new physical incarnation. These life-death cycles continue until the soul breaks all mortal bonds, becomes liberated, and returns to God. (See *astral world* and *reincarnation* in glossary.)

to drink the infernal liquid, even with the conscious knowledge of probable death from liver damage.

Though the pure consciousness of the soul maintains a continuity of remembrance from one life to another, the body-identified consciousness does not. The fact is, memory after death cannot survive under the following conditions:

(a) if there is attachment to the body;

(b) if there is attachment for past possessions, family, or friends;

(c) if there is a strong entanglement in bad karma, and if one has not risen above the effects of both good and bad actions.*

If, as in *(a)* and *(b)*, the newborn soul remembered and was attached to its previous body, possessions, family, or friends, imagine the agony and frustration the soul would feel in a new incarnation! It would not like to begin a different life amidst a new environment, a new family, and new friends. The soul is a brother to all — to all mankind. Imagine how narrow it would become if it loved only one small circle of human beings. It would not expand, and it wouldn't let those other souls expand, to reach the ultimate goal of unity. We must realize this oneness of our soul with all souls in the unity of the one Spirit, and it is impossible to do so unless the soul expands its sphere of family and friends to include all.

In the case of *(c)* above, the soul would be extremely discouraged, remembering past bad karma, struggles, and suffering, and wouldn't have the will to make new effort to progress. It would forget its transcendent nature. At the conclusion of each lifetime, death washes away all dark impressions, memories of failures and sins, and prejudiced conceptions, so that the soul can begin afresh to express itself in newer ways and make newer efforts to rise above and free itself from matter.

How to Cut the Cords of the Soul's Attachments

Following are the ways to cut the cords of the soul's attachments in order to release it:

* In the Bhagavad Gita, the Lord says: "Actions do not cause attachment in Me, nor have I longing for their fruits. He who knows My nature is also free from the (karmic) fetters of works" (IV:14).

1. Practice *titiksha* — the art of remaining even-minded while watching and analyzing bodily changes
   (a) during extreme heat;
   (b) during severe cold;
   (c) during a fever;
   (d) while suffering from a head cold (concentrate on the nasal cartilage and mucous membrane);
   (e) during pain from a wound or other bodily affliction; (Don't try to ignore it; watch it as a diminishing feeling of sensation, manifesting to you only as a matter of knowledge. You will find that the greater your knowledge about its specific nature, the less will be the feeling of pain associated with it. Thus learn to distinguish between knowledge of a bodily condition reported by the sensation of pain and the terrible fear, or agony, that is self-inflicted by the idea-habit of pain.)
   (f) during a sorrowful state of mind;
   (g) during the state of mind when it is overjoyed to possess a longed-for object.

The above teaches endurance and an objective nonattachment, and thereby produces a super-feeling, a superconscious phase of consciousness, by which changing bodily conditions are looked upon with an academic interest, and the restless excitement of sensations is neutralized.

2. Analyze and feel how the sensations of color and form, sounds, odors, tastes, and touch are transmitted through the channel of the nerves to the optical, auditory, olfactory, gustatory, and tactual centers in the brain. Watch the stimulus proceed from the tympanum as an auditory vibration in the nerves, or a vibration of taste proceeding from the mouth (as when eating tasty curries), or tactual vibrations coming from stimuli on the outer surface of the body.

3. Feel the movements of the diaphragm; the expansion and deflation of the lungs; the beating heart. Feel the circulation in the body. It is strongly felt after a leg or hand has been asleep. It can also be felt rushing to the brain during anger or other emotions. A man of keen perception and concentration can feel even normal circulation.

4. Learn to cause movements in each muscle individually through "muscle-will" exercise.*

5. Analyze the sensation of thirst; then drink hot or cold water and follow the sensation from mouth to throat, through the esophagus to the stomach. Watch the body states during a 24-hour fast; then observe how food goes into the system. Feel the closing of the epiglottis as the food passes over it and into the alimentary canal. Feel the movement of the stomach; feel the peristaltic action of the intestines.

6. Notice how smelling salts or perfumes strike the olfactory region, stir the brain cells into action, and become elaborated into perception and conception. Try this with various odors and tastes. Feel the immediate thoughts generated by a given sensation. See if you can separate sensation, perception, and conception. Try to distinguish between a given sensation and the memory of it through association of ideas; that is, try to distinguish between the flavor of a specific apple and that of previously tasted apples. Don't mix the two.

7. Distinguish in music, apart from its variations and undulations, the feeling engendered by it through the different notes, from lower to higher; its general vibrations on the tympanum, and on the whole body surface; its effect on the breath, and on the inner walls of the body; and its transmission through the tympanum to the brain.

8. Feel the sensation of the ingoing and outgoing breath in the lungs. Observe how breathing is affected by your surroundings, your thoughts, your actions. Conversely, scrutinize the thoughts and feelings generated in you by changes in the depth or rhythm of the breath.

9. Be aware of the perfect state and sense of well-being during good health. If pain of disease comes, before crying out, try to analyze what it is. Strive to separate the physiological malfunction from the mental process that translates sensation into pain through the habit of fear and imagination.

---

* The Energization Exercises originated by Paramahansa Yogananda and taught in the *Self-Realization Fellowship Lessons.* (See glossary.)

10. Above all, the greatest method is to hold more and more to the calm, breathless, conscious, powerful state that follows a long period of concentrated prayer, or deep positive thinking, or repetition of hymns or affirmations, or, highest of all, meditation: stilling body and mind with the Self-Realization Technique of Concentration, merging the consciousness with the sound of *Aum,* and magnetizing the spine and brain by practice of Kriya Yoga.* When the heart and breath are calm, when the heaviness of body weight disappears and you feel light, when sensations are neutralized and the mind is still, the soul begins to know itself as existing apart from the body.

The object of all the foregoing practices is to separate the soul from matter. Sensations must be of intellectual interest, with nonattached feeling. You must be able to completely disassociate and distinguish your own existence and happiness from the pleasant or unpleasant feelings of your senses and other bodily experiences. When you change the center of consciousness, perception, and feeling from the body and mind to the soul — your true, immortal, transcendental Self — you will have the yogi's mastery over life and victory over death.

* The Technique of Concentration and the *Aum* Technique of Meditation are taught in the *Self-Realization Fellowship Lessons.* Kriya Yoga, the highest technique of meditation, is available to qualified students of the lessons. (See glossary.)

How Feelings Mask the Soul

A Sunday afternoon class on the Yoga Sutras *of Patanjali,*
Self-Realization Fellowship International Headquarters,
Los Angeles, California, March 22, 1942

"Then the beholder (the soul) is established in its own state."
(Yoga Sutras I:3)

If at this moment you could completely calm your body, your thoughts, and your emotions, you would instantly become aware of your true Self, the soul, and of your great body of the universe, throbbing with the joy of God. The soul would be "established in its own state." Isn't it strange, that the joy of God is there, yet you cannot feel it? The reason you do not know His Bliss is that you are intoxicated with ego feeling (*chitta*).

If I put a screen before me, I will still be here, but you won't see me. Take the screen away and you will see me. So the screen of feelings arising from the ego (*ahankara* or body-consciousness) hides God's joy. Remove the screen through meditation and you will behold that joy.

Your real nature is calmness. You have put on a mask of restlessness: the agitated state of your consciousness resulting from the stimuli of feelings. You are not that mask; you are pure, calm Spirit. It is time you remember who you are: the blessed soul, a reflection of Spirit. Take off the mask of feelings. Face your Self.

Whenever you become angry or filled with hate you don a guise of evil. A person who gets angry enough wants to kill. He doesn't want to, really—that is, his soul doesn't want to—but because the soul has identified itself with feeling, his anger makes him think so. Therefore it is not good to remain in the ordinary state of human consciousness, subject to such violent emotions. You imprison yourself in various moods, and this is the cause of all your sorrows. To escape, you have to dissolve the feelings and emotions connected with body consciousness. Meditation is the way.

Feelings and Emotions Obscure the Soul

So long you have thought of yourself as having certain qualities, with their characteristic feelings and emotions. Patanjali says you are masquerading as these passions and desires because you have done it for so many incarnations that you have utterly forgotten your real nature. Once you realize that each day you are only impersonating different characteristics according to your changing feelings, you will not be the same person; you will be able to cast off these delusive states. When you realize that passion and anger are not part of your true nature, these emotions will no longer have any control over you. Every person is innately wonderful; he has only to rid himself of the mask of ego consciousness. Remember that.

If you put a diamond near a black cat, the diamond will reflect black. Can you then say the diamond is black? No. As soon as you remove the black cat and allow light to play on the diamond, it dazzles with its own natural luster. The black cat is your restlessness, which darkens your consciousness with emotions and obscures the light and joy of the soul. The very nature of restlessness is such that by the time you are feeling pleasure from one thing you are already looking for something different, a persistent discontent stirred by feeling. But bliss — the joy of God hidden in your soul — is always new, always constant in your consciousness. Because it gives complete satisfaction, there is no more restlessness in you. I hope you understand the value of what I am telling you today. It is the way to freedom from all sorrow.

Indulgence Enslaves the Soul

Perfect control of feeling makes you king of yourself. Never be addicted to anything or bound by any habit. Drinking coffee doesn't necessarily mean you are a slave to it; but if you have to have your coffee, then indeed feeling has enslaved you. As soon as you say, "No, I don't need it," let that be the end of your bondage. I never allow anything to bind me. I can eat or drink something enjoyable, and then dismiss all desire for it; the thought of it is gone in that instant.

Start by not catering to likes and dislikes. And give that same training to your children. You spoil your children when you say, "What would you like to eat? Do you care for spinach? You don't have to eat it if you don't like it." By such indulgence you make your child a slave of feeling.

You may say, "If we do away with our feelings and likes and dislikes, won't we become like dumb matter, useless to the world? Is that what Patanjali teaches us?" No. He says that when you have mastery of your feelings you abide in your true state. The true state of the Self, the soul, is bliss, wisdom, love, peace. It is to be so happy that no matter what you are doing you enjoy it. Isn't that much better than to blunder through the world like a restless demon, unable to find satisfaction in anything? When centered in your true self, you do every task and enjoy all good things with the joy of God. Filled with His intoxicating bliss, you joyfully perform all actions.

Many people think that the Hindus teach a sort of mental annihilation, the supposed result of the cessation of desire. On the contrary, the goal of Hindu philosophy is permanent bliss. There is no freedom or happiness in ceasing to exist. The very thought of it is painful. A joy that never grows stale is what you want; and that is what Patanjali teaches you can have, by becoming established in your true soul nature.

A Balanced Attitude Nurtures Soul Awareness

Then comes the question, how can we really take interest in anything if we neutralize desires and feelings? You have seen those who work without any interest in what they are doing. Their work and attitude show it. They don't care about the result so long as they can say they are doing their job. But the lover works very hard and conscientiously for his beloved; he will do more for the one he loves than he will for himself. This is the way to serve God, and this is how we will feel if we love God. We will work joyously for Him.

At one extreme, there are people who have the idea that to get ahead in life they must work nonstop, like automatons. But the other extreme is just as bad: as soon as these people become interested in spiritual matters, they lose interest in everything else. That is the wrong attitude. It is one reason India lost her freedom; she misused the doctrine of nonattachment. She thought, "So what if dirt accumulates in the hermitage? It is all right. Why bother? To do anything about it requires too much concentration on material concerns. Be nonattached. Renounce all material activity possible." Such an attitude hides mental laziness under a cloak of false spirituality.

I found that truly great masters are very interested in the world, but without any attachment. When Master [Swami Sri Yukteswar] was given something nice he was conscientious about looking after it. But if it was broken, he would only laugh. "My care is over. It has taken so much attention." He was truly nonattached.

I also feel the same way. I appreciate whatever God gives me, but I don't miss it when it is gone. Someone once gave me a beautiful coat and hat, an expensive outfit. Then began my worry. I had to be concerned about not tearing or soiling it. It made me uncomfortable. I said, "Lord, why did You give me this bother?" One day I was to lecture in Trinity Hall here in Los Angeles. When I arrived at the hall and started to remove my coat, the Lord told me, "Take away your belongings from the pockets." I did so. When I returned to the cloakroom after my lecture, the coat was gone. I was angry, and someone said, "Never mind, we will get you another coat." I replied, "I am not angry because I lost the coat, but because whoever took it didn't take the hat that matches it, too!"

Don't let your feelings rule you. How can you be happy if you are all the time fussing about your clothes or other possessions? Dress neatly in clean clothes and then forget about them; clean your house and forget it.

Once I was a guest at a very nicely arranged dinner party. I had much enjoyed the dinner, but our hosts were so nervous lest things not go right that it marred the whole affair. Those who are sensitive feel your nervousness. Why worry? Do your best and then relax. Let things go on in a natural way, rather than force them. Then everyone around you will be relaxed, too.

Activity is not life; it is the expression of life. But some people are so constantly active that they make themselves miserable, exploding with emotion. The ordinary person is like a pendulum, swinging back and forth from one extreme to another, always moving, always restless. This is little more than an animalistic state. The yogi, on the other hand, is always calm, centered in his true nature, like a stilled pendulum. When he is active he can go very fast, but when he stops, he is centered again in inner and outer calmness.

Work With Keen but Unattached Interest

So we must learn to work in this world with interest, but keep relaxed and unattached. I don't know how I could work without joyful enthusiasm. It is natural to have interest. Without it we have no spring for motivation. Have the utmost interest in doing everything for God. Love Him so much that your greatest pleasure is to work and plan for Him. Doing things for God is a very personal experience, so satisfying. I find such joy in fixing up this building for Him. But when something goes wrong, I am not upset, not the least bit. Why should I be? I did my best. Yes, I will try to do better, but I won't let adversity disturb my calmness. Isn't that a wonderful thought? Why not? You didn't create this world, God did. Why should you think you live in this world only to please yourself? To live for self is the source of all misery.

> There was a time
> When I looked at the flower,
> And enjoyed its fragrance,
> For me and mine.
> I heard the call of the brook,
> And it was for me and mine.
> Now I wake from that dream and hear:
> It was only for Thee and Thine.*

The yogi's thought is always "for Thee and Thine." He says, "I am here in this world for only a little time. Why form strong attachments? I don't know why I am here, but God knows. I will work for Him. I will try to follow not my own will, but what He wants me to do." It was this surrender to the highest wisdom that gave Jesus the strength to say, "Father, if thou be willing, remove this cup from me: nevertheless not my will, but thine, be done."† From this, many religionists have the idea that one shouldn't use his will. But if you didn't use your will you would

---

* A paraphrase of thoughts in the poem "For Thee and Thine," in *Songs of the Soul*.

† Luke 22:42.

die; for will power operates every physical and mental process. It is right to use your will, but with wisdom and direction from God. Otherwise, if you use your will wrongly you will fall into error and suffer the consequences. Krishna said, "Those who have mastered their minds become engrossed in infinite wisdom. Their minds thus relinquish all desire to concentrate upon fruits of actions. This insures them freedom...and enables them to reach that state which is beyond all misery-making evil."*

Motive Is Criterion of Right or Wrong Action

Watch your motives in everything. Both the greedy man and the yogi eat. But would you say that eating is a sin because it is often associated with greed? No. Sin lies in the thought, in the motive. The worldly man eats to satisfy his greed, and the yogi eats to keep his body well. There is a lot of difference. Similarly, one man commits murder and is hanged for it; another man kills many human beings on the battlefield in defense of his country and is given a medal. Again, it is the motive that makes the difference. Moralists make absolute rules, but I am giving you illustrations to show you how you can live in this world of relativity with self-control of feeling but without being an automaton.

Master used to give this example: "Suppose someone asks to borrow my nice field glass and assures me he will return it in fifteen days. But at the end of that time he does not return it. When I ask him where my glass is, he counsels me, 'You are a master, yet you are attached to a field glass!' I wouldn't loan it to him again. Another man may ask to borrow the glass, saying he will return it in perfect order. He is kind and thoughtful, takes care of it, and returns it promptly. To him I will loan it any time. It is not that I care that much about the glass; but if something is mine, it is for me to care for in order to keep it serviceful. The second man understood that I was saving the field glass so it could serve others as well as himself. The first man did not understand my motive, so he not only deprived me, but everybody else who could have used it. I didn't want the glass for myself; I was thinking of it for all."

Nonattachment gives great inner freedom and happiness.

* Bhagavad Gita II:51.

All the things I have cherished most I have given away. I enjoyed them through the joy of others. The joy I get out of whatever I do is impersonal, not for self. It lies in the joy of God and in making others happy.

In India I used to have a motorcycle. I rode everywhere on it, especially to visit my master in his Serampore hermitage. I enjoyed that motorcycle very much. So one day I asked Master, "Am I attached to it?" (He knew every tremor of my thought and consciousness.) "Certainly not," he said. Shortly after that, I gave the motorcycle away to someone who had a deep desire for it. And I never missed it. That is the kind of freedom Patanjali teaches you to have, so that at all times you are a god: absolute ruler of the kingdom of your consciousness. You let no dark forces enter your portable heaven. "Through my mind's iron bars no evil dares to pry."

Calmness Is the Parent of Right Action

When you attain freedom from slavery to feeling, you become spiritually sensitive; but you are no longer oversensitive to matter. You feel pain, but are untouched by it. You see this world, but know it isn't the ultimate reality. You are above every limitation of body and mind, centered in the calm nature of your soul.

But what poor training the world gives us you can well understand. Either the father is mad and takes it out on the children or the mother scolds without cause. What an example for the young! What a picture to place before them! It is better not to produce children unless you are willing to give them proper training. By withholding the right kind of discipline you make them miserable all their lives. They acquire habits that prevent them from being themselves, their true Selves. Of course, good habits are friends that help us, but wrong habits influence us to become demons. In the same house you may find one person tolerating everything with calmness and another who is all the time boiling with anger, jealousy, and other disturbing emotions. If you can always remain calm, isn't that much better? If God got impatient, think what would happen to this world! Fortunately for us, He remains calm. He has perfect control of feeling. One part of Him, His absolute nature, is never restless, even though as Creator He knows what is going on here, because He exists in all. So should we be, ever calm in our soul nature in spite of any turmoil around us.

When someone comes to me in a violent state, dancing with anger, I can see that he is suffering. No matter what I would say, he wouldn't understand because of his agitation. But if I have control over myself, I can humor him until I have calmed him and made him receptive to reason. I have never lost that calmness of my soul. If I had lost it, regardless of what excuse my mind might have offered, I would have lost with God. With God—that is where you must win. Inside, you should always be anchored in perfect calmness. When someone comes to you in anger, remain in charge of yourself. "I will not lose my temper. I will keep on expressing calmness until his feeling changes." Then you are demonstrating perfect control of *chitta*.

To have calm feeling doesn't mean that you always smile and agree with everyone no matter what they say — that you regard truth but don't want to annoy anybody with it. This is going to the extreme. Those who try in this way to please everyone, with the desire of getting praise for their good nature, do not necessarily have control of feeling. It is good to be pleasant and agreeable if your behavior is sincere. But agreeing with others all the time because you are afraid to speak truth, lest you displease, cannot be called control of feeling. Whoever has control of feeling follows truth, shares that truth wherever he can, and avoids annoying unnecessarily anyone who would not be receptive anyway. He knows when to speak and when to be silent, but he never compromises his own ideals and inner peace. Such a man is a force for great good in this world.

See Yourself as a Soul, Not the Physical Body

The truth is, we have all become like the proverbial prodigal son. We have wandered away into the dark lanes of bad habits and have forgotten how to keep the joy of God centered in our hearts. When the soul is not in its natural state, it puts on the garb of moods born of human feelings. But if we learn to remain inwardly with the Divine, we live and work in the blissful state of our true nature. In ordinary consciousness we think we are mortal human beings; but when we disengage ourselves from the ego, we see we are Spirit. Delusion causes us to imagine disease, fears, and all other limiting conditions of the body and mind. Can you imagine that you are not a man or a woman? Yet this is the truth. In the divine joy of the soul, the consciousness of sex is entirely lost. Even in childhood I used to see that I was apart from my body. I remember one day as a young child I was in that state of ecstasy and came from my bath unclothed. When my aunt saw me, she slapped me. I didn't realize why she had hit me until she sharply reminded me I had forgotten to put on my *dhoti.* Nothing God has created is sinful. Man created sin by his wrong thinking and misuse of the potentials God has given him.

The ordinary man thinks, "I and my body are one. I am so many pounds of flesh, with senses and feelings." But the divine man thinks, "I and my Father are one." He sees his body as a motion picture image. The picture on the screen is a product of a beam of light passing through a film. So the divine man sees his body as a product of the creative light of God passing through the film of *maya,* or delusion. He knows that he is not the body, that he is one with God's light.

An actor forgets he is acting and begins to live the part. We are like that. We have forgotten who we are and that we are only acting out a role on earth. When an individual doesn't remember his omnipresent blissful Self he masquerades in the garb of feeling and thinks himself a human being, limited to the body and subject to its suffering and death. See what a terrible transformation takes place! And throughout his whole life he searches for the happiness of that blissful Self which he already is.

The restlessness of the worldly man is such that he never tries to meditate, he never tries to introspect and know himself. To develop the mind is far better than to just work, eat, and sleep as the animals do. But to remain forever on the intellectual plane is also a sin against your true Self; for although you may get to the door of realization through intellect, you don't take the next step and open the door. Spiritual development is beyond the intellect. You can open the door of realization only through deep daily meditation.

Practice Deep Meditation and Retain Its Effects

And what you feel in meditation you must keep with you all the time. Too often, people meditate halfheartedly as a matter of habit; and as soon as they are finished with the mechanics of meditation they go back to their old state. You must plumb the depths of the peace and joy of meditation, and then hold on to the calm aftereffects. Then only will you change yourself.

The body reacts to the changes of the four transitional periods of the day: morning (the period around sunrise), noon, evening (around sunset), and night (between nine and midnight). It is very beneficial to meditate during these times.

Deep meditation and perfect control of feeling by holding on to the calm aftereffects of meditation—these lead to *samadhi*, the ecstasy of Self-realization and oneness with God. But the ecstasy of *sabikalpa samadhi*, in which you enjoy bliss within but lose external awareness of the body and the world, is not enough. What you want is *nirbikalpa samadhi*, or conscious ecstasy. That is the highest state, in which you remain outwardly fully conscious and active as well as inwardly fully perceptive of your God-union. It took me a long time to achieve that supreme level of consciousness. Lahiri Mahasaya and Master used to be always in that state. In *nirbikalpa samadhi* you can perform all your duties and face all the tests of life without ever becoming disturbed.

Thus success in meditation is the only answer to the mystery of overcoming the human nature so that the soul can become established in its own state, free from ego-created disturbances of feeling, centered ever in Bliss.

The Yoga Ideal of Renunciation Is for All

First Self-Realization Fellowship Temple,
Encinitas, California, January 18, 1942

What is God's will for man? Should he live as a wandering renunciant in the jungle, free from mundane concerns? Or should he live as a family man in the cities and be caught up in the affairs of this world with its fights and troubles?

The great masters have shown various ways through which one can know God. Renunciation is one way. It has been taught by Jesus Christ,* by Sri Chaitanya, by Lord Buddha. Once when a disciple of Sri Chaitanya received some fruits in his begging bowl, he ate a few and saved the rest for the next day. But because he was taking "thought for the morrow" — an attitude Christ also cautioned against† — Chaitanya told the disciple he did not want to see his face again. The training by my own master, Swami Sri Yukteswarji, was quite similar. "Live from day to day," he said, "remembering that all sustenance comes from God." Christ said: "Sell all that thou hast...and come, follow me."‡

I have lived in that way. In India for a time I lived the life of a divine gypsy, roaming free, absorbed in my love for God. I don't think I was ever more happy and carefree. Inwardly, I am always happy; but outwardly, as God's gypsy, I was as joyously free as could be, never even knowing or caring when or whence would come the next meal. That kind of training in total dependence

---

* "And everyone that hath forsaken houses, or brethren, or sisters, or father, or mother, or wife, or children, or lands, for my name's sake, shall receive an hundredfold, and shall inherit everlasting life" (Matthew 19:29).

† "Take therefore no thought for the morrow: for the morrow shall take thought for the things of itself" (Matthew 6:34).

‡ "Sell all that thou hast, and distribute unto the poor, and thou shalt have treasure in heaven: and come, follow me" (Luke 18:22).

on God is truly marvelous. Once a few companions went with me into the Himalayas for fifteen days. We made almost no preparations for our food. I was in my naturally joyous state.* One day during that pilgrimage I met a saint; I became so absorbed in talking with him about God that time passed without notice. My companions kept quietly urging me, "Come on, let's go and eat; we are hungry!" But I didn't feel hungry in the least. I was receiving food far more nourishing to my soul. In the Himalayas I saw many wonderful saints, healthy and divinely contented with only a little shelter, the simplest food, and scanty clothing. It is truly a spiritually beautiful life they lead.

Depend More on God

I know there is a law by which God directly supports that devotee who depends solely upon Him. If one lives the renunciant life sincerely, he will see how this law works. The true renunciant knows that everything comes from God, and that He is the sole support of life. A man may have plenty of food, but if his heart fails, food has no value for him. The Power that supports your heartbeat certainly knows your lesser needs. If you live solely for God and have faith in His power, He will give you direct help.

Some devotees thus renounce everything for love of God, and devote their lives to seeking and serving Him alone. Jesus Christ, the guru of the Western world, was an example of such renunciation. He said: "The birds of the air have nests; but the Son of man hath not where to lay his head."† He had no home, or place of his own; he had no money for food or clothes, yet he was maintained by God. Because he had given everything to God, he still had everything. He could demonstrate prosperity as no wealthy man has ever demonstrated it, feeding 5,000 people with a few loaves of bread and two fishes.‡ His many miracles showed his attunement with God and His power over all life.

People think of renunciation as denial. But relatively speaking, this is not so. I renounced small desires for the greatest

---

* The scriptures of India teach that God is ever-existing, ever-conscious, ever-new joy; and that the soul of man is a spark of God. The natural state of man, therefore, is infinite joy.

† Matthew 8:20.   ‡ Matthew 14:17-21.

Treasure in the universe. The saintly Nagendranath Bhaduri*
who had given up riches and material comforts to seek God was
being praised by one of his students for doing so. The teacher
replied: "Shortsighted people of the world are the real renunciants, not I. I left only a few paltry dollars and temporary
pleasures to gain an empire of endless bliss, and the greatest
prize of all—God."

God Appreciates One-pointed Devotion

Some will argue: "If everyone becomes a renunciant, what
will happen to the world?" The world is not going to come to an
end because *you* seek God. This is false reasoning, false
rationalization. There will always be many who will persist in
perpetuating the world—don't worry about that! Yet this world
is so filled with sorrow and hate and jealousy, it might not be a
bad thing if it were closed down and started anew! To bank your
whole life on the ways of the world and things of the world is
indeed a poor investment.

The way of complete renunciation is embraced joyously by
those who want to see God, and naught else but God. He reveals
Himself to those who live by the renunciant's creed: "God is my
life. God is my love. God is the temple that calls my heart to
unceasing worship. God is my Goal. No duty can be performed
without the power borrowed from God, so my highest duty is to
find Him." Without that attitude of devotion and determination
one cannot know God. In the Bhagavad Gita, the Lord says:
"Forsaking all *dharmas* (duties) remember Me alone; I will free
thee from all sins (accruing from nonperformance of those lesser
duties)."†

The outer (as well as inner) renunciation required of a
monastic is not possible for all; but in my childhood I resolved
that I would never give my allegiance to anyone or anything but
God; and I never have. In my heart I live only for Him. I want
nothing to stand between me and my God. Renunciation with
that ideal is very beautiful. And it is very wise to renounce in
this way for God, for He appreciates that one-pointed devotion.

Renunciation is considered by the masses as renunciation

---

* See *Autobiography of a Yogi*, chapter 7.

† XVIII:66.

of marriage, of a mate, primarily. Jesus Christ and Swami Shankara were such renunciants. And there was Gautama the Buddha, who was married and had a wife and child, but renounced them and went into the forest to seek God. His test was very much harder. A great saint in India used to ask those who came to him if they were married. If they said, "No," he would reply, "You are still on the safe side!" I know that many married people would say the same thing! Those who do not marry sometimes regret it; but those who do marry sometimes regret that. If one is not married, and has no strong desire for marriage, then he should seek God first, above everything else.

As soon as you are awakened to the importance of seeking God, look neither left nor right, but keep your mind upon your Goal. Once the desire for God is aroused, nourish it. Seek Him earnestly; seek Him first. Then if He guides you toward marriage, follow that way. "Seek ye first the kingdom of God, and His righteousness..."* Thus Christ admonished the multitudes. When you will have communion with God, you will know what He wants of you. That is the safest way to guide your life.

Yoga: The Universal Middle Path

The question then arises, "What about those persons who have already incurred obligations in the world? What chance do they have to seek and find God? Is there no escape for them?" Of course there is! Yoga offers a middle path between complete renunciation and complete worldliness.

Yoga means "union"; the path of Yoga is the science of uniting the soul with God. The practice of Yoga is not restricted to any particular type of life. Its goal is attainable by the monastic in the cloister or by the householder in the world. The purpose of renunciation is to pursue God. The purpose of Yoga is the same. In the path of renunciation the stress is on the physical relinquishment of everything that stands in the way of one's search for God. Yoga shows the way to *inner* freedom from such obstructions. Jesus referred to this when he said: "If thy hand offend thee, cut it off; it is better for thee to enter into life maimed, than having two hands to go into hell, into the fire that

---

* Matthew 6:33

never shall be quenched."* Jesus meant that it is better to be maimed of all desires, and thus be free to enter into eternal life, than to live in a "hell" of unfulfilled desires that keep one on the path of sorrow in this world. There should be nothing on earth that you cannot give up for God. If you cannot renounce at least some of your bad habits, moods, and materiality for Him, you are a weakling; and God cannot be attained by weaklings. Mental strength is absolutely necessary in order to find God.

It would be impossible, of course, for all people to leave the world and go into the forest to seek God alone. They would constitute such a large community that it would be necessary to build a city there to take care of their shelter, water, and sanitation needs. But we can renounce most of the luxuries and unnecessary things of life, and lead a more simple existence. If we do, we can and will be more happy, more peaceful. In fact, money brings unhappiness when it becomes the only standard of happiness. Jealousy and greed arise, creating divisions even within families. Life is much better for everyone when it is more simple. That is why the yogis teach that, when possible, it is best to live away from the big cities. The city dweller has no freedom of his own. He gets caught up in the rush and becomes just another automaton of urban life. In New York I have seen people who behaved just like cogwheels in a machine. One feels freer and more alive in smaller communities. But the flaw there is that if the townspeople do not strive to cultivate spiritual freedom and spiritual interests and understanding, they are likely to become gossipy, critical, and small-minded. Unless one brings God into his life, creating a dynamic balance, difficulties arise no matter where or how one lives.

Perform All Duties to Please God

The beauty of the Bhagavad Gita is that it is applicable to all human life. The Gita counsels simply and repeatedly that he who performs dutiful actions, not for himself, but for God, is saved. But how does one determine which actions are dutiful and which are not? The way is to follow the counsel of someone who has wisdom, for that quality is lacking in the devotee in the beginning of his spiritual quest. If one wants to be a lawyer, the

* Mark 9:43.

best course is to seek out a good one and learn his methods, the ways in which he trained his mind to deal in legal matters. So the same is true in seeking God. Follow a divine expert. In India we call such a one a guru: he who has followed the way and mastered himself, and therefore is able to lead others. A true guru is divinely guided, and if you follow him you will know what your duty is. What you want to do is not necessarily what you should do. It is easy to do what you want to do, but that is slavery. To act according to the dictates of wisdom is true freedom. But even this is just the first step toward being a true yogi. You must then perform those dutiful actions—physical, mental, and spiritual—with the sole wish to please God. Then you are a yogi.

The excellence of Yoga is that it points out both the Goal and the way. It says that you must be a renunciant in order to contact God, and shows that there is no excuse to say you cannot do so: Yoga teaches that whether living in the world or in a monastery, within your mind you can renounce everything, feeling that whatever you do is to please God. So in Yoga there are two kinds of renunciants: those who renounce everything, both physically and mentally; and those who remain in the world to fulfill their obligations, but mentally renounce all desires save the one desire to become united with God in meditation and in serviceful activity.

If you are inwardly watchful of your thoughts and your behavior, it becomes much easier to mentally renounce everything for God—and to renounce everything physically as well, when you wish to do so. You may renounce outwardly by running away to the jungle to seek God, but your undisciplined desires will go with you. Yet if you have renounced something in your mind, it is nothing at all to forgo it outwardly. I enjoy the food I eat, but inwardly I am aware that it is God who is eating through me. Therefore I feel no attachment to food. If I eat, all right; if I don't eat, I don't miss it. The idea is to learn to relate all experiences to God. This kind of renunciation can be embraced by everyone. Whether one lives in the world or secludes himself in a monastery, he who would find God must be inwardly a renunciant. Whoever performs his duties not for self, but to please God, becomes a true renunciant and a true yogi.

Play Your Role Well in the Drama of Life

It is wise to strive to do God's will in everything, because that is the way to peace of mind and happiness. If you deeply ponder it, you will see that this is a colossal thought. A vast cosmos of the different forces of nature is tied together by God's directing power. Everything works in mutual harmony with the Divine Plan. We are a part of that universal scheme — just as important as the sun and the moon and the stars. We have to do our part; we must play the role that is assigned to us by the Divine, not what we want to play. When you use your own willfulness in opposition to the will of God, you spoil this drama. You do not contribute your share to fulfill the great plan of this universe. Why not say: "Let me do what God wants me to do." I think you will be much happier, much more peaceful, much better off.

There will be greater joy in your life when you strive to please God, not self. When you awaken in the morning, affirm: "Lord, I offer this day unto You. The little ego no longer holds sway in this body; You alone dwell here." As soon as you begin to find God within yourself, you will also behold Him in others. Then you can't hate anyone, because you see Him enshrined in all body temples. It is a beautiful way to live. In everything we do we should think of God. In loving and serving our country, our family, and other loved ones, we should love Him above all else. He must be first in our hearts and in our lives. That is why He has declared, in the Ten Commandments: "Thou shalt have no other gods before Me."*

Be in the World but Not of It

The Lord did not create this world to torture us, but to test us. The purpose of this test is to see if in carrying on our material duties we can still keep our minds centered in Him, if we can learn to be in the world, but not of it—not absorbed or lost in its materiality. This is the example given to us by Lord Krishna, Lahiri Mahasaya, and King Janaka.†

---

* Exodus 20:3.

† A great saint and king in ancient India. He was renowned for wisely performing his outer duties of ruling his kingdom while inwardly keeping his consciousness centered on God.

The Bhagavad Gita says that he is not a yogi whose renunciation is solely outward; nor is that man a yogi who forsakes dutiful actions.* Some spiritual aspirants renounce sex, money, and material desires to enter a monastery or ashram, and then want to renounce constructive activities also. However, in the ashrams of my guru, Swami Sri Yukteswarji, we were given more work than we would do even for a family of our own. In family life, as a rule, one works primarily for himself and a few loved ones, whereas in a hermitage one works purely for God. But in the world, also, one can live only for God, if he changes the center of his consciousness.

Live in the Consciousness of God

Yoga is the art of doing everything with the consciousness of God. Not only when you are meditating, but also when you are working, your thoughts should be constantly anchored in Him. If you work with the consciousness that you are doing it to please God, that activity unites you with Him. Therefore do not imagine that you can find God only in meditation. Both meditation and right activity are essential, as the Bhagavad Gita teaches. If you think of God while you perform your duties in this world, you will be mentally united with Him.

Cease to think that you are working for yourself. Find God by striving to make your daily activities less identified with "me" and "mine" and more identified with God. Each one of you can feel that you are performing all your activities in the consciousness of God; for example, by eating not for yourself, but to look after the body temple in which God resides; by doing your work not with the idea of personal gain, but as a service to God, and with the thought of God. Feel that the care of those souls who are in your charge has been assigned to you by God's will.

The test of whether your life is lived for God alone is that you do not grieve over any frustrated personal desire, but only

* "The relinquishment of dutiful action is improper....Although performing the act of renunciation, such a person is unable to attain the results of that renunciation (salvation). When dutiful action is performed solely because it should be done (being divinely ordained), forsaking attachment to it and its fruit, that renunciation is considered *sattvic* (pure)" (XVIII: 7-9). "Worklessness is not attained simply by avoiding actions. By forsaking work no one reaches perfection" (III:4).

when you have displeased God. I take better care of others' things than my own. Because I perform all actions for God, I do them with more ambition and care than I would for myself. And if the results of those actions go wrong I don't suffer personally, because I acted only for Him. I did my best; and I will try again with greater joy and determination, but without attachment to my efforts and their outcome. If I were working for myself, I would be worrying all the time. But, since my object in working is only to serve God, the results are His, not mine. This is the way to transcend the law of karma.

Though I am called upon to perform all kinds of duties, I do not feel at all attached to anything I do, so I do not feel bound by anything. Every person should live in this way in order to know that this world is not his home; we are here for just a little while. So do not trust this life, for it will deceive you. Trust only in the Immortal, who is behind your temporal earth existence. You think that here is your home, here is your country, here are your loved ones; but when you leave this world, not even your body is your own.

You were not sent to earth to become hidebound in moods and habits, and enslaved to the environment in which you find yourself. If you had complete control over your life, I would say, "Go on, do as you please." But you do not have that absolute control. No one does until he becomes a master.* You were sent here to find God. But without direct contact with God, no one can know Him. So the real art of living is to be a yogi: he who has united his soul with Spirit in meditation, who has inwardly renounced everything, who practices the presence of God, and who performs all dutiful actions with the thought of God. You see that I am not telling anyone to neglect his duties. Look after everything entrusted to you, because God has given you those duties; but be nonattached. Realize, even as Jesus did: "My kingdom is not of this world."† That which lies beyond this creation of three dimensions is your real home. As often as I look upward into the spiritual eye, I am in that other world. Do you think it is impossible? It is not! Right here and now you can live in that other world. God is realizable. He can be coaxed to talk to

---

* One who has attained Self-realization and God-union. (See glossary.)
† John 18:36.

you. But to hear His voice requires spiritual effort and self-discipline.

Stand Unshaken Midst the Crash of Breaking Worlds

Periodically throughout its history the world has gotten into a mess. During times of war it becomes a torture chamber for millions of human beings. True happiness, lasting happiness, lies only in God, "having whom no other gain is greater." In Him is the only safety, the only shelter, the only escape from all our fears. You have no other security in the world, no other freedom. The only true freedom lies in God. So strive deeply to contact Him in meditation morning and night, as well as throughout the day in all work and duties you perform. Yoga teaches that where God is, there is no fear, no sorrow. The successful yogi can stand unshaken midst the crash of breaking worlds; he is secure in the realization: "Lord, where I am, there Thou must come."

When not all the pain of this world, nor even the sufferings of hades can affect you, you are a king. And that is what you must be. Breaking the limitations of this frail human body, you must manifest immortality. In his poem, "Marching Light,"* the great saint Swami Ram Tirtha wrote, "I hitch to my chariot the fates and the gods, in the voice of thunder, proclaim it abroad!.../Liberty! Liberty! Liberty! *Aum!*.../Hail, O ye ocean..../be dried up, depart!" That is to say, before the marching light of your soul the ocean will be dried up, and mountains will stand aside: "Beware, O ye mountains! Stand not in my way./Your ribs will be shattered and tattered today!" Think of that. Only the liberty of the soul is all-conquering; and it is all-satisfying and ever-newly joyous.

Do Not Be Frightened by God's Cinema

Be not afraid of the frightening dream of this world. Awaken in God's immortal light! There was a time when life, to me, was like helplessly watching a terrifying movie, and I was giving too much importance to the tragedies being enacted therein. Then, one day while I was meditating, a great light appeared in my room and God's voice said to me: "What are you dreaming

---

* A musical arrangement of the poem appears as "Swami Ram Tirtha's Song" in Paramahansa Yogananda's *Cosmic Chants*.

about? Behold My eternal light, in which the many nightmares of the world come and go. They are not real." What a tremendous consolation it was! Nightmares, however dreadful, are merely nightmares. Movies, whether enjoyable or disturbing, are merely movies. We ought not to keep our minds so absorbed in the sad and frightening dramas of this life. Is it not wiser to place our attention on that Power which is indestructible and unchanging? Why worry about the unpleasant surprises in the plot of this world movie! We are here for just a little while. Learn the lesson of the drama of life and find your freedom.

Make God the Polestar of Your Life

Make the Lord the Shepherd of your soul. Make Him your Searchlight when you move along a shadowy pathway in life. He is your Moon in the night of ignorance. He is your Sun during the wakeful hours. And He is your Polestar on the dark seas of mortal existence. Seek His guidance. The world will go on like this in its ups and downs. Where shall we look for a sense of direction? Not to the prejudices roused within us by our habits and the environmental influences of our families, our country, or the world; but to the guiding voice of Truth within.

Every moment I am thinking only of God. I have given my heart into the shelter of the Lord. I have given my spirit into His charge. My love, my devotion I lay at His feet of Eternity. Trust nothing before God. And then, through the inner direction of God, trust those who manifest His light. That Light is my guide. That Light is my love. That Light is my wisdom. And He tells me how His virtue is winning, and ever shall win.

God's Judgment Is Just

I used to worry about this war.* But I received great comfort when I prayed: "Lord, I am not the one to judge. Thou art the judge of mankind and nations. Thou knowest the karma of all. And what will be Thy decree, that is my desire." This thought took away my concern even for India, for I know God will protect her. We must learn to depend more on the judgment of the Lord. And that is known only after each act in the world drama is over. During the war His judgment may not be understood; but

---

* World War II.

in time we will see that His hand was in this conflict. The immediate outcome and what will come to pass thereafter will be according to His judgment, according to the karma that each nation and each individual within that nation has earned. Out of the fires of this war a greater world will come. Remember this: brute force is never the final victor. You will see that in this war. God's virtue will emerge triumphant.

Of all lands, America is blessed; and she will be blessed in spite of all the trouble she is now passing through, because there is no spirit of aggression in her heart.

Through the spiritual ideals of India and the idealistic material activity of America will come the great light of tomorrow. India's urge to meditate and commune with God, and America's urge to right activity that is meant to evolve and help the world —these are virtues of the true yogi. And these ideals of America and India will be the saviors of the world. They represent the true essence of the path to salvation for the individual and for the world in which he lives. Reducing these virtues from the national to the individual level, we have the essence of Yoga: meditation plus right activity, plus mental nonattachment. One who lives thus, whether his outward garb is that of a monastic or a householder, is a true renunciant and a true yogi, treading the sure path to enlightenment.

"With All Thy Getting, Get Understanding"*

Self-Realization Fellowship International Headquarters, Los Angeles, California, February 23, 1939

Understanding is the most precious possession of each soul. It is your inner vision, the intuitive faculty by which you can clearly perceive the truth — about yourself and others, and all situations that arise in your path — and correctly adjust your attitudes and actions accordingly. That is a big definition.

In this world, our understanding is often shortsighted. When our mental vision is thus impaired, it is impossible to see into the future to know what will be. Being blinded to the potential results of our actions, we frequently do the wrong thing. In order to get along well in this world, you must learn to perceive accurately your immediate circumstances and surroundings, and to perceive also what you are headed for in the distant future. You should have such keen and perceptive insight that you will be able to tell what your life is going to be, two years or ten years hence.

If your eyes are shortsighted, you can only see clearly things that are very near to you. And if you have longsighted vision, you can clearly see and distinguish objects in the distance, but not those close to you. Whether you are shortsighted or longsighted, the remedy is corrective glasses; otherwise, your vision will be blurred and you will not see things as they are. Similarly, if your understanding is shortsighted or longsighted, it is time for you to put on the mental glasses of attention—the ability to focus the mind so that its perceptions are clear and accurate. Thus the power of understanding is increased by attention.

---

* The title derives from Proverbs 4:7: "Wisdom is the principal thing; therefore get wisdom: and with all thy getting get understanding."

Conversely, restlessness—that which ruffles and diffuses the mind—blurs vision and causes misunderstanding. Emotion blurs your vision. Moods blur your vision. Most people act, not out of understanding, but according to their moods. Prejudices also blur your vision; these preconceived notions distort your understanding and prevent you from seeing clearly. In my experience with the great ones in India, the first thing I learned was to clear my vision of all forms of restlessness and mental prejudice that might blur my understanding.

It often happens that understanding has been prejudiced from childhood, according to environment and circumstances. Such a warped understanding cannot see any situation clearly. You should analyze the many prejudices that your understanding is subject to. Any time you are making a decision or taking action, ask yourself if you are doing it through understanding, or through emotion or some other prejudicial influence on your mind. As long as you are subject to greed or anger; as long as you are influenced by the wrong thinking of others; as long as you are affected by the misunderstanding of others, so long will your own understanding be unclear.

Seek the Help of a Spiritual Teacher Who Knows God

Because of prejudices, moods, emotions, you do not always see your own mind as it really is. Therefore it is wise to find some spiritual teacher or teachings that can show you how to analyze and correct your thoughts. They have real understanding who have fellowship with God. All souls who are of the Divine have clarified their understanding by attunement with His wisdom. Association with them will give you light. I respected my guru, Swami Sri Yukteswarji, not only because he was my spiritual teacher, but because he gave me that understanding. Any clarity in my vision I owe entirely to him, not to my family or anyone else. No one loved parents more than I loved mine; but the clarity of vision my guru taught me made me unshakable in the path of truth.

I remember when I left home and went to Banaras to renounce the world; I was after something much greater than money could afford. I had analyzed the lives of those who had money, and I didn't want to live their kind of life. I knew I would regret it if I tried. I saw that others had many things that I might have wanted, and I analyzed what would happen to me if I followed their path. I saw clearly that I would never have been happy.

While I was in Banaras, God led me to my guru. Later, in his ashram, I said to him one day: "I am called to my home. I must go to see my father. He loves me very much."

Master knew my family would try to hold me. "Better not go," he advised. "You may not be able to come back."

But I said, "Guruji, I promise I will return." For I knew there was no other life for me. Love for our parents and attachment to our parents are different things. Attachment clouds understanding; divine love is never blinded. I know that I love my parents more than anyone else in the family does, and that by giving my life to God I have done much more for them than I would otherwise have been able to.

When I went home, my father, who is not given to emotion,* was so grateful to see me that he had tears in his eyes. "You have come back," he said. "I am glad." In those few words there was much meant. His affection was so deep, he never wanted to express it outwardly. As a great saint once said, "The moment you utter your love, some of that pure feeling has flown from your heart and become mixed with the foulness of the mouth; the germs and taint of the lips have soiled it." God loves you more than anybody else. That is why He doesn't tell you. He shows His love silently through demonstrations. As I progressed on the spiritual path, I received more love from God than I ever could have from any human being.

But to get back to my story: As I stood before my father, he asked me to remain at home to take the place of my elder brother, who had passed on.† "Suppose I die?" Father said. "Who will look after your younger brothers and your sisters?"

"Father," I replied, "I love you more than anyone else in this world; but I love God more, He who gave me such a father."

---

* Paramahansaji's father was still living at the time of this lecture. He died three years later.

† Ananta Lal Ghosh died in 1916, after Paramahansaji had entered the Swami Order.

How could I leave the God who had blessed me with such a loving parent? If the Heavenly Father hadn't put that love in his heart, how could my earthly father love me? Duty to God fulfills duty to all, because without Him, we would not have any loved ones. This is true understanding.

Father couldn't say anything further. He understood. And when I went away again, singing "I am crossing the river of delusion; I shall not turn back lest I weaken," everyone in the house was weeping. By worldly standards it seemed very cruel to leave them, but through that renunciation the greatest blessing came to me—and to them. By serving God first, I could do far more for them spiritually than by any material aid I could offer.

A few years later, when I returned with illumination, I took Father to see my boys' school at Ranchi, and he said, "I am not worthy of you."

"No, no," I remonstrated, "I am not worthy of you."

Then he told me, "I am glad now that you didn't turn back to take the railway job I wanted you to accept."

Life Without Understanding Is Spiritual and Material Suicide

Blessed are those who have understanding. It is the greatest need on the spiritual path and on the path of life. Understanding is the searchlight that illumines your way and brings success. Before you can attain the crowning goal of this life, you must have that important faculty. So never be blind; never be misunderstanding. It is spiritual and material suicide.

Understanding should be your guiding force in every situation. No matter what your trials, try to understand. God never causes harm or suffering to anyone. It is we who, by understanding or misunderstanding, help or hinder ourselves. Pray to God that no matter what experiences come to you, you may have understanding. It is the only thing that will save you. When my trials become very great, I first seek understanding in myself. I don't blame circumstances or try to correct anybody else. I go inside first. I try to clean the citadel of my soul to remove anything that obstructs the soul's all-powerful, all-wise expression. That is the successful way to live.

To fly away from problems may seem the easiest solution. But you gain strength only when you wrestle with a strong opponent. One who doesn't have difficulties is one who doesn't grow. When you have understanding, you have no fears. In understanding lies security.

Many, many trials I have faced in life. The most difficult of all are those with human beings, because they do not understand. I have seen people I have loved, people to whom I have given my heart, misunderstand. But that has never created bitterness in me. If bitterness arises in your heart out of the nonunderstanding of others, you will lose your own understanding. Do not let yourself feel hurt when someone misunderstands you. Rather, pay more attention to helping that person. If you can neutralize your feelings toward those who misunderstand you, you will be ever ready to help anyone and everyone. All those who follow this path of Self-Realization must hold nothing but goodwill for all.

Understanding Must Have Both Heart and Head

Understanding is the vision of your inner being, the sight of your soul, the telescope of your heart. Understanding is a balance of calm intelligence and purity of heart. Emotion is not love; emotion is distorted feeling that will lead you to do the wrong thing. And understanding that is guided solely by the intellect is coldblooded; it too will teach you to do wrong. There are people you can't even talk to unless you rouse their emotion, and others you cannot move except by reason. Men sometimes become intellectually ossified, and women occasionally become emotionally unreasonable. You must have balanced understanding. If your understanding is governed by both heart and head, then you have clear vision to see yourself and others. You will also be able to know and assess what others are thinking of you.

True Understanding Tells You When You Are Right or Wrong

When you are right, someone may say you are wrong; and you can be wrong and somebody may say you are right. Now, if you have understanding, you know in your heart whether you are right or wrong. You have to watch and correct yourself. Suppose someone tells you that what you are doing is wrong. Then you should go into the inner sanctum of your heart and find out if you are in error. Analyze your motives. If you are wrong, correct yourself.

Those persons who have the greatest understanding are the ones whose opinions and guidance are to be trusted. That is why I trusted Master so completely. I could talk to him as openly as I could talk to myself. To cultivate that kind of understanding, learn to keep your mind free of all prejudices when you talk to people. If your understanding is clear, you can love and help others without being hurt or without hurting anyone else.

It is most wonderful when you can love all beings; when you can see their good and bad points without the prejudices of your own mind, and without the prejudices that others have. You will learn to love each one truly when your love is no longer conditioned by your personal desires. When you have that understanding, no one can hurt you.

Sorrow comes when a desire is not satisfied; pleasure comes when a desire is fulfilled. Thus our happiness comes and goes. That is why Lord Krishna says in the Bhagavad Gita, "Be even-minded in pleasure and sorrow."* He doesn't tell you to be callous or hard, like a stone. He tells you to learn understanding. When you live in that impregnable castle of understanding, no sorrow can touch you; no disease or tortures of the flesh can reach you.

Use understanding to chalk out your path and the future progress of your soul. It will enable you to find the right course without being prejudiced by anything. If you want to hold on to your understanding, love and respect all, but never be prejudiced by anybody or by your own thoughts, because it will be disastrous. As soon as the world is able to confuse you, you will be lost. But if you have a clear understanding, then no matter what clouds others try to create, you will see what is right.

My Guru's Guidance Made Me Clearsighted

Understanding is your savior. I remember the many who came to Master, and later left, because they were nonunderstanding. But I said to myself, "Many may come and many may go, but I will keep on forever." Master was a very strict disciplinarian. Others fled from his incisive wisdom. But I told him one day, "There is one person you will not be able to drive

---

* "Equalizing (by even-mindedness) happiness and sorrow, profit and loss, triumph and failure—so encounter thou the battle (of life)! Thus thou wilt not acquire sin" (Bhagavad Gita II:38).

away, and that is myself." I am proud that I kept that promise, because his guidance made me clearsighted.

Very few people know in what lies their own good. As a result of misunderstanding, they often do the very things that will hurt them. When I say something vehemently, it is not because of any hurt I feel from the actions of others, but because of the hurt those actions are going to do to them. If you are hurt by the wrong behavior of others, and let your heart go blind, then you cannot truly love those persons. But when you can keep your understanding clear, then you can help those you love. You can see the springboard of their actions, the course of their actions, and what those actions will lead to.

Some people readily respond to what I say; but others do not, because they don't understand in what lies their own good. Whenever I try to guide people, it is only because of an earnest desire to show them what is best for them. I never try to use any person for my own ends. No one!

Many people *think* they have understanding. But it doesn't hold up under testing. Put yourself in all kinds of adverse situations, get yourself talked against, be the butt of ridicule and hate, and watch your reactions. If you are not inwardly disturbed, if you can dismiss all feelings of hurt and injustice and keep only love in your heart, that is real understanding. In the ashram, my Guru used to constantly change me from one position of responsibility to another. He wanted my complete understanding in all circumstances, that my devotion to him and my peace of mind be not conditioned by any position in which he placed me. When I reached that evenness of understanding, it gave me unbounded happiness. It is wonderful to live that way.

Most of the time, people talk and act from their own viewpoint. They seldom see, or even try to see, the other person's side. If, lacking understanding, you enter into a fight with someone, remember that each of you is as much to blame as the other, regardless of which one started the argument. "Fools argue; wise men discuss." It is sarcasm that arouses anger. If truth spoken with kindness angers anyone, that can't be helped. They are your best friends who have true understanding, and who, when you seek their counsel, dare to tell you the truth. When your watch isn't keeping time correctly, you check it against a chronometer.

So mix with those who are wise and who are unafraid to tell you your faults. That is the value of your real friends. They are your chronometer.

Always be sincere. Never give others the impression that you agree with them when you do not mean it. You are a hypocrite if you outwardly agree with people rather than let them know your real thoughts. Violation of sincerity is a great sin. As soon as you deliberately deceive somebody, your understanding becomes clouded. As a result, you will attract hypocritical friends.

If you want understanding, you must give understanding. You must love all with the love you give to your parents, children, and other dear ones. That all-inclusive love is the most wonderful consciousness. Materially speaking, you are nobody to me, because we are not related by blood. But I have worked for you more than I have for my own family—night and day thinking how many souls will be happy if I can do my part to make them so. I know I have succeeded with some people; many, many have found salvation. But it is a very hard job, I tell you. When you try to enforce your authority, nobody wants to obey it. But if you exercise your authority with love and wisdom, it becomes the greatest guide to help others. That unshakable assistance I give to you is the searchlight on your path. It must not be blacked out by any prejudices.

Don't Oscillate in Keeping Your Good Resolutions

All good resolutions must be kept. The more you try to materialize your good resolutions, the stronger you will become. Be like the saint who said, "I made up my mind to have a walk every morning, but sometimes circumstances prevented it. On those occasions, even if it was late evening, I still went on that walk, lest my mind weaken in its resolution."

Before you make up your mind to do something, be sure that it is a good resolution to make. Once you have made up your mind, it is not good to oscillate, because to do so will weaken your will power. A resolution should not be changed unless the facts overwhelmingly justify it. Otherwise, wherever you go, your mental weaknesses will be with you. If you go to a forest, can you leave your weaknesss behind? No. Wherever you are,

there you must win your victory. You do not win by flying away
or giving up.

It is easy to make yourself miserable if you do not have
understanding. I could justly reason, "The world does not understand me. Why be in this materialistic land when I could enjoy
the greatest spiritual freedom in the Himalayas with Babaji?"
But if you have understanding, you say, "Wherever I am, I must
conquer." If you conquer your self within yourself, all of the
weaknesses of your mind, all the habits that beat you down, you
are a real conqueror. You must never admit defeat. Only when
you have admitted defeat are you defeated.

Stand By What Is Right

A little while we are here on earth, and then we are gone.
Don't be attached or bound to anything. When I was first asked
to be a citizen of this country, I refused because I didn't want to
be called a citizen of any country. My country is all nations; I am
a citizen of the world. My Father is God; my family is all mankind. Who can deny me that? If I fight, I will fight for justice. I
will defend America when she is right, and I will not fight for her
when she is wrong. I will fight for India if she is right, but I will
not defend her if she is wrong. Wherever your country is right,
support it. Wherever your family is right, stand by them. Wherever your friends are right, cooperate with them. You see how
clear it is? You cannot deny the correctness of this principle.
That is the divine spirit taught by Krishna and Christ and all
great ones. That is what is going to bring lasting peace in this
world.

I will tell you a little story. There was a Moslem judge who
was a very orthodox and prejudiced man. A Hindu villager was
brought before him, and the judge asked what the charge was. He
said, "Your Honor, I have to declare to you that your bull, fighting with my bull, broke the horns of my bull, so that he is
dying."

The judge replied, "Well, you know animals will fight. Case
dismissed."

Hearing this, the shrewd villager said, "Your Honor, I have
made a mistake. What I meant to say was that my bull has
broken the horns of your bull; it is your bull that is dying."

The judge was furious, and fined the man $50.00. When it was the judge's bull that was dying, his "judgment" became different. The moral is, always be a judge who is fair, who has understanding. Try yourself and your motives first. Whenever there is a doubt in your heart, judge yourself before your own inner tribunal.

Find Understanding Through Communion With God

Every day, analyze yourself; see how you are progressing. As you learn to analyze yourself impartially, you will be able to understand yourself and others. That is the true way of life. If you live and die in understanding, you will find immortality.

My aim is not just to build a large organization. I am trying to build the lives of people around the teachings of Self-Realization Fellowship. That is why I don't try to have big congregations in the temples. We want those who will commune with God. He cannot be known by intellectualizing or by hearing emotional sermons that create inner excitement.

What I have inside is something very sacred to me. I can't talk at random; I speak what I have verified by my own realization and experiences of life. That is why these truths are real to me. I don't come here to give you sermons, but to give you those truths that I garner from the garden of my experience. I come as the wind of heaven, bearing the fragrance of truth from the Father. I seek nothing from you for myself. My only wish is to give you that fragrance divine, and then disappear again in His bosom. What I give to you I want you to realize for yourself through your own personal communion with God. Nothing can match that understanding.

Criticism

Written circa 1928–1930

When criticized, analyze thyself. Take a thorough look at thy life's activities. Through the uncompromising eyes of thy censors, survey and criticize thyself. If thou dost find fault in thyself, correct it quietly and walk on. If thou dost not find in thyself the fault whereof thou art accused, smile within and go on thy way in stoic dignity. If persecutors continue to jeer at thee and demand a response, answer with love, not enmity.

If thou dost hold a position in which others look to thee for light, answer or battle for truth with love in thy heart, not for thine honor or for fear of a bad name, but to uphold the glory and purity of truth. Let thine actions and words be not for the sake of victory, nor for shaming others, nor to feed thy vanity, but only for truth. Love for truth, however, must always be tempered with the love of avoiding hurt to others. Defamation of others in the name of spreading truth, or for the sake of one's own benefit, is a sign of ego and inner weakness, a desire to make oneself appear taller by cutting off the heads of others.

Fight not, even for truth, if love is not in thy heart; hatred cannot be conquered by hatred; meanness cannot be overcome by meanness. If in the guise of defending "truth," hatred, or vengefulness, or an inflated ego precipitates in thy heart a desire to battle thy detractors, forsake the fight. First culture love. Love is thy strength and thy greatest ally. Its salve will heal the wounds inflicted by the hatred of thine enemies; and love is never defeated. Even death in the attempt to conquer hatred is love's victory for the immortal soul.

Those who hate and revile thee are not knowers of truth. Forgive them, for in their ignorance they know not what they do. As thou dost love to forgive thyself no matter what thou hast done, love to forgive others as readily. To those who criticize thee and wrongly accuse thee, knowingly and deliberately, give love unflinchingly. Let them be shamed by the steady gift of thy love in return for the poison they gave unto thee. Try to change them by thine unconditional love.

No one who knows the love of God can hate or express meanness to any of His children. How canst thou hate or hurt thine own erring brothers? Hateful or loving, they are still thine own. Brothers who act out of hate and spite know not that law. If thou hatest them in return, thou wilt drown them in the flood of hatred. Rather, show them the lighthouse of love that they might swim ashore. Let thy love tell them of the ignorance of their erring ways. Show them the example that thou lovest them in spite of their hatred.

Blessed are those who are criticized for doing good. A paradise of eternal bliss is theirs who live and die in right behavior. But woe unto them who out of jealousy, enmity, or self-interest malign and seek to harm the good name of those who are engaged in noble works. Sarcasm, slander, revengefulness, bias, untruth, are poison shafts of evil that boomerang to inflict great karmic injury to the soul of the criticizer.

Unkind and unjust criticism causes inharmony and factions of partiality, bias, and rebellion. Supported by those who love gossip, it becomes a crucifixion of the soul of the innocent, more painful than the crucifixion of the body. The love of gossip is the love to crucify the soul of others. But though gossip, lies, and slander hurt the criticized, they ultimately hurt the criticizer even more. The wrongly criticized becomes purer than ever, while the wicked accusers are condemned by the unfailing karmic law of cause and effect. In addition, they are convicted by their own conscience and condemned to live in a self-created prison-house of painful lack of inner peace. Those who sow error will reap the harvest of delusion and misery.

The divine way is to judge thyself, not others. Unless thou doest thine own housecleaning, thou hast no right to tell others their houses are unclean. If others sincerely ask thee for thine opinion, then judge them not with bias or personal aim, but with impartial love, and give them thy loving suggestions. No compromise with wrong acts. No mere pitying the wrongdoer. No unkind criticism of the transgressor. But tutor the error-stricken with unfathomable love. Say unto thy brother, "My heart bursts for the suffering caused to thee by thine own wrong actions. Mend thy ways. I love to see thee well." True words may be hurtful and bitter, so coat them with the sugar of love and kindness that they may be more easily swallowed by the one stricken with the fever of evil.

But if thy views are not welcome, maintain silence. Mentally send to the wrongdoer constructive thoughts, love, and prayers—without spoken words—for that is also beneficial and will help to awaken him.

He who is down needs not to be trampled on. He needs thy lifting hands of love. Think of others' woes as thine own and thou wouldst feel for all. Unkind criticism is a torturing enemy that delights in the downfall of others. Love is a saving friend that rejoices in others' happiness and well-being.

To offer criticism—even constructive criticism—is risky; but to be able thyself to stand criticism is of great benefit. It tests and reinforces thine armor of truth for use in the battle of life. Those who lovingly judge thee are thy best friends. Those who flatter thy faults are thy worst enemies. To receive impartial criticism is to tune in with the law of progress. But to succumb to flattery is to poison both material and spiritual advancement.

Harp not on the sins of others, neither on thine own—forgive and forget past error. Give no life and form to thine own or others' errors. Do not speak of others' faults. Never write about them or make them public. Do not engage in or repeat rumors and gossip. Do not make an untruth immortal by talking about it, by sounding thine own trumpet in the chorus of dissent. And do not draw personal conclusions and give voice to them when thou art not in a position to understand all sides.

Be busy in making thyself good. Thine example would talk a million times louder than words. Counteract criticism by humbly living the principles of truth. Reform thyself; and by watching thine example, let others be inspired to reform themselves. That is what is wanted and needed in this world: those who are criticizers of themselves, not others. Conquer vice by virtuous example, error by truth, hatred by love, ignorance by wisdom, fear by courage, narrow-mindedness by understanding, bigotry by liberality. Let these virtues begin with thyself. Be attentive to thine own mental housecleaning, and perchance others will be encouraged to get busy doing the same for themselves.

Where Is Jesus Now,
and What Is He Doing?

Self-Realization Fellowship Temple, Hollywood, California,
December 19, 1943

A merry Christmas to all of you. I wish you the best Christmas ever; and I know that in your hearts you send me the same message of love. Let us specially concentrate on his love today.

There are two aspects of Christ: Christ the man; and Christ the Spirit in the man. Worshiping Christ in Spirit is much more important than observing his birth materially and socially. Christ must be born within us in Spirit. He must be born anew in our consciousness. That is the "Second Coming" of Christ. It is an injustice to Christ to celebrate his birth only with feasting and presents. This is all right; but the lack of deep, devoted communion with the spirit of Christ at Christmastime is a serious omission in Christian practice. This is why once more I am reminding you to observe the spiritual Christmas on the 24th of December* by meditating many hours that day. And then have your social Christmas on the 25th. I am very happy that this message—to honor Christ's birth spiritually by long, deep meditation on him—has been received and followed by so many Truth seekers around the world. And it will be received by millions after I am gone.

Jesus said, "The harvest truly is plenteous, but the laborers are few." The blessings of the presence of God and Christ are there for those who will make the effort to commune with Them in deep meditation. If you follow the meditation techniques as given by Self-Realization Fellowship, you will know more about Christ than the millions of churchgoers who wor-

---

* In 1950, Paramahansaji began holding the long meditation on the 23rd of December, to allow devotees more time to dwell on the peace and joy of that day, before preparing for the customary festivities of the outer celebration of Christ's birth on the 25th.

ship him in sermons and external rituals, but don't take time to meditate deeply upon him. This Self-Realization movement was sent to the world to awaken the real spirit of Christ within you.

Wherever you are, pledge yourself to celebrate first the spiritual Christmas, and then the social holiday. These two you must always observe, for then you will see what a greater awakening will come. By striving to commune with God, Christ, and the great ones at Christmastime, you will prepare yourself for the way you are going to spend the new year that is shortly to come. It is a wonderful way to enter a new year. By greater spiritual effort, every day, you must redeem yourself by yourself. No one else can do it for you.

How Liberated Masters Watch Over the World

Perhaps you have wondered sometimes if great souls such as Jesus are lost to the world. Not at all. See how busy God is: He is always in His own ecstasy, yet He is busy running this universe. And all the saints and masters who have left this earth are also busy elsewhere, just as every one of them had something to do when here. The first time Lahiri Mahasaya called Babaji to materialize himself, to satisfy some doubting friends, Babaji didn't like it. "Do you call me for a trifle?" he asked. "I am very busy."* When a liberated master says that, he means he is busy with God, doing God's will. The great ones are all active; it is the mission of some to try to strengthen the good in this world. And to the extent that they are able to do so, through receptive minds, the devil's power weakens and God's power becomes stronger.

When a great saint is resurrected in Spirit, and yet takes a form in responding to sincere, receptive devotees, it means he has some part to play in the world's destiny. I know that Christ, in flesh and blood, is in communion with Babaji in India. Together they are watching over the destiny of the world.† They

---

* See *Autobiography of a Yogi,* chapter 34.

† "Babaji is ever in communion with Christ; together they send out vibrations of redemption and have planned the spiritual technique of salvation for this age. The work of these two fully illumined masters—one with a body, and one without a body — is to inspire the nations to forsake wars, race hatreds, religious sectarianism, and the boomerang evils of materialism." *Autobiography of a Yogi,* chapter 33.

tried very hard to avert this World War.* They and all other resurrected masters have a mission to perform. Who puts the powerful thoughts of peace in the minds of some souls? It is Christ and the great ones, for they are suffering very much in this war. They are not by any means happy with the state of this world. They are trying to establish peace and harmony on earth, and raise it to a higher spiritual level. But they can't if man doesn't let them.

God is almighty. He could stop the war tomorrow, but if He did, He would be a dictator. I used to wonder why He and the great saints didn't prevent this war. The answer is that they would have had to use miracles to do so; and God is so great, He will not impose His will on us. Nor does He punish or take revenge on us. He wants to convert His children not by force, but by persuasion and love. War is made by man, not God, and it is meant to teach us a lesson—the lesson of our innate godliness. But what a terrible way to learn this truth! God knows that we will never be destroyed, for we are immortal souls; but the lesson will never be learned by us unless we suffer. And is not God suffering also? Do you think He doesn't want us to be happy? He permits us to suffer from evil ways only that we might learn that the path to follow is the way of the good.

Christ Has Not Gone—He Is Watching You

If you want to know Christ as he was on earth, and as he has appeared to saints through the ages, you must live his life. Whenever it is necessary, he does appear to his devotees. And if you are in tune with him and live in your daily life even a little part of what I am telling you, you shall know him. Christ has not gone. He has given his philosophy, and he is watching those souls who are practicing it. You must live the ideals of Christ, and know that he is watching you all the time.

Why don't you see Christ or hear his voice? Because your physical eyes and ears are not attuned. You cannot see even television images or hear songs passing through the ether of this material world without the aid of television screens and radios. The static of spiritual restlessness keeps you from perceiving the still finer vibrations, which are highly delicate forces. That is

* World War II.

why you do not see Christ and the great ones until you learn how to tune in with them.

Christ is right here; he can be seen if you look within your forehead at the point between the eyebrows: the center of Christ consciousness; the seat of the single or spiritual eye. If you want to see Christ, concentrate at this point of spiritual vision; look through the spiritual eye. If you want to receive his universal intelligence, you have to feel his consciousness in the spiritual eye.

After death, Jesus resurrected his body and allowed hundreds of people to see him. To the doubting Thomas he said, "It is I; touch me." Why did he materialize his body? That others might behold him after resurrection and know that all who are in tune can behold him and know that he is. St. Francis said, "I meet Christ every night in flesh and blood." You too can behold him, if you can put yourself in tune, just as I have seen him many times.

There is a way to invite Christ. He doesn't want praise. Nor can he be bribed by wealth, by any sermon, or by mock devotion. He will be drawn only to the altar of your love. If there is sufficient love and devotion in your heart, then, and only then, will he come to you. He may actually materialize in person.

Christlike Behavior Is Difficult, but Rewarding

So remember that Christ is all the time working for you. And his throne is in your spiritual eye. When you are in tune with him there at the center of Christ consciousness, you can feel his presence, and see him sleeping on the bed of stars, dancing on the billows of your feelings, resting on the altar of your devotion. In every good thought is a secret home of Christ. That is where he is. But he will not come out of hiding so long as you have Satan with you, so long as you don't learn to love those who hate you and to live the other principles of Christ's life.

When Christ came on earth, he was born in the Orient. It is said that when he reached the age of fifteen, his family sought to arrange a marriage for him, as was the custom; but he chose to leave home, and went to India and Tibet, where he passed fifteen years with the masters. I have told you this before. You will recall that there were three Wise Men from the East who came to visit Jesus at his birth. He returned their visit during those years for which the Bible gives no record of his activities. Then he returned to Jerusalem to preach his message. But how few people appreciated him! Only when he was gone did some realize what he was; and succeeding generations began to build churches in his honor. Still, how very few people throughout the centuries have really lived the life of Christ. That is why millions who think of themselves as Christians are not happy or spiritually satisfied.

It is easy enough to learn about Christ and his teachings, but to practice what he taught is not so easy. I say it not from pride, but because I know, I have lived the life of Christ in every way that it has been possible. So I can truthfully tell you that the life he taught is the only way to true happiness. Many people think that to live Christlike is too difficult. It is hard indeed. It is also very difficult to become famous or wealthy; and great is your anguish when you find you can't fulfill your desire, even though you have made a great effort. But though you meet difficulty in trying to establish Christ-principles in your life, if you persevere, there is ultimate reward.

The Permanent Monument of Christ-love

Jesus was as perfect as a man could be. And what did mankind give him? Instead of being appreciated, he was crucified. You find intolerable the little abuse you get from others, but think what Christ suffered for giving love! Of all the miracles he performed, the greatest was when he said from the cross, "Father, forgive them, for they know not what they do." To that great Christ we give our tribute today—to him who has established in our hearts a permanent monument of love.

That same thing we must say during this wartime: "Forgive them, Father. Forgive them, for they know not what they do. Blinded by ignorance, they are murdering each other. They had no hate for those they now call enemies. Politicians led them to fight and kill one another." What will be the gain? The final result must be that man will understand that war does not pay. That is all. War will never solve any problem. Bombs will not settle disputes. Love alone disarms the enemy. Would any power on earth make me take a gun and shoot someone? No. I would not handle a gun for anyone.* We must remember the permanent monument Christ has left within us in his counsel: "Love one another." For we are all sons of the one God. That is what we have to learn. And universal Christ-love will become stronger than ever when the nations of the earth see their folly.

No politician or monarch will ever be worshiped as Christ is worshiped, because their rule is based on narrow interest, or greed, or hatred. It is the universal eternal principles that Christ and the great ones have lived that will change the narrow rules of politics. Humanity has gone mad because the example of Christ's life has been scorned or forgotten. He will not impose himself physically. We have to accept him spiritually; then alone will he bless us.

From My Indian Guru I Learned
the Real Meaning of Christ's Teachings

Live the ideals of Christ. It was from my guru, Swami Sri Yukteswar, in his ashram in India, that I learned about Christ and the real meaning of his teaching. And I never forgot it. I have been able to win in life because I applied those timeless principles.

In the ashram there was a younger boy named Kumar, who had come as a disciple shortly after I did. I thought he was Master's favorite, because he was rather quick and intelligent, and I was more slow in my ways. It was apparent that he wanted my position as the one in charge of the ashram. Guruji assigned him to my place and gave me lesser duties. Everyone complained to me, charging that Master had done me an injustice. But instead of taking their side, I took Master's side. I told them, "My relationship with Guruji is not conditioned by my title or what work I do. I have pledged to him my obedience. I didn't

---

* Christ said: "...all they that take the sword shall perish with the sword"— Matthew 26:52.

On another occasion during the war, Paramahansaji said, "I bless those souls who are courageously giving of their lives and limbs to resist evil and defend the ideals of justice and freedom. Killing is wrong, the use of force is wrong, but the sin lies in the evil of war itself, and in those who advocate violence as a means for settling disputes. We must work to change the hearts of men so that we remove the causes of war."

come here for praise or position. I came to humble my pride."

In the valley of humbleness the waters of God's mercy gather. Those who flatter you usually have a selfish objective. Never bribe, or allow yourself to be bribed, with flattery. Everything that happens to us is a test of God, to see how we behave. And this was my first test in my guru's ashram. I wouldn't be Yogananda today if I hadn't passed those tests with Master. I said to the devotees, "Master is right. I don't know why he has made this decision; but I know that if I were to feel hurt or resentful, I would be wrong."

So what happened? One day, when I was busy with the work assigned to me, Kumar went to Master to complain about me, and said, "You put me in charge, but everybody goes to him!"

Master replied: "That is what I wanted you to learn. You coveted his position; he never wanted it. They all go to him because he is naturally suited for it. And why did you ask Yogananda to clean your shoes, which he did? When he was the leader, did he ever ask you to wipe his shoes?"

I learned a great lesson from that experience. I had been tested, and in that test I had won. I did not follow Kumar's ways of pettiness. I not only said, "Father, forgive him," but I learned to love him. And later he followed me. That is the way of Christ.

Love Those Who Abuse You

Jesus said that if anyone smites you, turn the other cheek; give him love. It is a very difficult philosophy, but I have lived that life, and I know it is the only one that works. The way to practice Christ's philosophy is to begin with your family. Right in your own home he is watching whether you are following his ideals or the tenets of evil. In family life, the test of spiritual existence is to remain always calm and understanding. If someone wants to fight, remain quiet. Can anyone keep up an argument if you don't talk back? If you are married and your spouse goes wrong, love him all the more. Pour kindness and love on the wrongdoer. If your love is not understood, your loved one may leave you; but to the last day of life he will remember that he is the one who wronged you. It is better to live in the hearts of those you love as one who loved them unconditionally than to live in their memory as one who was hateful.

It is natural to love others who love you and are kind to

you. But Jesus said to give love even to those who abuse you. I have lived that philosophy. I have learned to love people in spite of their behavior. For those who fail this test, it is their doom. The fault lies with self, not with others. No matter how perfect you try to make a place, you will see that there will always be somebody coming to interfere. That is the law of this world. How many have tried to shake me and disrupt the harmony of my work, but have not been able to do so. Why? Because I follow the laws of Christ. No one can hurt me if I don't wish to be hurt.

Jesus had the power to destroy his enemies. I have that power, too. I could hurt others with just a thought; but I have never done it. I have never used that power for revenge. As you travel the spiritual path, your will becomes fiery. God gives His devotees great power as they grow. He doesn't give it to everyone, because people would destroy one another. But as one advances spiritually, his power increases. If he is tempted to use it to hurt others, however, he will destroy himself. The misuse of his power will be his end.

Jesus said, "If I would, I could borrow twelve legions of angels from my Father." But what did he do instead? He observed quietness. He didn't even try to defend himself. That is the divine way to overcome your enemies. If in a spiritual organization you are mistreated, give love. I have lived that. Remain quiet; for as soon as you help the wrongdoer with one word of quarrel, you have soiled your own thoughts; you have failed in your own ideals. When there is a fight, at least two parties are involved. So there can be no fight with you if you refuse to participate.

The only way to conquer your enemy is to follow the example of Christ-love. God has the power to destroy us in an instant; but He does not do so, even though we give Him plenty of cause. He gives love for hate. And He expects us to follow that example. Each one of us must live that life. No one can quarrel with me. That is the way I have conquered. If you want to know Christ you have to be victorious in every test, to conquer the ego self even in little things.

How a Quarrelsome Man Was Changed

In New York there was a Hindu writer who couldn't stand anyone else. He was always fighting with somebody. One day he became quarrelsome with me. He started by arguing with my friends, and then burst through the door into my room and began insulting me. "How is business?" he asked, implying that I must be getting a lot of money from my lectures and classes.

It is not the money itself that is good or bad, but the use of it that makes it right or wrong. You can use it for good or for evil. Everything that has come to me I have given to God's work.

As this writer continued to insult me in the grossest terms, my friends were giving me looks that meant, "If you just say the word we will usher him out the door!" I was worrying that they might lose their self-control and throw him out. So when he made further accusations, I started answering, "Maybe you are right." I didn't say he *was* right; merely, "Maybe you are right."

After some time, I asked my friends to leave the room. The writer slumped back on his chair and said, "For the first time I have been licked."

"Don't think I am not going to give it to you," I replied. "Tell me, why is it that an intelligent man like you behaves in this way? You were only advertising your bad behavior, and showing what kind of person you are. I was concerned only for you, that my friends didn't harm you."

"You are right," he answered. "Tell me more."

So I said, "You know, vultures soar high in the sky, but their whole mind is on the carrion on the ground below. They wait their chance; then swoop down to pick at that dead meat. That is the way you behave. Wherever people are gossiping and fighting, there you love to go and pick at the bones. You are known everywhere for your bad behavior."

"What should I do?" he asked.

I answered: "Wherever there is gossip or quarreling, leave at once; don't contribute to the fight. If someone insults you, or calls you a devil, that doesn't make you one. He who calls you a devil is being used by the devil. The best thing under such circumstances is to remain quiet. If you refuse to fight, then who can fight with you? And even if such a person goes a step further and slaps you, and you do not respond, that slap will burn in his palm throughout his life. But if you fight back, he will only want to strike you twelve times harder."

If You Associate With Skunks, You Cannot Smell the Roses

Evil people don't want to change their ways. The best policy is to stay away from them. There is more goodness than evil in the world, and there are more good people than evil ones. But if you associate with skunks, you cannot smell the roses. It only seems that evil is greater than good, because evil is hard to forget. If someone hurts you deeply, you remember it. But instead of concentrating on that, you should think of all the good things about the person who has hurt you, and of all the goodness that you have in your life. Don't take notice of the insults people give you. And never let anything bring you to a decision to fight, nor give anyone the opportunity to fight with you. If you do, you are a party to it.

Numerous are the scars I bear for doing good. And if they mattered I wouldn't be here; I would be in the Himalayas. But such scars are worthwhile, for they help you to grow spiritually. Only those who live the life of Christ and meet his tests find him. To them Christ comes. He would never have come to me if I had indulged in pride or anger; or if I had slapped back when others treated me unjustly. People will treat you unjustly—that is the way of the world. This earth is not a perfect place. Consider the mosquito. You would think it would be satisfied with drinking your blood; but no, it also injects a little poison into your system, and sometimes carries germs that cause disease and even death. Some human beings also are like that.

Greater Than the Wounds of Battle Are Wounds to Your Soul

I used to have a terrible temper when I was a boy. But one day I said to myself, "If you want to do good on earth, you must not lose your temper." I promised myself that I would destroy that enemy of my soul; and to this day I have never hurt anyone out of anger or spite. Greater than the wounds of battle are wounds to your soul. Let not your soul be wounded by anger and hate. Though it is terrible to see people maimed and killed in this war, there is consolation that on one side they know they are immortal souls; only their bodies have been hurt. The scars of the body perish with the body, but wounds to the soul on the spiritual battlefield are terrible. They are more deadly in their torture. Those who lose the battle of life by succumbing to hatred and meanness will lose themselves. Those scars remain on the soul; they will go with you beyond the grave and last for incarnations. If you are an angry or hateful person, who knows? You may come again on earth for many incarnations, hurting people and being hurt by them.

Wrath and hatred accomplish nothing. Love rewards. You may cow down someone, but once that person has risen again, he will try to destroy you. Then how have you conquered him? You have not. The only way to conquer is by love. And where you cannot conquer, just be silent or get away, and pray for him. That is the way you must love. If you practice this in your life, you will have peace beyond understanding. And then you will know what Christ is. Why shouldn't you be victorious in this way? Conquer dark qualities that cause great suffering and wound the soul. Get rid of them; pulverize them. These enemies I have destroyed, and now I am free. So must you destroy them.

Don't Soil Your Soul With Those Who Are Mischief Makers

Remember this: Don't soil your soul by mixing with those who are mischief makers. Bless them. Give them love, and learn not to let them draw you down to their level. Refuse to be insulted by anyone. Just remain quiet. God could speak, and shake the world, but He doesn't, because to do so would be to use force to make us behave. He has given us freedom to act rightly or wrongly, and He is silently waiting for us to change our wrong behavior. That is the way of all those who love God. They suffer silently. If anyone causes them suffering, they say, "All right, if you feel happiness in hurting me, go on." It is a marvelous ideal. I never had such joy in my life as through this philosophy.

Similarly, whenever you are hurt, remain silent. And inside don't feel hatred or anger. If someone speaks to you in hurtful language, remain quiet; or say, "I am sorry if I have done something to offend you," and then remain silent. What can that person do then? I have practiced these things in my life. Nobody can make me fight, even if he slaps me. I would go down on my knees and ask pardon. How can such a person fight you if you don't want to fight? He who believes in Christ should not retaliate when someone is trying to "get his goat." The example of

Christ is that we are here to love one another. We must never retaliate. You have no idea what strength comes from such self-control and love. You behold humanity as little children— they don't know what they are doing.

If You Would Come to Me, Live the Life of Christ

Whoever would come to me must come only in that spirit of harmony and love. Those who are in tune with me, as some souls have been from the beginning, have never had a cross word with me. Mrs. R—is one of these. Many have trod on her with unkind speech, but I have never seen her cold or angry. And never have I seen her without a smile. As a result, her seat is reserved in heaven. That is the kind of example I live. And all those who come to me, I want them to live the life of Christ.

If I can save one soul out of this crowd, I have done something much more valuable than the "converting" of thousands of people. I am speaking to your souls. I know many of you who come here will be saved through the words I have spoken here. But you must practice these ideals in your life. You must live more by the Christ-principles, instead of just talking about them. When you live Christ's example, you will be able to see him. He is like a fragrance, all-pervading. But it is only through receptive souls that he works. If you call to Christ with all your heart, and if you have learned the lesson that you must never fail to live in humility and love, and to meditate deeply upon God, Christ will come to you. You can see him in flesh and blood, even as he has come to Babaji, St. Francis, and others who are in tune.

Dear ones, this has been my Christmas message to you, that you might know where Christ is today, and what he is doing, and how you may know him. Christ-love and harmony I send to you all this Christmas. Let no one rob you of your peace and love.

And remember to set aside a day before Christmas every year in observance of the spiritual birth of Christ. I know millions of people will follow this path when I am gone, because it is the true teaching of Christ.

Do Souls Reincarnate?

Self-Realization Fellowship International Headquarters,
Los Angeles, California, September 5, 1940

Our theme tonight is the reincarnation of souls. Why should we be interested in reincarnation? Isn't one lifetime sufficient to worry about? In one sense, it is good to think that we live only once. And if it is so, we must not waste our time, but live every minute grandly and beautifully, in a spiritual way. It is true that no individual has been born on earth twice as the same person. This is according to God's wishes; and since the beginning of time He has not changed His policy. Shakespeare wrote of "The undiscover'd country from whose bourne / No traveler returns."* Once the hand of fate writes that you must depart, the decree is final and you are gone; and there is the end of your present form. So in that sense there is no return, because regardless of your identity in your previous incarnation, you start this life anew, with no recollection of who you were before. Because of that limitation on our consciousness, we see this life as the beginning and the end.

It may seem to you that I am teaching a philosophy contrary to that of the Hindus. But I am dealing with truth from the relative standpoint of God's creation. I read from the book of God, and from that library I speak to you. This is the way I learned from my Guru [Swami Sri Yukteswar], and the way he learned from his Master [Lahiri Mahasaya]. Without direct perception you can't really know at all if something is true.

Again, relatively speaking, if we incarnate only once, then we see in nature a devastating, iconoclastic method. Some babies are stillborn, or die after only a little while, without having had a chance to experience life. People of all ages are stricken with suffering, disease, and death. There is no certainty about life. Every year when new models of cars come out, there are always

* Hamlet, III, i, 56.

266

some that are "lemons," having mechanical defects. Is life like this, too? that somehow in the process of nature some souls are made with firm, sound bodies and minds and others are accidentally given weak bodies and defective brains? Are we just factory productions, with no control over what happens to us? If this life is the beginning of the end, then I say it is a terrible injustice. It is ruthless. We don't want to think of a God who would create such a life—this world would just be God's great zoo, with us as merely experimental animals, His human guinea pigs. If God deliberately made specimens with great talent and others with poor mentality, some beautiful and others deformed, then there is no justice, and no use in religion. And if this is the only life, with no existence hereafter, then there is no point in making any effort beyond satisfying our selfish whims of the moment.

We Have Made a Mess of God's Creation

God did not give us reason only to question but never be satisfied. The very fact that we can question shows that there are certain processes of evolution going on that enable us to gain greater and greater knowledge. We may not fully understand, but we instinctively know this much: there must be some justice in the law that creates the infinite differences among human beings. Is there any clue? We find it in the law of reincarnation, with its corollary of karma, the principle of cause and effect. God at some time started all souls in a fairly uniform way. We all had equal goodness and potential within us; but owing to the misuse of our intelligence and free will, we have created terrible disorder and lack of equality, lack of uniformity, in life.

You can't generalize about people, because God has given every individual freedom to make his own choices. No matter who we are or what we are—and even though we are somewhat bound by circumstances of our karma, the effects of our past actions—we can do anything we want to in our minds. In the vault of the mind lies all the chains of bondage, as well as the keys to freedom. All actions originate in the mind. Trouble comes because people have so many crazy thoughts, and wrong thoughts lead to wrong actions. In this country, everyone wants to be or to have something different from everyone else. People do whatever comes into their minds. They get married and divorced as often as they wish; they do just as they please without any thought for their fellow beings, or even for their own highest welfare. We stagger at the wild way the world is moving — so many different ideals held by so many millions of people, contradicting and conflicting with one another. One person or group wants one thing, and another person or group wants the opposite. There are so many customs to bind us, so many philosophies to confuse us. I often say that we are all a little bit crazy and we don't know it, because people of the same craziness mix with their own kind. It is only when people differently crazy come together that they find out their own craziness.

God wants to make something beautiful out of this earth, but there are lots of things that have gone out of control because we have misused the freedom He gave us. It is we who have made a mess of this world; and it is we, through opportunities in this life and in new incarnations, who must better our own lot as well as that of the world we live in.

We Feel Mortal Because We Lack Continuity of Consciousness

We are so identified with this present life and its travails that it seems to us we are mortal; but only the body is mortal. Our real self, the soul, is immortal. We may sleep for a little while in that change called death, but we can never be destroyed. We exist, and that existence is eternal. The wave comes to the shore, and then goes back to the sea; it is not lost. It becomes one with the ocean, or returns again in the form of another wave. This body has come, and it will vanish; but the soul essence within it will never cease to exist. Nothing can terminate that eternal consciousness.

To know firsthand about reincarnation you would have to have a continuity of consciousness during the transition period of death, the afterdeath state, and the prenatal state in the mother's womb, from one incarnation to the next. It is possible. I have experienced that. In my autobiography* that is coming out you will read how I felt when I was born, that helplessness of being confined in an infant's body; for my soul was developed and awake even when I was in my mother's womb. My soul rebelled against the limitations.

When the memory of the past comes while the soul is still

* *Autobiography of a Yogi,* published in 1946.

closeted in a helpless body in the womb, the soul feels very frustrated. Those memories cause the baby to move around with life; it wants to get out. The soul feels powerless in that confinement, remembering breath, yet unable to breathe. It struggles to be freed from the prison of the mother's body. When the baby is about to be born, an intense prayer-thought goes out from that soul. That is why some infants are born with hands folded as in prayer. But as soon as the child is born, it forgets its past. Only if the consciousness is highly developed will memories of the past be retained.

For instance, if you take a person from one house to another, he remembers it, because he was conscious during that transition. He may very well remember not only the different houses he went to, but also the route. But suppose an Eskimo in Alaska sustains a head injury that causes unconsciousness and amnesia, and is put on a train and brought to Los Angeles for treatment. When he awakens, if asked whence he came, his reply would be, "I don't remember." Also, under the spell of hypnosis you can be made to feel like a different personality, so that you don't remember your real name. At death a state of coma comes, in which you forget everything. But do you forget everything? That is the question. Your mind may not remember, but your soul does. When you are highly advanced spiritually, your soul remains awake and conscious from one life to another.

We Don't Want to Remember Troubles of Past Lives

I would plant one thought in your mind: Without God-realization, you wouldn't care to know about your past lives, lest you learn of the terrible happenings that have taken place in those previous incarnations. Think of the troubles and sorrows you have had in this life, and then think of your many past incarnations. Do not believe for one moment that you have not had equally painful or worse experiences in those earlier lives. Would you want to remember all you have gone through from the beginning of your creation? No. Because to do so would so depress and discourage you that from the beginning you would have no strength, no will, to keep on.

For instance, suppose you died of cancer in your last life. Would you want to remember that suffering now? Your fear of that experience might produce the condition again. If you had continuity of remembrance, and could recall that as John in your last life you were poor and died of a terrible disease; and that now you have come back in this life as Jack, and again you are afflicted with poverty and sickness, you would be hopelessly discouraged. It would paralyze your will to succeed.

We don't want to remember things that are unpleasant or evil. That is why nature obscures our memories from one lifetime to the next. In going from one body to another, something happens that makes us forget our past existence. God is good to us in that respect.

Of course, if we were wonderful in our last life, we might want to remember that, especially when facing some trouble in this life. People who go to fortune tellers or others to try to learn about their past incarnations really want to be flattered. They don't want to hear that they were an average or an evil individual. They want to be told they were a great king, a famous person, or a saint. False prophets tell people what they want to hear because they want to increase their following and the contents of their coffers. In one of my classes there were three ladies, each of whom confided to me that a certain fortune teller had revealed to her that she was a reincarnation of Mary, Queen of Scots. I brought the three "Marys" together and asked them to tell me which was the real one!

Live Rightly Now, Regardless of What Lies Hereafter

If there is a life beyond, and if you have lived this one well, you will carry that goodness on into your next life. If you haven't lived well in this life, you will still be reaping the results of your wrong actions in the hereafter and in your next incarnation. Even if there were no life beyond, to have lived this one rightly is still far better and more satisfying than living to the end of life in an unhappy, miserable state as a result of desultory behavior and wrong actions.

Once an atheist came to talk with me. He told me he didn't believe in an afterlife; it was his conviction that when we die, that is the end of our existence. I said, "Do you know for certain? Suppose there *is* life after death? Isn't it more practical to live rightly now? Then, if there is a hereafter, you will be rewarded for your good actions. Even if there is no hereafter, you will find inner peace and happiness in this life if you live it well."

We Are Not Products of Blind Chance

We are not products of blind chance; we are highly intelligent creations. Therefore it stands to reason that some great intelligence must have created us. There is no doubt about this. And certainly an intelligent God would not bring us on earth with so many inequalities without giving us equal opportunities to forsake evil and express goodness. He would give us time in which to practice that goodness and reap the blessings of right action. What is the use of scriptures, or of following divine laws, if this life is the end? Where is the love and justice of God if the hereafter is eternal heaven for a chosen few and eternal torment of hell for the error-stricken? God's law of reincarnation shows that when a person is evil—and no one can be so wholly evil that he can be forever barred from the kingdom of God—he is given a chance to work out that evil and to turn to goodness. Evil is like a graft; it is not a permanent quality in man, for everyone is a child of God. Every night God reminds you in sleep that you are not the body and its habits. You are free, you are happy. The purpose of reincarnation is to provide opportunity for man to go on working out all his desires and expressing all that he wants to express, until he realizes his true nature as a child of God, and understands that reunion with God is the true object of all his seeking, the Goal of all mankind.

We seek religion because we want to do away with our suffering forever. Worldly methods are not the answer. God is the answer; true religion that brings God-realization is the answer. So now is the time to wake up; take the sword of wisdom and slash away all bad habits. Most of you know the Bible story about the servants who stopped their work while their master was away. Only one of them kept on with his duties. When the master returned unexpectedly, and saw what had taken place, he dismissed all the other workers and rewarded the one who had faithfully continued to fulfill his responsibilities. So remember, the Lord has gone away for a time, but He says, "I will come back again, and I will see whether you have done your work or not. I will see whether I find you sleeping, or building up material desires, or if you are dutifully tending the house of life I have given you to care for."

Present Tendencies Reflect Temperament of Past Lives

The most important thing to know about reincarnation is that this life is a new opportunity given by God to destroy the evil and cultivate the good that you have brought from past lives. Every good quality you have is a heritage of the past. And those bad tendencies that seem to be beyond your control—tendencies that are staying with you in spite of all your attempts to destroy them—are also from the past; otherwise they would not grip you from the beginning of your life. Of course, you have acquired some new qualities in this incarnation, but the salient temperament of your past life has been brought forward into this one. That is why you find yourself a helpless victim of certain idiosyncrasies. But you can overcome them. You must free yourself from them now, otherwise they will pursue you into another life. Death won't make an angel of you; self-effort will.

If you have an angry temper, rid yourself of it now. If you are peevish or moody, overcome it now. Some people get angry without cause, no matter how kind or thoughtful you are toward them. Others habitually indulge in bad moods and negative thoughts. The most practical use of our God-given reason is to analyze what aspects of our nature we have brought from the past, and to rid ourselves of the bad habits now.

It is certain the bad and good tendencies that follow one since birth were not acquired in this life. Whence could they have come other than as a carryover from past existences? If you study children, you can see something of their past incarnations reflected in their behavior. Why are some so smart and others less keen? Why are some children born with a great talent for music, or mathematics? They have had no opportunity yet to acquire their talent in this life. It was highly cultivated in a past life. In some children you can see an old soul talking to you. Others are very infantile and cry over every little thing; they lacked emotional maturity in their last life. Early child training is so important because you can easily recognize those latent tendencies that should be nurtured or discouraged. After a child reaches the age of about five, it becomes more difficult to distinguish his past-life tendencies from those traits he is acquiring from present influences and the increasing awakening of his free will in this life.

Any time I have found something hounding me from the past, I have cut it out. As a child I had a very fiery disposition. And then one day I resolved that I was not going to carry this anger with me any more. I said, "Get out!" and from that day forth, I never felt anger again. I don't tell people I am not angry; I let them think I am, because sometimes a little fire is necessary. But inwardly I couldn't be angry if I tried. I have never willingly hurt anyone. Why exist with bad habits that we will carry from one lifetime to the next? Why not overcome them? That is why we have come into this world.

Your Divine Nature Is What You Must Cultivate

Remember, you are a child of God. Your divine nature is what you must cultivate. Do not allow your happiness to be conditioned by anything material. That is the first lesson you learn in the hermitages in India. Here, you want everything to be comfortable and just so. You must be able to forego anything without its disturbing your happiness. Learn to be even-minded, regardless of the conditions that arise every day.

Do not even allow yourself to be limited to the consciousness that you are a man or a woman: You are a soul made in God's image. Most souls born as women in this incarnation were women in their previous existence. However, if in this life they manifest strong manly tendencies, it is probable that they were born in a male body before. If one is a man now and has strong manly tendencies, he will be born as a man again. If you want to be a man in your next incarnation, cultivate reason more, and masculine interests; and if you want to be a woman, cultivate feeling, and interests that are more feminine. The wisest course is to remember always, "I am neither man nor woman; I am Spirit." Then you will rid yourself of the limiting consciousness of both tendencies; you will realize your highest divine potential, whether you are incarnate as a man or a woman.

Seek the Answer to the Mystery of Life and Death

Three kinds of reincarnated souls are of particular interest to us: our friends and loved ones; great souls such as Abraham Lincoln, and spiritual giants; and our own selves. Every hundred years, about fifteen hundred million people die. They are gone and forgotten, except those we love, and the great men and women who leave a permanent mark on history. We keep "contact" with them through our thoughts of them, so in that way they still live with us. But where are they, physically speaking? Where are the God-realized saints and great world citizens of the past? God has shown me the subsequent or present incarnations of many of them. Some are playing similar active roles on earth today. But God doesn't like to have these things talked about too much. It takes away the charming mystery of His play and would cause the actors to be stilted in their new roles.

Perhaps we wonder most of all about those we love. Where are they? Why are they spirited away from us? A brief goodbye, and then they disappear behind the veil of death. We feel so helpless and sad; and there is nothing we can do about it. Though all souls are born into a family of seeming strangers, their parents love them; but they don't know why. Are these souls sent for us to love just to cause us hurt when they are snatched away? If this is so, isn't it foolish to love at all? Isn't it foolish to be attached? Because you don't know when your loved ones will be taken from you, or when death will take you from them. When someone is dying, though he cannot speak, a desire is expressed in his consciousness. He is thinking, "I am leaving my loved ones; will I ever see them again?" And those whom he is leaving behind also think, "I am losing him. Will he remember me? Will we meet again?" That part is natural. Now, these thoughts would not have been given to us if there were no answer to satisfy our souls. It is only because it is so difficult to know these truths that you don't find the answer.

When I lost my mother in this life, I promised myself that I would never again be attached to anyone. I gave my love to God. That first experience with death was very serious for me. But through it I learned much. I searched undaunted for months and years until I found the answer to the mystery of life and death, and whether or not souls reincarnate. To you it is only a thought, just a belief, because you have no proof. But I am not talking to you from mere belief. I found proof of life after death, and of reincarnation. Therefore I can speak truthfully to you. What I tell you, I have experienced. I found in this life many souls that I knew before. That is what I meant in my poem, "On Coming to the New-Old Land of America,"* when I wrote: "Sleeping memories, of friends once more to be, did greet me—sailing o'er the sea.... " I can recognize souls whom I knew before in other lifetimes. You may ask how. God has given me that power because I first sought and found Him.

How to Recognize Souls You Have Known Before

There is a way that you also can recognize those whom you have known before. For example, we may associate with some people day after day, yet never really know them or feel close to them. But there are others with whom we feel immediately a deep harmony the first time we meet. It is not anything physical. It is a memory of the past. Many, many people that I have met in this country, and in India and elsewhere, I have known before. The friendship is even stronger now. It was not finished in past lives, and so it had to continue to evolve in this life. Friendship is the highest form of love. As such, it is meant to evolve into the divine manifestation of God's eternal love. Friendship is the highest relationship, because in friendship there is no compulsion; it is born of the free choice of the heart. It is God calling souls back to unity in Him. If you can be a friend to all, unconditionally, that is divine love.

Not many in this world find true friends; mere acquaintances are not to be confused with real friends. There is no attachment in true friendship, nor is it founded in selfish human love. It is an unconditional relationship between two or more souls: they may be unrelated, or family members, or marriage partners. It is best formed between souls who are seeking God or who have found God. Such was the friendship that existed between Christ and his disciples. Otherwise, relationships develop into attachment and remain on the plane of human love, taking the soul away from supreme friendship with God.

True friendship may be developed between woman and woman, man and man, or man and woman. The important consideration is that it be based upon soul qualities, not worldly qualities or attractions of the flesh. This can come only when you free yourself from the consciousness that you are a man or a woman.

* In *Songs of the Soul.*

If you are seeking such friends, pray to God: "Lord, lead me to those who are friends of the past, that I may continue with them the friendship that was interrupted through separation by death. Send such friends to me, because I want to help them with my thought of Thee." That is a wonderful ideal, isn't it? To have friendship not for idle talk and useless pastimes, but to develop the ultimate friendship with God. Only on that plane of sincere friendship will you find lasting happiness with any other soul.

Don't engage in too many socials. They are all right once in a while, but frequent socializing takes up too much valuable time. Enjoy divine thoughts with your friends. Use your time for God. If you find souls who will share that goal, then you can drink God together from the chalice of divine friendship. The highest duty God has given you is to develop His consciousness in yourself and to help true friends to do the same. So long as life sweetly sings with God, it will bring happiness to you and to others. Friends that harmonize spiritually with you are therefore very important.

No matter what difference of opinion there is between you and such friends, there is always understanding and communication. In that relationship, regardless of differing views, you have mutual respect and cherish your friendship above everything else. True friendship established in God is the only relationship that is lasting.

On one occasion, while I was traveling on a train, my attention was drawn to a man who was drinking and playing cards. There came a strange feeling that I must talk with him, that I had known him before. I sat nearby for a little while, and I felt the call of his heart. As I got up and passed down the aisle, he looked at me and said, "Can I talk with you?" We sat in a small empty compartment and talked for an hour. Then I told him, "God's blessing falls upon you." He cried and said, "Never will I follow evil ways again." Several years later we met in Kansas City. He stood to introduce me before my lecture, and right before the whole audience he shed tears and said: "The greatest blessing of my life was one hour spent in talking to Swami Yogananda on the train."

I am not speaking about myself, but to show how strong is friendship of the past. So, whenever you meet people, be watchful. Notice your first reaction to them. This tells you much about whether you knew those individuals before. It is not an emotion. When you feel in your heart a deep harmony with another person, then you know that you knew each other before.

Help Enemies of the Past Through Love and Forgiveness

Of course, I have also met some enemies of the past, but mostly friends. I remember another life centuries ago, when someone I loved very much was inimical to me and hurt me; but I triumphed over him. I met him again in this life, and again he became treacherous. But I have tried only to help him. He shall pursue me no more.

Forgiveness is more powerful than revenge. I have forgiven everyone who has knowingly or unknowingly tried to annoy or hurt me. I want nothing for myself any more. I have found such joy in my heart by giving everything to God and doing everything for Him. Those who do evil stew in their own evil. They can't really hurt you unless you let them. Even our enemies are all part of the tests of life. When an evil person tries to persecute you, remember that he has probably tried to harm you in some way in the past also. If you think of that hurt and how terrible that person is, that is a great mistake. When you give out hateful thoughts, that person receives them and hates you twice as much. Also, hate attracts, as does love. You don't want the magnet of your hate to draw your enemies near you. Never hate anyone. Love and forgiveness have a healing effect on yourself and on your enemies. And be grateful for all the wonderful friends God has given to you.

Never try to impose yourself, to force your friendship, on anyone. I give my love to all; and to those souls who are in harmony with me, I give my friendship unconditionally. When I receive the same, I rejoice, because in that friendship is the manifestation of God.

Seek God: He Will Show You Glimpses of Your Past

I also recall my own past incarnations, beyond all doubt. In the Tower of London, for example, I found many places that I remembered from a past life, places the present caretakers didn't know anything about. Because I was once an Englishman, in my childhood in India I preferred to eat with a fork and knife. When my family asked why I wanted to use these instead of my fingers, as is the Indian custom, I said, "I remember this from the past." They didn't understand, but I knew I had eaten in this fashion before. Such glimpses of past lives will be given to you as you advance spiritually. God will show them to you. And when you will be less curious about such matters, and your mind is filled only with God, you will know even more.

Remember, you are sent on earth to strive to destroy the bad tendencies and habits you have brought over from previous lives, and to avoid creating any more in your present incarnation, so that you may find God. Then you can walk out of this life saying, "Lord, my life's purpose is fulfilled. I don't have to come back again, unless You want me to come to serve You." As Christ said, "Him that overcometh will I make a pillar in the temple of my God, and he shall go no more out."*

You should seek God now; don't wait incarnations to find Him. He can be known in this life—*now*. And the more quickly you know Him, the better off you will be. You are foolish if you don't seek Him, because there is no other way that you will be satisfied. Having Him, you shall have everything.

If You Make the Effort, You Will Find God

God can never be given to you by somebody else. Why would He come to you unless you make your own effort? You must make love to God with all your heart, with all your mind, with all your soul. You must show that you want Him one hundred percent, and then He will come. The desire for God that you feel in this life you have surely had in your past life. This I can truthfully tell you. But it doesn't necessarily follow that you have the same degree of enthusiasm for God now. You must nourish that desire if it is to grow and be fulfilled. You don't know when you will be snatched away from this life and have to start all over again as a helpless baby. Years will go by before you feel again the desire for the Infinite.

How many of you make a sincere spiritual effort? You listen to my talks, but do you really try to know God? If you would sincerely try, you would find Him. It takes time and persistent faith: "Lord, I *know* You are listening to my prayer." If you stop

* Revelation 3:12.

calling to Him because you think He is not listening, that is your end.

You are walking on this earth as in a dream. Our world is a dream within a dream; you must realize that to find God is the only goal, the only purpose, for which you are here. For Him alone you exist. Him you must find. And Him you can know by continuously seeking Him; by steadfastness in your mind, harmony in your life, evenness in your temperament; by finding fault not with others but with yourself; by schooling yourself in the path of wisdom; by being humble, ever loyal to your friends and benefactors, appreciating the sincerity of all hearts, cooperating always with good and resisting evil, helping others, giving strength and understanding along the way—this is the royal way of living, the real way that leads to God. The recognition of the world doesn't matter; seek the approval of your own consciousness, and in that you will have the recognition of God. To be self-satisfied and make little or no effort to improve is to become stagnant. But to try unceasingly to progress, until you are sure that you are with God, is the way to live.

When God Comes, the Veils of Delusion Drop Away

This earth is a most imperfect place. When prosperity comes, war breaks out and sets mankind back centuries again. But don't take the ups and downs of this life too seriously. No matter what happens, inwardly say: "It is all right. I am only dreaming in God's dream—nothing can touch me. I am happy. Nothing holds me. I am ready every minute, Lord, to walk out of this dream, or to remain to do Your will." Then you will be free. That is a wonderful thought.

Anything you do with the thought of God is much different than the same experience without Him. The other day I was taken to see a movie, and the first thing I knew, I was in *samadhi*. Someone asked, "Aren't you seeing the picture?" "Yes," I said, "it is all movies—a movie within a movie." The theater, every motion, the people sitting around me—I could see them all as pictures on the vast screen of cosmic consciousness.

No matter what you are doing, when God comes, there is just complete intoxication. The veils of delusion drop away, and you know the answer to anything you want to know. In this state of consciousness I have seen far into the past and into the future. Generally I keep my eyes closed to these things, but when I am interested, I see them. And I see into the souls of those who come. No one can deceive me. I know each one inside out, but I never speak of this; I am not interested in the evil side of people, only in their good.

I don't encourage crowds of curiosity seekers, but I do encourage true souls in their individual romance with God. Such joy, such happiness! To have the love and protection of the Divine is the highest of all achievements, and you will find it here by making a little effort.

"I Come Only to Tell You of That Joy of God"

Of my own free will I give my time to serve you all. My reward is those souls who really love God and are in tune with this work of Self-Realization. I am not bound or attached to anything; any time I wish to walk out I can do so, for I have no illusions of name and fame—which only means to be beautifully eulogized and then buried. Whoever comes, freely I give of my time and my realization. And if you would receive, receive it. I am only too glad to give to you, for I know how hard it is to be without the Infinite Beloved. No matter where I am, you will receive from me that friendship and help.

The tiger of death is after you, and you must reach Home. If you value your souls, you will make the effort. Study the *Self-Realization Lessons*, practice the techniques, meditate deeply; and if you sincerely persist for seven years with intense concentration, you will have such spiritual satisfaction in your life that you will never forsake or forget this path.

So don't wait. I come only to tell you of that joy. And I ask nothing of you but that you tune in with me, so that I may give you that joy which is in me even as I talk—that joy of God. It is so personal and sacred, even to speak of it is sacrilegious; but He knows I do not say it to extol myself, but to help you. He knows I love Him above all else, and I know He loves me.

Hold to the thought that this earth life is like a motion picture. It is not real. To think it is real is to doubt God, and to be shattered by torments and death. But in the movies there is no actual life and death in the play on the screen, merely electrical shadows moving here and there. The bullet that is fired and the man who is shot—both are nothing but electrical images. A long time ago I went to see a movie about Abraham Lincoln. I was watching that great hero, and deeply appreciating his noble deeds, when suddenly he was killed. I felt very sad. But then I thought, "Why feel sorrow? I will wait until the picture starts again and he is 'reborn.'" So I sat through the showing until I had again felt the inspiration of his life. Then I said, "Now let me leave, before he dies."

This life is like that. Many whom I loved and have missed, God has shown to me again. So I sorrow no more. He is a wonderful God; you must know Him as I know Him. Once you see this life as God's dream, or cosmic motion picture, you will say: "There is no birth or death or tragedy. I am not afraid of these delusive changes made of light and shadows, for I am Thine immortal child. I have seen life and its dramas played well. It is an interesting play, but no matter what my role in it, I am Thy child, eternally one with Thee, O Lord."

Where Are Our Departed Loved Ones?

First Self-Realization Fellowship Temple,
Encinitas, California, August 28, 1938

Science has not created or invented anything; it has only discovered what is already existing in God. If we put our minds to it, we can similarly resolve the mysteries about which I am going to speak today.

When I talk to you about these things, it is not from what I have read or studied, but from my own direct experience of Truth. You may think it strange, but when I am speaking, I am at that moment seeing whatever I am describing to you. And why not? Through an X-ray machine, you can see the skeletal frame and all of the organs of the body. Certainly the human consciousness has much greater powers of perception than any machine. The little brainless radio can penetrate the ether and receive messages broadcast from miles away. Our consciousness is far more sensitive than this when we learn to finely tune it. Behind the body and all the thoughts identified with it is the subtle inner world, which is vitally linked with this world. You can behold this inner world when you have advanced spiritually.

The Unperceived World of Thought

We are accustomed to perceiving and responding primarily to gross manifestations that can be picked up by the senses. For the most part, we remain unaware of the subtle forces around us. Yet every thought we think sets up a particular subtle vibration. Do you know that because of this you can't hide from others what you really are? If you have done wrong, you know it. Even though you think you may be hiding it, the consciousness of having done wrong is present in your thoughts. People will find you out, because those thought vibrations will be reflected in some way in your behavior. The same of course is true of good thoughts. When you mentally utter the word "God," and keep on repeating that thought within, it sets up a vibration that invokes the presence of God.

Thoughts are so subtle that no instrument has been able to record them.* This is why we have voices; they enable us to convey our thoughts. But if you advance spiritually and cultivate deep calmness within, you will be able to feel and read the thoughts of others. When you are disturbed or restless, your mind radio is so out of tune it cannot receive their mental messages. If your consciousness is always fixed on externals—the body, desires, what somebody else has or is doing—it will never be aware of the subtle activities that are going on within and around you.

The five senses are extremely limited. The eyes can behold only certain vibrations of light. The ears can receive only certain rates of sound vibrations—any vibration too high or too low is not perceived. Unheard by most people, the whole universe is sending forth music: the great sound of *Aum* or Amen, the Holy Comforter, emanating from all creation. "They seeing see not; and hearing they hear not, neither do they understand."† Thus Jesus referred to the limited nature of the senses.

Man is the inventor of instruments that can perform miraculous tasks he himself cannot do. The microscope gives him a supersense through which he can see many things invisible to the naked eye. The radio has made available more knowledge about the world than any other modern invention.‡ But remember, it is man's mind that has discovered the universal principles which made possible the microscope and radio. It is the power of the mind you must cultivate. When you develop spiritually, your sight and hearing—each one of your senses—become so refined that you can perceive all the subtleties of which I speak. You will perceive the vibrations of thought, which are the true essence of the gross vibrations to which the limited physical senses are attuned.

---

* Brain waves resulting from thoughts may be recorded, but not the thoughts themselves.

† Matthew 13:13.

‡ This talk was given in 1938. The subsequent development of television has vastly increased the scope of world communication.

You will be able to see right through others' outer pretenses and perceive their thoughts. But it won't influence your attitude against those persons. You won't judge them, because you will understand them. God knows all the thoughts—good and bad—of every human being; yet He loves all His children just the same. If you are always looking at the world through a blue glass, everything will appear to be blue. So if you look through a blue glass of prejudice or hatred or emotion, you cannot behold people or conditions as they really are. As soon as you become ruffled by such feelings, your voice becomes harsh and you feel antagonistic and spiteful. But when you are calm and at peace within, you love everyone and feel friendly toward all. This is the harmony God intended for His creation. You should develop changelessness, even-mindedness, in this changing world; then the evil thoughts of others will not disturb or influence you. You will begin to feel the true subtle nature of human beings and the universe in which we live, and become more aware of the fourth dimension.

Where Is Heaven?

The fourth dimension is the sphere of lifetrons,* which can be perceived only through the sixth sense of intuition. As your senses become spiritually refined, they become intuitive, and you become more and more conscious of that other world. And where is that other world? Many people think it is far off in the skies, but this is not so. The fourth dimension, the astral world —heaven—is just behind the gross vibration of this physical realm. On the astral planets, life is not dependent upon breath or food or oxygen. This is not a fantasy of an overwrought imagination; it is the finding of my own experience. But one must develop spiritually in order to experience and understand the higher forces and laws of life. One such exalted soul was Trailanga Swami.† He used to float on the Ganges for days together, and sometimes would remain under the water for several hours or days. And why not? When you understand life, you know that it is more than its physical components. Realized

---

* The astral world. (See glossary.)

† More about the life of this saint may be found in Paramahansa Yogananda's *Autobiography of a Yogi,* chapter 30.

souls can operate the laws of the higher realms even though incarnate in a physical body. Because you don't see these things, you think they can't be true. But you must realize that your realm of experience is but an infinitesimal part of the Lord's creation.

We Are Made of God's Thoughts, Which Death Cannot Destroy

You are beholding only the middle of life; you do not see the beginning or the end. It isn't even reasonable to assume that death is the end—that we who are so intelligent and full of life cease to exist as soon as we fall asleep in death. The whole human being is a cluster of the creative thoughts and consciousness of God, which physical death cannot destroy. If death were the end, then there is no God, and there are no realized masters—it is all a pack of lies. The great ones wouldn't urge you to become better, for what would be the use if, good or bad, we are all junked at the end of life? What would be the value of the scriptures? Why should good men try to be even better? There would be no justice whatsoever if this present existence is all there is to each individual life. What of those souls who lived only a few years, or lived in blind or crippled bodies?

Know the Right Way to Find Your Loved Ones

True spiritualism is a wonderful science. It enables us to know that there is a life beyond this world, and that all of our loved ones do, indeed, continue to live on, though they have shed the physical body. But the modern practice of spiritualism has ruined the meaning of the real search for knowledge of the spirit world. Many who believe themselves to be spiritualists don't really know what they are talking about. Some have a little understanding, but too often they are victims of their own imagination; or worse, they become subconsciously possessed by disembodied tramp souls* seeking a human vehicle. These tramp souls delude and misguide the medium and, indirectly, those who seek his counsel.

Once I was sitting with some students in a gathering where a gypsy was present. Everyone was flocking around this fortune-

* See pages 289-90.

teller. I was quietly observing her. Soon I realized she was not actually answering what they asked her, but rather some queries she was cleverly putting to them. The students urged me to have my fortune told. The room was rather dark, so the gypsy couldn't see me too clearly. In a high squeaky voice I asked, "When will I divorce my husband?" She quickly responded, "Right away." Then I stood up, and she saw my trousers below my robe. "You deceived me!" she exclaimed angrily. Supposedly she was reading our minds; but I had read hers. Because of my long hair she had thought I was a woman, and that is why I tested her with that question.

So in spiritualism, as in any other field, there are some frauds; and among those that do have some psychic development, there are many who are well-intentioned but whose psychic powers are not guided by wisdom and Self-realization. In any case it is unwise, and can be dangerous, to toy with the spirit world through seances and mediums. You cannot contact saints through such channels; and if any spirits are invoked, they will be for the most part from the lower astral realms. But if you are truly sincere, it is possible by meditation and spiritual development to contact departed loved ones or great saints.

The Astral World Has Many Spheres

When we awaken in the morning, we find we are exactly the same as before we went to sleep. Similarly, when we and our loved ones awaken in the astral world after death, we are exactly the same; only generally we may be more youthful in appearance and free of disease.

We don't become angels merely by the instrument of death. If we are angels now, we will be angels in the hereafter. If we are dark, negative personalities now, we will be the same after death. Just as there are slums and beautiful parts of the country here, so it is in the other world. According to the way you have lived your life on earth—whether you have lived a good, pure life, or a mean, ugly one—you go to a better or a darker region in the astral world. Jesus spoke of these different regions: "In my Father's house are many mansions."*

* John 14:2.

The astral planes are of differing atmospheres, or vibrations, and each soul that passes on from this earth is attracted to whichever atmosphere is in harmony with its own particular vibration. Just as fish live in the water, worms in the earth, man on the earth, and birds in the air, so souls in the astral world live in whichever sphere is best suited to their own vibration. The more noble and spiritual a person is on earth, the higher the sphere to which he will be attracted, and the greater will be his freedom and joy and experience of beauty.

On the astral planets, beings are not dependent upon air or electricity in order to exist. They live on variously colored rays of light. There is more freedom in the astral world than in the physical world. There are no bones to break, because there are no solids there; everything is composed of light rays. And every-thing takes place by the power of thought. When souls in the astral want to produce a garden, they merely will it, and the garden comes into being. It remains as long as it is willed to. When a soul wants the garden to disappear, it goes away.

Communication With the Astral
a Secretly Guarded Science

Communicating with souls in the astral world is not a simple accomplishment. It is a science secretly guarded by nature. God does not want us to limit our love to the members of our family, but to learn to give that same love to the whole world. It is to teach us this that the members of our family are taken away one by one; thus we learn to turn our love to others. But if we love purely and unselfishly, and develop spiritually, we can learn the secret science of maintaining a link with our loved ones after death.

The human heart is so strong, and often so unreasonable! A boy meets a girl; they fall in love with each other. They grow up, marry, have children, and think, "These are mine." Possessive-ness makes people forget they were strangers before they met, that death will sever their present relationship, and that the children they call their own have only been given to them to look after during one lifetime. When their loved ones are snatched away by death, they grieve and wonder what life is all about.

The attachment of human affection is such that losing our loved ones brings a severe longing in the heart, and often creates rebellious thoughts within. Though I was still a little boy, I knew deep in my consciousness, long before her death, that my mother was to go. When she passed on, I cried and cried. I searched everywhere, but I couldn't find her. "Divine Mother," I prayed, "if You are here, You must answer me. Why did You make me love my mother so much, and then take her away? Was it to punish and torture me?" The answer came when the Cosmic Mother said, "Who gave you mother, who gave you father? It was I who gave you your beautiful mother." When I realized it was because of God that I had such a wonderful mother, I thought, "God alone holds the key to this mystery of life," and I began to search deeply within and to pray. Divine Mother answered and told me why my mother was taken away: "It is I who have watched over thee, life after life, in the tenderness of many mothers! See in My gaze the two black eyes, the lost beautiful eyes, thou seekest!"

After I found Divine Mother, I also found my earthly mother again, in the astral world, and talked to her. Such communication is possible. You can convert yourself into a broadcasting instrument or a receiving set. If you seek a departed loved one by very strongly and continuously meditating on that soul, you will receive an answer. But if your desire is not strong enough, your restless thoughts will disturb your meditative concentration. If your thoughts are running hither and thither when you are broadcasting your heart's message to a soul, your broadcast will be short-circuited. You must have a tremendous desire and powerful concentration in order to contact a soul who has gone into the other world. And you must send your thoughts to that soul continuously. Also, the one to whom you are broadcasting must be developed enough to receive and be able to respond to your call. It is easiest to contact souls that are on your level or plane of consciousness, and with whom you have had a deep affinity and close relationship. Communing with highly evolved souls requires much more powerful concentration.

The Saints Cannot Come to the Spiritually Unprepared

You cannot tune in with great saints unless you are spiritually receptive. If the person who is invoking the presence of a holy personage is not spiritually ready, that saint cannot communicate with him. Suppose you are invoking the soul of Jesus Christ, or Krishna, or Buddha. Divine ones such as these won't come until your consciousness has become so refined through meditation that you can receive them. The vibratory power of their manifestation is so intense it could burn the body and brain of one not attuned. I have seen these *avatars* and many saints; you can, too, when your own spiritual vibration becomes very strong. These divine souls are all present in the ether—no one has ever become nothing after leaving the physical body. They respond to your prayers and bless you. They live in the astral world unless they have reincarnated on earth or on other higher planets where the evolution of man is further advanced.

So you should develop yourself. Strive to be more in tune with the divine ones, such as Christ, Krishna, and the great Gurus of Self-Realization. If in deep attunement you inwardly see one of these great ones, beneficial changes will begin to take place within you, through their blessings. These are not simple matters we are discussing.

You must never be negative—that is, never sit quietly and make your mind blank in order to become "open" to messages from the other world. This practice makes one receptive to tramp souls that are roaming in the ether, seeking human vehicles for expression and experience in the physical world. These souls are of low type, with strong attachment to this world, which prevents them from natural adjustment to the better life in the astral world. Instead of remaining in the astral world, they hover between the astral and physical planes and are occasionally successful in possessing someone whose mind is weak and dwells on a low level of consciousness. The "devils" that Jesus cast out* were tramp souls.

The man Hickman, who murdered a little girl many years ago, was possessed. I have studied him thoroughly. He was a good boy, but abnormal sexual drive and abuse weakened his brain, and a tramp soul took possession of his body. This is the reason he killed the girl in such a vicious way. Souls trapped in

* "When the even was come, they brought unto him many that were possessed with devils: and he cast out the spirits with his word, and healed all that were sick" (Matthew 8:16).

human forms not their own usually destroy the brain — the personality—of the one they have possessed. This is why many mediums go wrong. Good departed souls do not possess you; they do not even come without a proper invitation—one that is issued from a high level of consciousness.

In order to draw good souls, you must have deep concentration and lift your consciousness to a pure, spiritual plane. In the superconscious state, you can consciously direct the trend of your experiences. So if you are meditating, you are on a high plane of thought; tramp souls, or negative or evil souls living on the lower astral planes, cannot get in touch with you.

One who is highly developed, and has mastered all levels of consciousness, can see into all realms of the astral world, high and low; and he can spiritually help the souls on those planes to work out some of their karma. That other world is as real to me as this one. Sometimes when I sleep on my left side, I see all kinds of dark souls dancing around. I bless them, and they go away. I rarely see such souls when I sleep on my right side, because the right side of the body is the positive side. There is a stronger flow of divine life current there, whose spiritual vibration serves as a screen blocking off negative forces. This is why, during practice of the Self-Realization *Aum* Technique,* the meditator is taught to concentrate on the cosmic vibration in the *right* ear.

When you are thinking of God or meditating upon God, or concentrating at the Christ Consciousness center at the point between the eyebrows, no astral beings can intrude on your consciousness. God is deeply respected in the other region— even by lower astral beings, who cannot stand high spiritual vibrations.

Technique of Sending Thoughts to Departed Souls

To send your thoughts to loved ones who have passed on, sit quietly in your room and meditate upon God. When you feel His peace within you, concentrate deeply at the Christ center, the center of will at the point between the two eyebrows, and broadcast your love to those dear ones who are gone. Visualize at the

---

* Taught in the *Self-Realization Fellowship Lessons. (See glossary.)*

Christ center the person you wish to contact. Send to that soul your vibrations of love, and of strength and courage. If you do this continuously, and if you don't lose the intensity of your interest in that loved one, that soul will definitely receive your vibrations. Such thoughts give your loved ones a sense of well-being, a sense of being loved. They have not forgotten you any more than you have forgotten them. There is still the dim memory in their consciousness of the loved ones they have left behind.

When you want to feel a response from such souls, concentrate at the heart center.* When you concentrate deeply enough, they may first appear in dreams. It is possible for them to do so. Sometimes you may have the same significant dream several times. So not all dreams are meaningless. If your mind is calm and attuned, you will know someone is trying to get in touch with you through that dream. As you develop spiritually, your loved ones may appear to you in visions in meditation. And when you are very highly developed, you can behold those souls right here in front of you. St. Francis used to see Jesus Christ in the flesh every night. But you must be really advanced before you can have such an experience. If you deeply meditate on God, He will show you all of these things.

Instead of weeping and feeling a sense of loss after the death of those who are dear to you, always send them your love. By doing so you can help the progress of their souls, and they can help you. Never drag them down by unreasonable feelings of selfish attachment and sorrow. Just say to them, "I love you."

Send your thoughts of love and goodwill to your loved ones as often as you feel inclined to do so, but at least once a year— perhaps on some special anniversary. Mentally tell them, "We will meet again sometime and continue to develop our divine love and friendship with one another." If you send them your loving thoughts continuously now, someday you will surely meet them again. You will know that this life is not the end, but merely one link in the eternal chain of your relationship with your loved ones.

* The *anahata chakra*, the subtle dorsal center and seat of feeling in the body. See footnote on page 4.

We Can Find Loved Ones Who Have Been Reborn

Ordinary souls remain in the astral world for a karmically predetermined time, and then reincarnate on earth. Highly advanced souls can remain in the astral heaven as long as they wish. But what if the souls of some that you loved are reborn on earth while you are still seeking them? As you go on sending them your love, they will feel your thoughts. When they are asleep—that is, when their conscious mind is asleep and the subconscious is awake—they will receive your love. In time, those souls will be aware of the vibrations you are sending them, and they will remember and understand. Furthermore, you will surely be attracted to one another again, and will feel the closeness of your previous relationship.

If you are spiritually developed, you will consciously recognize souls you have known before, just as I recognized my master, Swami Sri Yukteswar, when we met in this life. He had been broadcasting to me. This is why Master was often in my thoughts, and how I came to know him long before I ever met him in this life. Many times I had seen him in dreams and in meditation. When I was sleeping or meditating I got the vibrations he was broadcasting to me. So when I met him, I recognized him at once. Similarly, when your loved ones are reborn on earth, if your love for them is strong they will be brought back to you. They will be drawn into your life once again, in this incarnation or the next.

Generally, in each new incarnation, nature makes us forget the particular personalities and relationships of souls we knew in previous lives. What a blessing! Imagine how confusing it would be if you remembered all the roles you and your loved ones played in past lives. You wouldn't know which mother, father, spouse, or child to love. God prevents this chaos by dimming our memory so that we are free to perfect the relationships of our present incarnation.

True Love Draws Souls Together Life After Life

But even though we may not remember anything specific about previous-life relationships, love between souls—or even a deep attraction of hate—draws those souls to one another life after life. This is why, in this incarnation, you have felt strongly attracted to certain souls and not to others. You always feel naturally drawn to those you knew before. A close friendship is impossible with anyone you have not met in former lives. This is a fact. When you think of someone as a friend, it is because you have known that soul before, and your previous relationship makes you feel closer to that person. By reaching out to know and understand others we should increase our treasure house of friends and loved ones from one incarnation to another.

When in this life you are attracted to souls whom you like, but with whom you have quarrels and misunderstandings—as sometimes happens between family members—and you have to strive constantly to get along with one another, it means that in your previous life your relationship was half as friends and half as enemies. An example of this was Judas, who betrayed Jesus. Judas had known Christ in other lives, and was destined to be in that wonderful family of disciples. Even though he betrayed Christ, Jesus loved him unconditionally, as the mother loves even a wicked son. Jesus knew all of the twelve disciples before, and they had known him. This is why there was instantaneous attraction and acceptance. Lord Krishna similarly recognized his most beloved disciple: "O Arjuna, many births have been experienced by Me and by thee. I am acquainted with them all, whereas thou rememberest them not."*

The relationship between disciple and guru is the most beautiful because it is unconditional and everlasting: through all incarnations they are in touch with one another. And at the time of death, the guru comes to guide the disciple through the transition from the physical body to the astral heaven.

I have met in this life many, many souls I have known before, and they have also recognized me. In previous lives they were mine, and I was theirs. Most of those who have come to me in this life are souls I knew before.

We may remember not only people we knew and loved in previous lives, but places as well. When I came through London on my way back from India, I visited many localities where I had been in a former life. The memory of those places was stored in my consciousness. You may have had similar experiences: a new

---

* Bhagavad Gita IV:5.

area seems so familiar to you that you feel certain you have been there before.

The Soul and Its Joy Last Forever

There is so much more to life than what the ordinary man perceives and feels. Life and death hold no more mysteries for me. I know that I and all souls are ever-living manifestations of the one Life, God. The physical body and its comforts and pleasures do not last, but the soul and its joy last forever. I don't care about my body anymore. When you have finished your dinner, the plate no longer has a purpose. I am interested only in Spirit, who can make a thousand Yoganandas if He wants to. The body, which is so dear to the ordinary man, is no longer important when you find God. I never pray for my body. I have given it back to the Lord. His love is so great, it has taken away all attachment to this physical form. In His love all my desires have been satisfied many times over. I want nothing more. In my heart I can find but one wish: "May Thy love shine forever on the sanctuary of my devotion, and may I be able to awaken Thy love in all hearts." This is my only desire.

Dear ones, don't waste your time. You are wasting time, and you know it. I speak frankly and freely to you, because I have nothing to gain from you except your own highest spiritual welfare. You can't reach happiness or God by anyone else's assurance. You have to work for it yourself.

Wherever I find souls who are receptive, I try to speak to their minds. To those who are not interested I say little, because they don't want to listen at all. But those who are sincerely seeking God I try to reach through their thoughts, and draw them to Him. In God, you and your loved ones have existence and joy everlasting.

Reflections on Love

Written in 1940s

Love is a golden mansion in which the King of Eternity homes the entire family of creation. And at God's command, love is a mystic fire that can melt the grossness of the cosmos into the invisible substance of Eternal Love.

Like a river, love flows continuously through humble, sincere souls; but it bypasses the rocks of egotistic, selfish, sense-bound souls, because it cannot pass through them.

Love is an omnipresent spring with countless founts. When one of its heart-openings is clogged with the debris of wrong behavior, we find it surging from some other heart. But to think love dead in any heart is ignorance of the omnipresence of love. One should never block with wrong actions the channel of love in his own soul. Then he will drink with countless mouths of soul-feeling from the divine fountain of love coursing endlessly through all open hearts.

Love may exist in the presence of passion, but when passion is mistaken for love, love flies away. Passion and love together are a bittersweet mixed drink that produces some joy, but mostly an after-sorrow. When pure love is quaffed, the taste for passion loses itself in the sweetness of true feeling.

Droplets of love sparkle in true souls, but in Spirit alone is found the sea of love. To expect perfection in human love is folly unless one seeks to perfect that love by feeling within it God's love. Find God's love first; then, with His love, love whatever or whomever you like.

Do not limit your love to one being, however lovable, to the exclusion of all else. Rather, with the love you feel for the one you love most, love all beings and all things, including the one you love. When you try to imprison Omnipresent Love in the form of one soul, it will escape and play hide-and-seek with you until you find It in every soul. Increase the intensity and spiritual quality of the love you feel for one or a few souls, and give that love to all. Then you will know what Christ-love is.

Love is wonderfully blind, for it dwells not on the flaws of the beloved, but loves unconditionally through eternity. When dear ones are parted by death, mortal memory may fail to recall the pledges of love they made; but true love never forgets, nor does it die. For incarnations, it escapes from the heart of one form and enters that of another, pursuing the beloved, fulfilling all its promises until the emancipation of those souls in Eternal Love.

Grieve not for lost love, whether it is through death or the fickle fluctuations of human nature. Love itself is never lost, but just plays hide-and-seek with you in many hearts; that in pursuing it you might find its ever greater manifestations. It will keep hiding from you, and disappointing you, until you have quested long enough to find its abode in the One who resides in the deepest recesses of your own soul, and in the heart of everything. Then you will say:

"O Lord, when I resided in the house of mortal consciousness, I thought I loved my parents and my friends; I fancied I loved birds, beasts, possessions. But now that I have moved into the mansion of Omnipresence, I know it is Thee alone I love, manifested as parents, friends, all creatures and all things. By loving Thee alone, my heart expanded to love the many. By being loyal in my love to Thee, I am loyal to all I love. And I love all beings forever."

I see life on earth as only a scenic backdrop behind which my loved ones hide at death. As I love them when they are before my eyes, so does my love follow them with my ever-watching mental gaze when they move elsewhere, behind death's screen.

Those whom I have loved I could never hate, even though they grow uninteresting through ugly behavior. In my museum of recollections, I can still behold those traits that caused me to love them. Beneath the temporary mental masks of those whose behavior I dislike, I see the perfect love of my great Beloved, even as I see it in those worthy souls that I love. To stop loving is to stem the purifying flow of love. I shall loyally love every being, every thing, until I find all races, all creatures, all animate and inanimate objects embraced by my love. I will love until every soul, every star, every forsaken creature, every atom, is lodged in my heart; for in the infinite love of God, my breast of eternity is large enough to hold everything in me.

O Love, I see Thy glowing face in the gems. I behold Thy shy blush in the blossoms. I am enraptured, hearing Thee warble in the birds. And I dream in ecstasy when my heart embraces Thee in all hearts. O Love, I met Thee in all things—only a little and for a while—but in Omnipresence I clasp Thee entirely and forever, and I rejoice in Thy joy evermore.

The Known and the Unknown

Written in the early 1920s

We exhaust the known by knowledge and enjoyment of it; then we turn to the exploration of the unknown, because the known does not satisfy us permanently. If it did, we would not have survived so long on this planet. Permanent satisfaction with the known, with no vision for the future, no effort to improve, no initiative to explore, no impulse to interpret, would have meant stagnation of the human race, and hence annihilation.

The terms "known" and "unknown" are relative. What is unknown to the savage is known to us. Both are links in the chain of life. When a link is still on the reel it is unknown. When the reel unwinds and the link comes out, it is known. What was unknown to a boy comes to be known to the man that the boy becomes. What was unknown to the average person twenty centuries ago is common knowledge to the average citizen of today. Man can know more and more because there remains at every step of knowledge something unknown. If there were not always this unknown quantity, the phrase "progressive knowledge" would be a contradiction.

How to Develop Your Talents

Consider the seemingly unfathomable depth of the human personality. Like bubbles, the many facets of our being rise to the surface, coming from somewhere deep below. A one-year-old child has hardly any coordinated finger movement. He practices the violin for many years and becomes a Kreisler.* Can everyone, given the same opportunity, become a Kreisler? Yes and no. Yes, because each person is the same as everybody else in essence, and can become as accomplished as anyone else in actuality. The infinite possibilities of the soul are the same in all

* Fritz Kreisler (1875–1962), famous violinist and composer.

persons. And no, because time is needed for the possibilities to come forth as actualities. If someone is still scratchy on the violin after many years' training, it will probably take him several lifetimes to become a Kreisler.

Talent is the unknown quantity of personality born with the person. It may not be full-fledged. Training brings out talent that is already within. It cannot bring forth sprouts if seeds are not already there. Training not only encourages the seed to grow into a plant, it has the additional merit of improving the quality of the seed through culture. The enhanced seed then makes for further improvement. Thus, when talent is improved through training, it becomes the father of further accomplishment. The fact that talent can be improved proves the latency of its potential, just as it proves the importance of training to make it fully manifest.

Talent, therefore, has various stages of expression, which can be observed in the development of a personality to its consummate expression in that human being. Every man who comes into the world carries within a general chart of his life, the details of which he fills in throughout his lifetime. The highways, and some byways, are already in the chart when he is born. These are the traits he brings with him from previous incarnations. He accepts them as his basic nature; and then connects them with alleys, and makes some additional byways. Sometimes he also extends the highways far beyond their original limits, if he has real dynamic driving power. If he lacks this dynamism, he moves for the most part along the limited maze of paths that he had in his chart at birth, and in the few new pathways he has drawn in his present daily life. He does not push himself further. He is a common man.

But he cannot remain so circumscribed forever. He cannot always be common. He will have to expand. He will have to move out toward new vistas. The cosmic law of evolution will not let him rest. He may be idle for a while, but the law of soul-progress is eternally active. God is always on the job; His idleness or sleep would spell death to the universe. He will, through the material working of His law, arrange circumstances that will at first coax the apathetic individual to turn in the right direction and move forward with positive action. If he does not heed, God will have to let him wander through the stinking open graveyard of his own follies, until he wagers his very life to get out of his abysmal condition and resolutely follows the proper road to progress and true happiness.

Recognize the Tendencies That Make You Unique

"Above all, to thine own self be true." This statement is the climax of a famous list of advice given by Polonius in Shakespeare's play, *Hamlet*. Narrowly speaking, it means to be honest with yourself; do not do a thing that you inwardly feel to be wrong. Truly, to have a clean conscience, even if the whole world doubts you, is a joy and a strength worth all the treasures of the universe.

But the words of Polonius hold a great deal more meaning than this. Conscience is not the only companion of our selves that we have to care for. There are others, too. A party of peeping desires, a group of half-sleeping tendencies, a company of live-wire wishes, compose the crowd. In order to be true to ourselves, we cannot push aside these traveling companions with whom we started life. We have to be at least attentive to them, too, if we do not want to lose in life's game. There may be some in the crowd that need shackling—the appetites, jealousies, and others that are apt to choke our growth or hurt others. Some, such as selfish desires, may need strong doses of advice and treatment. There are others that are safe enough to be relied on, or at least tolerated, such as the self-preserving and social instincts. A special few need to be deliberately spurred on — sympathetic tendencies, spirit of reverence, service, love of truth. We have to attend to each propensity in a way that is most suitable. That is the proper education of the inner being.

In other words, we must be true to ourselves, not in the sense of bringing flower offerings to every tendency we have, even the baser ones, but in the sense of recognizing the place of every one of them in the scheme of our life, and checking and subordinating, or guiding and directing, each one of the crowd in such a way as to make it contribute to the general well-being and happiness of the whole.

Though some tendencies have been cited and generalized, they are only a small part of the whole potential crowd from which each individual has gathered his own host of tendencies. In childhood his collection remains in the backyard of his personality as an unknown quantity. The progressive expression of his personality is the result of those tendencies' becoming known, added to, or banished from his life.

In this way, every individual is a species unto himself. Though each person is a human being, one does not resemble another any more than the dress of a native Burmese resembles that of an American. The fabric may be essentially the same, both being made of cloth, but the design and style are significantly different.

Mass Education Must Allow for Individual Development

To recognize difference is as important as to discover similarity. To legislate or to enter into a contract is an evident attempt to standardize human relationships by considering the similarities of human nature. If every person were radically different from every other, if there were not a single point common to them, laws that would apply to all or the majority of a group could not be passed nor could there be fairness in any binding contract. Noting similarities is all right, for human interaction would be impossible without some common basis. But there must also be consideration of the differences.

Modern civilization—with its inventions, discoveries, and larger contacts; with its forms of government, and its devices of popularizing culture through books, newspapers, radio; with its vast arterial systems of transportation and commerce—leans toward the standardization of the mind of man. The par is more important than personalities; the average more important than the exceptional.

In medieval and more ancient times, personalities overshadowed the par; the exceptional eclipsed the average. The overall intellectual level was lower than today; but in each age there were towering personalities, as were Newton and Milton in their time. There were many ignorant or illiterate persons to one Solomon or Shakespeare. Now there is more attempt than ever before to raise the average human being to a desirable level of culture; but there is always the accompanying danger of cramping the genius in the straitjacket of the mediocre.

There is an element of good in either point of view, emphasizing the par or the exceptional. One encourages the upliftment of the ordinary multitude; the other makes people revere the bright men. A happy mean is best. It is as foolish to try to make all people the same—however high the level of sameness may be—and overlook the exceptional genius, as it is to prepare the ground for the growth of only the exceptional to the neglect of the average.

To return to our point, observing similarities may be good; and standardizing the human mind—if the standard is high—may be partly justifiable. But it would be a grievous psychological crime to standardize methods of education or training by ignoring the differences in the personalities of the learners. Because of the similarities among people, some set standards may be used, up to a certain point, with respect to the system of education. But if education according to such set standards is carried beyond that point, we crush the man to save the standards.

In an attempt to bring below-average children up to the average level, a teacher may stunt the growth of the bright ones. What is true of secular education is also true of inner psychological training. There is no stereotyped way of promoting spiritual growth. There is no spiritual mill that can grind non-spiritual persons into Self-realized souls by the turning of a motor. Everyone has to work out his own salvation according to hints from his inner self after he has been started on the right road by stereotyped suggestions, standardized spiritual advice: be reverential, be patient, be contented, be self-controlled, be meditative, and so forth. The crowd of tendencies that one is born with then needs slightly different handling in different people. Some of the inclinations are to be curbed, some tolerated, some developed, some sparingly fed, some starved out. The tactics applied in the case of each individual will therefore necessarily vary according to the set of traits he possesses.

Past Desires Produce Present Tendencies

What is the origin of a tendency in a man? A conscious desire that he entertained in this life or a previous incarnation. If you do not believe in reincarnation—and by the way, if you don't, it will surely be uncomfortable for you to give any satisfactory explanation of the discrepancies in the conditions and talents of people—then you will have to blame the desires that your forebears entertained as having crystallized as hereditary tendencies in you. This latter explanation is certainly not wholly satisfactory.

Training of innate talents or tendencies enlarges the scope of their influence. A man with diplomatic ability ingrained in his nature will be a diplomat, no matter whether he is an ordinary laborer dealing with fellow workers or members of his family, or whether he is one of a board of select men—a member of the legislature or a plenipotentiary in an international peace parley. Education or political training and opportunity will only sharpen his inborn diplomatic tool, and extend the scope of its use. The difference in the capacity of talent in different people, even when increased by training, is therefore due not only to the scope of the training, but also to the inborn possession of that ability and its prior degree of development.

If there were no possibility of change inside, wherein are sheltered the seeds of what we are to become, we would be unable to alter the unknown part of our nature. But we do have the opportunity to influence what we become. Early training has much to do with stimulating or paralyzing the growth of this unknown part of our self. As the seeds send forth their messenger-sprouts, we should look after the fertilizing, weeding, loosening of the ground, watering, and protective fencing. And we must also do pruning and uprooting of undesirable growth. The fruits of the garden of our life will be large, small, or medium-sized, healthy or diseased, according to how we attend to their rearing. That much lies within the scope of human freedom. If we turn our free-choice activities to the best use, the outer result will be desirable; and there will also be new and better seeds gathered in the unknown part of our nature, and these will in turn determine the future known expression of life.

How Much Free Will Do We Have?

Though man is made in the image of God, somehow or other there is a lot of foreign matter in his makeup that he will have to replace or spiritually alchemize before he will have the right to a place anywhere near the throne of God. Our tendencies are the foreign matter. They are what make us throw in our lot with surroundings and circumstances. If it were not for these inclinations, there would be no meaning as to why each person attracts different circumstances. As a matter of fact, through an inexorable law, our tendencies attract our companions and environments for the most part. The law of affinity is a matter of correspondence between what we are potentially and actually, on the one hand, and the broad world on the other.

The cue to our conduct is always supplied from the known and unknown within. What we are going to be is about seventy-five percent foreordained by ourselves. That "horoscope" of tendencies from past incarnations attracts our present hereditary condition as well as the other circumstances we will draw to ourselves. Fatalists, and some inept astrologers who try to compute the unknown, are greatly mistaken in their belief that life is one hundred percent foretold and can be astrologically charted. They leave no margin for the freedom of the individual: free choice to change himself this way or that, free choice to decide between two courses of action. In most cases, though, the free will of man is nothing more than a slave—in the guise of freedom, but fettered to past tendencies.

Yet everyone knows there is such a thing as an unconditioned decision that we make after rationally balancing the pros and cons of a certain matter. Having made such a decision, if we exercise our will, we can change many things in our lives that appeared unchangeable, or that may have been predicted to be incontrovertible. This willing is freedom of will. Free will does exist. If it were not so, none could escape the vicious circle of his fate once he had drawn it. Growth would be circumscribed. Newer channels of activities would have little scope. The evolution of human beings would hardly emerge from the level of savagery.

The conception of new social orders, progressive ideas in political government, advanced methods of scientific exploration, new departments of research, sallies of literary activity— all prove the ability of man to exercise free choice in every line by the power of will.

As previously stated, you are born with about seventy-five percent of your life predetermined by your past. You will make up the remaining twenty-five percent. If you yourself, through your own free choice and effort of will, do not determine what that twenty-five percent will be, the seventy-five percent will make the twenty-five percent for you, and you will become a puppet. That is, you will be ruled absolutely by your past, by the influence and effects of your past tendencies. This is why spiritual training is vital. It takes into consideration not only the seventy-five percent of our lives that we already are, but also designates the methods to mold the brand new twenty-five percent that we ourselves are going to create by the exercise of our freedom.

Cosmic Law Is Activated by Our Decisions

The Cosmic Law is not the doer of things, but the evolutionary mode of operation of cause and effect. This law works changes when activated by the agency of our decisions, which are determined either by our past tendencies, or by our present free choice. The motive of Eternal Good that is interlinked with the Cosmic Law is in every atom, and in us too. It is what inherently urges us to learn from past mistakes, and to use our free choice and will to initiate those positive causes that produce everlasting good effects.

What we do automatically is within a predetermined realm of the law of cause and effect. That is, when habit—psychological or physiological—determines our conduct, the habit is the cause, and our conditioned response is the effect. What we do with a distinct motive decided upon by free choice is within the realm of "final cause." When we act in accordance with a forethought of a distant purpose, such as to realize a goal or attainment of an object, and we harness our habits and will-initiated actions to serve as the means to that end, we are acting according to the "final cause." Every motive is a "final cause," and every "final cause" starts the series of ordinary cause and effect. President Wilson wanted world peace. He boarded a ship, crossed over to France, and gave his "fourteen points." The thought of world peace is the "final cause," or motive; the preparation for the trip, taking the boat and crossing the Atlantic, delivering his speech, and so forth, are the series of ordinary causes and effects started by the "final cause."

All our impulsive and habitual acts, and motive-caused acts (that is, actions initiated by "final causes"), are the chariots that carry the will of the Lord, the Cosmic Law, the Divine Final Cause. In other words, everything happens according to the will of God as expressed in His Cosmic Law. We are instruments for the fulfillment of that Law. Our part is to make the right free choice so that our instrumentality is used to fulfill the good effects rather than the unpleasant ones that cause suffering as a means of teaching man to avoid wrong actions. When our chariots run into the ditch because they were hitched to wrong actions, they have to be pulled out by strenuous effort of our will and God's will as expressed in the Cosmic Law.

Frankly speaking, from the highest metaphysical point of view, the truth is that the Cosmic Law has its hand in everything that we have done or are going to do. Fortunately, we do not realize that. If we try to fathom with our crude understanding that greatest mystery by which the universe is governed, we would become paralyzed from self-induced fatalistic blows to our psychological make-up. Do not let your dream of life be broken by fatalism when it is not yet time for you to wake in the daylight of God. You will be puzzled by your wrong judgment of God's ways. The first step toward understanding is to use your will to make those choices that are in harmony with the Eternal Good within the Cosmic Law.

Live Life for God

When you live life, not for God but for itself, every moment of it is incurring a debt to Him. Those debts pile up, day after day. Borrow from the commonly unknown bank of God, the universal Spirit, and clear your debt to Him. You can get the loan only for the asking. And you will not be hounded for payment of interest either. This is the only bank that makes loans and does not worry the recipients with the demand of interest, because the Universal Bank is always ready to invest in the betterment of its own property, the world, and to look after the interests of its tenants. This is a form of banking that none but God allows. If you do not pay off the debts you have contracted by your life in matter, isolated from God, suffering will be your jail sentence.

What is the loan you should ask? The loan of spiritual wisdom: the eye to see every event of life as God sees it, to feel every detail of life as He feels it, to live every moment of life as

He lives it. When you ask God for this wisdom, the loan comes to you written off as a gift.

Every event, fact, action, or thought of a God-man such as Jesus or Krishna is the meeting point of the same wisdom coming from two sides—from God and from the God-man living in God. It is like a dot on a circle that you can approach from either side. God fulfills His aim through the God-man, and the God-man knowingly acts to fulfill God's will.

We do not know that He does the same thing through us, so we suffer and lament the bankruptcy of our so-called freedom. This is not narrow determinism. It is true idealism. We are absolutely free when we reach the Absolute. Until then we are relatively free; and it is a sin and source of suffering not to use wisely our relative free will. Working our way through relative freedom, we come to the Absolute Freedom. Then the whole of the Unknown becomes the Known; there is nothing more to know, and the knowing is all-satisfying and ever-new.

Controlling Your Destiny

Encinitas, California, January 1, 1938

With the beginning of the New Year, let us with concentrated resolve and spiritual determination enter into a new era of our lives. Please pray with me: "We are entering a better life, O Father, through the portals of the New Year. May it be a year of greatest communion with Thee, the Giver of all gifts. Be Thou the only King sitting on the throne of all our desires, directing our lives through our intelligence. In the past year desires often led us astray. Bless us that henceforth all our aspirations be in consonance and harmony with Thy will. Bless us that every day be a new awakening in Thy consciousness, physically, mentally, morally, and spiritually. We thank Thee, O Father, and the Great Ones who are all blessing us and coaxing us to Thy kingdom. *Aum. Aum. Amen.*"

This is my New Year's wish for you: that you all reach the land beyond your dreams, where there is peace and joy eternal. May you realize the fulfillment of whatever strong good wish you release in the ether.

Let us meditate: Think of the beautiful happenings of the last year. Forget the dark experiences. Sow the good you did in the past on the fresh soil of the New Year, that those vital seeds may grow in an even better way. All past sorrows are gone. All past deficiencies are forgotten. Loved ones who have died are living immortally in God. We are in Eternal Life now. If we realize this we shall never know death. Waves rise and fall in the ocean; when they disappear, they are still one with the ocean. Even so, all things are in the ocean of God's presence. There is nothing to fear. Link every state of the mind with God. It is only when the wave separates itself from the ocean that it feels isolated and lost. Think constantly of your connection with Eternal Life, and you shall know your identity with the Supreme Eternal One. Life and death are but different phases of being. You are a part of the Eternal Life. Awaken and expand your consciousness in God so that your concept of yourself ceases to be limited to the little body. Meditate on this. Realize it. Your consciousness has no circumference. Look ahead millions of miles: there is no end. Look to the left, above, and below: there is no end. Your mind is omnipresent, your consciousness unlimited.

Pray with me: "Heavenly Father, I am no longer bound by the consciousness of the past year. I am free from the cramped consciousness of the body. I am eternal. I am omnipresent in the chasm of eternity above and below me, on the left, on the right, in front, behind, and all around. Thou and I are one.

"We bow to Thee, O God, to Guru, and to the saints of all religions. And we bow to all souls in every nation, for they are made in Thine image. In the new year we wish peace for all nations of the globe. May they realize their common brotherhood under Thy Fatherhood. Bless them with this understanding, that they forsake fighting and live peacefully with one another to make a heaven of this earth. And bless us all, that we may help to build Thy heaven here by remodeling our lives spiritually, and by example inspiring others to do likewise. We love Thee, our Father, and we love all races as our brothers. We love all creatures, for they reflect Thy life. We bow to Thee, templed in everything.

"Heavenly Father, make us strong in this new year, ever guided by Thy constant presence, that in body, mind, and soul we may reflect Thy life, health, prosperity, and happiness. As Thy children, may we become perfect even as Thou art perfect. *Aum, Peace, Aum.*"

Each day do some good. Give to a worthy cause, it doesn't matter how much; or help some individual. God is watching to see if you feel for His suffering in others. Make up your mind to be of service to someone every day. You can often help others just by giving them a little understanding. Never gloat over the faults of wayward brothers if you wish to reform them. See God in everyone, as I see Him. Do not ridicule an erring person. God is sleeping in that soul; you must lovingly awaken Him. Mentally put yourself in the position of others, and then with the utmost kindness you will be able to understand and help them. There is no greater joy. Just as I am always trying to improve myself, I feel for others in their aspirations to be better.

The one thing that will help to eliminate world suffering—more than money, houses, or any other material aid — is to meditate and transmit to others the divine consciousness of God that we feel. A thousand dictators could never destroy what I have within. Every day radiate His consciousness to others. Try to understand God's plan for mankind—to draw all souls back to Himself—and work in harmony with His will.

The greatest blasphemy is to create divisions in God's church. If there were a hundred Gods there could be a hundred different religions, but there is only one God and one truth. It is not dogma and "churchianity" we are to follow, but the spirit of truth and realization that is within every soul.

Our Acts, Past and Present, Forge the Chain of Our Destiny

Picture the New Year as a garden you are responsible for planting. Sow the seeds of good habits in this soil and weed out worries and wrong actions of the past. If you are not a good gardener you will have to come back on earth to try again.

You will never find happiness so long as you are controlled by destiny. By "destiny" I do not mean "fate." There is no such thing as fate. Destiny comprises those forgotten past causes of present effects that you have created in your life. You may say, "I was destined to be greedy." But no, you are not. The first day you started eating you were not a greedy person. You created that habit. The drunkard was not a drunkard the first time he tasted alcohol. When you repeat actions without judgment, you find they begin to usurp your thought and will and make your body obey their dictates. Then you say it is your fate to be a weakling or a failure. That binding chain was forged by you, link by link. You are not destined to be anything except what you have made of yourself. You alone preordained yourself to be good or bad when you repeated in the past certain beneficial or harmful actions.

Each soul is therefore controlled both by a destiny created by himself and by present freewill-initiated actions. It is good to know how much of your life is controlled by destiny and how much you govern it as you want to. Most mornings when you awaken you make up your mind to do something, but you don't

do what you had planned. Modern life is an unbalanced existence. Everyone is racing for something he does not really want
when he gets it. Before you create compelling desires, discriminate carefully. If you are driving a horse that is running away
with your carriage, your first need is to control the horse.

Analyze your actions and find out whether your life is
similarly uncontrolled, pulled toward certain destruction by the
wild steeds of your senses. If there is any harmful habit you have
not yet tamed, learn now to control it. Slavery to habits such as
drinking or sex indulgence will destroy you. Start now to master
them. To stumble and fall into wrong ways is only momentary
weakness. Do not think yourself wholly lost. The same ground
on which you fall can be used as a support to help you get up
again, if you learn from your experiences. But to stay fallen is a
grievous weakness. Your soul must ultimately be redeemed, and
the only real sin is in ceasing to strive toward that goal.

The Hindu scriptures say that each soul is individual and
independent. It is not governed by heredity, but rather attracts a
certain family and heredity because of some similarity to its
own ego or pseudo nature; or because of other attractions created by certain past habits and desires. Your disposition may be
either sweet or sour, but God did not make you that way. If He
arbitrarily created you as you are, you could not be held responsible for what you do. The prevailing system of law is defective
in that it does not penetrate the inner man. The punishment
may fit the crime, but unless it fits also the particular karmic
pattern of the inner man, the criminal may neither repent his
wrongdoing nor desire to mend his ways.

No matter what his present state, man can change for the
better through self-control, discipline, and following proper diet
and health laws. Why do you think you cannot change? Mental
laziness is the secret cause of all weakness. The mentally lazy
man is the most hopeless. He does not even want to make an
effort to succeed.

Man must change his slothful mental habit and cease to
think his present status is predestined. Even the consciousness
of being male or female can be completely forgotten. In sleep this
consciousness goes: you are a free individual. Every morning
God awakens you with the consciousness that you are free, but

as your day begins you again put on all the binding habits of worldly consciousness.

Do not live day after day in the same sorry state. If you pray, and believe what you pray, you shall receive God's blessings and help. If you have a bad habit, create a mental antidote and continuously apply it until the poisonous habit is neutralized. Tell yourself resolutely that you are going to be different, that you may be weak now, but you are going to be strong. The minute you *make up your mind* to correct yourself, you will change, you will be different. Suppose you are a greedy man. If you are mentally determined, then as soon as you think self-control, you have self-control. So long as you think you are strong, you can mentally resist temptation. If you anger easily, resolve that you will not become angry today. Even if at first you can control your anger for only a few minutes, you will conquer if you persist.

The Example of Great Men Shows
That Our Destiny Is Not Fixed

Try to remember and concentrate on all the beautiful and positive qualities of your life, and do not affirm your deficiencies. The greatest enemy of yourself is yourself. You alone are responsible if you cannot get out of the ruts you have made. You must make a firm determination to do so. No one keeps you tied to destiny but yourself. The example of great men should make you begin to disbelieve that your destiny is fixed. They became great by changing their attitude. You can do the same. Usually those who have achieved great things in life have also had great failures. But they refused to be downed by them. Those who have achieved won many battles, and lost others, but they did not give in to a negative "destiny."

As a young boy I had chronic indigestion. I kept a chest full of medicines for the malady. The first time I talked about it with my guru, Swami Sri Yukteswar, he said, "Why not try divine healing? You don't have to suffer like this." I had been convinced that nothing would work, but when he spoke to me in this way, his conviction impressed my mind. From that day on I was healed.

You sympathize with yourself, believing your weaknesses and difficulties are inescapable. Change that kind of thinking.

Reject the consciousness that you are a mortal beggar. Always remember you are a child of God. I know I can will anything I want to, and Nature will obey me.

Be Mentally Dissociated from the Body's Limitations

Begin by controlling your physical habits. They come from the influence of the habits of your family, of your forefathers, and of the whole world. Resist those influences. While trying to rid yourself of a physiological habit or condition, do not give in to it even mentally. Do not let your mind accept any limiting suggestion from the body. Look after the body, but be above it. Know that you are separate from your mortal form. Put up a great mental barrier between your mind and body. Affirm: "I am apart from the body. No heat, cold, or sickness can touch me. I am free." Your limitations will become less and less. But if the body convinces the mind of sickness, then suffering becomes doubled. If you neglect your body and do not strengthen your mind, you may acquire chronic disease. Never let your mind be controlled by your body; this is extremely important. Make up your mind you will not accept any conditions imposed on it by the body. But denial alone is not enough. You must train your mind to be completely apart from body consciousness. This does not mean you should neglect a broken arm, affirming that there is no arm. Give it the proper physical treatment but do not be mentally disturbed by the bodily discomfort. Be dissociated from whatever happens to you. You will find then that no pain can ever again hurt you.

Health and sickness are dreams of the mind. You are Spirit. You are above them both. Though you are temporarily jailed in the body, mentally rise above imprisoning thoughts of health and sickness. In the constant fear of sickness, you are concentrating on it and attracting it to you. Make your mind impervious to all bodily sensations. I do not even feel the need for sleep when I remind myself that I am Spirit, and that Spirit does not sleep.

Almighty Power Lies in the Mind

The mind is the miracle of all miracles that God has created. No person is truly ignorant, but he may appear so if he is deeply asleep in delusion. We do not see the fine mechanisms of the mind. Almighty power lies therein. We can realize this with the help of a guru, one who has acquired this mental strength. If you want to be an acrobat, mix with acrobats. If you want to be strong-minded, mix with those who have strong minds. Stay away from useless company, those persons whose influence paralyzes your will and mind. Silence and seclusion are the secrets of success. In this modern life of activity there is only one way to separate yourself from its ceaseless demands: get away from it once in a while. Only weaklings give in to environment. The kingdom of your destiny, and its creator, is yourself.

Be an angel inside. It is the easiest thing to do. Every time you feel anger, go within and say, "I am the peaceful child of God. I am whatever I make up my mind to be. The stars and angels and all creation must bend to work my will." Try your mental power in small things first, and you will strengthen it for greater endeavors. If you have a strong mind and plant in it a firm resolve, you can change your destiny. I know I was to have died long ago, and the sickness I was to have died of.

The power to attain success lies in the mind. You will realize this truth if you can hold to this conviction against the disbelief of the whole world. Take up some hobby or project that others think you cannot do, and then do it. Start with modest aims, and gradually your mind power will become more developed. The world and your family label you in a certain way; but mentally, constantly, work to change yourself for the better. There is no limit to the power of your mind. Concentrate on that thought. Fill your mind with the resolution to accomplish, and work toward your goals with positive actions. Keep driving the mind toward higher attainments. Acquire spiritual prosperity, and every other kind of prosperity will be your slave. My life is a testimony to that.

Whenever you are sitting still, without any demands on your attention, be away in your mind, using it constructively every moment. Great things are produced first in the mind. I keep mine at work all the time, and put its creative thoughts into action the moment I see an opportunity. Then the results come. Every day you should try to do something creative. Improve your destiny. Take your health, or your moral life, or spiritual life—one thing at a time—and change it as you desire. Whatever I have wanted to accomplish in this life, I have been able to do. Matter has come out of mind, hence the mind has no physiological limitations. Therefore if you can control the mind, the whole world will gravitate toward you. Everything I have ever wanted, I have received. One thing I craved above all else was the ever new happiness of God. As the result of disbanding all other desires, this also I have attained.

Do not be a helpless failure. Control your destiny by changing your thought. Do whatever you make up your mind to do. To concentrate the mind in this way does not cost you a thing. Inwardly determine to change yourself, and you can change your destiny according to your will.

Guests—Good and Bad

Circa 1930

Mankind is tied up, steeped, in bad habits. They are constantly being fed, while good habits are starved. The undesirable bad-habit guests have been allowed to fill the seats in the auditorium of your mind, whereas the good ones are hardly granted an audience, and so go away, discouraged.

To develop good habits you must nourish them with good actions; and to do this it is necessary to seek good company. Environment (in particular, the company you keep) is very important, for it is stronger than will power. Most human beings are traveling matterward, and encourage you to follow their example. The searchlight of the mind of such persons is constantly directed outside, whereas its beam should be focused inside. People are running, running, but there is no place in the world to which they can flee to escape themselves. Ultimately, each one must face himself; and that is why you should seek association with saints and friends who turn your mind toward Self-realization and away from the delusive influence of bad habits.

If you pray for spiritual or material success, but entertain thoughts of possible failure, it is like sending someone on an errand, only to have him attacked by bandits on the way. The thieves who prevent your success are your own bad habits. You send your prayer-children to God without protection, and they are waylaid by robbers of habitual restlessness and doubt before they can reach God. He hears your prayers, of course, for God is everywhere and all-knowing; but under certain conditions He does not answer those prayers in the way you have asked Him to.

I will tell you a story. Once there was a king who told one of his subjects that unless he could answer a certain question, he would be hanged. The man said, "Tell me the question." The king then asked him: "Where does God sit, and which way does He look—north, south, east, or west?" The subject went home to think, and told his servant that he would be killed unless he answered the king within a fortnight.

The servant said to his master, "Let me go for you. I will answer the question." So the servant went to the king and explained his errand. "First," he said, "let me sit on your throne, for while I answer your question I am your teacher." The king surrendered his throne to the servant, and then asked him: "Where does God sit, and which way does He look — north, south, east, or west?"

The servant responded with a request, "Bring me a cow."

So a cow was brought. Then the servant said, "Where is the milk?"

"In the udder," said the king.

"Nay, Sire," said the servant, "the milk is not only in the udder, but throughout the cow, for the milk is in the essence of the cow."

Then the servant asked that a bowl of milk be brought; and when it was set before him, he asked the king: "Where is the butter?"

The king said, "I see no butter."

The servant answered, "The butter is throughout the milk. Just churn the milk, and the butter will become separated from it. Therefore, as the milk is all through the cow, and the butter is present throughout the milk, so is God everywhere."

Thus did the wisdom of the servant save the life of his master, for the king received the correct answer to his question.

If you ask yourself this same question, you will receive a like answer, for you must milk God's presence from the vastness of all nature, and you must churn Him from the matter-diluted mind by your heart's longing and inspiration in deep meditation.

A Letter to God

God-realization is not a monopoly of yogis and swamis. He is in the heart and soul of every being. And when you open within yourself the secret temple in your heart, then with the all-knowing intuition of the soul you shall read the book of life. Then, and only then, will you contact the living God. And you will feel Him as the very essence of your being. Without this feeling in your heart, there will be no answer to your prayers. You may attract what your positive actions and good karma permit you to have; but to receive conscious response from God, you must first attain divine attunement with Him.

When I was a child, I wrote a letter to God. I was so little I could hardly write, but I thought I told Him a great deal. I did not ask anything for myself. I asked to be told something about Himself. Every day I waited for the postman to bring me the answer to my letter, never doubting that it would come. And one day it did come. He came to me in a vision. I saw the answer of God written in letters of shining gold. I could scarcely read, but the meaning came to me. He said: "I am Life! I am Love! I am looking after you through your father and mother!" Then I understood. I *felt* God!

If through sincerity and unconditional devotion your prayers reach God, it matters not if your sins be deeper than the ocean and higher than the Himalayas. He will destroy those karmic obstacles. For a time, perhaps, you may sink under a stratum of darkness; but still you are a spark of an Eternal Flame. You can hide the spark, but you can never destroy it.

God is in everything. When you have Him, you have everything. Whatever I wish for now comes to me immediately. So I must be careful in my wishing. First and last, I wish for God. When I wish for others, I have to struggle, for I have to fight their karmas.* In seeking God you must be careful not to be secretly wishing for something else when you wish for Him, saying to yourself, "First I will wish for God; then surely I will get the automobile I want." That is not right. You cannot fool God.

We must seek union of our consciousness with God's consciousness. When we have that, our prayers will not be waylaid. We are not beggars. We are sons of God.

Never pray for anything of this world until you have first prayed successfully to know God. Pray until you have attained God; then your prayers will be guided by wisdom, not by the inclinations of habits. Do not fool yourself. Wake up and say to Him: "I will forsake all lesser desires; I yearn only to know

---

* A God-realized guru such as Paramahansa Yogananda may compassionately help other souls by spiritually mitigating, or taking upon himself, the karmic effects of their past wrong actions. (See *karma* in glossary.)

Thee." Of course you should pray for others who are suffering, but do not pray for "things" of the world until through deep meditation and love for God you feel your identity with Him. He knows what you need. Seek Him until you find Him, until your whole being throbs with His power and glory.

Ask Him to reveal Himself to you. Do not rest until He answers. Ask with all your heart, again and again: "Reveal Thyself! Reveal Thyself! The stars may be shattered, the earth may be dissolved, yet my soul shall cry unto Thee, 'Reveal Thyself!'" The inertia of His silence will be broken by the steady, persistent hammering of your prayers.

At last, like the invisible earthquake, He will suddenly make Himself manifest. The walls of silence holding back the reservoir of your consciousness will tremble and crumble, and you will feel that you are flowing like a river into the Mighty Ocean, and you will say to Him: "I am now one with Thee; whatever Thou hast, the same have I."

You will be consciously face to face with your Self at last. The auditorium of your mind will be crowded to overflowing with the holy guests of your own divine thoughts. Beggars of grief and discord and pain will not be able to enter there, and their wails and sighs will be drowned in the harmony of an ever-singing and never-weary choir of happiness and peace.

How to Free Yourself
From Bad Habits

*Self-Realization Fellowship Temple, San Diego, California,
June 1, 1947*

During my absence from the temple, I have missed you all; but I have accomplished much writing. That is my joy, for through my pen I can give to you what God gives to me. Seclusion is the price of finding God. Sometimes I am more with you in God when I am away than when I am with you personally. During this period of seclusion I have been immersed in the wondrous dynamic presence of God. My whole room was ablaze with His Being. You don't know how thrilling night is when you are alone and practice His presence. He is omnipresent, moving in space as a great auroral mist, the Light out of which all things are formed. You must make the effort to experience Him yourself.

Saint Francis taught simple devotion; but as his monks became more and more organized, they felt it necessary not only to cultivate devotion to commune with God, but to study theological books and to acquaint themselves with the arts and sciences of the time. Saint Francis warned them repeatedly that studying would not get them to God; that they must rather have love for Him.*

God can never be found through philosophical abstractions. If you have love for God and practice Kriya Yoga and meditate deeply, you will find Him. Don't wait, for waiting is dangerous. Present good health may produce in your consciousness a happy complacency. But who knows whether or not your head may be

---

* "My brethren, my brethren! The Lord has called me by the way of simplicity and humility, and this way has He pointed out to me in truth for myself and for them who are willing to follow me....But with this wisdom of yours you will not reach your goal and will return to your vocation for all your fault-finding, whether you want to or not." — *The Saints That Moved the World*, by René Fülöp-Miller.

on the block waiting for death? Krishna said, "Get away from this ocean of suffering and misery."* He meant that we must go where we can find real happiness. It can be had only from God's hands. But the greatest obstacle in our path is our bad habits. Habit is both our best friend and our worst enemy. And that is the theme of this morning's service.

Habit Defined

Habit is an acquired aptitude or inclination to a particular action, instilled by repetition. It can decrease, or resist, or facilitate the force of action. The mental mechanism of habit was given to us to simplify the process of our actions. Without its aid, we would have to learn the same things over each new day. For instance, the writer works daily at his writing until he is able to express his thoughts clearly and interestingly. If that habit were not established, he would have to relearn repeatedly the basics of composition. Similarly, if you had no such power of habit, then every day of your life you would have to relearn everything you do, even how to say your name. In other words, you would remain like a helpless infant.

Habits are necessary, but we misuse their power. Habit is like a parrot: If you teach it to sing good songs and say good words, it will repeat them over and over. And if you teach it to swear, it will do the same, whether you want it to or not, embarrassing you and others. Likewise, your bad habits will make not only you, but everyone around you, uncomfortable; whereas your good habits will be a joy to you and to others also. Therefore, it is tenable that you should prefer good habits and destroy bad ones.

Habits are formed gradually, by repetition of an action. It is said that it normally takes the average person about eight years to firmly establish a habit. But habit formation can be quickened. In childhood especially, the mind is more pliable, and it is then easier to form good habits. However, in ancient India, our teachers who specialized in training the young knew the importance of understanding the predisposition of the child's nature in addition to providing proper education and environment.

* "Him will I swiftly lift forth from life's ocean of distress and death, whose soul clings fast to Me. Cling thou to Me!" (Bhagavad Gita XII:8, Sir Edwin Arnold's translation).

They selected children according to the good karma and habits they brought with them from past incarnations. You have probably seen some children who from the earliest age were absolutely unwilling to be good. This is because they had developed bad habits in previous lives. On the other hand, many children are naturally inclined to right behavior because of good tendencies developed in former incarnations.

Older people reflect the inner influence of past-life habits just as children do. When persons who were spiritually inclined in the past take up the spiritual path, they keep on going with youthful enthusiasm to the end. Others who have brought with them anti-spiritual habits will not take to the spiritual path in spite of repeated urgings, unless in this life they wake up and begin to realize that God is the only source of happiness.

Watch Out for Hidden Bad Habits of Past Lives

Since you do not know what good or bad habits you have established in previous lives, you should be careful about what you do in this life, lest the slightest stimulus give a fresh hold to some bad habit that has been trailing you through incarnations. This explains how it can happen that a person may take just one drink, and his old habit of former lives awakens and catches him; before long, he has become an alcoholic. Therefore, one shouldn't even try such experiences as those produced by alcohol and drugs, which are not only useless, but potentially harmful. Don't flirt with unproductive, dangerous habits.

The word "karma" means action; also, the effects of actions. The nature of those effects determines whether you have reaped good or bad karma. When you say, "It is my karma that has brought this evil event upon me," you have not distinguished between good and evil karma. Good karma brings good results, and predisposes one to repeat good actions. Evil karma produces evil results, and is the fertile soil for more evil actions. If you have a particular bad habit or karmic inclination, don't mix with those who have the same kind of bad habit. If you tend to be greedy, avoid the company of others who are greedy. If you have a desire to drink, stay away from those who drink. People who support your bad habits are not your friends. They will cause you to throw away your soul's joy. Avoid the company of wrongdoers and mix with those who are good.

Train Children to Develop a Preference for Right Habits

In this modern age, everybody needs to be trained, because they have so much temptation placed before them. All parents should train their children to develop a taste for better habits. Consider more seriously the responsibility of guiding your children. Many bad habits are imposed on them in the environment of the schools! Influenced by other children, they feel they have no choice; if someone doesn't join the crowd and smoke or drink, he is considered a sissy. Youngsters thus succumb to all kinds of wrong behavior. I know so many boys and girls who have taken to drink and smoking, and even worse. Those young children that I have taken into the ashram for training I consider my own, and my heart goes out with them when they go into the environment of the public school. I tell them, "Don't be a doormat. Dare to be different, and to say *no* when others try to persuade you into wrong ways."

Coeducation is a total failure. You will learn this sometime. Coeducation for college-age students is less questionable. I was once going to write about these things, and then I thought, "Why should I? Who will pay any attention?"

The very fabric of your family life is being destroyed because of the lack of moral and spiritual education at home as well as in the schools. You must do your part to teach your children to resist evil. You have here such a great nation, but the abuse of freedom is the road to destruction. When I was a child in India, we were given strict moral and spiritual culture at home. Mother used to tell me, "Never desire wealth." I asked why, and she said, "It will make you a slave." We were never permitted even to utter the word "wine," because drinking was recognized as an evil habit. Reason with your children. Remind them that by developing wrong habits they are wading into the cesspool of error. If they should go on in that way, it will be too late for them to come out of it. All the joy of life will be over for them.

I know a young couple who were married just four weeks ago, and already they are unhappy and coming to me for advice. It isn't academic education alone that makes people happy. It is "how-to-live" education—how to develop a harmonious, moral life, stronger will power, and spiritual understanding—that will bring happiness. The women in this country have much devotion and spiritual inclination, but as mothers few of them properly train those ideals into their children. The boys here would be wonderful if taught how to develop their "won't" power.

When You Say *No* to Temptation, Mean It

When you say *no* to temptation, you must mean *no.* Don't give in. The spineless weakling all the time says *yes.* But great minds are full of *no*s. The weak-willed become doormats for everybody to walk over and trample on; they deserve this treatment for giving in to their weaknesses. Remember, temptation may appear to offer something very pleasurable in the beginning, but it leads to restlessness, always seeking something different, always seeking new thrills. Resisting temptations isn't the denial of all the pleasures of life; it is to have supernal control over what you want to do. I am showing you the way to real freedom, not the false sense of freedom that in fact is compelling you to do what your habits lead you to do.

Don't Cater to Likes and Dislikes

Catering to your likes and dislikes is also to be avoided. They, too, are cultivated habits. When I came to this country and tasted olives for the first time, I didn't like them; but everyone was saying how good they were, so I ate them until I also learned to like them. To follow what you *should* do, irrespective of likes and dislikes, is what brings lasting happiness.

Many times we dislike certain things that we should like because they are good for us. This is particularly true of our eating habits. If you mix sand and water and then plaster a wall with it, the mixture will stay put for a while. But when the water dries, the sand will fall away from the wall. In the same way, what pleases your taste does not always satisfy the needs of your body. If you could actually see its complex workings and how it is affected by what you feed it, you would not down coffee and doughnuts every morning as a substitute for a balanced breakfast.

Most people are heavy meat eaters, and neglect fresh fruits and vegetables in their diet. As a result, their kidneys and intestines are affected, and all kinds of troubles develop. Meat is not an essential to health; in fact, it is harmful. The cow is supplied with all its nourishment merely by eating grass. The elephant and the horse get their strength and stamina from a vegetarian diet. Why do intelligent human beings cultivate such bad eating habits? Why do you persist in wrong eating, even when you know better? Because you were not started out with the right habits. No matter what anyone says, you want to eat the wrong things because the habit of liking those foods has been established. That is the misuse of the power of habit. If from the beginning you form the habit of eating the right foods, you won't crave white bread and lots of sugars and starches and fried foods; you won't be used to them.

Bad Habits Are Like an Octopus

Bad habits are like an octopus—they have many tentacles to hold you in their grip. And once they enwrap you, those octopus-like habits feed on you; they will destroy you. But if good habits have a hold on you, they will nourish you.

Don't at all let your mind tell you that it is so hard to be good and so easy to be bad. It is much easier to be good than to suffer the consequences of wrong actions. It is a little difficult sometimes to resist temptation, because your senses try to entrap you. But once you get into the habit of being good, it is very hard to be bad; because you know you will be beaten up within and without by doing something you know is wrong. There is no fun in having bad habits; evil destroys all the fun. It satiates the mind so that soon there is no longer any joy in over-eating, in sexual over-activity, in over-indulgence of any of the senses. If in anything you overdo, remember, you are under the influence and in the grip of bad habits. For instance, if you have ulcers of the stomach, and through habit continue to eat meat, or hot or fried foods, which further irritate the stomach and take away the scabs formed by nature to heal the ulcers, the ulcerated condition will worsen and may develop into cancer or a hemorrhage. Rather, you should eat puréed and soft foods, and other foods that do not irritate the stomach lining. Why let habit make you eat those things you know will harm you?

Just as crime doesn't pay, so bad habits don't pay, because they will destroy your health and happiness and peace of mind;

and they will also set a bad example for those you love. You must strive to conquer harmful habits now. Don't be a weakling. Stay away from the things that stimulate your bad habits. And always choose good substitutes that will bring you peace of mind and a sound, healthy body.

Temptations are charming and strong, but you are stronger, because the image of God is within you. No matter how many times you fall, you can rise again. But when you admit defeat, then you are lost. And lost is your peace and happiness.

Train Your Will to Be Unenslaved

Saint Ignatius of Loyola was called the saint of will power. He was not satisfied to wait for the grace of God to descend. He trained his will so that he could commune with God at any time. He said, "I can find God at all times, whenever I wish, and any man of good will can do the same. As the body can be exercised by going, walking, and running, so the will of man can be trained by exercises to find the will of God." That is what I believe—to train your will, to have complete mastery over your will, so that you can do the things you ought to do, with the will unbound by bad habits.

One should have freedom even to cut his own throat if he wants to; but he certainly should not use his freedom, his free will, to do any such thing! It seems, however, that in the name of freedom it is human nature to want to do the very things that are not good for us. Tell the self-willed person to do something that is good for him, and he will want to do exactly the opposite. People who behave in this way are childish and immature. When one is ripe with wisdom, then he is a truly mature human being. Age has nothing to do with it.

A slave is a slave. No matter how he tries, he can't do without the thing he is a slave to. Never allow yourself to be enslaved by anything. You have all the will power in the world to break any habit. The power of divine will is always with you, and can never be destroyed. But you allow it to be eclipsed by your bad habits and other wrong influences.

When you make up your mind to do or not to do something, never give in — unless you see you are wrong; then quickly change your mind. Otherwise, don't give up, because weakening of the will takes away your most valuable treasure. Persons you associate with may want you to be like them; but it is you, not they, who will have to bear the consequences of what you are.

There is a story about the fox that lost its tail in a trap. He called a meeting of the other foxes and told them how wonderful it was to be rid of the tail. But one wise old fox got up and said, "Mr. Fox-without-a-tail, would you advise us to cut off our tails if you still had your own?" All the other foxes then saw the trick. The moral is that if others want you to take on their bad habits, just say *no*. For example, if anybody wants you to drink, because he likes to drink, be firm: "No thank you. I am very happy and having a good time without it." There is no real fun in being drunk and behaving like a fool; and not even remembering, when you are sober again, how badly you behaved. Besides, drink can destroy forever your nerves, your peace of mind, and your happiness.

So never let anyone weaken your will. Others will test you, but when you have made a resolve, keep your word. Above all, keep your word with yourself. If you find that you are unreasonable, that is different. Then you must be able to change at once and do that which is right.

A Story of "Won't" Power

When I like a particular food, I eat it until I decide to give it up. I don't create a dislike for it, I just leave it alone. For instance, as a child in India I used to like very much a small vegetable called *patol*. I would eat it morning, noon, and night. One of my friends said, "Don't you get tired of it?" "No," I responded. "When I like it, I like it." He said, "Then you are a slave to it." I thought, "Maybe he is right." So I vowed that I would not touch it for one year, and I didn't. You must develop that mulish "won't" power by which you will not budge, no matter how you are urged. Some months after I had made that resolution, my friend invited me and other friends to dinner. *Patols* were served; I ate everything except that vegetable. My friend said, "We are sorry that you won't eat it." I replied, "First of all, you decided to test me. For me to give in and weaken my will would be foolishness. And secondly, I have said that I will not touch this food for 365 days, and as a result I have no taste for it. I enjoyed *patols* before, but now the wish for them is gone."

Remember, you must get rid of every habit that enslaves

you. And don't associate with those who in the guise of friend-ship work with Satan to delude your will. Those friends who inspire you are your guardian angels. Those who love God are your protectors. If you want to be an artist, you should mix with artists. If you would love God, associate with those who love Him.

By Concentration, Habits Can Be Installed at Will

As weak-minded people can fall into bad habits easily, so strong-minded persons can learn to create good habits at will. How? By concentration. I will give you an illustration.

Years ago, in Boston, I was invited to someone's home for dinner. I was enjoying the meal very much until Roquefort cheese was served. I was very suspicious of those dark spots in the cheese. But I saw that everyone else was eating and enjoying it. I took some cheese in my mouth, and suddenly my stomach turned and all the contents inside said, "If you let Mr. Roquefort in, all of us will rush out at once!" I was gagging, but I said mentally, "Be quiet. I am the boss." One of the guests looked at me and said, "What is the matter?" I didn't dare to open my mouth. I watched everyone else enjoying the cheese, and I said to myself, "I command my mind to establish immediately the habit of eating Roquefort cheese!" And I found that I was eating and enjoying it. To this day I am very fond of Roquefort cheese. Later someone suggested that I install the habit of eating Lim-burger cheese; but I said, "Nothing doing." I didn't see any reason to inflict its awful smell on myself and others.

Introspect to Know Yourself as You Are

Be more serious about your life. Every night, introspect to see whether you are being swept down the current of bad habits or whether you are developing your will power and "won't" power in order to be master of yourself.

St. Ignatius had a wonderful method. He taught his monks to keep a daily record of all their good and bad actions by making a graph of dots and dashes. Many who never thought they could overcome their bad habits were helped by his suggestion. By watching the graphs of your mind, you can see whether you are progressing every day. You don't want to hide from yourself. You must know yourself as you are. By keeping a diary of your introspection, you keep watch on your bad habits and are better prepared to destroy them.

But no matter how you have sinned in the past, never call yourself a sinner, because that is the greatest sin against the image of God within you. It is better that you always affirm to yourself that you are a child of God, because that is what you are. As soon as you say you are a sinner, your mind accepts that decree, the will gives up, and you are done for. God seeks willing hearts who want to be free; and if you are willing, all the years of your past errors will not stop you from getting back to Him.

Perennial Peace and Joy Lie Within, Not in Externals

As a child of God, your real nature is to be happy; you will never be satisfied with anything less than true happiness. And it will not depend on anything outside yourself. Drink and dope will give you the false notion that you are having a good time, while they are actually destroying your body and mind and stifling the soul. The scripture tells us that on the day of Pentecost, the disciples of Christ were all drunk. They were drunk not with the alcohol of wine, but the ecstasy of God. It is this divine ecstasy, this divine happiness, that your soul is seeking.

You spend so much time in decorating your homes or working to buy a new car; and that is all right. But you must be able to renounce all things inwardly. Why? Because it gives freedom from enslavement to possessions. Just think about that. You bemoan not having what others have. You don't know what it is to be free. The contrast of the happiness within your soul outbalances all the pleasure that you can get from your senses. So don't spend too much time seeking and caring for possessions. Yes, it is good to be neat, but don't be overly fastidious; after you have cleaned things, they are soon dirty again. Be spotless within. Make your inner self a temple of God. Make it a temple of the mystic life of the universe. Then you are king of everything, and not attached to anything. That inner renunciation is the greatest way, greater than merely following the path of outer renunciation, undergoing forced discipline with the inner self still attached to the body and possessions. Change your heart, for therein you can make an altar either for the devil of misery, or for the Heavenly Father. Perennial peace lies within, not in outer possessions and conditions.

God alone is sufficient, for in Him lies all love, all life, all happiness, all joy, all peace — everything that even in your wildest dreams you could not imagine. Cultivate a relationship with Him. Practice the presence of God every day, and never go to bed at night until you have practiced your Kriya and are filled with that joy. Have that eternal peace within and without; then whoever comes to you shall feel your peace and be uplifted by it. You don't want to be a human skunk, driving away by your obnoxious behavior, your bad habits, whoever comes into your presence. You want to be a human rose, a flower of bliss, a bird of paradise. As soon as God touches you, all the fragrance of every flower is manifest within you. All the goodness and purity of God is within you. That is why it was said of Jesus: "Never man spake like this man."* You cannot fathom the real nature of those who know God, because they are depthless. My gurudeva, Swami Sri Yukteswar, was like that. He was apart from everything. The teaching of being united with God, and thereby nonattached to everything else, is Yoga.

The Time to Create Spiritual Habits Is Now

Since it may take eight years to form a habit, if you want to be spiritual, you must begin to cultivate the right habits now. All of your life you have been restless for things of the world. You sit to meditate and you become more restless. Then you say, "There is no use in meditating." But that is foolish reasoning. You have to live those eight years anyway, so why not use that time to perfect your practice of meditation? The more concentration you put into it, the sooner you will develop that habit. Your mind will then be saturated with the habit of silence. And when that habit is formed, you will feel restless, not for the world, but for God.

No matter what your work or responsibilities, you must keep your most important engagement — with God in meditation; for all things will betray you if you betray Him. That is why I never miss my appointment with Him, especially at night. Don't go to bed until you feel the joy of God within and without; then all day long He will be with you. Nothing can match that joy.

* John 8:46.

Develop the habit of communion with that great joy which is beyond the state of sleep. Deep, dreamless sleep is an unconscious way of contacting the peace and joy of God, and meditation is the conscious way. The satisfaction of ten million sleeps does not begin to describe the bliss you feel in conscious communion with God. Remain in that blissful calmness within your soul. When all things worldly and all secular concerns completely vanish and dissolve in the light of Spirit, then you shall see Him.

Don't wait until later to change your habits. Procrastination fosters more bad habits until the will is a prisoner, and you think you can't change. Do not allow yourself to reach that state. So long as you are willing, God will help you.

Technique for Creating and Destroying Habits

When you want to create a good habit or destroy a bad one, concentrate on the brain cells, the storehouse of the mechanisms of habits. To create a good habit, meditate; and then with the concentration fixed at the Christ center, the center of will between the eyebrows, deeply affirm the good habit that you want to install. And when you want to destroy bad habits, concentrate at the Christ center and deeply affirm that all the grooves of bad habits are being erased.

I will tell you a true story of the effectiveness of this technique. In India, a man who had a bad temper came to me. He was a specialist in slapping his bosses when he lost his temper, so he also lost one job after another. He would become so uncontrollably irate that he would throw at whoever bothered him anything that was handy. He asked me for help. I told him, "The next time you get angry, count to one hundred before you act." He tried it, but came back to me and said, "I get more angry when I do that. While I am counting, I am blind with rage for having to wait so long." His case looked hopeless.

Then I told him to practice Kriya Yoga, with this further instruction: "After practicing your Kriya, think that the divine Light is going into your brain, soothing it, calming your nerves, calming your emotions, wiping away all anger. And one day your temper tantrums will be gone." Not long after that, he came to me again, and this time he said, "I am free from the habit of anger. I am so thankful."

I decided to test him. I arranged for some boys to pick a quarrel with him. I hid myself in the park along the route where he used to pass regularly, so that I could observe. The boys tried again and again to goad him into a fight, but he wouldn't respond. He kept his calmness.

Make-believe Pleasures Cannot Substitute for the Bliss of God

You should wish for a thousand million deaths rather than enmesh yourself in bad habits from which you cannot free yourself. Money, sex, and wine were created as make-believe pleasures. They could never substitute for the bliss of God. Even if you do no more than pray sincerely to Him, His great joy will eventually come upon you. Naturally, God wants to test you with the taste of temptation and the lure of your bad habits to see if you really want Him more than the enticing pseudo-pleasures of the body. If you give in, you will get nowhere. If you keep pouring water into a pot, you cannot expect the pot to dry out. You must dry up the water of bad habits in the sun of good company, wholesome activity, introspection, and will power; and, above all, meditation and God-communion. No one can help you unless you are willing to help yourself. As I said, if you are willing, then God Himself will help you.

When Jesus prayed to the Heavenly Father, "Lead us not into temptation, but deliver us from evil," he meant, "Leave us not in the pit of temptation wherein we fell through the misuse of Thy gift of reason." Temptation cannot lead us unless we misuse our God-given reason. If once you taste the sweetness of God in meditation, you shall not be touched by temptation any more. You will throw off your bad habits and go after Him. If you truly seek God, you will find Him.

The Garden of Flowering Qualities

Inspirational message* preceding Sunday Service
First Self-Realization Fellowship Temple, Encinitas, California,
May 3, 1942

I behold civilization as a garden in which I see all kinds of flowering human qualities. Like a bee, my mind seeks out the blossoms of good qualities. So many people behave like flies, "buzzing" intently about God until something attracts their senses; then off they flit, even if the lure is spiritually unwholesome. The bee seeks only those flowers that yield pure honey. You must be a divine bee, tasting nothing but the sweetness, the goodness, of the honey of God. Remember that, and try to absorb in yourself the good qualities of others. By adoring and tasting human goodness, we can find God. He is the honey, and in His honeyed qualities in others we will taste His presence everywhere.

Everything that is good is God. Whether it manifests in nature or through noble qualities in human beings, it is God whom we are beholding. God the Beautiful is manifest in the synchronized scenery of nature. His breath is heaving in the wind; His divinity is smiling at us in the flowers. The qualities of love and peace and joy that grow in the garden of human hearts are reflecting His goodness, His beauty. He who looks for evil sees evil everywhere. He who looks for goodness sees goodness everywhere. Let your eyes behold only that which is beautiful, so that the ugliness of evil will disappear from your consciousness.

By seeking out evil, by being negative and affirming to yourself negative thoughts, you see this world as a forest of fear. By seeking goodness, being good, and affirming good, you see

---

* During the opening meditation at the Sunday temple services, Paramahansaji often received deep and beautiful inspirations from God, sometimes in response to another's spiritual need, which he shared in his opening remarks before speaking on the sermon topic for the day.

this world as a garden of beauty. The Bhagavad Gita teaches that he who thinks negatively and beholds evil in the world is the enemy of his Self, and the Self acts as his enemy. And he who beholds only goodness is a friend to his Self, and the Self acts as his friend.* If you are your own enemy, picking up evil from everywhere, your true Self will be your enemy. And if you befriend yourself by absorbing good qualities from everywhere, your true Self will be your friend. So in this world seek only that which is good, do that which is good. Constantly seek God instead of indulging in negative thoughts and actions, and you will find peace of mind and happiness in your life. Sometime you will have to rid yourself of evil. Why not now?

No matter how you have been enwrapped in negative thinking and negative behavior, those wrong habits cannot enslave you forever. We think we can't rid ourselves of harmful sense temptations and jealousy and anger; but there is no emotion that can forever hold your soul. So, dear ones, let no one call you a sinner. You are sons of God, for He made you in His image. To deny that image is the greatest sin against yourself. And if you are a sinner against yourself, God shall be against you. Rather say to yourself: "No matter if my sins be as deep as the ocean and as high as the stars, still I am unconquered, because I am Spirit Itself." Darkness may reign in a cave for thousands of years, but bring in the light, and the darkness vanishes as though it had never been. Similarly, no matter what your defects, they are yours no longer when you bring in the light of goodness. So great is the light of the soul that incarnations of evil cannot destroy it. But the self-created temporary darkness of evil makes the soul miserable, because you suffer in that darkness. You can drive it away by opening your spiritual eye in deep meditation, filling your consciousness with its all-revealing divine light.

No one else can save you. You are your own savior as soon as you realize, "I am Light Itself. Darkness was never meant for me; it can never cover the light of my soul."

* "Let man be uplifted, not degraded; let him transform his self (ego) into the Self (soul). The Self is the friend of the (transformed) self, but the enemy of the unregenerate self" (Bhagavad Gita VI:5-6).

Oriental and Occidental Christianity

A class for Self-Realization students in 1926

Spirit is the infinite reservoir of wisdom. Each human life is a channel through which that divine wisdom is steadily flowing. Some channels are wide and others narrow. The larger the channel, the greater the flow of God-power.

We are unique channels, for it lies within our power to make ourselves narrower or wider. We have been given freedom of will and the power of choice. Some choke the channel of their lives with the mud of accumulated ignorance, never allowing themselves to be cleansed by the dredge of knowledge. The ocean of truth attempts fruitlessly to flood in greater volume through such narrow openings.

There are others who keep on digging, widening, deepening the channels of their lives by self-discipline and culture, thus inviting an ever larger volume of God-wisdom to pass through. Jesus the Christ was one of the greatest channels through which the cosmic wisdom flowed. We must remember that each channel is finite and has its limitations. I daresay there shall never be born a prophet who can contain or exhaust the whole ocean of truth in his short span of life. Other prophets shall always come to express truth anew. Though infinite truth must thus suffer measurement even at the hands of prophets, these great souls nevertheless serve to widen the channels of smaller lives, inundating those shores with their unbounded wisdom.

True Christianity

True Christianity (the divine principles taught by Christ) should not be confused with some of the forms that cloak it. True Christianity is neither Oriental nor Occidental, nor is it the teaching of Jesus and his saints alone. Its eternal principles belong to every truth-seeking soul. Jesus the son of man lifted himself to the state of being a son of God. That is, he rose above ordinary human consciousness and entered the cosmic Christ

335

Consciousness, the pure reflection of God present in all creation. When St. John said that "as many as received him, to them gave he power to become the sons of God,"* he meant that anyone who could receive that Christ Consciousness, who could increase the capacity of his consciousness to hold that infinite ocean of truth, would become, as did Jesus, a son of God—one with the Father.

This offers hope to every seeking heart, for there would be no incentive in following the example of Jesus if we could not be like him. Jesus was not sent to us to symbolize an unattainable goal. He came as a living inspiration, demonstrating what we all may successfully seek and achieve. If God created all men in His image, as stated in the Bible, He could not give more to one than He gives to all the rest. He cannot be accused of partiality, which would make Him less divine. We are all His children, created by the power of His being—endowed with that power to become His true "sons."

Nor did God alone make Jesus the spiritual giant that he was. If God creates prophets as unique beings, ready-made in a spiritual factory, then we might justly think it needless to struggle, and would expect Him to remold us and do our spiritual thinking for us. The gift of reason and choice, the power to exercise free will, is peculiar to man and is sufficient to demonstrate to us that we must acquire our own spiritual growth by individual effort and achievement. Jesus struggled, fasted, prayed, disciplined himself in every way. We admire Jesus the more that, being born a human, he became divine.

Spiritual truth is one: interpreted by Christians it is called Christianity; by Hindus, Hinduism; and so forth. Narrow-mindedness confines religion to church or temple worship and sectarian beliefs, mistaking the form for the spirit. Truth has suffered constriction in all interpretations, narrow and liberal. We must reach the goal of Self-realization of truth, wherein man-made interpretations no longer limit us.

The aim of Yogoda† (Self-Realization) is to teach the prac-

---

* John 1:12.

† The word *Yogoda*, used in this article by Paramahansaji, is the name by which his work in India is known: Yogoda Satsanga Society of India. He also used this term in America in the early years. (See glossary.)

tical methods, the exact techniques, of widening the channel of human consciousness, so that truth might flow in continuously, endlessly, without obstructions of dogma or unproved beliefs. Yogoda points out, not only the words and personalities of saints and prophets, but the path of concentration on a practical system. It teaches the step-by-step progression from belief to personal realization and individual attainment of divinity.

Oriental Conditions of Life Were Different

"Sell all ye have and give to the poor," "Take no heed for the morrow .... what ye shall eat, what ye shall put on," * and other spiritual injunctions of Jesus would not admit of strict practical application in the Occident today.

What Jesus preached can be understood only by developing the inner consciousness, spiritualizing the inner self. Christianity originally placed less emphasis on the outer formalities of religion. Jesus taught an Oriental† people, in an Oriental setting and atmosphere. The truths he spoke were interpreted by the Oriental mentalities that surrounded him. If the New Testament had been written by Jesus, rather than his disciples, it would have been very different. The spiritual experiences of the Biblical characters, however transcendental, or intuitional, when expressed through Oriental mentality and terminology, took on an Oriental hue. Soul experiences cannot be fully expressed through words, and when language half-lisps them, they assume a distinguishing individual stamp.

The shunning of all material possessions as taught by Jesus was especially applicable to and possible in those times and conditions. If Jesus were preaching today to Americans, his essential message would be the same, but expressed differently than 2,000 years ago to a people in a land where living conditions and climatic and social factors made it possible to live much more simply than is generally practical today. Then, a little labor would suffice to gain the necessities of life. The warm climate

* Ref. Matthew 19:21, 6:25,34.

† When this talk was given, the terms "Orient" and "Occident" were commonly used to designate the East and West. The Orient included those countries east of the Mediterranean; thus Paramahansaji's reference to Jesus and his followers as Orientals.

simplified the problem of clothing and housing. Less attention was needed for the physical side of life. Oriental Christianity taught plain living, outdoor living, meditating on the lap of Mother Nature. Jesus did not preach a mode of living far removed from the customary life of that day. Nor would he today advocate a radical change in our routine of life.

This is a different age; the purposes of the Creator demand that the world's evolution proceed through ever new and varied conditions. So Jesus would not concentrate today on a drastic departure from the practical forms and conditions of our life. Now, as then, he would point out that formalities of life are secondary; that the only worthwhile change, the only permanent advance, is the inner evolution of man toward spiritual perfection. The outer conditions of life will never be perfect until the inner condition is perfect. The effect cannot precede the cause. Christ's teaching, interpreted by and adapted to Occidentals, is thus different, and this we can call Occidental Christianity.

Through a misunderstanding of Christ's teachings, his early followers conceived a contempt for, and disregard of, the progress of material life. They did not attempt to translate inner growth into outer achievement. This has been the case throughout the Orient generally. But God's laws do not respect any man-made interpretation. Whenever and wherever man, as a Christian or Hindu, or as any race, breaks God's physical, mental, or spiritual laws that govern the spiritual, mental, social, industrial, and materially progressive conditions of life, he is punished with war, plague, famine, material poverty, and spiritual ignorance. History teaches us that man must develop his life in an all-round manner, neglecting neither the physical nor the mental and spiritual sides, if he would achieve perfection.

Why Christianity Changed in the West

However, we must admit that because of a spiritual emphasis the Orient generally, and India in particular, has been the breeding-ground of the world's greatest prophets and saints — Jesus, Buddha, Krishna, Shankara, Chaitanya, my Master and paramgurus, and many others. Strangely, we do not find in the West any prophet of such eminence. If we could take statistics of the world's mentalities, we would find that in general the Orientals are more spiritually inclined, and the Westerners more materially and industrially minded. That is why Oriental Christianity, as taught by Jesus and his disciples, underwent a distinct change in form after arriving in the Occident. Jesus' exhortation to the Oriental multitude, "Seek ye first the kingdom of God," was changed for all practical purposes in the West to "Seek ye bread first and the kingdom of God later." "Sell all ye have and give to the poor" became "Buy all ye can at cost price, then sell at top price and invest wisely the surplus."

But even if people today desired to carry out literally the instructions given by Jesus to those of his time, they would not be able to do so with a good conscience. Family responsibilities in most cases would prevent a man from selling all his goods and giving the money to the poor. If he took "no heed for the morrow.... what ye shall eat, what ye shall put on," he would not be acting correctly toward those dependent on him, who have a right to expect his support and protection. But the fact that people in the more complicated modern world cannot always follow literally the precepts given by Jesus does not prevent them from being in every respect true Christians, following faithfully the inner teachings and true essence of Christianity. They can spiritualize their ambition and their wealth by using them for the good of others. They can avoid the greed of luxury, and satisfy only their real needs.

Jesus was able to preach to the multitudes on mountaintops and other outdoor places. News of his meetings spread by word of mouth, for in his day people did not depend on newspapers. But such delightful freedom from hall-rents and advertising expenditure is not possible today. The teacher may be willing to preach on the mountaintop covered with snow, or inaccessible by subway or bus, but the audience is not willing to come there to hear him. In the West, they want large steam-heated and centrally located meeting places. So the teacher who is sincerely desirous of sowing the seeds of spirituality in the hearts of the multitude ought to be willing also to accept the conditions of life in the country and age in which he finds himself. As Bruce Barton has pointed out in his wonderful book, *The Man Nobody Knows*, Jesus would employ the methods of the successful businessman; he would be a large user of newspaper columns as a means of communication, for example, if he were preaching today in America. The means do not greatly matter; getting the message to the people is the main thing.

Costly big churches have to be erected today to house the religious multitudes, with consequent concentration on financial problems. Once a man came to me after my first lecture in his city, and said, "Swami,* many times I have come to different lectures here, sat on one of those hard, uncomfortable chairs of the auditorium, and been forced to leave after a half-hour of discomfort. But tonight, I am glad to tell you, your sermon completely erased the hard-chair consciousness from my mind during the whole two hours. Just the same, you should arrange always to provide your audience with comfortable seats, as otherwise an American audience will not stay!"

Real God-Communion Is Needed

Churches in the Occident have done untold good by their efforts to remind people of their spiritual obligations and of God's laws. But churches have become form-bound, lacking in the spirit of deep meditation and real God-communion that Jesus and his disciples so plainly manifested in their lives. Today, the congregation at church is there in body, but in mind it is often somewhere else. During the sermon, or at the time of prayer, how many are thinking instead of the chicken dinner awaiting them, or of a business deal! Such mental waywardness is not the fault of the churchgoer, for he has never been taught the art of directing his mind, of withdrawing it from the realm of sense-distraction and focusing it on God. Indeed, the average man does not even know or believe that it is possible for him to communicate personally with God. God can be contacted by the practice of specific techniques of concentration and meditation on the Cosmic Vibration.† He will become as real and near as

---

* In 1935, Sri Yukteswar bestowed on his beloved disciple Yogananda the spiritual title "Paramahansa." Prior to that time he was known as Swami Yogananda. (See *swami* in glossary.)

† *Aum*, the Holy Ghost, Amen, the Word: Invisible divine power, the outward manifestation of the omnipresent Christ Consciousness. *Aum*, the blissful Comforter, is heard in meditation and reveals to the devotee the ultimate Truth, bringing "all things to ... remembrance" (John 14:26). (See *Aum* in glossary.)

one's own thoughts and body. Yogoda has been sent to teach this art of communion, of personal God-contact, of coming into conscious touch with the Source of all light, all power, all bliss.

Religionists limit truth by claiming to monopolize it, one calling the other "heathen." Many Christians think the Hindu and the Buddhist to be "heathens"; the Hindu and the Buddhist, if bigoted and lacking in religious courtesy, feel the same about the Christian. But true religion is not exclusive. Its essence is twofold. First and most important, it consists of certain inner principles of attunement with God that make life progressive, permanently happy, and beautiful in every way. Secondly, it has material and mental forms of routine and discipline that are required to bring those inner principles into manifestation in man's material life. Religious customs and forms are like husks, necessary to protect the kernel of truth. But if the husk covers no seed of life, it is useless, barren. The sacraments, conch shells, temple bells, the cross, the crescent—such exteriorizations have been necessary to symbolize certain spiritual truths. But with time, people's minds became concentrated on the form of the service or ritual, the personality of the preacher or priest and his method of delivery, the architecture and size of the church or temple, the number of followers and their social status and possessions. On the other hand, those with iconoclastic ideas want to destroy all form. Their error is that their zeal to do away with form is itself concentration on form, or outer precepts. Thus the symbols and outer forms of religion act as red flags to excite the bull of religious fanaticism.

Yogoda offers a remedy, a solution. It asks the different religionists to live together in harmony by concentrating on the one Reality behind form, the Truth that is the kernel of every religion. Yogoda has come, not to unite all churches and religions into one church and one form, nor to destroy individual expressions of religion, but to show the scientific methods by which the utility and truth of the church and creed may be proven and demonstrated. Change of religious customs, or fusion of all forms into one common form, would not alter the essential religious attitude. Nothing but proven truth, religious truth that has been tested and experienced individually, will ever satisfy completely the mind of man and do away with religious bigotry and ignorance.

East and West Need Balance

In the West, because of the lack of scientific methods for directly perceiving truth, there has not been an overwhelming interest in spiritual inquiry and research. On the other hand, in India, where a host of saints and men of realization have testified to the truth that all men may know God through a definite series of steps and methods of concentration and meditation, we find that religion has always played a prominent part in the daily life of the multitude. But East and West alike suffer from overdevelopment of one phase of life and underdevelopment of other phases. India in her religious one-sidedness broke God's laws governing the material part of life, and as a consequence has had to suffer from famine and plague. In the West, worship of the god of wealth and ignorance of God's spiritual laws have produced nations without inward peace, manifesting outwardly in the horrors of the World War. Thus East and West have failed in one respect, and succeeded in another. Wise men of the East have a wealth of spiritual insight and peace that no outward circumstances of suffering can destroy. And materially scientific men of the West have conquered plague and famine. Each needs the other's help to achieve perfection.

Westerners need not blow up their factories, give up their banks and businesses, and retire to the jungle in order to be spiritual. But they can accept the scientific methods of inner realization from the East; and can pursue their progressive worldly activities for the good of others, instead of for selfish purposes. Nor need the East accept wholesale the industrial materialistic methods of the West. All that is necessary is an acceptance of the Western spirit of progress and development in reference to the betterment of material life. Thus each may benefit by the example and teachings of the other. The East must see the Supreme in wholesome progressive material things of life, and the West must not forget the spiritual Goal in its enthusiasm for worldly activity. A balance must be struck.

No matter what religion you follow, ask yourself, "Am I happy? Am I making others happy? Have I found the answer to the supreme question of life? What is my highest duty? How can I find peace and bliss?" Yogoda (Self-Realization Fellowship teachings) provides a practical technique of God-realization, of spiritualizing the body-cells through a definite system of physical development, of keeping in touch with the Supreme Source of cosmic supply that governs all aspects of our material and spiritual life. This is the practical message for which Occidentals have been hungering — those who are not content with blind belief and long to prove truth through their own personal experience. This is the message — one of actual God-communion — that will fill again the empty churches. People today frequent the movie-houses, but the churches are comparatively empty. Why? Because there is something tangible to interest and delight the mind in the former. The Yogoda science of meditation will supply this interest in the latter. It will show each seeker that the most interesting thing in all the world is the Bliss-God within. It will give him the key to enter into this realm of unparalleled joys. All the pursuits of life offer only partial happiness, even if crowned with utmost fulfillment. But in finding God we have the reservoir of perennial, unending, unsatiating bliss. For He can give what the whole universe cannot give. He is the Whole; the universe is but a part of Him.

Knowing God Scientifically

Once Occidentals know real communion with this great Bliss-God, their whole attitude toward religion and the church will change. No sermon will be dull then, no church empty. Seekers will hold the key to prove the truth of His existence. They will be listening to words about One whom they have experienced and know to be true, to be near, to be living. They will be devotees of God because they have met Him, and not because theoretically it seems that such a Being exists and should be worshiped.

Nothing can ever fully satisfy the heart of man except living proof. Yogoda brings that proof to man's door. Just as it is necessary for the astronomer to look through a telescope in order to see distant stars, so it is necessary for the questioner of God's existence to look for Him through the instrument of scientific meditation. If one proclaimed or denied the existence of a distant star, and yet would not look through the telescope to see if he were wrong or not, his opinion would be worthless. He cannot prove his stand unless he has confirmed it through available instruments of knowledge. Similarly, no one may rightfully deny, or positively affirm, the existence of God unless he has practiced the methods of approaching Him.

Yogoda meditation is a telescope through which you can see God. Without it, you must rest your belief in God on unproved faith alone. With it, you can challenge anyone to disprove that God can be known.

To control the mind by psychophysiological methods, to direct it Godward, to be its leader, not its slave—that is Yogoda ("that which yoga imparts") whether you give it that name or not. All life's labors are in vain unless you know how to shift your attention from failure to success, from worry to calmness, from mental wanderings to concentration, from restlessness to peace, from peace to conscious Divine Bliss within. If you have attained this control, then the purpose of life has been gloriously fulfilled.

(Paramahansaji concluded with the following lines, which he had composed:)

> Whether in the prison house of loneliness
> Or heaven of blissful solitude;
> Whether fettered by the chains of labor
> Or resting idly in the peace of long-deservèd rest,
> I care not,
> If Thou art with me.
> Whether in mosque, church, or temple
> It matters little,
> If I love not Thy house and its creed
> More than Thee.
> In the revolving wheels of factories
> I want to feel Thy pulsing, marching life.
> If Thou art in the factory,
> I prefer that to Heaven without Thee.
> Whether in Himalayan caves
> Or crowded subway,
> Whether in jungles of Hindustan
> Or of modern life—
> Wherever we go,
> Teach us to discover Thee
> In all Thy secret nooks,
> East, west, north, south,
> Everywhere.

A World Without Boundaries

Opening talk at a banquet at the Self-Realization Fellowship Second Temple, * *Los Angeles, California, February 26, 1939*

Wherever different minds meet in the spirit of fellowship, there we find a great harmony, peace, happiness, understanding, and cooperation in life's activities. With so many troubles plaguing this earth of ours — a miniature world war going on in Europe, nation tearing at nation — never before was there a greater necessity for peace than now.

I believe there will always be wars, until perchance we all become so spiritual that by the evolution of our individual natures we will make war unnecessary. No matter what their differences, if great minds such as Jesus, Krishna, Buddha, Mohammed, sat together, they would never use the engines of science to try to destroy each other. Where there is understanding, peace reigns. Why must people feel it necessary to fight? The power of guns evokes no wisdom, nor has it ever accomplished lasting peace.

War is like poison in the system. When we have toxins in our body, that impurity has to get out somehow. So we suffer from disease. Likewise, when there is too much selfishness in the international system, that poison breaks out in the world as the disease of war. Many people are killed, and then for a little while there is a lull. But war comes again—and will come again and again—so long as there will be ignorance, and so long as the individual man has not become a perfect citizen of the world.

God gave us intelligence, and He placed us in an environment where we must use that intelligence. The universe is like a shell, and we are like little chicks moving about within it. But what is beyond this shell of matter? What is beyond its three dimensions? We must penetrate space and know the workings of that other world out of which this one has come. We should use

* See footnote page 97.

our intelligence to analyze the mysteries of life and to explore the secrets the Heavenly Father has hidden behind nature. How much better use of intelligence this would be, than the creation of bigger and more destructive instruments of war. We must use our intelligence to have peace among ourselves.

Understanding Must Be Freed From Prejudices

Why not follow a process of education in which, rather than nurturing hatred toward nations that are different from our own, we try by love to create understanding? Understanding is extremely necessary. But just as some people are shortsighted and some are farsighted, so is our understanding. It is often clouded by many prejudices. Our vision is obscured from our very birth by the prejudices of family, race, and nation. Prejudice is a principal cause of war between brother nations. We shall never understand ourselves or others unless we keep our understanding free from all clouds of prejudice.

We so love our own thoughts that we can't always understand what the other person is thinking. We are cooped up in a little pen of our own concepts; just like the little frog that lived in a well: When a frog from a huge lake fell into the well and told him about his vast home, the little frog only laughed and wouldn't believe him. He had never seen anything beyond the confines of the well, and was thoroughly convinced that his home was the largest body of water there could possibly be. This is the limited attitude of nations as well as individuals. Each nation thinks its views are best.

We have to learn to give unceasing understanding to all, even to those who misunderstand us. I give you an illustration: C can analyze D fairly well, so he thinks he can understand everybody else. But he knows nothing about B, who is sitting behind C and D, and thinks he understands both of them. And behind B is A, who sees B, C, and D, and therefore thinks he understands everyone. It is human nature to think we know better than anyone else. But the only way to truly know anything is by cultivating divine understanding.

Love the World as You Love Your Nation and Family

International understanding is much clouded by lack of realization that individual happiness is included in family happiness, family happiness in community happiness, community happiness in national happiness, and national happiness in international happiness.

Love of family is inherently strong. Through family love, God became the father to love you through wisdom, and He became the mother because He wanted to give you unconditional love. God became the lover and the beloved to unite souls in an expanded love. He became the friend to unite souls in a pure, impersonal love that makes no demands. In friendship there is no compulsion; it comes through the choice of the heart. Such friendship should exist between husband and wife, child and parent, in all human relations. Friendship is a great factor in bringing peace in the international family of the world.

No one can love his nation without learning the first lesson in love, which is to love his family. The baby's initial cries are for milk, but soon it invests its love in the mother and father. Then, as it grows older, it learns to love its country. When that soul becomes Christlike, it begins to love the world.

You are a member of the worldwide human race. Don't forget it. You must love the world as you love your nation and your family. This is difficult to learn, but the task of Self-Realization Fellowship is to show you how. We teach that it is by fellowship with God that fellowship with man must be established; because only when you know God and see Him in all can you love the Jew and Christian, Muslim and Hindu, with the same spirit. I was taught this as a child, but it was more or less a forced intellectual concept. It wasn't an understanding from within. I tried to love the whole world, but it was not easy. As soon as I looked at my family, my love lost itself there. But one by one, many of those dearest to me died. I thought that nature was very cruel. Then I began to realize that my love was undergoing discipline; that I was to expand my love, not limit it to my family. God showed me that it was He whom I loved in my loved ones. Then, from within, my love began to expand to all. I could no longer feel partiality toward family. When I returned to India in 1935, I saw that this was true. Except for the love Father gave me, I felt like a stranger when I visited the family home.

Therefore, through family life and then through national life, God is schooling every individual to understand his interna-

tional family, that we may have a United States of the World
with Truth as our guide.

International Understanding Dissolves Divisive Boundaries

We are all aliens here. No territory belongs permanently to
any country. The hand of time eventually erases all nations.
Their boundaries don't last, because they represent divisions
that have been carved out by force. I believe a time will come
when in greater understanding we shall have no boundaries
anymore. We shall call the earth our country; and we shall, by a
process of justice and international assembly, distribute unselfishly the goods of the world according to the needs of the people.
But equality cannot be established by force; it must come from
the heart. The greatest blessing would be to develop international understanding by which we may realize this truth.

These ideals should be taught in all the schools. Just as it
would be a sin to teach everyone to "love your family; it doesn't
matter what happens to your country," so it is a sin to teach love
of country that militates against your greater world family.
When in every school love of country is over-emphasized, it
sows the seeds of misunderstanding and even hatred toward
other nations. How dare we spoil children by teaching them the
kind of patriotism in which there are seeds of hatred! Unless you
love your country, you cannot love the world; but children
should be taught also to love other countries as they love their
own. That is the principle of God.

Peace Will Come When We Learn to See God in All

So you see, we must dissociate our wisdom from all environmental influences. If we can learn to understand others,
and to free our minds from all prejudices born of environment,
we begin to express the perfect image of God within us and to
find it in all. "But as many as received him, to them gave he
power to become the sons of God."* The light of the sun falls
equally on the diamond and the charcoal; but the diamond, by
its transparency, reflects the sun more. Bhagavan Krishna taught
that because the wisdom in man is covered by ignorance, and
because man chooses to misuse his independence to nurture

* John 1:12.

that ignorance, he doesn't reflect the true image of God that is within him. But in all those who use the power of the mind to be good, the power of Spirit will manifest. If we can *receive* that power of Spirit, then we become true sons of God. And we must learn to see the light of God falling on both His good and bad children. Peace will come when we discipline our hearts to see God in all, not just in those who love us or whom we think of as our own.

Peace is not something that you and I or a few great souls can create at once, by command. Even a million Christs or Krishnas could not do it. Try as he would, Lord Krishna could not prevent the great war between the Pandavas and Kauravas, which is described in the *Mahabharata*.* All humanity has to become Christlike to bring peace on earth. When each one of us shapes his life according to the wisdom and example of a Christ, a Krishna, a Buddha, we can have peace here; not before. We must start now, with ourselves. We should try to be like the divine ones who have come on earth again and again to show us the way. By our loving each other and keeping our understanding clear, as they taught and exemplified, peace can come.

Peace Begins at Home and in the Schools

Each individual in a family and community should strive to live peacefully with others. Peace must begin in the home and in the schools. In the classrooms we must teach international patriotism—to love the world as Jesus, Krishna, and the great masters have taught, and not to do anything that would lead to international discomfort. It is not our nationality or our color that we should be proud of, but our understanding. We should cultivate our understanding and use it to determine what is truly best for family happiness, national happiness, and international happiness. International happiness should include the well-being of the nation, the community, and the family. The standard of legislation should be merit, not color of skin or any other class distinction. These are the ideals to be taught to children.

So long as God's children differentiate, "We are Hindus and

* Hindu epic poem, eighteen chapters of which make up the scripture, Bhagavad Gita—"Song of the Lord." (See *Bhagavad Gita* in glossary.)

you are Americans; we are Germans, you are English," so long will they be bound by delusion and the world divided. Much war and suffering and destruction will be prevented if we cease to emphasize differences and learn to love all without distinction or prejudice. Be more proud that you are made in the image of God than that you are of a certain nationality; for "American" and "Indian" and all the other nationalities are just outer coats, which in time will be discarded. But you are a child of God throughout eternity. Isn't it better to teach that ideal to your children? It is the only way to peace: Establish the true ideals of peace in the schools, and live peace in your own life.

Without Selfishness There Would Be No Wars

If we analyze individual psychology, we find that all human beings are passing through one of four states. When a desire is fulfilled we are happy. When a desire is contradicted we are unhappy. Between these two states is indifference; we are neither happy nor unhappy. Beyond these three states is peace. If we can clear our understanding of all selfish prejudices—individual, family, national—we can reach that state of peace.

Just think, if Hitler and other dictators and world aggressors had had no personal or national selfishness, how many wars would have been averted. I would like to see one qualified person attain to the presidency just for the sake of the country. Lincoln was such a one. I cannot think of him without thinking of his aspirations for all mankind. But most politicians seek office for their own advantage, and the advantage of those communities and causes that are closest to them personally. The love of nation of a Lincoln or a Gandhi is based on wisdom. The ambitions of puny politicians do great harm against the permanency of this or any country.

So patriotism must not bring wars and troubles in its wake. What is the value of a patriotism that destroys life, that kills innocent men, women, and children? War is supposed to show the nation's love of country. But that is not the right way to show it. The way to demonstrate true patriotism is to behave as children of God, and to give divine understanding to all people. "All they that take the sword shall perish with the sword."*

* Matthew 26:52.

Divine Love is greater than the power of the sword. Greater than all the swords in the world is understanding.

Today, the best country to live in is America. I am not saying this to flatter you, but because it is the truth. Here you have freedoms and material advantages and opportunities unknown in many other nations. Don't abuse those privileges and blessings. Remember that the only justification for life is to unravel the mysteries of this universe. The only justification for human existence is to find God. The Lord hopes you will learn to love the Giver more than all His material gifts.

Yoga Meditation Reveals Our Divine Nature

Out of the cosmic tomes of truth, India developed the Yoga system, the science of oneness—oneness of the soul with God; oneness with the principles of eternal righteousness; with the universe; and with all mankind. The sage Patanjali formulated the Yoga system into eight steps for achieving the goal:

1. Avoid unrighteous behavior—*yama.*
2. Follow certain moral and spiritual precepts—*niyama.*
3. Learn to be still in body and mind, for where motion ceases, there begins the perception of God—*asana.*
4. While concentrating on the state of peace, practice control of the life force in the body—*pranayama.*
5. When your mind is your own, that is, under your control through *pranayama,* then you can give it to God—*pratyahara.*
6. Then begins meditation: first, concentrate on one of God's cosmic manifestations such as love, wisdom, joy—*dharana.*
7. What follows in meditation is an expansion of the realization of God's infinite omnipresent nature—*dhyana.*
8. When the soul merges as one with God, who is ever-existing, ever-conscious, ever-new Bliss, that is the goal—*samadhi.*

The joy of God can never be exhausted. He is sufficient; the purpose and the aim of existence. True understanding comes when we feel God as the great bliss of meditation. And peace is the first proof of His presence.

To have peace we must love more, but we cannot love people unconditionally unless we know God. The soul is absolutely perfect, but when identified with the body as ego, its expression becomes distorted by human imperfections. If human beings were only these imperfect bodies and minds, there would be some justification for prejudices and divisions. But we are all souls, made in God's image. So Yoga teaches us to know the divine nature in ourselves and others. Through yoga meditation we can know that we are gods.

If Everyone Learns God-Communion, Peace Will Reign

I believe that if every citizen in the world is taught to *commune* with God (not merely to know Him intellectually), then peace can reign; not before. When by persistence in meditation you realize God through communion with Him, your heart is prepared to embrace all humanity.

I am neither a Hindu nor an American. Humanity is my race, and no one on earth can make me feel otherwise. Prejudice and exclusiveness are so childish. We are here for just a little while and then whisked away. We must remember only that we are children of God. I love all countries as I love my India. And my prayer to you is that you love all nations as you love America. God created a diverse world to teach you to forget your physical differences with other races; and, from the debris of misunderstanding and prejudice, to salvage your understanding and use it to make an effort to know Him as our one Father.

Therefore, my friends, resolve that you will love the world as your own nation, and that you will love your nation as you love your family. Through this understanding you will help to establish a world family on the indestructible foundation of wisdom.

Follow the ways of God. Set a time apart each day to meditate on Him. When you commune with God, you shall feel toward everyone as toward your own. No one can ever make me feel he is not mine. All human beings are God's children, and He is my Father.

To Know God Is to Love All

*Closing talk at a banquet at Self-Realization Fellowship
Second Temple, Los Angeles, California, February 26, 1939*

Self-Realization means "to know the Self as soul, made in the image of God." *Fellowship* stands for "fellowship with God, first, and through Him, fellowship with man." As soon as we learn in meditation to love God, we shall love all mankind as we love our own family. Those who have found God through their own Self-realization — those who have actually experienced God — they alone *can* love mankind; not impersonally, but as their blood brothers, children of the same one Father. That is my experience. When we have fellowship with God, and through Him true fellowship with all, we find no differences in race, class, or creed. When God is our religion, the dross of dogmatism is removed from our understanding and we see the Truth, which is in every soul and in every religion.* I hope you will all remember this fellowship, this divine friendship with all Truth-seeking souls, and practice it with one another. We want to give you this spiritual inspiration.

There is no excuse for preaching division in a temple of God. Churches must be places for communion with God. When we know the Father, sectarian divisions vanish. All the divine prophets and *avatars* have declared that God is One, and this is the point emphasized by Self-Realization. Religion is far more than morality; it is communion with God. To preach God and to encourage devotees to commune with Him is the only real purpose of a church or temple. If religion loses sight of communion with God, it has failed in its duty. But I think we are coming to that time when more and more people will want to truly realize the presence of God, and to feel the brotherhood of man.

---

* "Wherein lies happiness? In that which becks / Our ready minds to fellowship divine, / A fellowship with essence; till we shine,Full alchemiz'd and free of space. Behold / The clear religion of heaven!"—From Keats' *Endymion.*

A God of Love, Wisdom, and Beauty

Now is the time for you to make the effort to know God. In meditation, again and again throw the bombs of your deep yearning against the bulwark of silence, until its walls are broken down and God is revealed. *Feel* the love of God; then in every person you will see the face of the Father, the light of Love which is in all. You will find a magic, living relationship uniting the trees, the sky, the stars, all people, and all living things; and you will feel a oneness with them. This is the code of divine love.

The Heavenly Father can be known as cosmic love, cosmic light, cosmic bliss. He is also infinite beauty. When we look at a rose, we shouldn't analyze too much, but rather concentrate on its beauty. If our thoughts are engrossed in the chemical and botanical characteristics of the rose, we lose sight of its loveliness. Rather, we should bathe our spirits in the deep, pure feeling that stirs within us when we gaze on the glories of His creation. This is the way to know God as beauty. And God is poesy. It is another expression of His beauty. He is the Infinite Poem, and the Joy we feel when we hear inspiring poems. Poetry itself is "a thing of beauty and a joy forever." If we love God, we love poetry.

To establish God's kingdom on earth, we must follow the path of wisdom, beauty, and love. We must cultivate wisdom, and learn through our wisdom to love the beauty of God in all souls and in all things.

God-Contact Answers Every Question

It is wonderful when people of divergent views come together, not to emphasize their differences, but their points of unity. From this gathering tonight you must carry away with you something worthwhile. Every speaker here has affirmed that we must not think of war, but of peace; and really live it. We can know true peace when we realize God. When we know the Heavenly Father, we will have the answers not only to our own problems, but to those that beset the world. Why do we live, and why do we die? Why the present happenings, and why those of the past? I doubt there will ever come on earth any saint who will answer all the questions of all human beings. But in the temple of meditation every riddle of life that troubles our hearts shall be resolved. We will learn the answers to the puzzles of life, and find the solution to all our difficulties, when we come in contact with God.

The season of life is very short, and within this span we must try to reap the richest harvest of realization. All that is necessary is that we make the effort every day to meditate and practice the presence of God. If we live with noble thoughts as our companions, we are trying to be better. The effort is all that God expects of us. No doubt it seems a most difficult accomplishment to remember God in the pressure of our many activities. But the Bhagavad Gita says: "He who perceives Me everywhere, and beholds everything in Me, never loses sight of Me, nor do I ever lose sight of him."*

See how the Lord is assuring us! He says: "He who watches Me always, and who looks for Me during the little gaps of leisure hours, who seeks Me in the hearts of flowers, who probes into the Source of the infinite movies through the tiny star of the spiritual eye at the Christ Center, who searches Me out in friendship and in filial and divine love — he shall find Me. I am with him always. He shall never lose sight of Me, nor will I ever lose sight of him."

He Who Is Mentally Undefeated Finds God

Your own problems are the most important ones for you to solve, for if you better your own life, you will have helped to resolve the enigma of this existence for others — example speaks louder than words. You should so love God, and have such implicit faith in Him, that even though the world may consider you a useless soul because you have fallen, or are physically weak, still you can say: "Father, I want to go to Thy temple, though my legs are paralyzed. I want to hear Thee, Lord, though my ears are deaf. I want to speak of Thee, though my lips are dumb. I have not given up, Lord. My mind and my heart are inwardly racing toward Thee."

There is no reason your mind cannot be with God. Sever the delusive fetters of materialistic attachment, which you yourself have created, and which bind your thoughts to worldly consciousness. Within your heart stand aloof: in the world, but not

* VI:30.

bound by worldly ways. Pray to the Father: "I want so much to know Thee, and to solve the mystery of life. Though my flesh is weak, my spirit is willing. Within my heart day and night I have a consuming desire for Thee. In the light of my love I want to behold Thee." Then the Beloved of the universe responds: "Though the world says you are lost, you are still My little one." So remember, he who is mentally undefeated is the one who finds God within the temple of his heart.

No matter what your obstacles, this you can do: In the secret sanctuary of your heart you can seek God; and you can love Him with all your heart. Whenever there is a little time between duties, retire to the cave of silence within. You won't find silence amidst crowds. Seek time to be alone; and in the cave of inner silence, you shall find the wellspring of wisdom.

The Garden of Truth Is Found in God-Communion

I searched throughout India and found blossoms of truth in all teachings. But the whole garden of truth is found in communion with God. Only when you hear truth from His lips will you be fully satisfied. When you commune with Him, you will know what you should do about any problems, and you can truly say: "I understand the will of my Father," or "I can see the love of my Father behind all that happens to me." By feeling the love of God and following the love of God you will come to love everything and everyone. You will be able to transcend all limitations; for the love of God is the solution to life, to war, to struggle.

I saw and felt this love of God in the true masters I met in India. I remember when, as a young boy, I saw for the first time Master Mahasaya, a very great saint.* He was meditating, gazing into space into another world. He hadn't even spoken to me; but the instant I came into his presence I was entranced, because I knew there was something real in him: I saw that he was one with God. I started to speak to him, but he turned to me and said, "Please be seated. I am talking to my Divine Mother." When I heard these words, something happened within me. I realized I was standing before one who was actually communing with God. At that moment, the love I felt for the Divine Mother

---

* The story related here, and other incidents in Paramahansaji's relationship with Master Mahasaya, are recorded in *Autobiography of a Yogi*, chapter 9.

was a thousand million times more than I had felt even for my earthly mother, the dearest person in the world to me. It was overwhelming.

I pleaded with the saint: "Please, please, sir, ask Divine Mother if She loves me. She will tell you; She is listening to you now." Day and night this prayer had possessed my heart. Now I *had* to know the answer. He agreed to intercede on my behalf.

Early the next morning, I ran back to Master Mahasaya and asked him if Divine Mother had said anything about me. He looked at me and said, "Naughty little sir."

I persisted. "Did you ask Divine Mother what She thinks of me?"

Again he said, "Naughty little sir." Then he added: "Must you test me? You know the answer already. Didn't She come to you last night and tell you that She loved you?"

My heart was overjoyed at these words of confirmation, for indeed it was so. Divine Mother had appeared to me in deep meditation, and told me of Her love for me. I could never forget that experience: a great light, and Her divine presence. The brightest light of this world is only darkness compared to the light of Spirit. "The light shineth in darkness."*

After my first meeting with Master Mahasaya, I had gone directly home and started to meditate, long and deeply. The darkness of this world disappeared and space opened. In the brilliance of the inner divine light, I saw the form of a woman with the most beautiful face I have ever seen. In the light of her eyes, the entire universe opened up before me.

I asked, "Are you the Divine Mother?"

Her sweet voice replied, "I am."

I cried, "Mother, do You love me?"

"Always have I loved thee, ever shall I love thee."

Oh, what joy I felt, such great ecstasy! I experienced a oneness with the Love in everything.

I had gone back to Master Mahasaya the following morning just to hear from him that my vision was true. He precisely described the time I had had the experience, and the exact words

---

* John 1:5.

I had heard from Divine Mother. How did he know? Such power
is greater than telepathy. It is oneness with the omnipresence of
God. Such mysteries can be understood only by talking with
God. When through your own efforts you feel for God the love
that a miser feels for his money, and a lover feels for his beloved,
then God will come to you.

Look to Your Spiritual Welfare

You are not a bird or a beast; you are a human being, a son of
God, and you must express your true Self. Remember this. You
are here to break the bonds of delusion, and to tear open the veil
of nature and assert your divine power as a child of God.

Time is slipping away. Why do you let yourself forget God?
Why leave this earth without knowing the mystery of life—why
you are here and whither you go? When I went back to India in
1935, I visited Bodh Gaya and sat under the tree where Buddha
sat in meditation until he received enlightenment. I could exactly feel his feelings, his thoughts, his ecstasy. When realization
comes, what freedom! what joy!

All life is a school of experience that points in one direction: Godward. Seek until you find Him; for until you do, you
shall never be able to solve the riddle of life, nor be free from the
miseries that are a part of mortal existence. At night, don't go to
bed until you have felt communion with God in meditation. You
know it is the naughty baby who cries the loudest that gets his
mother's attention first. So be like the naughty baby and cry for
God. Be satisfied with nothing less than God. To love the gifts of
creation more than the Giver is folly. Within your heart renounce everything; seek God, give yourself completely to Him.

Remember that one day even those dearest to you will be
taken away—not to punish you, but to remind you to give your
love to all beings as your own. And greater than this, to help you
to learn it is God alone who has loved you through your loved
ones. The purpose of life is that you find God and receive directly from Him His all-satisfying eternal love.

So, dear friends, in the nighttime, when you are free from
your material duties, look to your spiritual welfare. Meditate,
pray—pray again and again. Practice the meditation techniques
of Self-Realization to master the restlessness of the mind. Fol-

low the great Gurus of this path: through these teachings they found God. Knowing God—this is what the Self-Realization teachings are all about. I have come with but one purpose: to give you the love of God.

How You Can Approach God

Special Convocation held December 26-27, 1937,
Self-Realization Fellowship Second Temple,
Los Angeles, California

[Paramahansa Yogananda responded to remarks of introductory speakers in the following words:]

I thank every one of you who has cooperated with this cause to help make this occasion a success. I pray that you all profit by the things God has said to us tonight through those that love Him.

Anyone who does not respond to love is not fit for the name of human being. Those who do respond to love receive the message of God that passes to them through the words of others. I feel this very strongly. In the words spoken tonight, God has blessed us. And I am humbled by the kindness addressed to me. Praise does not make me any better; blame does not make me any less. I only know that God is reflected in all. Because of the happiness I feel in the joy of Spirit, I want to impart His love to all who come to me; and I shall continue to do so as long as I live. This is my greatest desire, for which I live now.

Very few people understand how to proceed in their efforts to contact God. Many reason, "Well, whether we think of Him or not, He sustains us; He gives us food and other necessities of life in this world He has created. So why worry about seeking Him now; that is for the afterlife." Some think, "I pray, but I don't know if He is listening; I didn't receive what I prayed for, so why bother?" Others say, "When we die, *then* we will be angels." But remember, my friends, if you are not angels before sleep, you will not be angels after sleep. Similarly, you will not be given wings and a halo just by virtue of the sleep of death unless you have earned them here. Whatever you want and expect to be, you must be that now. You must work for it today.

We must be practical in spiritual matters, just as material success requires systematic application. The practical aspect of

Self-Realization teachings has changed the lives of thousands. True Self-realization has transformed Saint Lynn* more than I have yet seen in any other Westerner. We have a wonderful exchange of spiritual vibrations such as the ordinary person never dreams of. Because God is reflected in his countenance, his very face sends me into the inner spiritual ecstasy of God's presence. If you live God, you are able to make others feel His presence, in the same way that you make others feel your enmity if you hate them. You must use your power to be an instrument of God. Sincerity is a transparent diamond through which the light of God shines in our lives.

But how can you know how to approach God when there are so many religions, each one claiming that it will send you to heaven? You have already tried one or many paths, but do you feel that you are in heaven or any nearer to it? Your own Self-realization of truth, not blind dogma, must be the only binding force in your spiritual life.

I do not want to hold anybody by my personality; for if I do, when death shall cut that string, the flower garland of those souls will be strewn and trampled by time. I am here to serve souls, and the only bait that I shall use is my love. Flattery I shall never give. Anyone who will sincerely practice the methods of this path will remain with me, bound by his own Self-realization. It is in your own interest that you should open your eyes of intuitive understanding and follow truth, not dogma or religious charlatanism. Have goodwill toward all religions; love them in your heart, but be faithful to the path to which God has drawn you. Don't take my word or anyone else's. Ask the Father; He will tell you. Pray to Him, "Heavenly Father, lead me, that I be not deluded." If you are sincere, you will find that He will guide you, and that you can prove through your own experience the truth of my words.

The Monkey Trial—And Its Sequel

It is appalling how we human beings abuse ourselves in so many ways. There was a famous trial in Tennessee when a

* Rajarsi Janakananda (formerly Mr. J. J. Lynn), first successor to Paramahansa Yogananda as president and representative spiritual head of Self-Realization Fellowship/Yogoda Satsanga Society of India. (See glossary.)

school teacher there began teaching his class Charles Darwin's theory of evolution.* It raised great controversy as to whether man was created by God or evolved from apes. One side said, "Suppose we did come from monkeys. We have come so far; that is good." The other side said, "We won't accept the absurd idea that our forefathers hung from trees by their tails!" While this trial was going on, the head monkey in the world is said to have gone to heaven with his delegates to see God. He addressed the Lord: "Your Majesty, we have come to register a protest. The race of human beings has been known to engage in all kinds of evils — lying, cheating, committing adultery and murder, waging wars. Now there is a sect that is trying to establish that these creatures are our relatives. We are insulted!"

We don't always have reason to be proud of ourselves as human beings, but neither should we be discouraged by our mistakes. Always look to the silver lining in every experience, learn from your mistakes, and look to God no matter what happens.

If you believe it when someone tells you that you can get to heaven without effort, you will be sadly disillusioned. You must know the method by which you can find God; how you can please and approach God. There is prayer, affirmation, following moral ways, concentration, meditation. The Kriya Yoga path I am giving to you is a science that includes all of these.

If scientists got together and only prayed for inventions, would they get them? No. They have to apply God's laws. So how can a church or temple bring you God just by blind prayer or ceremony? You should go to the church or temple not for socials or because of beautiful music or lofty sermons, but for God, and for your own spiritual development, which will give you God-consciousness.

I am not trying to lure or hold anyone by the bait of false promises. If you come here for God, and if you stick to what you receive, and practice it faithfully, then you will find truth through your own Self-realization.

Jesus taught that the greatest commandment is to love

---

* The famous Scopes trial held in 1925. For a more detailed discussion by Paramahansa Yogananda on evolution, see page 21-22.

God "with all thy heart, and with all thy soul, and with all thy mind, and with all thy strength."* Christ's apostle St. Paul summarized that teaching in the words, "Pray without ceasing."† Buddha taught, "Meditate on God." Bhagavan Krishna proclaimed, "He attains the Supreme Effulgent Lord, O Arjuna! whose mind, stabilized by yoga, is immovably fixed on the thought of Him."‡ Zoroaster and all prophets of true religions gave the same teaching.

Proof of the Existence of God

The proof of the existence of God as proclaimed by the great ones is not in books, nor in the words of others. It is within yourself. When you sit quietly and pray, and nothing happens, you have not contacted God. Blind prayer, and praying with the wrong motive, do not work. If you pray five hours daily from today that you might become a Henry Ford, that prayer will not be granted. But if you pray to God, "I am Thy child. I am made in Thine image. Make me one with Thee," that prayer will be fulfilled.

The wave cannot say, "I am the ocean," because the ocean can exist without the wave. But the ocean can say, "I am the wave," because the wave cannot exist without the ocean. It is correct to say the ocean has become the wave. Similarly, it is the greatest delusion to say, "I am God." You must in truth know within, from your own experience, that you are one with Him and can work His miracles. When you can feel your consciousness in every atom, in all space, and beyond creation, then you can rightfully say, "God and I are one"—but not until then.

Once you reestablish your lost relationship with God, then you will have everything. Was not Jesus richer than Henry Ford? He had everything the Father has. His home was the universe. His consciousness was omnipresent. That is why he said: "The son of man hath not where to lay his head."§ Jesus demonstrated that he was one with God. He said, "Thinkest thou that I cannot now pray to my Father, and he shall presently give me more than twelve legions of angels?"** But he would not use his powers to destroy those who were crucifying

* Mark 12:30.   † Thessalonians 5:17.
‡ Bhagavad Gita VIII:8.   § Matthew 8:20.   ** Matthew 26:53.

his body. That is where he expressed his godlike qualities. For God does not punish us for our wrongs; we punish ourselves by reaping what we alone have sown. So when Jesus said: "Father, forgive them; for they know not what they do,"* he represented God by his humility and by his refusal to use his tremendous power to punish others.

The Way to Know God

What, then, is the way to know God?† You must follow those moral principles of right living that are common to all true religions. First of all are the "Thou shalt nots": Don't steal, don't lie, don't kill, don't commit adultery; don't commit any evil act. Everything has a purpose, and you should understand the reason behind moral rules. For example, if you are a slave to sex and misuse its power, and forget its divine purpose—to create children—you will lose energy, and destroy your physical and mental health.

Secondly, follow the positive rules, too: be kind, sincere, truthful; love your fellow man; practice introspection and self-control.

But in themselves, the first two steps are not enough to know God. After adopting the right methods of living, you must learn to quiet the body and mind, and this begins with right posture. Always sit upright, with the spine straight. This is particularly essential for meditation. Mastery of the restlessness of the body produces great mental power.

The fourth step is to switch off the life force from the body, so that the attention is freed for inner contemplation on God. You cannot commune with God by emotional or muscular demonstrations. When the life force is shut off from the muscles and senses, sensations cannot reach the brain to disturb one's inner concentration. Why do you feel peace in absolute physical and mental stillness? Whence comes the peace you

---

* Luke 23:34.

† From this point Paramahansaji follows the general outline of Patanjali's eightfold path of Yoga: *yama* (moral conduct), *niyama* (religious observances), *asana* (right posture), *pranayama* (control of *prana*, subtle life currents), *pratyahara* (withdrawal of the senses from external objects), *dharana* (concentration), *dhyana* (meditation), and *samadhi* (superconscious experience). See *Yoga* in glossary.

Paramahansa Yogananda with Madame Amelita Galli-Curci, world-renowned operatic soprano, Washington, D.C., 1927. Paramahansaji's guru, Swami Sri Yukteswar, had assured his disciple when he came to America: "Everywhere you go ... you will find friends." Indeed, the Guru's wisdom and practical "how-to-live" teachings attracted devotees and friends from all walks of life — including prominent figures in science, business, the arts. Mme. Galli-Curci wrote: "The teaching of Yogananda gives to life a purpose, joy, happiness, and bliss. It is the science of living, and is applicable to all our daily problems and activities." *(See pp. 8 and 57.)*

Swami Sri Yukteswar and Paramahansa Yogananda in religious procession, Calcutta, 1935. Paramahansaji had returned to India for a last visit with his Guru, whose spiritual training had prepared Sri Yogananda for his worldwide mission.

experience in sleep at night? Something cannot come from nothing. The answer is that God is behind the state of sleep. That peace felt in sleep, during muscular and sensory relaxation, comes from God. So the masters have said we should practice *pranayama,* which means methods to control the life force in the body.

Pranayama brings results much faster than simple prayer or other methods of diverting the mind from sensory distractions. In one life you can attain God-consciousness by Self-Realization techniques. Meditation, which is possible only after achieving interiorization, is to experience consciously, with the full possession of your mind, that state of divine peace and joy which you feel subconsciously in sleep. So the masters teach that by switching off the five sense telephones of sight, smell, taste, touch, and sound, through *pranayama,* you can produce that consciousness at will, enhanced a thousandfold. As every mental state has a corresponding physical state and every physical state has a corresponding mental state, the practice of *pranayama* for Self-realization is aided by right eating, right thinking, right behavior, and proper exercises to oxygenate the system.

After successful *pranayama,* your consciousness becomes interiorized. This interiorization is the fifth step. You will find your mind fully alert and concentrated within, ready to enjoy the divine peace and presence of God in deep concentration and meditation, the sixth and seventh steps. When you are in this way able to close off distracting sensations, you will be at the altar of God.

Apply the test. No matter what path a devotee follows, he will ultimately have to retrace his way back to God by these successive steps.

I can keep my mind fully concentrated on anything I choose. When you can shut out restless thoughts at will, and put the attention wholly on God, that is the real beginning of divine communion. Unless you are able to do that, you have not reached God.

Those who love God are always thinking of Him. If you love Him deeply enough, you do not have to fly away from the world. You can fulfill any responsibility and still think of Him.

Just as the pianist is always thinking of music, so the lover of God is always thinking of Him. A divine joy feeds the brain, the heart, and the soul. That joy is God; He is ever new Joy.

I remember when Master [Swami Sri Yukteswar] said to me: "If the whole world were given to you, you would grow tired of it. No power or miracles can compare with the joy that is God. That perennial happiness is what everyone is seeking. God is ever new joy unto eternity. If you have that joy, it will never grow stale." From that day, that joy has never left me. Whether conditions make me feel externally sad or pleasant, whether I am laughing or crying, the silent river of God's joy has been continuously flowing beneath the sands of my thoughts and all the experiences of life. I don't talk about it; I feel it. The whole universe holds no attraction for me, for when I behold that great silent river of joy within, I am satisfied.

In India these truths have been proven. God has not been so much talked about as proven by the great masters. You must do likewise.

I can say, "God, God, God," and go into the state of ecstasy. I can enter that state by meditation, or by seeing beautiful scenery, or by looking at someone whose countenance shines with the presence of God. When you have mastered the steps by which you reach the highest *nirbikalpa samadhi* state, you can return to it at will by any method. Test these truths in your meditations. But do not delude yourselves. Many people get caught by the ego and think they are already there. But to them I say, "If you break your hand, can you heal it at once, as Jesus could restore wholeness to his crucified body?" If you cannot do that, do not think that you have attained the state of Christ-oneness with God. You must still labor for it.

To His devotees, God sometimes reveals Himself as a great light; or as the cosmic sound of *Aum,* or Amen; or as boundless joy, love, or wisdom. His light spreads like wings, all over eternity—such light that sometimes I see this earth in it like a dream. This world *is* a dream.

God is in the intelligent, creative, vibratory sound of *Aum* or Amen that devotees hear. He often talks to me through that vibration. In it I feel His creative intelligence and power.

God is love. When you feel unconditional love for all, that is

God. In devotees, of course, you feel the love of God more manifest, but still you love all, because even though hidden, He dwells in all.

By constant communion with Him, everything but God vanishes. I have no consciousness of nationality, no consciousness of India or America. I love you all just as I love my own family. Good or bad, I love all alike, for they are my brothers and sisters. Naughty or good, we are His children.

We must manifest that love now; we must practice that love now. Patriotism that teaches everyone to love all nations as well as their own is the right form of patriotism. But that patriotism which teaches us that to love one's own nation one must be the enemy of other nations — patriotism that espouses aggressive domination and bloodshed—is wrong.

One who does not love all as God's children does not have true patriotism, for as I wrote in the poem, "My India,"* "God made this world; and man made its confining countries with their fancy-frozen boundaries."

You insult yourself when you take pride in the color of your skin, or in race or creed. I prophesy that some day the races of Europe shall be dark and Asians shall be white. Be proud of what is beneath the skin and flesh and bones — the image of God within you. Be proud of That alone. It is a strange paradox: you in the West have accepted Christ, who was an Oriental. He was born in the Orient, amidst downtrodden nations, to show that you should love all nations and races alike.

So the last or eighth step is *samadhi* or oneness with God as Light, or Cosmic *Aum*, or Joy, or Love, or Wisdom — and not only oneness, but expansion of that oneness from the limitations of the body to the boundaries of eternity. If you have attained this God-union, I bow down to you. I sit at the feet of anyone who has fully realized God, as do all souls who have felt God.

Be loyal to what you have received, and work at it earnestly. Otherwise you shall never know the wondrous blessings of this path. One cannot keep transferring from one to another of five cars, each traveling by a different route, and expect to get any-

* In *Songs of the Soul.*

where. Take up one method that you know to be truth and follow that. You must realize God yourself. He is the only real Friend whose love is unconditional and everlasting. Before you were born, when no one else was with you, He was with you. When earthly friends bury you, He will still be with you.

Every night when you sit to meditate, pray to God unceasingly. Tear the silence with your longing. Cry to God as you would cry to your mother or to your father: "Where are You? You made me; You gave me intelligence to seek You. You are in the flowers, in the moon, and in the stars; must You remain hidden? Come to me. You must! You must!" With all the concentration of your mind, with all the love of your heart, tear at the veils of silence again and again. As constant churning brings hidden butter out of milk, churn the ether with the ladle of your devotion and it shall produce God.

The Cosmic Lover

Written circa 1930

None I behold as stranger. I rejoice to love all with the God-given pure feeling of human attachment. I care not how many holy men howl, "Be attached to no one!" I am attached to all. Nonattachment is necessary if one's love encompasses only one or a few, excluding all others. Never could my attachment be exclusive, omitting any from my circle of love!

To love all with genuine attachment, as one's own, is beautiful, enjoyable, heart-thrilling, heart-awakening. It is He, the Cosmic Lover as the Cosmic Trickster, who comes to us garbed in the forms of those we love—father, mother, child, beloved, friend, acquaintance. In teaching us to give love through parental, conjugal, and friendly attachments, the Cosmic Lover surreptitiously imbibes from us in those forms the attachment-fragrant love of our hearts, even as He gives attachment-perfumed love to us in His guise of parent, child, beloved, friend.

Why then does He cruelly break our hearts with His game of hide-and-seek, making us love some of His forms as our own beloved ones and then causing them to vanish silently behind the impenetrable screen of dissolution? He thinks we take His entertainments amiss. He doesn't wish to hurt us with pangs of separation; He wants us to love Him, not flesh-bound in one or two finite bodies, but with all-embracing attachment to His infinitely diverse forms in all incarnations and ages. He seeks our steadfast love—pure, spiritual, wholehearted, with perfect abandonment—as He displays His entertaining new forms on the stage of life. He appeals to us to love Him unconditionally in His multifarious roles—in a healthy or a diseased body, as a rich father or poor mother, kind friend or treacherous foe, king or servant, protector or enemy, admirer or caustic critic, brother or beloved, son or daughter, doctor or minister; as a bird, a beast, a flower; as the skiey star-bosomed beauty above, or the wave-breasted blue brine below.

The Infinite Entertainer forbids that we love Him forever in only select forms of our choosing, lest we fail to appreciate the entertainment of His ever-changing, infinite variety of forms. But to teach us what love is, the Cosmic Lover invites us in the beginning to love Him in any way we please, until through the silent coaxing of His courtship, our love becomes purified, free from taints of selfishness, individual attachment, sense blindness, finiteness, mortal limitations, pangs of separation, temporality, meanness, emotionalism, fickleness, human indifference and forgetfulness, blasts of death and oblivion.

Let us be not afraid to love our dear ones, foolishly fearing to lose them in the mists of death. Love them so dearly, so truly, so purely, and forever unlamentingly — even in temporary, love-kindling separation—that you find in them the everlasting true love of God. Finding Divine Love you will find beneath Its canopy all your loved ones of all incarnations, and with omnipresent love you will embrace not only them, but all heretofore unseen, unknown forms of the Cosmic Lover.

Personal and Impersonal God

Self-Realization Fellowship International Headquarters,
Los Angeles, California, December 21, 1939

Tonight's talk will bring home to your consciousness the significance of the coming of Jesus Christ on earth. Though a few doubt what happened twenty centuries ago, his presence in this world was real—many came in contact with him personally. Some understood his greatness; others ignorantly helped to crucify him. In the drama of his life, Jesus showed us what God Himself would be like, and how He would behave, if He came on earth in flesh and form. In Jesus, as in other divine incarnations, we have been able to behold and know the visible God.

The God of some scriptures is a revengeful deity, always ready to punish us. But Jesus showed us the real nature of God. Time and again Jesus said: "I and my Father are one."* The Spirit within him was one with the Infinite Spirit. He who is one with God is God Himself. Jesus proved this in his life. And yet, though one with all-powerful God, he humbly let himself be crucified through the ignorance of certain men, rather than retaliate against them. As a son of God, a reflection of Cosmic Consciousness, he had dominion over all forces in creation, but he never used his power against anyone. He who could raise the dead, who realized that his body was not physical but ethereal, could certainly have saved himself from the cross. He said, "Thinkest thou that I cannot now pray to my Father, and he shall presently give me more than twelve legions of angels?"† But instead, he hid his omnipresence and allowed his body to be crucified. He did not destroy his enemies with "twelve legions of angels," but rather overcame evil with the power of divine love. His actions demonstrated the supreme love of God, and the behavior of those who are one with Him.

Don't you prefer a God who with infinite love is ready to

---

* John 10:30.   † Matthew 26:53.

371

say: "I forgive you, for you know not what you do"? You may be worried about the wrong you have committed, but God is not. What is past is past. You are His child, and whatever wrong you have done came about because you didn't know Him. He doesn't hold against you the evil done under the influence of ignorance. All He asks is that you not repeat your wrong actions. He wants only to find out whether or not you are sincere in your intention to be good.

God shows His loving forgiveness to us every day. He could punish us by hellfire for our errors, but He doesn't. Hellfire is an imaginary creation of man's vengefulness, which he ascribes to God as well. But revenge is not God's way. In His greatness He is ever loving toward His children. We never have to fear Him. We should fear only ourselves, our own wrongdoings: those actions performed against the dictates of conscience. Before the tribunal of the conscience the evil man convicts himself. Jesus said: "Repent: for the kingdom of heaven is at hand."* That is, repent of the mischief you have done, and you will attain the kingdom of God. So remember that God does not condemn you; you pass sentence on yourself by your own actions. You punish or reward yourself through the karmic results of those deeds.

The great problem is that God knows too much about us! I often say to Him: "Lord, it is not fair that You know everything about us, and we don't know anything about You." If you knew that God is with you all the time, you wouldn't do many of the things you do. But He doesn't want to interfere with the free will He has given to you. He wants your spontaneous love. He has given you freedom to do good or evil, to cast Him away or receive Him on the altar of your heart. You may do whatever you choose; He doesn't intervene. But those who willingly choose good actions are on their way to becoming manifest representatives of God, just as Jesus was a perfect representative of God.

Jesus said: "Many prophets and righteous men have desired to see those things which ye see, and have not seen them; and to hear those things which ye hear, and have not heard them."† It is only from time to time, in different ages, that great souls are sent by God with a special mission to declare His glory. Their

---

* Matthew 4:17.   † Matthew 13:17.

lives reflect the various attributes of God: Krishna manifested the love aspect of God; Jesus' life represented the devotional and active, or serviceful, aspects of God; Swami Shankara reflected the wisdom of God; Chaitanya,* the love; Buddha showed us God's benign intelligence, working through *dharma* or cosmic law. Hence, though God Himself is invisible, He can become manifest in the bodies of such great masters.

It is significant that when we think of God in human form, we visualize Him according to our own familiar concepts. For instance, the Chinese make the image of Buddha with a flat nose and almond-shaped eyes; the Hindus represent him with an aquiline nose. Such is man's need for a personal God in a form to which he can easily respond.

God Is Both Personal and Impersonal

Many devotees who worship a personal aspect of God shun the concept of an impersonal God; and devotees of the Unmanifest sometimes reject the idea of a personal God. But I say that God is both personal and impersonal. He is the Absolute, beyond form, but He also makes Himself manifest in many ways. If there were no blue sky, no vast space, no beautiful scenery, no moon or twinkling stars in the heavens, we would never have suspected the existence of God at all. The wonders we behold in this universe suggest to us the immanence of God. He is visible everywhere, in everything He has created, and in the workings of His intelligence governing all creation.

When we see pictures of tragedy and drama and comedy on a movie screen, we forget that all the characters and their characteristics are nothing more than electricity, vibratory forms of light. So it is when we see all the different things about us—the earth, the sky, the trees, other human beings, and myriad creatures—we forget that they are nothing but God, the Cosmic Electricity. We must realize that all of us are playing a drama of good and evil in this world, and that our flesh, the bulb and the electricity that illumines it, the vast ocean, the wood, the iron—

---

* A brilliant scholar in India, Sri Chaitanya in 1508 had a spiritual awakening and became inflamed with love for God, whom he worshiped as the *avatar* Lord Krishna. His fame as a *bhakta* (devotee of God) spread throughout India in the 16th century.

all are made of God. Do not forget this. Everything is composed of the subtly vibrating cosmic energy of God.

The visible universe is thus a vast personal representation of the invisible Spirit. Everything is a part of Him, even the smallest speck of dust. The wood that appears to be inert matter is the living light of God. In seemingly empty space there is one Link, one Life eternal, which unites everything in the universe — animate and inanimate — one wave of Life flowing through everything.

The wave is the same as the ocean, though it is not the whole ocean. So each wave of creation is a part of the eternal Ocean of Spirit. The Ocean can exist without the waves, but the waves cannot exist without the Ocean.

Therefore, you see, God is both personal and impersonal. He is the Uncreated Absolute; and He is manifest in creation, peering at us through the twinkling stars, breathing on us His sweet fragrance through the flowers, and talking to us through his saints.

Even the Finite Is Infinite

Now, just behind the universe is the infinite presence of God. And because God cannot be bound by any form, even His personal aspect in the universe is also infinite. So what we call finite and infinite are both right before our eyes. But our eyes deceive us, because they cannot see all there is. What we call finite is infinite in essence. Therefore, we cannot conceive the depth of the heavens, of space. The space in this room is about eighteen feet, measured by what confines it; but space itself cannot be seen or measured. When you stand on a mountaintop and look up at a clear night sky, you see only a few thousand stars. But uncounted trillions more lie beyond your vision. If you look through a telescope you can see a few of them; you can see the moons of such planets as Saturn and Jupiter. The light of the distant stars takes aeons to reach the earth. And what is beyond the farthest star? Man does not know. Space is infinite. The ordinary human mind cannot comprehend this truth.

If you trace the origin and end of matter, you find it is infinite. Trace the origin and end of human beings, and again, you find they are infinite. You may say, "My name is John. I am finite." But who were your parents? And who were their parents?

Ask this of each preceding generation, and eventually you come to Adam and Eve. And whence did they come? From God, who is infinite. Creation was infinite in the beginning, and is infinite in the end. At the moment you are in the middle, or manifested state, of that infinite change. Therefore you are infinite too; there is no beginning or end to you.

In this sense, nothing is finite; nothing is personal. Everything in essence is the ever-living Absolute who has become personal and visible to us for a time through this cosmos. It is His life permeating the universe, rotating the suns and moons and stars in mathematical order. God is visible as these created forms, yet that very visibility makes Him invisible: Gross vibrations hide His infinite nature, His omnipresent invisibility in which everything has its beginning and end. To illustrate, steam is invisible, but when condensed it becomes visible as water; condensed further by freezing, it becomes ice. Steam is a gas; ice is a solid; how different, and yet the same. Similarly, the impersonal God is personal, and the personal God is impersonal. All matter is Spirit, and Spirit has become matter. There is no essential difference. Reasoning thus, it is easier for us to conceive that invisible God can have a visible aspect.

The Absolute Cannot Be Described

The impersonal God cannot be described, or even understood with the intellect. The only way you can know the Absolute is to be one with Spirit. It is only the personal God that you can think of or worship. I would ask any human being if he can convey what God is like without employing any personal concept; he can't. When you think of God's love, you think of the human love you have felt in your heart, and you picture God's love as greater than that. Because goodness, love, wisdom, have been embodied in persons you know, or more perfectly so in the lives of the saints, you are able to conceive these as qualities of God, and to say that He is kind and good and beautiful, that He is wise and loving. Do you see how tangible He is? But without a personal example of God's divine qualities, we could not conceive of Him at all. So long as we are identified with our own body-consciousness, God will be more real to us in the personal aspect than in the impersonal. So it is easier to strive first to realize Him as the personal God.* In fact, we *should* approach Him through the visible, because that is more tangible to us. For this reason are great ones such as Jesus sent on earth. Though one with God, they have a body of bones and flesh. In this way, God takes a body at will to guide and inspire His children. But He cannot be confined to any one body because that would mean He is born and He dies; He would be limited, not limitless. He would not be God.

God Manifests in Human Incarnations

In the beginning, before creation, God was invisible; but He wanted to become visible, and to enjoy His infinite nature through many forms. Electricity is in the air around us, but you don't see it. Unmanifest, it is impersonal. But when it is brought into a bulb, it becomes visible, even though it is the same electricity. So it is with God. You are all gods†—the Divine Electricity made visible in body-bulbs—though you don't know it. Thus my God not only remains unseen behind the stars, hidden in the sky, but He is visible right before me—a God who has taken the forms of more than a billion beings on earth. "Know ye not that ye are the temple of God, and that the Spirit of God dwelleth in you?"‡ But though He has made a personal representation of Himself in each human being, some reflect His light more than others. These are His great saints and avatars.

To cite again the example of Jesus, his body that was crucified and that he recreated, or resurrected, was manifested from the invisible God. And that resurrected form didn't die a second death, but was dissolved in Spirit after Jesus had appeared to his disciples. This demonstration proves that God can make Himself visible and appear in any form at any time. Since God is not limited to any one manifestation, it is all right to visualize Him in whatever form is dearest to your heart. He will appear to you in a form representative of one of His divine attributes, such as those personified in the deities of the Hindu scriptures, or as any avatar, saint, or great soul that you love. The first step in drawing

---

* "Those whose goal is the Unmanifested increase the difficulties; arduous is the path to the Absolute for embodied beings" (Bhagavad Gita XII:5).

† "Is it not written in your law, I said, Ye are gods?" (John 10:34).

‡ I Corinthians 3:16.

that divine response is to visualize, with eyes closed in meditation, the image of the deity or saint. If your meditation is deep and your effort is persistent, you will draw God to you.

Throughout twenty centuries, God incarnate in Jesus has appeared to many devotees, including St. Francis of Assisi. And because St. Francis so completely identified himself with Jesus, he lived the crucifixion of Jesus in his own consciousness, and the stigmata appeared on his body. I saw the same miracle in Therese Neumann;* her hands and feet showed clearly the wounds of the nails. Such are the testimonials of God.

The Guru Is a Model of God

In India we emphasize very strongly that God can be received only through the proper spiritual representative. In the West the emphasis is on filling the church, without much concern as to the inner spiritual qualifications of the preacher. In India we search everywhere for one who is a visible representative of God: one who knows God and communes with Him. When we find such a model, when in such a one we see God in action, we call him "guru," and follow him faithfully. Guru is he whom God appoints to lead you out of the darkness of ignorance into the land of His eternal light. A seeker may have had many spiritual teachers, but he can have only one guru. When he finds his guru, he follows him solely and steadfastly. God is visible in the lives of those who love Him and are in tune with Him. Thus whoever attunes himself with his guru finds God. Do you see how important it is to follow one who can show you the way to God through his example? When you are in tune with your guru, the visible representative of God, He will come to you in that form while you are meditating. Then you will know that God is real and that He works through the guru.

Before his passing, my great guru, Swami Sri Yukteswar, told me to wear a certain kind of bangle as a special protection. With faith in his blessing in the bangle, I put it on. When I was in Bombay just before returning to America, I realized that the satanic power was trying to destroy my life, to prevent me from

---

* The Catholic stigmatist of Bavaria (1898-1962). See *Autobiography of a Yogi,* chapter 39.

fulfilling the mission given to me by God and my guru. I wasn't afraid; I knew God was with me and I remembered Master's promise of protection. I put a little light on in my room, because the evil forces do not like light. For a little while I sat meditating, watchful of my spirit. And then I felt sleepy. As I opened my eyes and looked toward the right wall of the room, I saw the black form of Satan, horrible, with a catlike face and tail. It leaped on my chest, and my heart stopped beating. Mentally I said: "I am not afraid of you. I am Spirit." But still my heart wouldn't work. Suddenly I glimpsed an ochre robe, and there stood Master. He commanded Satan to leave; and as soon as he spoke, the evil figure vanished and my breath started to flow again. I cried out: "My Master!" He said: "Satan was trying to destroy you. But fear not. I am with you evermore." I could even smell the familiar, gentle fragrance that emanated from Master's form, just as when he was incarnate on earth.

Such experiences convince you that the forces of good and evil do exist, just as radio vibrations are present in space. If you dig into the ether with a radio receiver, immediately you can hear songs that have been broadcast from another point in space. Likewise the saints, by tuning in their minds to God, have drawn Him from the silence of space. He and His saints are right here, hidden behind the ether. Tuning in with Them is not simple, but unless you learn to do this, how are you going to convince yourself that God *is*?

There are sixteen qualities of God that are manifest in great incarnations. Krishna and Christ, and also Babaji, Lahiri Mahasaya, and Sri Yukteswar, had all sixteen qualities: the power of omnipresence, power of projection, power of omnipotence, joy, and so on. In lesser prophets there are lesser manifestations. When God's sixteen qualities are fully manifest in a human being, he is one with God Himself.

Those Who Are One With God Can Appear in Form Any Time

A master who is one with God can appear in form any time he wishes, just as my guru appeared to me and as Jesus used to visit his beloved disciple St. Francis every night. Just think what your life would become if you had even one experience like that! You would see this whole world as it really is. But you are not willing to make the effort to explore the depths of meditation.

God's presence is there in abundance, but you don't work for it; you don't use your intelligence and God-given freedom to find Him. When I started my search for God in this life, I found that what the great teachers say is true, and I went after God in earnest.

One night, another student and I decided to meditate on Krishna; we wanted to behold him. After several hours my companion said, "Come on, let us go to bed now." His whole thought was of sleep, because he didn't really believe Krishna would come to us. But I said: "You go to bed if you like, but I haven't given up hope. I shall go on meditating." As I said that, there was a sudden blinding flash of light, and in that light I saw the divine face of Lord Krishna. I cried out: "Krishna is here!" I touched my friend, and he beheld him too.

So you see, on the one hand, it is the hardest thing to find God, and yet it is also the easiest if you are sincere and determined. God is not impressed by great temples or well-planned sermons; He doesn't enter the gates of pride and material pomp; He cannot be known through a mechanical relationship. God responds to a sincere call from the heart. "A humble magnet call, a whisper by the brook, on grassy altar small—there I have My nook."* Such was my temple even in childhood. I used to seek a quiet outdoor nook, and there I would pray until I saw that the blades of grass were the sinews of God, the water was the light of God, and in the laughter of the brook I heard His voice.

Realizing God Requires Unflinching Determination

But most of you don't make the effort necessary to go all the way to God. Some say a little prayer, and conclude there is nothing but darkness behind closed eyes. Some say they are getting God through art, playing the piano or the violin, or through painting. But God is not that easy to attain. Only when you sit in meditation with unflinching determination, crying for Him day after day, night after night, will you know Him; not until then. Realizing God requires this supreme effort.

"He who perceives Me everywhere, and beholds everything in Me, never loses sight of Me, nor do I ever lose sight of

---

* Excerpt from "Where I Am"; a poem by Paramahansa Yogananda in *Songs of the Soul*.

him."* The Lord says: "I play hide-and-seek with my devotee. As he keeps on watching Me, I am watching him. I hide behind the ambitions of man. But when My devotee says, 'Lord, even when I pursue my ambitions, I am seeking You behind them and some day You will be caught in the net of my devotion then I respond."

It is so easy to slip away from God in the busyness of the world. But if you are idly lazy, He won't come, either. He wants you to work constructively, servicefully, but thinking all the while of Him. And he wants you to think of Him also in quiet, deep meditation. Work hard, but when the time for silence comes, surrender yourself completely to God in meditation.

So you must get busy. The depth of your concentration and the length of time that you spend in meditation are both important. Just saying a brief prayer will not bring an answer from God, nor will praying to Him while thinking of something else. The Lord will never come if we seek Him only halfheartedly. When you meditate, concentrate at the Christ center between the eyebrows, and don't think of time or anything else but the object of your meditation. Don't be like those who go to church on Sunday mornings, listen absentmindedly to the sermon, and wait impatiently for the service to be over so they can have their Sunday dinner. Be eager to know God. In India we sit attentively at the feet of the guru; he talks, and we listen. When he doesn't talk, we sit quietly and meditate.

The Right Meditation Techniques Are Necessary

The great battle of meditation is with restless thoughts. Only when the thoughts quiet down in meditation and you concentrate on God alone can you contact Him. The radio of the ordinary mind is full of static; but when the static is eliminated by concentration and devotion, God will come in. Have you been able to shut off your restless thoughts when meditating? No? This is why the teachings of Self-Realization Fellowship are invaluable. As soon as you tune out restlessness by these scientific techniques, the personal aspect of God will come to you.

The first signs of response that God gives to you as you seek Him sincerely are peace, light, or the sound of *Aum*; or you feel a

* Bhagavad Gita VI:30.

great joy in your heart. You may see the spiritual eye,* or hear the voice of God or of one of His saints. And you will know that God is with you.

People who have a strong imagination or a very weak nervous system may be susceptible to hallucinations. By following the Self-Realization techniques one avoids hallucinations and receives the blessing of true spiritual experiences. This is why I strongly urge you to learn these techniques and to practice them with great diligence. Apply yourself. It is not enough just to read the instruction for the techniques, think they are nice, and then lock them away. You must use them daily in your meditations.

Don't Put Off Your Search for God

Before this life is snatched away, make the Infinite visible to you now. Don't put off your search for God until your old age, or hope somehow to reach Him when you die. A thief is a thief before sleep; after sleep he is a thief still. Similarly, we don't become angels, introduced to God, when we die. We are the same after death as before. Make God visible to you in this visible life. When He comes, you will know such joy, such love, such wisdom, such understanding!

A negative state of desirelessness is not the goal of life. The goal is eternal fulfillment of all desires. The trouble is, you allow lesser desires to prevent you from fulfilling the only lastingly meaningful desire — for God. Once you find Him, all other desires are satisfied.

If you will use your nights for meditation, when everyone else is asleep, you will find God. Never go to bed without making that effort. What of it if you lose a little sleep? The great sleep of death will get you anyway. But it will be worthwhile if you can reach the deathless state before the Grim Reaper catches you.

Seclusion is the price of greatness. To realize God, to see Jesus and the great ones, you must have time to be by yourself. You cannot have divine communion if you mix with people all of the time. But once you have achieved God-contact, then no matter where you are or with whom, you will be drunk with the presence of the Lord.

* See glossary.

I am always inwardly intoxicated with that Joy. But in the West I have rarely shown my inner spiritual feelings. It would not be understood by many here. People in India understand these things more. Many times there, in ecstasy, my body has fallen as I lost awareness of this world in the great inner bliss of God. But if that happened here in America, some would say, "What is going on?" In the West I have heard teachers claim that they can enter cosmic consciousness; yet when supposedly in that state, their breath was heaving like a bellows. In *samadhi*, breath disappears; it melts away and the body is sustained by the Cosmic Life. When the symphony of God's song comes into the heart, thought of body-consciousness also melts away. The body and all its processes are absolutely still when the Lord is with you.

Through the Self-Realization teachings, you can experience these truths of which I speak. But no one can give such experiences to you unless you yourself make the effort.

So, from tonight, get busy! Pray with all the devotion of your heart, and you will see God; you will see Jesus or Krishna or the saints. But you must make the supreme effort to behold Them in meditation, or you will not be able to reach that divine state. I hope that you will try. When a halfhearted man plays the piano, the result is halfhearted, without inspiration. But when an individual who has practiced and practiced and practiced plays the piano, everyone says, "Oh, how wonderful!"

When an ordinary man puts the necessary time and enthusiasm into meditation and prayer, he becomes a divine man. My Master used to say: "The little cat that goes into the jungle becomes a wild cat." The little man with small thoughts who goes into the jungle of books becomes absorbed in intellectualizing about God; he doesn't find the nectar of God-realization. But the little man who meditates, who constantly thinks of the joy of God, who constantly prays to Him, becomes one with the Infinite.

When once you have heard the voice of God, you are on the way to the highest states of consciousness. You will know God as immanent and transcendant, personal and impersonal. You will worship Him as Spirit, and love Him in manifest form as the Nearest of the near.

How to Find a Way to Victory

Self-Realization Fellowship International Headquarters,
Los Angeles, California, February 16, 1939

This earth, which once seemed such a big place, I behold now as a tiny ball of atoms, spinning in space, warmed by sunshine, with nebulous gases playing around it—a little ball of clay on which various life forms grow. The Word* of God, the Voice of Spirit—the manifestation of the Infinite—is in everything. The disastrous upheavals that take place on this finite sphere are caused by human selfishness; by man's inharmony with man, and with the hidden Spirit in man and in all creation. Because mankind has not learned the lesson of these catastrophes, the earth continues to suffer devastating storms, earthquakes, floods, diseases, and, worse than these, the clouds of war.

There is a way to conquer this world—to conquer nature and to conquer life, with its poverty, disease, wars, and other troubles. We must learn this way to victory. Great leaders such as Napoleon, Genghis Khan, William the Conqueror, attained wide dominion over other men and lands. Yet their victories were temporary. The victory that Jesus Christ attained is everlasting. How to achieve this permanent victory? You must start with yourself. You may think it is hopeless to try to conquer hatred and inspire mankind to Christlike ways of love, but never was the need so great as now. Atheistic ideologies are battling to drive religion out. The world is marching on in a wild drama of existence. Trying to stop the raging storms, we seem no more than little ants swimming in the ocean. But do not minimize your power. The real victory consists in conquering yourself, as did Jesus Christ. His self-victory gave him power over all nature.

Science approaches the mastery of nature and of life in another way. Yet the initial promise of scientific discoveries

---

* Cosmic Intelligent Vibration, which structures and enlivens all creation. (See *Aum* in glossary.)

often fails to yield anything permanent. The beneficial effects are felt only for a little while; then something worse comes along to threaten man's happiness and well-being. Total victory will not come by applying the methods of science alone, because these methods deal with externals, with effects rather than their subtle causes. The world will go on in spite of disasters, and science will again and again make new conquests. But only spiritual science can teach us the way to complete victory.

The Mind Must Remain Undefeated

According to spiritual science, the attitude of the mind is everything. It is sensible to conquer extreme heat by the use of artificially cooled air, and extreme cold by artificially produced warmth; but while trying to conquer discomfort externally, train the mind to remain neutral to every condition. Mind is just like blotting paper, which readily takes on the color of any dye you apply to it. Most minds take on the color of their environment. But there is no excuse for the mind to be defeated by outer circumstances. If your mental attitude changes constantly under the pressure of tests, you are losing the battle of life. This is what happens when someone in good health and with a good mind goes out into the world to earn a living and immediately gives in to failure when he meets a few obstacles. It is when you *accept* failure that you *are* a failure. Not he who is handicapped by illness, nor he who is constantly trying in spite of repeated setbacks, but he who is physically and mentally lazy is the real failure. The person who refuses to think, or reason, or discriminate, or use his will or creative energy, is already dead.

Learn how to use the psychology of victory. Some people advise, "Don't talk about failure at all." But that alone won't help. First, analyze your failure and its causes, benefit from the experience, and then dismiss all thought of it. Though he fail many times, the man who keeps on striving, who is undefeated within, is a truly victorious person. No matter if the world considers him a failure; if he has not given up mentally, he is not defeated before the Lord. This truth I have learned from my contact with Spirit.

You are always comparing your lot with that of others. Someone is more alert and successful than you are; therefore you are miserable. This is a paradox of human nature. Don't bemoan your fate. The minute you enviously compare what you have with what someone else has, you defeat yourself. If you only knew the minds of others, you wouldn't want to be anyone but who you are!

We should envy no one. Let others envy us. What we are, no one else is. Be proud of what you have and what you are. No one else has a personality just like yours. No one else has a face like yours. No one else has a soul like yours. You are a unique creation of God. How proud you should be!

Evil Is Anything That Obstructs God-realization

To say there is no evil is unrealistic. We cannot escape evil by ignoring it. What is evil? Anything that obstructs God-realization. God is aware of all our wrong thoughts and doings and the troubles we are in. If He doesn't know that evil exists, He must be a very ignorant God! So, good and evil, the positive and the negative, both exist in this world. While trying to keep the consciousness positive, many people become unreasonably afraid of negative thoughts. It is useless to deny that negative thoughts exist, but neither should you fear them. Use your discrimination to analyze wrong thoughts; and then dump them.

Once the poison of a negative thought takes hold in the ego,* it is very hard to get rid of. A story is told of a man who was trying to drive an evil spirit out of a woman. He threw mustard seed at her, which was supposed to make the spirit depart. But the evil spirit just laughed: "I got into the mustard seed before you threw it, so it doesn't work against me." Similarly, when the poison of negative thoughts has thoroughly permeated your mind, the power of the mind doesn't work anymore. The "evil spirit" of negative thoughts gets into the "mustard seed" of your mental force. Thus, if you have been sick for a month, you tend to think you are going to be sick always. How can that one month of illness outweigh the fact of the many years of good health you have enjoyed? Such reasoning is unfair to your mind.

---

* Human consciousness, identified with the body and hence with mortal limitations. The divine consciousness of the soul is identified with God and is impervious to negative influences.

Deep metaphysicians probe into the consciousness of the soul, and with its divine power drive out all traces of evil from their lives. This is the Yoga way of destroying all obstacles to the union of soul with God; it is not imaginary, but scientific. Yoga is the highest way to God. Through Yoga you leave behind all negative thoughts and realize the ultimate states of consciousness. Yoga is the path of the spiritual scientist. It is pure science throughout, a complete science. Yoga teaches you to look yourself honestly in the eye and find out what you are, and then, with all the strength of your soul, to destroy the evil in you. You cannot just deny evil away. No matter how much persistence it takes, the spiritual scientist is never discouraged. He knows there is no trouble formidable enough to overpower the strength the Lord has given him.

The Conquest of Self Is the Greatest Victory

Learn to analyze yourself, looking at both the negative and the positive: how did you come to be what you are? what are your good and bad points, and how did you acquire them? Then set about to destroy the bad harvest. Remove the tares of evil traits from your soul and sow more seeds of spiritual qualities, to increase the crop of good harvest. As you recognize your weaknesses and scientifically remove them, you become stronger. Therefore you must not allow yourself to be discouraged by your frailties; to do so is to acknowledge yourself a failure. You must be able to help yourself by constructive self-analysis. Those who don't exercise their discriminative faculty are blind; the native wisdom of the soul has been eclipsed by ignorance. This is why people suffer.

God has given us the power to remove ignorance and uncover our innate wisdom, just as He has given us the power to open our eyelids and perceive light. Introspect every night, and keep a mental diary; and now and then during the daytime be still for a minute, and analyze what you are doing and thinking. Those who don't analyze themselves never change. Growing neither smaller nor bigger, they stagnate. This is a dangerous state of existence.

You become stagnant when you let circumstances override your better judgment. It is all too easy to waste time and forget about the kingdom of God. Thus you dwell too much on petty things, and have no time to think about Him. When you analyze yourself each night, be watchful that you are not becoming stagnant. You came into the world not to lose yourself, but to find your true Self. God sent you here as His soldier to win victory over your life. You are His child, and the greatest sin is to forget or to put off your highest duty: to win the victory over your little self and regain your true place in the kingdom of God.

The greater your troubles, the greater the chance you have to show the Lord that you are a spiritual Napoleon or a spiritual Genghis Khan — a conqueror of your self. There are so many imperfections within us to be surmounted! He who becomes master of himself is a real conqueror. You must strive to do what I am doing — constantly winning within myself. And in this inner victory, I find the whole world at my command. The elements, which seem so mysterious, the scriptures, which seem so contradictory — all things are made clear in the great light of God. In that Light everything is understood and mastered. To gain this wisdom of God is the only purpose for which you were sent here; and if you seek anything else instead, you are going to punish yourself. Find your Self and find God. And whatever life demands of you, do it to the best of your ability. By discrimination, by right action, learn to conquer every obstacle and attain self-mastery.

So long as you question whether you will win or lose in your battles with life, you will go on losing. But when you are intoxicated with the happiness of God within you, you become more positive—and more humble. Don't go backward, and don't stand still. The majority are either stationary or engaged in a tug-of-war between their good and evil tendencies. Which will win? Temptation is the voice of Satan whispering within your mind. Satan is always trying to bungle matters for you. To be stricken with weakness is not a sin, but the minute you give up the effort to overcome it, you are lost. So long as you are trying, so long as you pick yourself up when you fall, you will succeed. It is not the victory itself that brings pleasure, but the power and the satisfaction that come when you conquer a weakness.

Study the lives of the saints. That which is easy to do is not the way of the Lord. That which is difficult to do is His way! Saint Francis had more troubles than you could imagine, but he didn't give up. One by one, by the power of mind, he overcame those obstacles and became one with the Master of the Universe. Why shouldn't you have that kind of determination? I often think that the most sinful action in life is to admit failure, for in doing so, you deny the supreme power of your soul, God's image within you. Never give up.

Develop a liking for those pursuits that will help you to have greater mastery over yourself. Real victory is to carry out your good resolutions in spite of all difficulties. Let nothing break your determination. Most people reason, "Let it go today; I will try again tomorrow." Don't deceive yourself. That kind of thinking will not bring victory. If you make a resolution and never cease trying to carry it out, you will succeed. Saint Teresa of Avila said, "Saints are sinners who never gave up." Those who never surrender eventually attain victory.

Be Secure in Your Innate Goodness

One day you will be gone from this world. Some will cry for you, and some may say a few words against you. But remember that all the bad thoughts you have had, as well as your good ones, will go with you. So your important duty is to watch yourself, correct yourself, do your best. Ignore what others may say or do against you, so long as you are sincerely striving to do right. I try never to antagonize anyone, and within my heart I know I have done my utmost to be kind to all. But I care not about man's opinion, whether praise or condemnation. God is with me, and I am with Him.

It isn't a boast, but I have experienced in my own consciousness the great joy of the sure feeling in my soul that no one can provoke me to revenge. I would rather slap myself than be mean to anyone. If you hold to your determination to be kind, no matter how people try to ruffle you, you are a conqueror. Think about it. When you are threatened, and you remain calm and unafraid, know that you are victorious over your little self. Your enemy cannot touch your spirit.

I could not think of being unkind, even to a mortal enemy. It would hurt me. I see so much unkindness in the world, and there is no excuse for me to add to it. When you love God, and when you see God in every soul, you cannot be mean. If someone behaves hurtfully toward you, think of the best ways to behave lovingly toward him. And if he still refuses to be considerate, remain withdrawn for a time. Keep your kindness locked up within, but let no demonstration of unkindness mar your behavior. One of the greatest victories over the little self is to be sure of your capacity to be always thoughtful and loving, to be secure in the knowledge that no one can make you act differently. Practice this. The entire Roman government could not have roused unkindness in Christ. Even for those who crucified him, he prayed: "Father, forgive them; for they know not what they do" (Luke 23:34).

When you are certain of your self-command, your victory is greater than a dictator's — a victory that stands immaculate before the tribunal of your conscience. Your conscience is your judge. Let your thoughts be the jury and you the defendant. Put yourself to the test every day, and you will find that as often as you take punishment at the hands of your conscience, and as often as you strictly sentence yourself to be positive—to be true to your divine nature—you will be victorious.

Age is no excuse for not trying to change oneself. Victory lies not in youth but in persistence. Cultivate the persistence that Jesus had. Compare his mentality, when the time came for him to give up his body, with that of any seemingly successful free man walking the streets of Jerusalem. To the very end, in every test—even when Jesus was imprisoned and crucified by his enemies—he was supremely victorious. He had power over all nature; and he played with death to conquer death. Those who fear it allow death to be victorious over them. But those who face themselves, and try every day to change for the better, will face death with courage and win the true victory. It is this victory of the soul that is most important.

For me there is no longer any veil between life and death, so death doesn't frighten me at all. The embodied soul is like a wave on the ocean. When someone dies, the soul-wave subsides and vanishes beneath the surface of the ocean of Spirit, whence it came. The truth about death is secreted from the consciousness of ordinary people, who make no effort to realize God. Such persons cannot conceive that within themselves is the kingdom of God, replete with His wonders. There, no pain, no poverty, no worries, no nightmares can ever delude the soul. All I have to do is open my spiritual eye, and the earth is gone and another world appears. In that land I behold the infinite God. This state comes through a balance between activity and meditation. Tremendous activity is necessary; not with a desire to serve oneself, but with a desire to serve God. And equally necessary is daily effort to realize Him through deep meditation.

Do Not Neglect God for Work, Nor Neglect Work for God

Your being a very busy person does not justify your forgetting God. Devotees on the spiritual path have even more tests than those who follow a material path, so don't use your worldly obligations as an excuse to ignore God.

You should not neglect God for work, and you should not neglect work for God. You must harmonize both activities. Meditate every day, and be thinking of God as you carry your heavy bag of worldly duties. Feel that you are doing everything to please Him. If you are busy for God, then no matter what tasks you are performing, your mind will be always on Him.

In the difficult struggle to maintain balance between meditation and activity, the greatest safety lies in the consciousness of the Lord. Everything that I do with the consciousness of God becomes meditation. Those who habitually drink can work while they remain under the influence of the alcohol. So, if you are habitually intoxicated with God, you can work without interrupting your inner divine communion. In the state of deep meditation, when your mind has withdrawn from everything and you are one with the consciousness of God, no stray thought will cross the threshold of your memory. You will stand with God behind the strong iron gate of your concentration and devotion, which neither gods nor goblins dare pass through. That is the most wondrous state of victory!

Get away from everyone now and then, just to be with God. See no one. Introspect, study, and meditate. Night is the best time for such seclusion. You may think you can't change your habits and practice this because so many duties occupy your time. But you have the whole night to yourself, so there is no excuse not to seek God. Don't be afraid you will lose your health if you lose a little sleep. Through deep meditation you will gain greater health.

After a certain hour at night, my mind is not with the world at all; I am mentally away from everything. Sleep is a very small consideration in my life. At night I try to feel sleepy like others; I tell myself I will sleep; but a great Light comes, and all thought of sleep vanishes. When I don't sleep, I never miss it. In eternal wakefulness I see there is no sleep. The joy of divine wisdom enthralls the consciousness.

I feel the drama of God that no one else can feel, save those to whom He reveals Himself. I am part of this world drama, and I am apart from it. I behold you all as actors in this cosmic play. The Lord is the director. Although you have been cast in a particular role, He has not made you an automaton. He wants you to perform intelligently and with concentration, and with the realization that you are playing your role for no one but Him. This is how you should think. God has chosen you for a specific work in this world, and whether you are a businessman or a housekeeper or a laborer, play your part to please Him alone. Then you will be victorious over the sufferings and limitations of this world. He who has God in his bosom has all the powers of the angels with him. His victory cannot be stayed.

God Doesn't Teach Through Mystery but Through Illumined Souls

When you are moving blindly through the valley of life, stumbling in darkness, you need the help of someone who has eyes. You need a guru. To follow one who is enlightened is the only way out of the great muddle that has been created in the world. I never found true happiness and freedom until I met my Guru, he who was spiritually interested in me and who had the wisdom to guide me.

Within your heart cry constantly for God. When you have convinced the Lord of your desire for Him, He will send someone—your guru—to teach you how to know Him. Only he who knows God can show others how to know Him. When I found such a one, my guru Swami Sri Yukteswarji, I realized that God doesn't teach through mystery, but through illumined souls. God is invisible, but He becomes visible through the intelligence and spiritual perception of one who is in constant communion with Him. There may be many teachers in one's life, but there is only one guru. In the guru-disciple relationship a divine law is fulfilled, as demonstrated even in the life of Jesus, when he acknowledged John the Baptist as his guru.*

He alone who is God-realized, and who has been commanded by God to redeem souls, is a guru. One cannot be a guru merely by thinking he is. Jesus showed that the true guru acts solely at God's behest, when he said: "No man can come to me, except the Father which hath sent me draw him."† He gave all credit to the power of God. If a teacher is without egotism, you may know that God alone resides in his body temple; and when you tune in with him you are in tune with God. Jesus reminded his disciples: "Whosoever shall receive me, receiveth not me, but Him that sent me."‡

The teacher who accepts personally the adoration of others is merely a worshiper of his own ego. To find out whether a path is true, discriminate according to what sort of teacher is behind it, whether his actions show that he is led by God, or by his own ego. A leader who has no realization cannot show you the kingdom of God, no matter how large his following. All churches have done good, but blind belief in religious dogma keeps people spiritually ignorant and stagnant. Many times I have seen vast congregations singing God's name, but God was as far away from their consciousness as the distant stars. No one can be saved just by attending church. The real way to freedom lies in Yoga, in scientific self-analysis, and in following one who has traversed the forest of theology and can lead you safely to God.

Success Lies Within the Seeker

So be serious about studying these Self-Realization Fellowship teachings. They have been sent to give you illumination. Many souls have been saved from the darkness of spiritual ignorance through this work. Others, who didn't apply themselves, strayed away; and I know that some of them have fallen spiritually by the wayside. The fault lies within the seeker if he

---

* "Then cometh Jesus from Galilee to Jordan unto John, to be baptized of him. But John forbade him, saying, I have need to be baptized of thee, and comest thou to me? And Jesus answering said unto him, Suffer it to be so now; for thus it becometh us to fulfill all righteousness. Then he suffered him" (Matthew 3:13-15).

† John 6:44.   ‡ Mark 9:37.

does not succeed on this path. If one makes a sincere effort to change, and steadfastly follows Self-Realization, he will find his way out of the dead forest of theology and the endless miseries of this world.

Make up your mind now to put forth greater effort to know God. I don't come here merely to give you lectures on philo-sophical or theological ideas about God, but to encourage you to *know* Him. This is why I don't obligate myself to hold these meetings. I would not come unless I felt the inspiration flowing from the Father. Divine inspiration has no beginning or end; I feel the same surge of inspiration with which I started. No matter how many drops you take from the ocean, it remains the same. God is a spiritual ocean. Take everything out of Him and still He is the same; beginningless, endless, infinite. He can never be exhausted.

Whatever I say to you, I speak for my Father—not for my will or my ego — to help you on the path of emancipation. Self-Realization Fellowship marches on in all lands. I know it is God who speaks through my voice. The voice of Self-Realization is the voice of God. Follow it. Great souls, those who are hungry for God, are following this path and drinking the nectar of His presence. Practice these teachings, and you also shall see how beautiful life becomes.

Rejoice in God's Bliss, and Serve Others

It is not my wish to develop a large, mechanical organiza-tion, but a hive filled with the spiritual honey of God. A minis-ter should never try to attract a large congregation solely to fill the seats of his church. The desire for crowds and big temples melted away from me like snow. I rejoice only in God's bliss and in serving those whom He directs me to help. Do your part. Spread the work of Self-Realization through your words and example, through your devotion. It is not that I am breaking under the load of my work, but I am anxious to help all who are desirous of help; and it is your duty, also, to spread these teach-ings to others through your spiritual vibrations, that they too may receive this truth. I see the great avalanche of truth that is passing through this humble self, and I am very grateful that God would honor such an insignificant one as I with the duty to spread His message. Those who will sincerely follow this path will surely find redemption.

Self-Realization is the work of Christ and Babaji. It saddens the heart of Jesus when in his churches Satan diverts the minds of people to activities that are not related to realizing God. "Churchianity," with its social diversions and bigotry, is taking them away from the spirit of Christ. We should go to church for one purpose only: God-communion. That is why you come here. If you will grow used to quiet, deep meditation at home and in church, you will someday realize what it has done for your life. You need quiet places for communion with God. This is the real purpose of churches and temples.

To Win God Is the Ultimate Victory

So remember, don't think you cannot change and improve. Every night, analyze yourself; and meditate deeply, praying: "Lord, I have lived too long without You. I have played enough with my desires. Now what is to become of me? I must have You. Come to my aid. Break Your vow of silence. Guide me." Ten times He may remain silent; but in between, when you least expect it, He will come to you. He cannot remain away. So long as you harbor an unholy curiosity He will not come; but if you are really sincere, then no matter where you are, He will be with you. This is worth all the effort you may make.

Seclusion is the price of greatness. Avoid going too often into noisy places. Noise and restless activity keep the nerves excited with emotion. That isn't the way to God; it is the way to destruction, for that which destroys your peace draws you away from God. When you are calm and quiet, you are with the Lord. I try to remain by myself most of the time, but whether I am alone or in crowds, I find seclusion in my soul. Such a deep cave! All the sounds of the earth fade away, and the world becomes dead to me, as I stroll in my cave of peace. If you haven't found this inner kingdom, why are you wasting your time? Who will save you? None but yourself. So lose no more time.

Even if you are crippled, blind, deaf, dumb, and forsaken by the world, don't you give up! If you pray, "Lord, I cannot go to Thy temple because of my helpless eyes and limbs, but with all my mind I am thinking of Thee," then the Lord comes and says: "Child, the world gives you up, but I take you in My arms. In My eyes you are victorious." I live in the glory of that consciousness of His presence every day. I feel a wonderful detachment from everything else. Even when I try to feel a special wish for something, I find my mind detached. Spirit is my food; Spirit is my joy; Spirit is my feeling; Spirit is my temple and my audience; Spirit is my library, whence I draw inspiration; Spirit is my love and my Beloved. The spirit of God is the satisfier of all my desires, for in Him I find all wisdom, all the love of a beloved, all beauty, all everything. There is no other desire, no other ambition left for me, but God. Whatever I sought, I found in Him. So will you find.

Don't Waste Your Opportunity to Seek God

Waste no more time, for if you have to change your bodily residence you will have to wait a long time for another opportunity to seek God earnestly, passing first through rebirth and the travails of childhood and the restlessness of youth. Why squander your time in useless desires? It is foolish to spend your life seeking things you must forsake at death. You will never find happiness that way. But every effort you make toward the contact of God in meditation will bring you an everlasting gift of the soul. Start now—those of you who are real lovers of God, seeking not your own glory, but the glory of Spirit.

Each one has to win his own victory. Make up your mind that you are going to be supremely victorious. You don't need an army or money or any other material help to gain the highest victory attainable; just a strong determination that you are going to win. All you have to do is sit still in meditation, and with the sword of discrimination cut off, one by one, the advance of restless thoughts. When they will all be dead, God's kingdom of calm wisdom will be yours.

Every one of you who has heard this sermon, and who makes a sincere effort to change, will find a greater communion with God, and in Him the true and lasting victory of the spirit.

"I Am Blessed to Behold Him"

Self-Realization Fellowship International Headquarters,
Los Angeles, California, January 3, 1937

[A speech given at the banquet closing a special Convocation honoring Paramahansaji on his return from an extended visit to India, and celebrating the twelfth anniversary of the founding of the Self-Realization International Headquarters on Mt. Washington in 1925.]

I cannot express in words my appreciation for all the kind things you have said to me tonight. I am deeply grateful for your devotion and strength of spirit, and for the words that came from your hearts. I pray you bless me that I may always be worthy to serve you. I am proud to be with you, and I am always happy to be reminded of my great duty to you and to all my brothers and sisters of the world.

What has been spoken here of Yogananda is not of me, but of Him who is within me. I only know that you are all images of Christ. When you watch the wave, you don't see the ocean; but when you watch the ocean, you see it is the ocean that becomes the waves. It is the same ocean beneath all the waves. I see that ocean of Spirit beneath the lives of you all. I bow to you.

I am not worthy of the wonderful things that you have said of me. Little as I am, I can only say it is a manifestation of the blessings of God that makes me so loved in your eyes. My life on earth has not been in vain. May God bless you for your words, and may I be more and more worthy of what you have said.

I am overwhelmed by the many inspirations of this occasion wherein we have felt divine joy, divine understanding, and divine communion in which we have forgotten all limitations and differences. I pray that such communion through understanding and beautiful festivities and kindness reign all over the earth, that on the altar of unity the kingdom and omnipresence of God may be expressed. By the pickax of such occasions, the

---

Opposite: Paramahansa Yogananda, 1951

Administration building at International Headquarters of Self-Realization Fellowship, established by Paramahansa Yogananda in 1925. From this twenty-five-acre site located on the summit of Mt. Washington overlooking downtown Los Angeles, the science of Kriya Yoga is disseminated worldwide.

Aerial view (taken with wide-angle lens) of Hermitage grounds overlooking the Pacific Ocean at Self-Realization Fellowship Ashram Center, Encinitas, California. An SRF Retreat with a year-round retreat program provides an opportunity for Self-Realization members and friends to share in the tranquil beauty and spiritual atmosphere of the Hermitage environs.

rocky and useless crusts on our souls are broken—the Divine Spring gushes forth and brings to us new purity, new joy, new love.

A Fresh Beginning for the New Year

We have begun the New Year with a renewed consciousness. Every day let us endeavor to supplant wrong habits and tendencies with good habits and actions. May we all realize the joy of such occasions as this Convocation, and receive such upliftment from these experiences that the darkness of ignorance may be forever dispelled by the beacon light of that joy. I am blessed to behold Him on this occasion and to behold His inspiration in all of you. I am boundlessly blessed to have heard Him speaking through the lips of these divine souls.

It was God who spoke to me His appreciation. You are all gods, if you only knew it. Behind the wave of your consciousness is the sea of God's presence. You must look within. Don't concentrate on the little wave of the body with its weaknesses; look beneath. Close your eyes and you see the vast omnipresence before you, everywhere you look. You are in the center of that sphere, and as you lift your consciousness from the body and its experiences, you will find that sphere filled with the great joy and bliss that lights the stars and gives power to the winds and storms. God is the source of all our joys and of all the manifestations in nature.

God has not to be earned. "Seek ye first the kingdom of God ...and all these things shall be added unto you. Nor be ye of doubtful mind."*

Awaken yourself from the gloom of ignorance. You have closed your eyes in the sleep of delusion. Awake! Open your eyes and you shall behold the glory of God—the vast vista of God's light spreading over all things. I am telling you to be divine realists, and you will find the answer to all questions in God. Meditation is the only way. Beliefs, reading books, cannot give you realization. It is only by meditating in the right way that you can have that great realization and joy. If you follow that way, you shall know that God is not moved by blind prayer or flattery, but He can be moved by law and devotion and the love of your heart. Together with practice of the meditation techniques, you

---

* Matthew 6:33, Luke 12:29.

must surrender yourself to God. You must claim your divine
birthright. Your constant prayer, your boundless determination,
your unceasing desire for God, will make Him break His tremendous vow of silence, and He will answer you. Above all, in
the temple of silence He will give you the gift of Himself, which
shall last beyond the portals of the tomb.

The Movie Drama of Life

When you see a motion picture or a stage performance, if
you know the plot beforehand it will not be so interesting. It is
good that you don't understand this life, because God is playing
a movie drama in your life. It wouldn't be interesting if we
knew what was going to take place before it happened. Don't be
anxious about what is to be in the end. But always pray to God,
"Teach me to play my part in this drama of life—weak or strong,
sick or well, high or low, rich or poor — with an immortal
attitude, that at the end of this drama I may know the moral of it
all."

Do not waste your time. You are God's greatest creation,
greater than all else He has made. You are blessed with the
power to think and reason. God says, "I gave you will; I gave you
freedom and free choice. Perchance you will forsake all things
and love Me, who gave those gifts to you." I at last found all the
silver streamlets of my desires leading to that great Ocean of
Consciousness. Many of you swim toward that Ocean, but stop
by the shore. If you keep on following the good in life, you shall
flow down the river of desire into the ocean of God's consciousness. All life's "realities" that stand before you will be unreal.
Today we are, and tomorrow we are not. We must remember our
utmost duty to that great Power which is behind all our lives. In
acting out our part in this drama we must not forget our highest
duty to Him. If we want to understand this life, we must realize
the fine work God is doing in the flowers, the flame of His mind
that is burning in our thoughts, the life from Him that is pouring
through our souls, and the worlds upon worlds that are spread
out over the great vastness of the cosmos. How boundless is that
God, and yet we feel Him in our consciousness. Our lives are the
reflection of that Spirit. No wave can exist without the ocean
behind it; so we must realize the great Ocean of Life throbbing
behind our lives.

Realization From Mountains or From Living Souls?

It is the living examples of divine souls that can give you the consciousness of God. Once, long ago, I wanted to go away from hermitage duties to seek God in the solitude of the Himalayas. Master [Swami Sri Yukteswar] tried to tell me that I would not gain there the realization that I would receive in meditation under his guidance. But I didn't listen to his strong hint. I went away. In a short time, though, I came back to my Guru. I thought he would rightly be very much displeased with me. But instead, when he saw me, he said casually, "Let us find something to eat."

I asked, "Are you not angry with me, sir?"

He replied, "Why should I be angry with you? I would not use you for my own ends. You have come back; and my love for you is the same. When you went away, that was your pleasure, and I had that same love for you then." Then I knew the meaning of unconditional divine love, and that God in the form of my guru on earth was giving that love to devotees.

One day, shortly after I had returned, I was trying to meditate deeply, and Master called for me. I didn't want to go. He called me again. I answered, "Master, I am meditating."

Then he said, "I know how you are meditating. Come." I went to him, and as I looked at his eyes I saw he was gazing at me with great divine compassion. "Poor boy," he said, "mountains cannot give you what you want." Suddenly, he touched my chest. I had heard of transmission of divine perception, but in the experience Master gave me I realized it. Everything melted; all was light. My breath went and my body was rooted to the ground. I felt I was free of the body; I was Spirit. I had a thousand eyes. I could see everything in front of me and behind me, for miles around. I could see through solid substances; I could see the sap flowing through the roots of trees, and I could see through buildings, walls, and everything. I tested myself to see if the experience was real, and I saw that it was; for I could see all things around me with either open or closed eyes. Such a joy, for which I had hungered for years, Master gave me by that single touch. There was a tremendous bliss of divine communion—no words can describe the joy and happiness that came to me. (I had never fully appreciated my Master's greatness. I was so sure of him. I didn't realize that he would work so many divine blessings in my life.) God has no eyes. He sees through the pores of space—the same way I saw all things independently of the eyes. Everything in the universe was happening within me.

After half an hour of bliss and wonderful visions, Master touched me again and I found myself once more circumscribed by the limited body. Mountains indeed could not have given me what God gave me through my Master. He was the embodiment of God on earth to me. He said, "Come, let us go for a walk now." But he made me sweep the balcony floor before we went. What a contrast! A lesson in balanced spiritual living. He and I then walked in silence by the banks of the Ganges. He was humbly indifferent whenever I wanted to express my gratitude for the spiritual vision he gave me. That was my great Master.

The Resurrection of Sri Yukteswar

Master is free, like the radio vibrations that travel all around.* His presence is ever sweetly haunting me. He was never so real as he is now. Frequently I see him standing near. Everything that he said to me has come true. He had predicted, "I shall leave the body when you come back to India." I shall never forget. So many years he had waited for my return. So many years [since 1920] I had been here in America; but he waited patiently and didn't recall me until two years ago. Then I wrote to St. Lynn, "Master is calling me. He won't wait for me any longer. I must go." St. Lynn was so spiritually understanding and intuitive, he immediately cooperated with a generous donation to send me to India. I went there and Master fulfilled his tryst with Immortality. He left his body; and then, to my greatest surprise, he came to me in resurrected form.† It is not imagination, my friends. Today's common phenomena of radio and so on would have been viewed with skepticism an age ago. God has so many wonderful demonstrations to show you if you will tune yourself to see these manifestations. It is worthwhile to try. You must put your heart and soul into meditation. If you give a couple of hours morning and evening to meditation, you shall find that great God who is behind all things.

---

* Swami Sri Yukteswar left his body March 9, 1936, during Paramahansaji's visit to India.

† Recounted in *Autobiography of a Yogi,* chapter 43.

"Among thousands of men, one strives for spiritual attainment; and among the blessed true seekers that assiduously try to reach Me, perhaps one perceives Me as I am."* It isn't necessarily those who come first who shall find God; it is those who last on the path that shall be blessed. They shall receive Him.

God Is More Tempting Than Temptation

I found God more tempting than temptation. Side by side I compared Him with all material desires, and I found Him more desirable than anything else. I am anchored in that Spirit. I find my home in Mt. Washington or in an auto; in India or America or anywhere. The joy of material things fades away, but the joy of God never fades. It is an eternal romance with the Spirit. It is joy indescribable. Although you find glimpses of the Divine, don't be satisfied; go deeper within, and you will sit at the brink of eternity facing God. There, in the land beyond all your dreams, where the well of God is eternally springing, in the heart and soil of your soul, there you can go in the ark of silence. God is waiting. And you are dreaming about this dream. Turn your attention from this world to the kingdom of God which is within. I live in that kingdom, that joyous sphere where stars and planets are floating in the vastness of my consciousness.

"O God, I see Thee painting Thy beauty on the canvas of the sky, on the canvas of nature, and on the canvas of my consciousness. O how blessed I am! I, who am unworthy to utter Thy name."

I see Him with my eyes closed in meditation, and I see Him with my eyes open. That eternal freedom you too must find. You shall, if you make the effort. It is better to enter into life maimed—having cut off all lesser desires—than to live without God.† Awaken yourself! Be anchored in the Spirit of God, in the realization of the Infinite Being that flows like an ocean through all creation. It is worthwhile in this short season of life to make the effort to gain God-realization. Joy will flow constantly. I feel this great Ocean of Life and I say, "O God, this little being Thou hast blessed with Thy joy. And I know now why Jesus was willing to bleed for all, and to give his life: He was anchored in that joy in Thee."

* Bhagavad Gita VII:3.   † See Mark 9:43.

All of you must bring your body, mind, and soul under discipline, and pray with might and devotion to God. If you follow the way of meditation that we teach, you shall find that one day, when you are least expecting it, God will drop both His hands to lift you up. It is not only that you are seeking God, but that God is seeking you—more than you are seeking Him. But He has given you independence to cast Him aside if you wish. You must help your Father. Come back to your home; and as with the biblical prodigal son who returned home, He shall kill the fatted calf of wisdom, eternal bliss, and divine understanding as a feast for you. And you shall find Him with you evermore.

God, Guru, Paramgurus, devotees, I bow to you all. I bow at the feet of all humanity, for all are the children of God.

Take God With You Through Life

Extracts from a talk given at Self-Realization Fellowship International Headquarters, Los Angeles, California, August 17, 1939*

Because of God, everything else is. Because of Him, you exist. Because of Him, you have material abundance and conveniences, and all the satisfactions that go with them. So unto God your gratitude should be great. Why then do you not remember His supreme importance to you? How can you sleep away each day in ignorance of Him? There is no excuse. Why give so much importance to material life? Attend to your earthly obligations, but all the while think of God. For every day the demon of fate is snatching people from this temporal land; at any moment you may be taken away.

Perform your duties in this world conscientiously, but keep your engagement with God without fail. I work hard to serve all, but when I am alone meditating, I allow no one to disturb me. Other matters can wait; the engagement with God must never be neglected. One saint in India would not interrupt his worship to read even urgent messages. In your life, also, you must give supreme importance to daily communion with Him. Otherwise you will never keep your engagement with God.

Great teachers will never counsel you to be neglectful; they will teach you to be balanced. You have to work, no doubt, to feed and clothe the body. But if you allow one duty to contradict another, it is not a true duty. Thousands of businessmen are so busy gathering wealth, they forget that they are creating a lot of heart disease too! If duty to prosperity makes you forget duty to health, it is not duty. One should develop in a harmonious way.

* Paramahansaji sometimes digressed at length during a lecture, often in response to unspoken thoughts and questions of his listeners. The material in this article is such a spontaneous digression. The lecture proper, "Looking at Creation With Seeing Eyes," appears in *Man's Eternal Quest.*

There is no use giving special attention to developing a wonderful body, if it houses a peanut brain. The mind also must be developed. And if you have excellent health and prosperity and intellect, but you are not happy, then you have still not made a success of your life. When you can truthfully say, "I am happy, and no one can take my happiness away from me," you are a king—you have found the image of God within you. Be proud of that Image within. If you rant and rage through life, constantly irritated by everything and looking down on everyone—and if you die with that consciousness—you won't have even begun to realize that God is within you, that He is your Self.

Once an Indian saint and a few disciples were bathing in the Ganges when another man arrived and began to wash his horse near the holy man. As the intruder tended his horse, he was intentionally careless in splashing water on the saint. The angered disciples wanted to strike the offender. But their guru said, "No, let him alone." Suddenly the horse kicked its master, knocking out some of his teeth. The saint went over and lovingly helped the injured man. The inexorable laws of nature, not the saint, had punished the wrongdoer. God and His cosmic laws work unfailingly for the benefit of those whose actions are ever in tune, and for the awakening, through suffering, of those who are not true to the divine Self within.

Man Is Made in the Image of God

You are an image of God; you should behave like a god. But what happens? First thing in the morning you lose your temper and complain, "My coffee is cold!" What does it matter? Why be disturbed by such things? Have that evenness of mind wherein you are absolutely calm, free from all anger. That is what you want. Don't let anyone or anything "get your goat." Your "goat" is your peace. Let nothing take it away from you. And blame no one else for your unhappiness; blame yourself. If you are mistreated by others, seek the fault in yourself, and you will find it much easier to get along with everyone. Jesus looked upon his enemies as little children. If a child hits you, you don't hate him for it. You forgive him, realizing he didn't know better. When people persecute you, do not desecrate the image of God within you by vengeful retaliation. If you want to realize His image within, remember *now* that you are a god, and behave like one.

Most people are victims of moods, and unless one controls them, they will control him. A person who is not self-controlled is not fully "sane," and he doesn't know it! He who masters his moods becomes a more balanced individual. It is a strange phenomenon that no one can be tempted to do willingly something he feels is against his own highest interest; yet of his own volition, spurred by moods, whims, and habits, he does many things that are contrary indeed to his welfare.

Always think first of what you are about to do and how it will affect you. To act on impulse is not freedom, for you will be bound by the unpleasant effects of wrong actions. But to do those things your discrimination tells you are good for you is all-freeing. That kind of wisdom-guided action makes for a divine existence. Then you find and reflect the image of God within you. When you make up your mind to do or not to do something, and you carry out that resolution—in spite of contrary influences of moods or bad habits—that is real freedom.

The teachings of the great ones of India are not a Sunday affair, to be forgotten the rest of the week; they are to be practiced daily. Mere belief is not sufficient; self-discipline, control of moods, is also essential. The training given by India's masters is meant to show the disciple how to be unconditionally happy, untouched by suffering and change. For that training and understanding I deeply thank them.

God Will Not Force Himself on You

If one is sincere in his search for Truth, God helps him to find a book or a teacher to inspire and encourage him. When the seeker is deeply in earnest, God sends him a guru. A guru is a God-knowing person who has been divinely appointed by Him to take the seeker as a disciple and lead him from the darkness of ignorance to the light of wisdom. Through the guru's pure perception, God teaches the devotee. For the Lord has taken a vow of silence, and He does not address the disciple directly until that devotee has attained a considerable degree of spiritual development. God's silence does not mean that He is cruel or indifferent. On the contrary, in His humility and love He has given man freedom to work out his own destiny. God does not wish to interfere with that free choice. He wants us to use our freedom to find Him, but He does not want to force Himself upon us.

Because God gave us independence, and because we misused it, we have become estranged from Him. Until you know God, until you have heard His voice, no matter what spiritual path you are following, you have not attained real communion with Him. His voice *can* be heard. He *can* be known. He is more real than all the things you perceive with your five senses. But you must work at finding Him.

The Guru Is Sent by God

For success in the divine search, as in every other aspect of life, it is necessary to follow God's laws. To understand the secular knowledge available in a school, you have to learn from a teacher who knows it. So also to understand spiritual truths it is necessary to have a spiritual teacher, or guru, one who knows God. Even if you cannot be in his physical presence, or even if he is no longer incarnate on earth, you must follow the teaching of such a teacher if you would find God. Just any teacher will not do. There is only one guru uniquely the devotee's own. But if you turn away from the emissary of God, He silently asks: "What is wrong with you, that you foolishly leave the one I have sent to help you learn the divine science of the soul? Now you shall have to wait long, and prove yourself, before I shall respond again." He who cannot learn through the wisdom and love of his God-ordained guru will not find God in this life. Several incarnations at least must pass before he will have another such opportunity.

An understanding of the divine law of the guru-disciple relationship is necessary. We learn this in India. It is very simple, but very important: you have to find the guru, first; then real spiritual progress begins. It is not that I am trying to make you loyal to me personally. I am only stating a fact: if you want God, you must be loyal to the one God has sent to help you.

Besides attunement with the guru, there must be day and night a consuming desire for God. The ardor of a thousand million loves must be gathered in your heart for Him, and the consciousness of urgent necessity: as the miser seeks money, as the lover longs for the beloved, as the drowning man gasps for breath, so must you desire God. Cry for Him constantly: "Am I going to find You? I want only You!" As you pray and pray, perhaps you will see a little glimmer of His light, to encourage you. But God wants to know if you will persist, if your will cannot be weakened by any temptation. Mistakes you have made do not matter. If nothing can change your love for God, He will come to you.

But how many of you meditate deeply enough to receive Him? If you do so in the right way, if you mean business with God and want only to please Him, you will find Him; and He will talk to you through your conscience and through your awakened spiritual perception.

God's Answer to His Devotee

During one period about seven months ago I was absolutely bogged in activity, lecturing every night and talking to people all day. There was no time to be alone with God, and so He seemed far away. I became very dejected. "Lord, what is this?" I prayed. "How can I think of You? Shall I fly away from these classes?" (I ask Him all the time if He wants me to leave everything to think only of Him.) I felt that my whole soul and brain were about to burst with longing, as I went on praying and crying for Him: "What You do with me I don't care. People have perished for money and for women. I don't mind if I perish for You, my God! But I must know You are here with me. How can I see You? How can I go on without You? I love to work. I love to help people, but not at the cost of losing You. Lord, my only thought has been to serve You in Your work, so why is it I feel I have once in a while lost Your contact?" When I refused to give up until He responded, the most beautiful answer came. The Lord said: "When you are not meditating, isn't it true that in your thoughts you are missing Me and thinking about meditating? When you meditated you thought of Me, and when you didn't meditate you missed Me; therefore the thought of Me was always predominant."

From that day I have had seven months' ecstasy! Even though talking to people while I continued with the classes, or otherwise working, I have felt every minute that bliss of God-contact. This divine state has not left me these many months. No matter what I am doing, I find the needle of the compass of my mind always turned toward God. Such is the devotee's consciousness.

You must similarly pray until you get His answer. He will respond to you, even as He responded to me. There is always some particular desire lurking constantly in your consciousness. Find out what is uppermost in your mind: Is it health, or money, or love? Perhaps your health has not been good, and in your mental background is a constant yearning: "Lord, if only I could be healthy again!" Why shouldn't you long for God in the same way? By remembering that He is ever with you, and is your greatest necessity, you can keep God uppermost in your mind.

A Loving Message for America

It is easy to remember God in India, because there everybody talks of Him. Here, if you talk about God anywhere except in church on Sunday you are regarded as a fanatic! But America is advancing rapidly in spirituality. There is more understanding and desire for God here than in most other parts of the world. And I believe that a great blessing is going to come upon you. You must cultivate those qualities in your souls that will make all nations look up to you. The two most important commandments to be obeyed are these: "Thou shalt love the Lord thy God with all thy heart, and with all thy soul, and with all thy mind, and with all thy strength.... Thou shalt love thy neighbor as thyself."* "Neighbor" means whoever is drawn into your path. When you have followed these two commandments, all others will be kept automatically.

He who is humble and loves God is the greatest of all. It is easy to rationalize and say that you have no time for God, but in your heart and in the background of your mind you can always pray unceasingly: "Reveal Thyself, come to me! Thou art my life." Hold these thoughts no matter what you are doing. Whether struggling with a problem or enjoying some accomplishment, let God be ceaselessly in the background of your mind: "I love Thee alone, I seek Thee alone. Reveal Thyself." Then God will come to you.

Thoughts are like the honeycomb; the love of God is the

---

* Mark 12:30-31.

honey. If you are really sincere, God will come to drink the honey of your devotion from the honeycomb of your thoughts.

Our Destination Is God

The desire for God does not come of itself; it must be cultivated. And without that desire life has no meaning. When you sleep you say good-bye to this world, to your family, your name, everything. Even your body is forgotten. You do not know when you may have to say a more permanent good-bye to the world. You are on a journey, stopping here for just a little while. Life is like a great caravan passing by. Your first interest should be to learn the purpose of this journey, and its destination. That destination is God. It could not be anything else.

The Lord comes to the devotee who lives for Him and dies in Him. He touches that soul and says: "My child, wake up. You are just dreaming. Death has not touched you at all." Then the devotee knows that all his earthly experiences were meant not to torture, but to teach him his real soul nature. The soul cannot be burned. It cannot be drowned or stabbed or shattered.* The devotee realizes: "I am not the body. I am formless. I am Joy Itself." Remind yourself of this truth each morning as you awaken: "I am just coming from the inner perception of my Self. I am not the body. I am invisible. I am Joy. I am Light. I am Wisdom. I am Love. I dwell in the dream body through which I am dreaming this earth life; but I am ever eternal Spirit."

A Controlled Mind Lessens Pain

Whenever you are in misery, physical or mental, practice this spiritual consciousness. During sleep, you do not feel even a broken bone. And if in waking consciousness you keep a very controlled mind, three-fourths of any pain you experience will likewise disappear; for there is no relation between pain and the body except through the mind. When a stranger is hurt, you don't feel as much concern as you would if he were your brother. A mother watching over her suffering baby feels greater pain than she would if it were another's child. Similarly, physical

---

* "No weapon can pierce the soul; no fire can burn it; no water can moisten it; nor can any wind wither it....The soul is immutable, all-permeating, ever calm, and immovable—eternally the same" (Bhagavad Gita II:23-24).

suffering in your own body is intensified because, through identification with it, you are more in sympathy with your body than
with someone else's. You must be better able to detach your
mind and feeling from the body. That is why Jesus said: "Take no
thought for your life, what ye shall eat, or what ye shall drink;
nor yet for your body, what ye shall put on."* Love for the
body, love for the senses—these are harmful to your spiritual
development.

If you want spiritual illumination, practice these truths.
They are so beneficial that they ought to be applied by
everyone. Once in a while, try getting along without food and
other comforts in your daily life. Fast for a day or two,† and
deny yourself some of the pleasures and conveniences you are
accustomed to, and see whether or not you are just as content
without them. The really freeborn person is master of himself.
He is led by the inner wisdom of the soul, uninfluenced by
others or by the dictates of his own habits or moods. This kind
of freedom requires rigid self-control and a deep understanding
of the Self. But it is not difficult to attain this freedom. It is
your true nature.

One should maintain a constant mental state of devotion to
God. I have tried every form of activity, but no matter what I am
doing, my mind remains with God. You should enjoy this creation, without being enslaved by it. I know from experience that
the pleasure of finding God is the most enjoyable. Yet people are
so steeped in delusion that they will not make the effort to know
Him. They would rather engage in worldly interests, or passively
seek Him through reading books and wandering from one religion to another. People do not follow the real way of God-
perception because that way lies in continuously praying to
God, in seeking Him day and night, and in conquering all forces
that keep the mind away from Him.

Yoga is most wonderful because it gives step-by-step methods that lead to God-realization. In college you may earn a D.D.
and be proclaimed a Doctor of Divinity, and still be a Doctor of
Delusion! *Practice* of religion, not just intellectual understanding, is most important—practice of the *perception* of God.

---

* Matthew 7:25.   † See footnote page 159.

The successes of some religious teachers are like spiritual mushrooms, growing overnight but having no firm foundation. Qualified teachers have divine realization, and are guided by the blessing of God and their own God-realized guru.

You cannot save others' souls unless you have saved your own. In the Orient, true seekers strive to attain their own salvation and do not proselyte to save others. In the West, many teachers aspire to save others' souls without first having saved their own. I have met such a one. He was a man of the flesh, through and through; yet he had a large following as a religious teacher. He pretended to be what he was not—a deeply spiritual man. Because I was born in India, he considered me a "heathen" and, deeming himself a "good Christian," he therefore felt it his duty to tell me that I didn't know anything about Truth. But when I asked him to describe what he experienced when he went into ecstasy and communed with God, he could not answer; his greatness was as shallow as the flattery that proclaimed it. Then I "gave it to him": "Your experience of God and the true nature of your Self is severely limited, because you are too identified with the senses to develop much spiritually. The adulation of many followers is not the measure of one's realization. That others say you are great does not make it so. Such flattery is insincere and meaningless. If you concentrate on receiving true love from people, drawn by your own merit, you will never again fall for flattery; you will see right through it. Flattery is poisonous because it is a distortion of truth, and hence misleading. So long as you enjoy your band of flatterers, you will have no real friends."

There are some who expect flattery from me, but I never give it. I cannot be insincere to the God I behold in all, even in those who are in delusion.

Test yourself every day to see if you are behaving according to your true soul nature. Do not be discouraged in your efforts, thinking that God is not listening to your prayers, or is not aware of your striving. If you study the lives of the masters and saints you will see that they had much more trouble than you have. Not only did they have to conquer self; they also had to take on the problems of others. Each one who comes to the guru thinks he is the only one the teacher has to look after. He wants the guru to respond to him according to his own preconceived desires. And in addition, in this country, the expenses of an organization and of supporting disciples are such that the spiritual teacher has also to be a checkwriting machine! But God blessed me, through the understanding souls He sent to help me accomplish what He had brought me here to do.

Follow Those Who Have Found God

Follow the spiritual paths recognized by the masters who have found God. If you practice the Self-Realization yoga methods you will reach God much faster than if you travel the blind routes of theology. India specialized in finding God. If you follow her truly great masters you will reach the Goal much quicker. In my early seeking I tried all methods; I know which is faster. Someone said to me: "Everyone claims that his path is best. How am I to know?" "Test them," I said. "It is only by tasting water that you can tell whether it will quench your thirst. Rationalizing about water won't do it." Pray that God lead you. If you are sincere, God will show you the right way for you.

So, dear ones, remember: Day and night seek God. Do not be controlled by moods or habits, but use your free will to do always the right thing. All the time, no matter what you are doing, mentally pray to God. Do not be absentminded; do things with concentration, but in the background of your mind ever be calling to Him: "Lord, reveal Thyself. Come unto me. Thy love is all-satisfying. I want Thee alone!" And at night meditate; practice the techniques taught by the masters of Self-Realization, and you cannot fail to find God. Make the determination with me:

"O God, we make within our hearts a solemn promise not to fall into the sleep of delusion, but to remain awake in Thee; to make every effort to pray unto Thee unceasingly in the background of our minds, until we find Thee; and to follow the Self-Realization path of yoga, and through our example help others to come into Thy kingdom. Father, help us to find Thee, for Thou art our own."

The Aurora of Bliss

Written in the early 1920s

Bliss is the polestar to which all mariner souls, storm-tossed on the waves of tumultuous sorrow and exciting pleasure, look for guidance.

Bliss is God's consciousness—His being, His supreme quality, His infinite life. Feeling an ever-increasing bliss in attentive meditation is the surest sign of His presence. The greater the bliss, the deeper the contact with God.

There are two ways of experiencing bliss: by *sabikalpa samadhi* and by *nirbikalpa samadhi*.

In the *sabikalpa* state, the meditating devotee becomes so inwardly immersed in bliss that thoughts, feelings, memory images, all sensibilities of the world, fall from the consciousness. Just as one who is deeply engrossed in reading an interesting story does not see or hear what is going on around him, the devotee becomes so absorbed in the enjoyment of bliss within that his awareness is wholly absent without. It is not unconsciousness or a mentally chloroformed state in which there is simultaneous disappearance of consciousness both internally and externally, but a supernal state of heightened inner divine perception.

In *nirbikalpa samadhi*, or complete union, the yogi enjoys simultaneously the transcendental bliss of the Absolute beyond creation as well as Spirit's blissful omnipresence in all universal manifestations—the unmanifested ocean of Spirit and Its manifested waves of creation in the universe. In this state, with closed or open eyes, while walking, talking, sleeping, meditating, the devotee consciously contacts the all-pervading bliss as the *summum bonum* — transcendent, but also immanent in all creation. He realizes that bliss—conscious, intelligent, everlasting, all-pervading, ever new joy — has frozen itself into the primordial causal, luminous astral, and gross physical creations.

As one becomes immersed in bliss by deeper and deeper silent meditation, he finds the fountain of bliss spraying through the pores of his consciousness, thoughts, feelings, and sense-perceptions.

I remember the day when for the first time, unlooked-for, from behind the clouds of the drudgery of routine meditating habits, the aurora of bliss suddenly burst upon my consciousness. It surpassed all my expectations. Joy indescribable! The light of bliss illumined all the dark corners of consciousness, clearing away the shadows of all questions, passing X-raylike through gross objects and showing me all things lying beyond the horizon of mortal gaze—east, west, north, south, front and behind, above and beneath, within and without, all around—everywhere.

In the light of this aurora I saw the entire motion picture of the cosmos. Dead memories of ages past were resurrected. Bliss lit the hall of the universe, and all at once I beheld in it all my blood relations—soul-kinsmen of the past, present, and future: stardust, gems, flowers, birds and beasts; mothers, fathers, sisters, brothers; saints and hoary sages.*

After such an awakening, the yogi silently says:

"Peering through the dark nights of my unfruitful meditations, looking steadfastly wisdomward, at long last I found the aurora of bliss suddenly bursting within my consciousness. Its brilliance, which had dimly twinkled behind the clouds of countless incarnations, scintillated through my unfulfilled aspirations.

"Unveiled splendor! The beautiful scenes on the canvas of the sky are painted with the varied colors of bliss. The music of violins, birds, spheres, atomic vibrations, all play together the grand symphony of bliss. The perfumes of flowers are saturated with the fragrance of bliss; their petals, fashioned from the beauty of bliss. All joys are inspired by bliss. The wine of the gods, thirst-allaying cool drinks from fresh streams, the honey of flowers, fruit nectars, all flow from the winepress of bliss.

"My thoughts with open mouths seek to drink of bliss in all activities of life. My wild fancies dip their curiosity-parched

* See also "My Kinsmen" in *Songs of the Soul.*

lips in the golden river of bliss. My feelings swim on waves of ever new bliss. My intuition, spread like the ubiquitous ether through everything, mingles with the all-pervading, inly flowing bliss.

"I listen to the enthralling music of bliss. I smell, taste, think, feel, the sense-surpassing delights of bliss. I behold bliss everywhere, in all things. I embrace bliss in every form and particle of creation. From bliss I come, for bliss I live, and in bliss I merge. Bliss is the ocean in which all the waves of my desires, dreams, ambitions, sense-cravings, actions, devotion, wisdom, have melted into one sea of fulfillment.

"Past, present, future, drop their veils. I behold the molten rays of the ever-changing, everlasting aurora of bliss pass through the sextillions of thoughts that coursed in the brain of each one of the myriad beings who had lived, hoped, and died. The aurora passes through the lightless-light cosmos of causal thought-forms* hidden behind the walls of earthly sunrays, moonbeams, and inhabited planets. From this thought-womb, the one life-blood of bliss flows down through the arteries of thoughts of all contemporary individuals. Astral bliss-electricity shines in all animate and inanimate bulbs of being. All dreams of art, literature, science, of religion and scriptures, of thoughts, activities, and inventions, yet to be dreamed in the brains of future earth or other planetary generations, wait for the help of the omniscient bliss to weave their storied tapestry.

"In the hall of bliss, in the dream mansion of cosmic aurora, I behold mountains, starlets, denizens of civilized and wooded jungles, thermal-magnetic-electrical laws; man, beast, thoughts, spiritual perceptions — all singing together in perfect harmony the song of universal brotherhood."

* See *causal world* in glossary.

Answer the Call of Christ!

All-day Christmas Meditation,
Self-Realization Fellowship International Headquarters,
Los Angeles, California, December 24, 1939

The conception of Christ was not ordinary, but immaculate. For us his birthday is therefore a very special day to celebrate, knowing and feeling as we do that in Jesus' immaculate conception the Heavenly Father prepared for the birth of a perfect being.* The true celebration of Christmas is the realization in our own consciousness of the birth of Christ Consciousness.

Do away with all wandering thoughts and feel your oneness with the spirit of Christ. I invoke the Spirit of Jesus, and of the Masters who are one with him in Spirit, that the perfect one who was born on earth nineteen hundred years ago may manifest his consciousness within you now. This I pray earnestly today, with all the unctuous fervor of my soul. All things are possible through prayer. Jesus said, "What things soever ye desire, when ye pray, believe that ye receive them, and ye shall have them."† Believe that your prayer for his visitation is granted, and it shall be so. The love of Christ becomes manifest in you not merely by peace of mind nor even by burning zeal; but by calm, devotional will for perfection. "O Christ, come unto us! Manifest thyself unto us! Naughty or good, we are thine. Deliver us from the bondage of restlessness and receive us as we are."

May all those who are in tune with us today (whose

---

* In the Bhagavad Gita, IV:7-8, the Lord speaks thus of the coming on earth of the Divine Consciousness in the form of the Great Ones: "Whenever virtue *(dharma)* declines and vice *(adharma)* predominates, I incarnate as an *avatar.* In visible form I appear to destroy evil and reestablish virtue."

† Mark 11:24.

thoughts I feel coming to me)* be blessed with the presence and the consciousness of Christ. "Heavenly Father, Thou dost grant those prayers that come from our heart; and this is my heartfelt prayer, that all of us here be visited by Thy presence, Thy glorious presence. O Infinite Light! all the candles of our devotion are burning. Come! Come unto us!"

The love of God cannot be described. But it can be felt as the heart is purified and made constant. As the mind and the feeling are directed inward, you begin to feel His joy. The pleasures of the senses do not last; but the joy of God is everlasting. It is incomparable! Today you can understand the spiritual gains you have made here as a result of long meditation conducted with continuous devotion. You have already meditated four hours and it has seemed like only minutes to most of you. In the consciousness of some, I see, there has been a nibble of response from God; and in others the Divine has wholly swallowed the bait of their devotion.

Forget everything else! Just lay yourself at God's feet. There is no time like the present to surrender yourself unto Him. At first He bestows a glimpse of joy that comes after a little meditation, and stays but a little while. That is when most people misunderstand, give up, and are lost again in worldly snares. But great joy and happiness are to be had if you go on until you realize the spirit of Christ and experience the bliss of contact with the Great Ones. No pleasure of the senses can ever give that comfort and happiness. Even the movies with their entertaining variety may become tiresome, but God never is. Once you get to God and experience His bliss, He becomes more real to you than all else, His contact more joyous than any pleasure of the senses, more tempting than any other temptation. Until you feel His joy you can never attain His glory; you cannot know what happiness lies in becoming a king of kings, a prince of light.

That is why you should use all the strength of your soul to find God. He is not the monopoly of anyone; nor may He be bribed. God doesn't need our praise. That approach to Him implies some strain and effort — like a lover's praising the

---

* From SRF students throughout the world who held all-day Christmas meditation-meetings on this day in 1939.

beloved all the time just to keep her pleased. God doesn't want that kind of relationship with you. But divine, unconditional love is so beautiful. There is no other gift you can give Him but the gift of your love. If God could ever be said to beg from us, it is for our love. If He wants anything at all from us, it is our love. The smoke-screen of delusion has come between us and Him, and He is sorry that we have lost sight of Him. He is not happy seeing His children suffer so much—dying from falling bombs, terrible diseases, and wrong habits of living. He regrets it, for He loves us and wants us back. If only you would make the effort at night to meditate and be with Him! He thinks of you so much. You are not forsaken. It is you who have forsaken your Self. You are the greatest transgressor against your own happiness. God is never indifferent to you.

You have meditated deeply today. And so should you meditate every night. But instead you pass your time in foolishness, wasting opportunities to be with God. Forget useless pursuits. Neglect minor duties, if necessary; but do not neglect God. He is not merely a name. God is the life that is surging within us; the life by which we see and love one another. For a little while we behold one another here. "Today" is but a thought of God, a moment in eternity. Time and again God has shown me that this whole creation consists of nothing more than His dream-thoughts.

We are in a dream state. The only way to wake up is to refuse to recognize anything as reality except God. Otherwise you will again and again sink to your knees in a mud of suffering that is of your own making, until you realize that neither good fortune nor evil fortune is real, that He alone is real. Then all earthly delusions (disease and health, joy and sorrow, life and death) will pass away. So many people have come on this earth and have left it; still we live as though we shall be here forever. Only he is wise who lives in constant remembrance of God. To think of Him always is to find freedom from this earthly dream of birth and death.

May you all be so filled with the love of God that in your heart you know nothing else, day or night, but His peace and joy. Again and again I have talked to God, and again and again I have reproached Him with what has happened to this creation. For here we are first tempted by Satan. If only we had been first tempted by the Lord, we wouldn't want to follow satanic ways. Misery is the word for this creation with all its delusion and suffering; and one by one we are taken away, we know not whither. Is there any happiness in this? No, happiness comes only in realizing that the nightmare of creation is not real, and that God is real.

Let those who want this world worship it. But you go on to find the supreme joy of Spirit. The love of the Lord is everlasting. If you but once get to Him, then—just as the compass-needle, no matter how you turn it, always points to the north—your mind will ever turn to the love of the Spirit. There are no words to describe that love.

No joy is real except that of the Spirit. But unless your heart cries for God, you cannot know Him. The hearts of worldly people become dry as dust. Why? Because they cry for everything except God. You must cry for the Lord! Cry for Him who, if you would but realize it, is already yours. The sole purpose of creation is to compel you to solve its mystery and perceive God behind all. He wants you to forget everything else and to seek Him alone. Once you have found refuge in the Lord, there is no consciousness of life and death as realities. You will then see all dualities like dreams during sleep, coming and going in the eternal existence of God. Forget not this sermon, a sermon He is expressing to you through my voice. Forget not! He is saying:

"I am just as helpless as you, for I, as your soul, am tied in the body with you. Unless you redeem your Self, I am caged with you. Dally no more, groveling in the mud of suffering and ignorance. Come! bathe in My light."

It is because God wants you that I am here with you, calling you to come home, where my Beloved is, and where Christ, Krishna, Babaji, Lahiri Mahasaya, Sri Yukteswarji, and the other saints are. "Come," the Lord is saying, "they are all rejoicing in Me. No worldly joys—the taste of food, the beauty of flowers, the passing pleasure of earthly love—can compare with the divine joys of My home. Come! Come! Come! Every night in meditation you shall live with Me in eternal love. Remember Me! Remember My love!" Thus the Lord is calling you. There is only one Reality. It is He. Forget everything else.

Make the *Self-Realization Fellowship Lessons* your daily

study, and meditate every night. Don't go to bed until you have communed with God. In the silence of the night, in the bower of your consciousness, beyond the reach of the noisy senses, renew your romance with God. In the bower of Infinitude, beneath His moonèd Joy, have eternal communion with the Beloved of the universe.

Divine Mother's face is bright like lightning. She is with us today. How happy we are! How joyous we are! "And every day, O Mother, be Thou with us, that we go about our duties filled with the fragrance of Thy Presence; that we be lured away from the stinkweed of the senses. Father, Mother, Friend, beloved God, Jesus Christ, Bhagavan Krishna, Mahavatar Babaji, Lahiri Mahasaya, Sri Yukteswarji, saints of all religions, we bow to you all. Come unto us, that we may bathe in Thy glory!"

[Paramahansaji here began to chant, "Come, Listen to My Soul Song,"* and a period of meditation followed. Then he spoke again.]

God is nearer than the beat of our hearts, nearer than our thoughts. Love Him! When a prodigal soul returns to God, after having run away into the world of matter, there is rejoicing in Heaven; the fatted calf of wisdom is prepared for the homecoming celebration for that soul in the kingdom of God. If you would but look within, you would find that God is a wonderful host, offering every kind of entertainment! In Him there is no time, no space, no limitation of any kind.

"Jesus and the Masters, be with us! Inspire us all with thy glories! We are not worthy of Thee, O Spirit! Our lips have wasted time in worldly speech. Now our soiled lips are talking of Thee. Divine Spirit, bless us that within our hearts we speak only of Thee evermore. No matter what we say with our tongues, our hearts will ever be repeating Thy name. Divine Beloved, Thou art ours. Bless all who are here that they drink of Thy joy, glory in Thy joy, and thus forget this earth-dream altogether. We are just moving in a dream. We may be working and experiencing life's passing scenes, but it is not real. Only when we feel the joy of Thy Being are we awake in Reality. *Aum,* glory. *Aum,* glory. *Aum,* Christ. *Aum,* Christ."

[Another period of meditation followed, after which Paramahansaji related the following experience.]

* A song in *Cosmic Chants* by Paramahansa Yogananda.

I saw a great blue valley. The mountains were like shim-
mering jewels. Here and there mist sparkled around these opalescent mountains. A silvery river of silence, diamond-bright,
flowed by. And there I saw, coming out of the depth of the
mountain, Jesus and Krishna walking hand in hand — the
Christ who sang by the river Jordan and the Christ who sang by
the river Yamuna. Krishna with his flute and Christ with his
song came hand in hand, and they baptized me in the river. My
soul melted in the flaming-bright waters. The shining mountains and the river and the sky all began to emit flames. My
body and the bodies of Christ and Krishna, the opal mountains
and the glowing waters and the sky all became dancing lights,
and atoms of fire flew. Finally nothing remained but mellow
light. In that Light I behold all creation trembling. Thou art
that eternal light of Spirit wherein all forms commingle. Thou
art That. *Aum*.

[A period of meditation followed.]

There is no way to find God's love other than to surrender
to Him. Master your mind so that you may offer it to Him.
There are four steps or states of consciousness. The ordinary
man is restless all the time. However, when he practices meditation he becomes once in a while calm, but most of the time
he remains restless. As he practices meditation more he feels
half the time calm, half the time restless. And when he practices meditation deeply and regularly, he is most of the time
calm and only once in a while restless. Finally he reaches a
state wherein he is all the time calm, and never restless.

The trouble is that you do not meditate long enough, and
hence you fail to reach the state of complete calmness. But if
each night, when everybody else is asleep, your mind is praying
to Him continuously like a steady stream, then God answers
you. Pray to Him, "Lord, this life is Thine. I cannot live without
Thee. Thou must come to me." What is the use of praying unless
you mean this? Prayer that is merely habit is a mockery, and is
wrong. Today you have been so absorbed in Him that you haven't
even been aware that you have been meditating for seven hours.
It seems as if we had just started. This is the way you should
always pray. Day and night, sometimes for weeks, I am not really
conscious of this world. That is true. I am always drunk with the

joy of Eternal Spirit. "Whosoever will save his life shall lose it; but whosoever shall lose his life for my sake and the gospel's, the same shall save it."* You must be willing to lose it for God.

May this Christmas be the greatest holy day you have ever had. Want nothing but the love of God. That alone is real. Never go to sleep unless you feel that divine consciousness. I can't sleep until I have had that contact. Dear friends, don't wait 365 days to meditate deeply again as you have today. For during those 365 days some of you will leave this earth. This life is like a ship. You are on that ship, watching the passing scenes; then suddenly you hear the stopping-throbs of the ship's motor, and the journey is over for you.

The whole world is pulsing with the power of God: indescribable, infinite happiness; wave after wave of bliss. Your heart is like the shore, and the Ocean of Infinite Love is breaking on the shores of your heart. I hope you all consciously experience that. Think of the millions of people who are getting drunk with wine today to "celebrate" the birth of Christ. What a sacrilege! Satan tries to keep man's attention tied to everything but the Divine Joy. But on your calendar the engagement with God must be supreme.

In the beginning of my spiritual training with my master, Sri Yukteswarji, when we would sit together in meditation in the evenings I would become restless as the time approached for me to leave the Serampore hermitage in order to catch the last convenient train back to Calcutta. Disregarding my state of mind, Master, I found, would not dismiss me as early as I thought he should. I would have to run fast each night to reach the train in time. As I discovered that my worry about train schedules was not influencing Master, I made it a point to banish the restless feelings that had previously been disturbing me. My Guru immediately began to dismiss me in ample time to catch my train.

Sri Yukteswarji gave such wonderful training! I wish the churches in this country might in time give that kind of training, too. If the poor minister has to entertain you every Sunday, the entire purpose of the church is missed: for God begins

---

* Mark 8:35.

where motion ceases. I had to talk to you today in order to help you feel what I am feeling. But the masters in India don't teach by talking. They just have the disciples come and sit with them in meditation.

Make every night a Christmas night by meditating until you are full of the divine consciousness you have felt today. Instead of making sure of God you have been making sure of money. Tomorrow you may be gone from this earth, taking with you no imperishable riches. But if you have made time for God, and have experienced Christ Consciousness, when death comes you may truly say, "I am king over life and death. Joyously I plunge into the Infinite!"

Some people think of America as a materialistic land, but I have found many wonderful souls here. I am glad to see so many here today, to chant and meditate with me. It is you, and souls like you, who are the real saviors of this country. By your devotion to God you bring blessings on your whole nation.

The only way to attain salvation is to have complete loyalty to God. This dream of life will be taken away from you one day; the only thing that is real is the love of God. Nothing else; all are false dreams. Get away from them. Every minute I see how necessary that is. But He has tied me to the SRF work, and so I tell Him: "I shall work for You alone." Then I feel within His supreme joy.

How kind He has been to this unworthy devotee! I could never have imagined that I might win God. Indeed I used to pity myself, saying: "Lord, You love Your saints, but why don't You love me?" Then I found that He loves all alike. But first you have to show Him that in your heart you have forsaken everything else. Unless you give up desires for body-comforts, sleep, and every other desire, you cannot know Him. Day and night you must think of the Divine Beloved. Then your heart will always sing. Follow the *SRF Lessons.* Practice the presence of God. And meditate.

My greatest Christmas gift to you is this day in which we have spent many hours together drinking in the love and joy of God. Make the most of this time. Feel joy and forgiveness for all. Dance in the joy of God. Preach God. Bless America, bless the whole world, with the love of God.

My body shall pass but my work shall go on. And my spirit
shall live on. Even when I am taken away I shall work with you
all for the deliverance of the world with the message of God.
Prepare yourselves for the glory of God. Charge yourselves with
the flame of Spirit. Forsake slavery to the desires of the flesh.
Until you have established your spiritual mastery over the
body, the body is your enemy. Always remember that! Have no
other desire than to spread His name and to think and sing of
Him all the time. What joy! Can money give us this joy? No! It
comes only from God.

The Lord wants us to escape this delusive world. He cries
for us, for He knows how hard it is for us to gain His deliverance. But you have only to remember that you are His child.
Don't pity yourself. You are loved just as much by God as are
Jesus and Krishna. You must seek His love, for it encompasses
eternal freedom, endless joy, and immortality. Experiencing
the bliss of God, you see that there is no such thing as time, and
know you shall never die. Every day I enjoy that consciousness.
I don't like to show it outwardly. Indeed I can't show it—it is
too delicate and precious. I have caught Him in the net of love. I
hope you all have felt the presence of Jesus the Christ this day
as I have felt it. Jesus appeared to me at one time today as a
little boy; but then he didn't appear in form any more, remaining with me instead as formless Joy eternal, Light eternal.

I tell you these experiences in order to encourage you, but
you should not talk to others about your sacred feelings. Keep
them in your heart. Use your nights for talking with God.
Forsake sleep—it doesn't matter. Don't worry about "tomorrow." Every night and all day long have this joy that you have
felt today. Lazy people shall never enter the kingdom of God.
Don't be afraid to work hard. Thrash the body mentally. And
meditate all the time. While you are working, ever be thinking,
"Lord, I must not forget Thee." Want Him so deeply that you
could roll on the ground with anguish for Him. Cry for Him.
Don't watch the clock. Don't care whether He does or does not
answer, for that puts a condition on your love. He is aware of
your every cry; and when your heart's full surrender has been
made and the *danse macabre* of karma is over, He burns up His
veil of *maya* for you and then where is death? where is old age?

where is sorrow? Nothing remains but His light. This is the truth.

Falter no more, you who have heard these words. Follow the truth that God has sent through Self-Realization Fellowship and you shall be forever blessed. God is ever calling you through the flute of my heart. I urge you—forget Him not! Our bodies may perish, but let our souls forever blaze like eternal stars in the heart of God.

Make a solemn resolution today with me: "Heavenly Christ, Krishna, Babaji, Lahiri Mahasaya, Sri Yukteswarji, saints of all religions, we pledge our lives to the cause of our own Self-realization, that we may realize through the Self the infinite Christ, the infinite Presence of God. Heavenly Father, forget us not, though we forget Thee. Remember us, though we remember Thee not. Be not indifferent unto us, though we are indifferent unto Thee. Bless us as we make this solemn vow: 'We shall make a continuous effort to experience the spiritual Christmas every night and every day.' Cast us not into the jaws of death, into the pit of our own self-created ignorance. Make us realize that the only important engagement in life is our nightly engagement with Thee. Keep us from laziness and make our flesh work every moment for the redemption of the world, that Thy consciousness descend on every man. Be Thou with us, O Christ and the Masters! We pray with all the intensity of our hearts, O Lord, that we may never forget Thee. Be with us evermore. Tomorrow we celebrate thy birth in festivities, O Christ, with friends we love. But today we have celebrated thy birth in the spirit of true remembrance of Thee. *Aum. Peace. Amen.*"

This way of keeping Christmas is sorely needed all over the world. I hope that no matter where my body is, you will daily celebrate this kind of holy day, but especially on the day before Christmas, when you should meditate all day long. Then you will realize that the real Christmas lies in the experience of Christ Consciousness.

May you remain in the eternal glory of Christ every night and every day of the year. You will be blessed whenever you become so intense in your love for God that you forget the body while meditating. The body then becomes purified. Be intoxicated with God. Make a resolution to study your *Self-Realization Lessons* with deep interest. Then you will be able to do something worthwhile in this world. What is the use of being a "soap-box orator"? You should talk only from your experience of God and Christ. I want teachers who will be able to talk of God and Christ as they actually feel Their presence, and see Them. Pray with me:

"Heavenly Father, charge my body with Thy power. Charge my life with Thy life. Charge my soul with Thine eternal love. We surrender ourselves unto Thee. May Christ Consciousness be born in the cradle of our flesh, in the cradle of our souls. Heavenly Father, Mother, Friend, beloved God, be Thou with us evermore. This is our earnest prayer: 'Be with us evermore.'"

Divine Communion
With God and Christ

An ecstasy experienced by Paramahansa Yogananda during a meditation service in the chapel of Self-Realization Fellowship International Headquarters on December 24, 1940

Noting in the West the festive outgoing consciousness, often lacking in depth of true spiritual feeling, which accompanies the seasonal celebrations of Christ's birth, Paramahansa Yogananda in 1931 began in Self-Realization Fellowship the custom of holding one purely spiritual observance of Christmas, an all-day meditation service, before the social festivities on December 25th. Similar observances are held by Self-Realizationists on the birth anniversaries of Bhagavan Krishna and the Self-Realization Gurus, for such times are particularly auspicious; then, special blessings flow from the Great Ones into receptive hearts.

During these long meditations led by Paramahansaji, he often entered *samadhi*, ecstatic communion with God and the Great Ones. Sometimes he talked aloud with God, bestowing on all present a glimpse of the Divine Love. You may share with them now the inspiration imparted by the outpourings of a heart aflame with love for God and mankind as Paramahansaji prayed and talked with the Divine during the meditation in 1940. The following words were spoken during intimate moments of his long communion with God, during which he was experiencing the Infinite Christ Consciousness, and beholding also that Infinite Christ in the beloved form of Jesus.

Do your utmost today to coax God and Jesus Christ into the secluded, silent temple of your heart. Set aside all restlessness and idle thoughts, banish impatience, and plunge into the Infinite. Greater than sleep is the refreshment that comes from deep meditation. In our meditation today we must consciously approach Christ; we must feel his presence, we must see him! Be satisfied with nothing less.

Let us all pray together:

"Heavenly Father, Jesus Christ, Bhagavan Krishna, Mahavatar Babaji, Lahiri Mahasaya, Sri Yukteswarji, Guru Preceptor, we bow to you all.

"Heavenly Father, we pray with all our hearts that You grant us this day the vision of Christ in form and in Spirit.

"O Christ, receive the fervent message of our hearts; come unto us, appear unto us. Jesus Christ, Lord and Master—Lord of millions and Master of creation—in the cradle of our devotion manifest unto us consciously. Reveal your presence in bodily form as you were on earth, and manifest yourself as Spirit—joy ineffable, peace indescribable; calmness, omnipresence, and bliss eternal.

"Beloved Lord, with so much joy and happiness unending locked in our souls, why do we beg for this and that from the world? Bring us to the boundless shores of all-fulfillment in Christ Consciousness. *Aum. Peace. Amen.*"

[After a long period of deep meditation and devotional chanting, Paramahansaji prays alone. With the naturalness of a child the blessed Master, wholly absorbed in divine communion, ardently addresses the Lord as "Thou" and "You" in a sweet mingling of reverence and intimacy.]

"How many hours, days, and years have passed in material pursuits and attachments! O Lord, break down the imprisoning walls of vanity and ego. Destroy the desire for name, fame, and power. Everything we lay at Thy feet, Beloved One, for we came here on earth to glorify Thy name alone. What is the use of our existence here if You do not come unto us? Many incarnations have been wasted; let it not be true of this one! Bless us to help us make the greatest effort to find Thee in this life.

"O Lord, You have the power to kindle divine love in all hearts. You can bless Your devotees with longing for Thee night and day. Give us Thy love, that we no longer have to call entreatingly to You; that the instant we think of You, our hearts and souls will be choked with Thy love divine.

"I pray for all Thy devotees, that morning, noon, and night they sing Thy name, Thy holy name; naught else. How blessed we are if even for a moment we have sung of Thee. In the light of Thy name all our sins vanish, and we dream no more the mortal dream of delusion. We are Thy children; the birthmark of infinity is on our souls. Thy kiss of immortality is on our brows. The blessing of Thine outstretched hands rests eternally upon us.

"Make us realize our oneness with Thee. Awaken us permanently from the dream of delusion that we may remember unceasingly that we are Thine immortal children. Though the nightmares of death and delusion dance around us, we are untouched by them.

"Let Satan not delude those who are seeking Thee. He is strong, but Your love is greater, omnipotent. One touch of Thy grace can drive Satan from the hearts of all. Father, one or two of those devotees You sent to me have slipped away into delusion's mire. I pray for them. Let none succumb to Satan. I pray that for many here this long deep meditation today will mean the last of Satan in their lives.

"With folded hands, with hearts full of joy, we bow to Thee. Oh, such joy! Beloved One, what have I done to deserve this great bliss that fills my being? I desire to live only to drink Thy name from the chalice of all hearts. Naught else do I crave but Thee. All other desires I have renounced. Everything I lay at Thy feet, for Thy love alone. Bless me that I may give Thy love to all, that they also may know Thy love and my goodwill toward them.

"I have renounced the world and family. And no more disciples do I want, O Lord. I am but Thy student, Thy disciple. I am here only to speak of Thy love, of remembrance of Thee. Oh, what glory! What joy!

"Why, O Lord, have I to do this organizational work? I don't want position or honor. I don't want anything; only You; and to be with those devotees who help me to remember You. I don't want to teach anyone, or offend anyone with discipline. I want only to discipline myself. But it is not I, it is You who love and speak to them, You who bless all through me. It is You who think, feel, move, love through me, O Spirit Divine, O Beloved One, Glorious One, Beloved God, Guru of gurus.

"What is there in anything, Lord? Everything is but a dream to me. Where is my body? I see it too is but a gross dream. All desires have vanished. I have no more desires even for the organization; only the desire for Thee alone. All that I do, I do to please You. I shall labor in ditches if You want me to; but You must promise that You will be always with me, and with those devotees who love You.

"You gave me the responsibility to work in the earth.* I felt You in the sand and in the sun. I felt Your caress in the breeze and Your strength in the handle of the spade with which I shoveled. You were all around me, gently blessing me. With every thought You spoke to me.

"O Beloved, O God, O Father, Mother, Friend, all the mother-love of incarnations is crushed into Thy one love. You are the Beloved behind all beloveds, the Lover behind all lovers, the Friend behind all friends, the Relative behind all relatives. I cannot recognize any relationship as greater than my relationship with You. All human relationships are dead without Thee. Make all realize that Thou art the only love, the only reality.

"I stand on the brink of eternity, ready to jump from the world of delusion into Thee. But I want to take the world with me. Let me not see any face that does not reflect thoughts of Thee and love for Thee, my beloved God. I love all, even those who avow themselves my enemies; for I see Thee in every being. Bless me that my hands and feet, my speech, thoughts, and feelings be always busy for Thee. May I speak of Thy love to all when it is Thy will that I speak of Thee.

"Let me spend not a moment away from Thee. Destroy me if I forget Thee for an instant. I do not want to live without Thee. Delude me not with anything. I will not have it. I will not have it!

"Divine Spirit, what glory, what joy Thou art! Omnipotence! One glimpse of Thy grace can destroy the darkness of ignorance and all bad habits. Save us all. In the presence of Thy greatness, I am a little child. I want not to be a teacher, only a humble child at Thy feet, O God. I lay everything at Thy feet, Beloved One.

"O beloved Christ, is it only a day, a few short hours, that we

---

* Paramahansaji is referring here to his habit of working along with the ashram residents, cleaning the grounds, planting trees, directing construction of new buildings. He taught that no duty was to be considered great or insignificant in serving God. He lived what he taught.

have passed in this deep joy of meditation? What a sweet memory of thy presence lingers with me. I pray that all may feel thee. May they make the mightiest effort to tear away the veil of delusion and restlessness hiding thee, that they may enjoy at least once each year, at Christmas, thy blessed presence. For me, every day is a Christmas of joy. Every day, whether I am traveling in the car, or am in solitude in the ashram, or working, or meditating, thine infinite consciousness is born within me anew. O joy ever new!"

[Beholding a vision of Christ and Sri Yukteswarji, Paramahansaji addresses those present:]

Jesus Christ is here, blessing you all! And I behold my Guru, hiding in space. Guru, Guru, Guru!

[Paramahansaji continues his divine communion with God and Christ:]

"O Universal Christ, what joy You have given to us. Why doesn't mankind receive Your glory, for without You, the Christ Consciousness, no man can live. O Infinite Christ, in You I see all the saints shining in starlike luster. You are the sky in which they are glimmering. You are the One, the only *One*. What joy!

"O Christ, this day we have called you with all our hearts, and you have come and blessed us all. You have been born to us in physical form and in Spirit in the cradle of our devotion. What joy I feel; joy, happiness eternal. O Christ, we bow to thee.

"Beloved God, we pray that every devotee have this experience of divine communion. We cannot live without Your presence, without Your guidance. You are the power in our hands and speech. You are in every niche of our thoughts and feelings. Yet how You love to hide from us! My beloved Lord, You are all-compassionate, so You understand and don't mind my scolding You for hiding Yourself. Maybe we, Your children, are naughty; but You must not hide from us, for therein begin all of our miseries. Reveal Thyself unto us, be with us. Hide no more, beloved Lord, hide no more. With folded hands and bowed head and heart, we stand before Thee. Receive our humble devotion. Come to us in any form You like, that we may feel Thee tangibly. The little time we have left in this life must be spent in conscious awareness of Thee.

"Mentally I have renounced everything. I give no importance to any lesser duty, but have devoted my attention wholly to Thee—to loving Thee and serving Thee. I love not crowds, but crowds of souls who love Thee. Bring no one to me who loves Thee not, who does not want to love Thee. Draw only those souls who are seeking Thee, or in whom the desire for Thee can be kindled. I want naught from other human beings but to talk with Thee in them, and to quaff Thy love from the cups of their hearts. I pray that whoever comes to Mt. Washington or Encinitas seek only Thee, know only Thee, love Thee alone.

"We thank Thee, O Spirit, for sending Jesus Christ to us on earth; for sending Krishna, Babaji, Lahiri Mahasaya, and Sri Yukteswarji, for through them You have called us. Whoever comes in contact with the very soul of Self-Realization Fellowship will find Thee and the blessings of these Great Ones. Receive us, O God and Gurus, that we may rejoice with Thee in heaven, free from disease and death, sorrow and troubles, problems and hatred, war and suffering. May all these dream delusions vanish before the light of our communion with Thee. Father, Mother, Friend, Beloved God, knowing Thee, being entranced with the eternal joy of Thee, we have no interest in temptations, no fear of any of Your tests. Divine Mother, naughty or good, we are Thy children. You love us unconditionally; and we unconditionally love You. We come to You not as beggars, but as Thy children; and we demand that You reveal Thyself unto us; reveal Thyself, reveal Thyself!

"Sunder forever the cords of karma that bind us. Nothing can hold us, for we are Thy children, heading for our home in Thee. With Your grace and blessings on our efforts we shall find Thee at last. We promise before Thee to strive to give up all lesser desires, that we may concentrate our attention on love for Thee, weeping tears of joyous longing at Thy feet. Bless us with the devotion to cry for You in the silence of the night; that Satan will fly away from us, frightened by our cries for Thee, frightened by Thy response.

"Protect us in the castle of Thy presence. Let not Satan delude us ever. By Thy glance of grace, dispel Satan's power and drive him away forever. Our hearts are Thine. This is but the beginning of our acquaintance with You, O Lord—the beginning unto eternity. We love Thee with all our hearts, with all our minds, with all our strength, with all our souls.

"We surrender ourselves unto Thee that our bodies, minds, and souls be purified by Thy presence. Forget us not, though we forget Thee. Remember us, though we remember Thee not. Be not indifferent unto us. Free us from all-consuming delusion, and entrance us with Thy love alone. Lift us on Thy lap, O Mother. Cast us not at death's door.

"All dreams of delusion are finished. For me, the dream of this world is over. Lord, Thou art the only reality behind this dream world. Thou art the only ambition of my soul, the only goal of my life. Thou art the Guru, the Master, and the Lover; the Friend and the only Beloved I seek.

"Let the glory of the Universal Christ descend upon us. May we feel that Presence pouring through our hearts, trickling through our minds, and our hands and feet. O Eternal Light, may we behold the Infinite Christ within and without. We celebrate that Christ in Spirit, and we pray that every day be a Christmas of divine rejoicing. *Aum. Peace. Amen.*"

The Eternal Romance

*Self-Realization Fellowship Temple, Hollywood, California,
January 10, 1943*

Whenever I pray, I find God with me. Sometimes He tells me things that are astonishing. All the complexities of existence are gone. In the simplicity of just pure knowing, I find His Presence.

Thoughts are rivers flowing from the reservoir of Spirit. To connect your life with Spirit is the most important duty. God listens to the language of your heart—language that comes from the very depths of your being. People think God doesn't respond to their prayers because they don't understand that God sometimes answers differently from what they expect or ask for. He will not always answer according to their wishes until they have fulfilled His desire for their perfection.

Once I was riding in a car and God showed me the future, when all the present occupants of the houses we were passing were gone. They had been so certain of this life. God said, "I didn't create this world just for people to indulge in human emotions. I created temptations to see if My children would instead be tempted to seek Me, their Creator." That experience was so satisfying. I saw that all the responsibility belongs to God. He knows that He got us into this trouble!

We think God is invisible. When we see a watch, we know it was made by someone, somewhere. Now the little "watch" of this universe—with sun, moon, stars, the earth, and so on—how was it made, and by whom? You just chew your food, but some intelligence in the body converts it into all the elements the body needs. Who gave you air to breathe, and who created the relationship between air, life, and body? God. How can you doubt Him? He is present behind everything. Him whom I looked for in the clouds and everywhere, I find in every motion of my body, and enthroned on the stillness of my mind.

Whenever I want to know something, God talks to me; He

guides me or tells me what to say. Or people tell me things, and I suddenly realize it is He who is talking to me through them. When I conducted the service last Sunday, as soon as I prayed, He came as a great Light before me. They said I gave one of my best lectures that day.* Then came the afternoon class, and finally the evening lecture. Everyone thought I would be tired and would leave then; but we sat down and meditated until one a.m. I was as fresh and wide awake as if I had just had a good sleep. For about fifteen days now I have had very little sleep. His light sustains me.

God Stands at the Door of Your Consciousness

These are some of the experiences I am having. They are real, and they begin to multiply when you know God is with you. He will not give such experiences just to attract you, but only when you convince Him that you refuse anything less than proof of His presence. It isn't that He is partial to me. He would do wonderful things for you if you would only love Him. He loves all. He stands at the door of your consciousness, but you will not let Him in. I am seeing increasingly that He is seeking us far more than we are seeking Him. He is not indifferent to us; we are indifferent to Him. So you must seek Him sincerely with great intensity of mind. You may think He is not answering you, and that is when most people become discouraged and stop. But it is He who has kept you going that far, and you must not give up. When doubt comes, say, "Well, how am I moving my hands? How is my digestion working? How does my breath ebb and flow? He *must* be there. He *is* there." Since you are so dependent upon that Power, why not turn to that Power? When you are persistent every day in showing that you love Him above all things, then whenever you wish anything, it will happen.

God Yearns for Our Love

I asked God why He made this creation. "Was it necessary for You?" He answered, "No, but I had no one to share My joy." And so He became the Creator, but with one condition: He would impose on Himself the same yearning and seeking that He imposes on His creatures. Everyone is seeking something

---

* Scheduled for future publication.

for the happiness he hopes it will give. But people don't find true happiness because every avenue of material gain ends in a blind alley. You want a thing only until you have it. When you get it, the pleasure diminishes until the joy is gone. Most people think there is nothing more to life than to be born, to marry, to produce children, to make money, to grasp at elusive pleasures, and to die. But that is not so. God says, "I have imposed the same difficulty on Myself as on My children. As they are not finding fulfillment, so have I not found what I want." And what is God longing for? Our love. Our attention. He has made it very difficult for Himself, because He gave man free will to seek Him or reject Him. He says, "I am pursuing every heart, waiting for My children to spurn My creation and turn toward Me." What a grand thought, to realize that He has imposed on Himself the same "exile" that He has imposed on us, that God is seeking something too—our love.

When we talk of God, many people think of a venerable Being sitting on a throne in the remoteness of Heaven! They reason, "How can I feel love for this unknown God? Let us eat, drink, and be merry now!" But behind every rosebush of pleasure is a rattlesnake of unhappiness. There is no permanent pleasure in the world. Your body may be beautiful, but suddenly disease comes, and nothing can heal it. You may be very wealthy, but then the stock market crashes and you lose everything. Why should we suffer these disappointments? Well, God is similarly disappointed, because He wants us, and we have denied Him our love. So He is suffering too, because He has caused this separation. And unless we choose to go to Him willingly He cannot free us or Himself from suffering.

The Desire Behind All Desires

For a little while you can be happy with worldly things, but inside there is a void. Everything bores you in time. I realized that even in my childhood. I envisioned myself in every kind of situation. And when I could not picture an experience for myself, I looked at someone else who lived that life which I thought seemed nice, and I saw unhappiness and discontent. That is why I didn't get caught in any of those traps.

I saw that Somebody is using our hearts to enjoy things and to love others. But then He takes away that object of our love, as in death, or suddenly the love grows stale and is gone. Where is that love? It is God playing hide-and-seek with us; it is He whom we should seek.

I don't bow to a God we have to fear. I say, "Thou art nearest of the near, dearest of the dear, closer than the closest." I tell Him anything that is on my mind; and He answers me. Who else could love like that? He was always behind me, knocking at the gates of my life, waiting to get in. I found that no matter what I had sought in this world, through incarnations, it was He whom I really sought. Every time I satisfied a desire, there was no joy in it any more. "Ah, fondest, blindest, weakest, I am He whom thou seekest!"* "I" means that joy eternal—God.

In the desire for money, sex, human love, people are really seeking but one thing—happiness—and that is God. I remain drunk with that Happiness day and night. It is not an abstract state of mind; that Happiness can talk to you. It is just behind the ether out of which all creation sprang. That Happiness is God, and it is folly to seek or limit your love to anything else. I could never give my love completely, even to my mother, whom I loved so dearly, because I knew that behind her was Someone who loved me through her.

Ignorance Means Not Using the Power God Gave You

One of the illusions of life is to continue to live helplessly. As soon as you say, "It's no use," it becomes so. The ghost of ignorance is right within you. Ignorance means not using the power God gave you. Why are you saying and doing the same harmful things over and over every day? To think you cannot change at will is delusion. You *must* be able to change, to expel harmful habits immediately when you choose to do so.

Most people always behave in a predictable, characteristic way because they have become habit-bound. But if a person inwardly changes his habit-patterns, others notice and say, "He is a different person!" even though outwardly his appearance has not changed. Don't remain the same day after day. Look within and see if you are still bound by the same old habits that people have recognized year after year. If you are, take the sword of wisdom and cut out those habits. Then use your God-given

* From *The Hound of Heaven*, by Francis Thompson.

discrimination to remake your life into a worthier image.

I made some resolutions for this new year, about little things I had neglected, and about removing from this mansion of my life unnecessary "luxuries" that fill up precious gaps of time. I did not tell anyone about them. The hardest tests came in the first eight days after I made the resolutions; everything seemed contrived to make me break them. But, on January first, with God's help, I had firmly removed all contrary inclinations from my mind, so nothing could bend my will.

You are your own greatest enemy when you say, "It can't be done." You will be surprised at how much freedom God has given you to change your life. Don't wait until the body is riddled with disease, until it can make the mind weak, for then the fight is harder. You are not flesh and blood. You are the Light in this body. Immortality is caged in this little form and it wants to get out. Recently two disciples were standing beside me, and suddenly I saw them as in an X-ray—flesh and bones and organs, everything—and a great light was coming from them. When God is with you, all matter changes into electric shadows. Everything becomes ethereal. These experiences are not figments of imagination. They are manifestations of truth.

God Is the Most Lovable Being

Never think that God does not answer your prayers. Every word you have whispered to Him He has written in His heart, and someday He will answer you. If you keep watching for Him and the many ways in which He does respond, you will know that in fact He answers you all the time. If you are very eager, He will answer in greater ways. Only by persistence can He be persuaded to come.

God is the most lovable Being in the universe. Everything that you want is in Him. To seek anything else is a great mistake. I am not wasting a minute of my time. I have cut out everything that diverts me from Him. Such happiness I could never find anywhere else. I am living in that state of God-consciousness; and where I am, I want you to come. I want to reciprocate the love of those whose love I have received by taking them with me into the love of my Father.

Once, when I was very young, my family tried to persuade me to marry. I saw the prospective bride, and I thought she had the most beautiful face I had ever seen. I heard God say, "Why don't you marry?" But I said to Him, "Are You not more wonderful? I do not want that face; I want You who are behind that face!" Years later, I saw how her beauty had faded with age, but my joy in God had increased a thousandfold.

Marriage is for those who do not feel inwardly the renunciant's conviction that God alone is sufficient. But those who are married are not barred from finding God—the purpose of the divine friendship of marriage is to help each other toward that end. In fact, no marriage can be completely successful without God's love. It takes unconditional love to make the marital relationship harmonious. What a hades husbands and wives make of their lives without that love, and without trust in each other.

Couples in even the closest relationships are very secretive and keep things to themselves. In the beginning they share everything, but when they start to have differences and quarrels, they withdraw and put up a wall around themselves. Where has their love gone? Two young people say they will die if they cannot be together. But if suddenly one of them became old and gray, where would that love be? What is it that they love, the soul? No, it is the face.

The point is, your first goal must be to know God. When you have found Him, when your heart is in tune with Him, then whatever He tells you to do is all right. But if you entangle yourself without first finding God, you have chosen the path of error.

You are alone on this earth and nobody will pay for your mistakes but yourself. So why should you follow the mistakes of others? You must live your life as you know you should live it. Don't keep feeding your bad habits with fresh actions that strengthen them. The weak man says, "I smoke, and now I can't quit." Well, before he smoked he never felt the need. Be free. When God's boundless joy and soothing light come, nothing else matters. Then outer experiences also will testify that what you see inside is true.

There Is More to Life Than Appears Outwardly

It is a great delusion to think there is no more to life than appears outwardly. Your real life is with God, and to go back to

Him is the reason we are here. He took the trouble to create this world to entertain us, and He wants us to see it as His play. "All things betray thee, who betrayest Me."* To go after worldly pleasure and forget God is to set a course to unhappiness. Evil promises happiness and gives sorrow. Would you pick a flower if you knew its mere touch was poisonous? No. The only lasting happiness is found in God. Sit quietly and pray deeply, devotedly. Talk to Him. Don't be afraid of Him. There is no other way to know Him than by meditation. You must never miss it. At the end of the day you are tired and want to lie down and sleep, but instead sit up and meditate intensely. You will see how it changes your life. After deep communion with God, four or five hours of sleep will be enough. Beyond that you drug yourself. Use the rest of your time to meditate.

I hardly see anyone these days; I want to be only with those who talk with God. The less you engage in idle talk, the better it is. The less you mix with others who just waste your time, the better it is for your spiritual life. Seclusion is the price of greatness.

This short season of life will be gone before you realize it. Reap the harvest of divine happiness that nothing can take away. It is not impossible; you have only made yourself think it is impossible. The power of God is within you, so when your mind tells you a thing can't be done, say to that thought, "Get out! It can be done." And it will be, if you make up your mind. Why waste your time on spurious pleasures? Go to the very Source. If you remain in that Happiness all the time, you will also be happy in the world; you will see that all disease and suffering are but short-lived nightmares of the body.

Every day is a battle, and you must fight. Saints have the greatest battles, but their struggles mean nothing to them after a while because they have found God. Think of the life of Saint Francis. Very few saints suffered as he did: painfully ill and blind, yet he healed the sick; and even after his own death, he raised the dead—such was the power of his love for God.

God Is Always With Us

God is not remote from His creation; He is always with us.

---

* Also from *The Hound of Heaven*, by Francis Thompson.

You don't see the breeze, but you know it is there. He who made the breeze and us, He is here. Every time I move my hands and feet I see it is He who is moving them. The whole universe trembles with His presence. There is no other reality.

This life is a cosmic motion picture. As soon as God comes, everything becomes light and dances in His light. When you see a motion picture and forget it is entertainment, you react to it as though it were real. But when you see it as a picture, you do not agonize over the portrayal of suffering, violence, and death. It is God's play of light and shadow that has made creation appear as it does to us. When you realize this, you see it as a dream motion picture. But, woe unto you if you don't realize this; you will be hurt and feel alone and forsaken. Wake up; know that God is with you, and that when death comes and no one can be there to help you, God and Guru will be there.

People who have earthly wealth have nothing without the riches of God. They can take nothing material with them when they die. But those who have cultivated good qualities are the truly rich, because they carry that treasure with them beyond the portals of the grave.

Many think they are not suited for the spiritual life, but that is Satan's greatest lie. Satan is ignorance. God tells me that the only path we are fitted for is the path that leads to Him! That is why nothing else satisfies us. So it is false reasoning to say you are not ready for God yet. Every heart is suffering, and everyone who suffers is ready.

A square peg does not fit in a round hole. This earth can be compared to the round hole, and your life is the square peg. Some day you will see that the "square hole" into which you fit is God. You are deluded into thinking that you belong to your family and your country. There is no America, there is no India, for me; all countries are mine because they are God's, and all families are mine because they are God's. I have never allowed anyone or anything to monopolize me. I have said to God: "My love I shall give to no one but You. I shall not give it to those who would limit it with selfish attachment, merely because they ask for it; nor shall I give it to any creature or to any thing. I will run away from all that would imprison my love, and will save it for

You alone." By giving my love to God alone, I have given it to all.

Don't be discouraged. Turn to God. How could there be any greater promise than what He told me? "Every whisper you utter to Me, I will answer." I would never have thought that, with all of the organizational responsibilities I have taken on, I could inwardly remain in such joy of God. It is because I never forgot one thing: my meditation. My only desire was to be with God, so I was always asking Him, "When are You going to release me from so much work?" Now, work or no work, it doesn't matter; by His grace, I am enjoying the greatest inner freedom and bliss.

Cut off the tentacles of habits and kill the octopus mind that says it can't be done. Just say, "It can!" and then do it. Get rid of your bad habits. Change yourself every day. Don't be overwhelmed by all your responsibilities. Life was given that we might find the Eternal Life. Peace was given that we might find the Eternal Peace. Desire was given, not to be used for material things but that our need for the Infinite be satisfied. If you would but seek Him a little more urgently, you would find Him. Doubt not!

Before I came to America, one day I prayed and prayed to God until I felt my brain would burst. I cried to Him: "I don't know what awaits me in America, but if anything takes me away from You I don't want to live! Give me a sign that it will be all right!" Suddenly there was a knock at the door; I opened it, and there a saint was standing. He said, "God tells me to tell you: 'Follow the behests of your Guru and go to America. Fear not; you shall be protected.'" When he saw that I wanted to go with him, he said, "Don't try to follow me." I tried, but found that my feet would not move. In America the saint's words have come true. I have loved nothing more than God, and because of that allegiance He has remained with me.*

One night in Boston, during a period of intense activity, I prayed to God that I wanted to run away, lest I lose Him in the midst of all the demands placed on me. But God said to me: "Keep on with your work, of course; you are doing it for Me.

---

* The saint was Mahavatar Babaji. The story told here is recounted more fully in Paramahansaji's *Autobiography of a Yogi*, on which he was working at the time this talk was given.

When you are busy, you are all the time telling yourself that you are wasting your time if you are not with Me. But you *are* with Me!" After that, I was in ecstasy for seven months; everything was going on just the same, but I was in the ecstasy of God.

A terrible pain comes when you feel He is gone—far worse than the anguish of a millionaire who suddenly finds he has lost every cent he had.

The Romance With God Is Eternal

These are not just sermons that I am giving you, but the truth that will free you. So, I want you to remember: Follow the *Self-Realization Fellowship Lessons,* for they contain the greatest message of the age. And at night pray continuously in the cave of silence. Never go to sleep without meditating. Sleep you can have any time, but not God. Whenever people leave you alone, in the little gaps of time between duties, sit quietly and pray to Him: "Reveal Thyself. You are here; you can't fool me. You are within me and all around me. I love You alone." He will come to you, in clouds, in light, in faces—in all kinds of ways. God talks to His devotees through intuitive feeling, through friends, through light-writing, and through a Voice heard within.*

Last night as I meditated, heaven opened up to me. Everything I see in His Light comes true. Then you know He was just hiding from you. The greatest romance you can have is the romance with God. Human love goes away in a little while, but your romance with God is eternal. Not one day must pass without seeing Him. That is why I wrote, "Through endless incarnations I called out Thy name, searching by the streamlets of all my silvery dreams."† I always tell Him that He is to blame for sending me out; but at last I realize that all life's illusions were to make me appreciate Him more, to excite me to seek Him. It

---

* In *How You Can Talk With God,* a booklet published by Self-Realization Fellowship, Paramahansa Yogananda elaborates on how God talks with the devotee through the *Aum* Vibration: "The Cosmic Sound that you hear in meditation is the voice of God. That sound forms itself into language intelligible to you. When I listen to *Aum* and occasionally ask God to tell me something, that sound of *Aum* changes into English or Bengali language and gives me precise instructions." (See *Aum* in glossary.)

† "Divine Love Sorrows," in *Songs of the Soul.*

was always He, the Father behind all fathers, the Mother behind all mothers, the Lover behind all lovers, that I sought through incarnations. He is the Lover and our souls are the beloved, and when the soul meets the greatest Lover of the universe, then the eternal romance begins. The love that you have been seeking for incarnations through all human loves is at last yours. You will never want anything else.

A Scripture of Love

Paramahansa Yogananda has been described by his beloved disciple Rajarsi Janakananda as a Premavatar, *or "incarnation of divine love." In the following prose, written circa 1936, Paramahansaji speaks first of his own search for that divine love; then from his at-onement with God as Love.*

I sought love in many lives. I shed bitter tears of separation and repentance to know what love is. I sacrificed everything, all attachment and delusion, to learn at last that I am in love with Love — with God — alone. Then I drank love through all true hearts. I saw that He is the One Cosmic Lover, the One Fragrance that permeates all the variegated blossoms of love in the garden of life.

Many souls wonder wistfully, helplessly, why love flees from one heart to another; awakened souls realize that the heart is not fickle in loving different ones, but is loving the one God-Love that is present in all hearts.

The Lord ever silently whispers to you:

I am Love. But to experience the giving and the gift of love, I divided Myself into three; love, lover, and beloved. My love is beautiful, pure, eternally joyous; and I taste it in many ways, through many forms.

As father I drink reverential love from the spring of my child's heart. As mother I drink the nectar of unconditional love from the soul-cup of the tiny baby. As child I imbibe the protecting love of the father's righteous reason. As infant I drink causeless love from the holy grail of maternal attraction. As master I drink sympathetic love from the flask of the servant's thoughtfulness. As servant I sip respectful love from the goblet of the master's appreciation. As guru-preceptor I enjoy purest love from the chalice of the disciple's all-surrendering devotion. As friend I drink from the self-bubbling fountains of spontaneous love. As a divine friend, I quaff crystal waters of cosmic love from the reservoir of God-adoring hearts.

I am in love with Love alone, but I allow myself to be deluded when as father or mother I think and feel only for the child; when as lover I care only for the beloved; when as servant I live only for the master. But because I love Love alone, I ultimately break this delusion of My myriad human Selves. It is for this reason that I transfer the father into the astral land when he forgets that it is My love, not his, that protects the child. I lift the babe from the mother's breast, that she might learn it is My love she adored in him. I spirit away the beloved from the lover who imagines it is she whom he loves, rather than My love responding in her.

So My love is playing hide-and-seek in all human hearts, that each might learn to discover and worship, not the temporal human receptacles of My love, but My love itself, dancing from one heart to another.

Human beings importune one another, "Love me alone," and so I make cold their lips and seal them forever, that they utter this untruth no more. Because they are all My children, I want them to learn to speak the ultimate truth: "Love the One Love in all of us." To tell another, "I love you," is false until you realize the truth: "God as the love in me is in love with His love in you."

The moon laughs at millions of well-meaning lovers who have unknowingly lied to their beloved ones: "I love you forever." Their skulls are strewn over the windswept sands of eternity. They can no longer use their breath to say, "I love you." They can neither remember nor redeem their promise to love each other forever.

Without speaking a word, I have loved you always. I alone can truly say, "I love you"; for I loved you before you were born; My love gives you life and sustains you even at this moment; and I alone can love you after the gates of death imprison you where none, not even your greatest human lover, can reach you.

I am the love that dances human puppets on strings of emotions and instincts, to play the drama of love on the stage of life. My love is beautiful and endlessly enjoyable when you love it alone; but the lifeline of your peace and joy is cut when instead you become entangled in human emotion and attachment. Realize, My children, it is My love for which you yearn!

Those who love Me as only one person, or who imperfectly love Me in one person, do not know what Love is. Only they can know Love who love Me wisely, faultlessly, completely, all-surrenderingly—who love Me perfectly and equally *in* all, and who love Me perfectly and equally *as* all.

PARAMAHANSA YOGANANDA:
A Yogi in Life and Death

Paramahansa Yogananda entered *mahasamadhi* (a yogi's final conscious exit from the body) in Los Angeles, California, on March 7, 1952, after concluding his speech at a banquet held in honor of H.E. Binay R. Sen, Ambassador of India.

The great world teacher demonstrated the value of yoga (scientific techniques for God-realization) not only in life but in death. Weeks after his departure his unchanged face shone with the divine luster of incorruptibility.

Mr. Harry T. Rowe, Los Angeles Mortuary Director, Forest Lawn Memorial-Park (in which the body of the great master is temporarily placed), sent Self-Realization Fellowship a notarized letter from which the following extracts are taken:

"The absence of any visual signs of decay in the dead body of Paramahansa Yogananda offers the most extraordinary case in our experience.... No physical disintegration was visible in his body even twenty days after death.... No indication of mold was visible on his skin, and no visible desiccation (drying up) took place in the bodily tissues. This state of perfect preservation of a body is, so far as we know from mortuary annals, an unparalleled one.... At the time of receiving Yogananda's body, the Mortuary personnel expected to observe, through the glass lid of the casket, the usual progressive signs of bodily decay. Our astonishment increased as day followed day without bringing any visible change in the body under observation. Yogananda's body was apparently in a phenomenal state of immutability....

"No odor of decay emanated from his body at any time.... The physical appearance of Yogananda on March 27th, just before the bronze cover of the casket was put into position, was the same as it had been on March 7th. He looked on March 27th as fresh and as unravaged by decay as he had looked on the night of his death. On March 27th there was no reason to say that his body had suffered any visible physical disintegration at all. For these reasons we state again that the case of Paramahansa Yogananda is unique in our experience."

AIMS AND IDEALS
of
Self-Realization Fellowship
As set forth by Paramahansa Yogananda, Founder
Sri Daya Mata, President

To disseminate among the nations a knowledge of definite scientific techniques for attaining direct personal experience of God.

To teach that the purpose of life is the evolution, through self-effort, of man's limited mortal consciousness into God Consciousness; and to this end to establish Self-Realization Fellowship temples for God-communion throughout the world, and to encourage the establishment of individual temples of God in the homes and in the hearts of men.

To reveal the complete harmony and basic oneness of original Christianity as taught by Jesus Christ and original Yoga as taught by Bhagavan Krishna; and to show that these principles of truth are the common scientific foundation of all true religions.

To point out the one divine highway to which all paths of true religious beliefs eventually lead: the highway of daily, scientific, devotional meditation on God.

To liberate man from his threefold suffering: physical disease, mental inharmonies, and spiritual ignorance.

To encourage "plain living and high thinking"; and to spread a spirit of brotherhood among all peoples by teaching the eternal basis of their unity: kinship with God.

To demonstrate the superiority of mind over body, of soul over mind.

To overcome evil by good, sorrow by joy, cruelty by kindness, ignorance by wisdom.

To unite science and religion through realization of the unity of their underlying principles.

To advocate cultural and spiritual understanding between East and West, and the exchange of their finest distinctive features.

To serve mankind as one's larger Self.

Other Books by
PARAMAHANSA YOGANANDA

Available at bookstores or directly from the publisher:
Self-Realization Fellowship
3880 San Rafael Avenue
Los Angeles, California 90065

Autobiography of a Yogi
Man's Eternal Quest
The Science of Religion
Whispers from Eternity
Songs of the Soul
Sayings of Paramahansa Yogananda
Scientific Healing Affirmations
How You Can Talk With God
Metaphysical Meditations
The Law of Success
Cosmic Chants

From the same publisher:

The Holy Science
By Swami Sri Yukteswar
"Only Love"
By Sri Daya Mata

Please request current catalog listing these and other
publications before ordering.

Free Booklet: *Undreamed-of Possibilities*

The scientific techniques of meditation mentioned in
The Divine Romance, including Kriya Yoga, are taught in the
Self-Realization Fellowship Lessons. For further information
please write for the free booklet *Undreamed-of Possibilities.*

GLOSSARY

Arjuna.   The exalted disciple to whom Bhagavan Krishna imparted the immortal message of the Bhagavad Gita *(q.v.)* around 3000 B.C.; one of the five Pandava princes in the great Hindu epic, the *Mahabharata*, in which he was a key figure.

ashram.   A spiritual hermitage; often a monastery.

astral body.   Man's subtle body of light, *prana* or lifetrons; the second of three sheaths that successively encase the soul: the causal body *(q.v.)*, the astral body, and the physical body. The powers of the astral body enliven the physical body, much as electricity illumines a bulb. The astral body has nineteen elements: intelligence, ego, feeling, mind (sense-consciousness); five instruments of knowledge (the sensory powers within the physical organs of sight, hearing, smell, taste, and touch); five instruments of action (the executive powers in the physical instruments of procreation, excretion, speech, locomotion, and the exercise of manual skill); and five instruments of life force that perform the functions of circulation, metabolization, assimilation, crystallization, and elimination.

astral light.   The subtle light emanating from lifetrons (see *prana*); the structural essence of the astral world. Through the all-inclusive intuitive perception of the soul, devotees in concentrated states of meditation may perceive the astral light, particularly as the spiritual eye *(q.v.)*.

astral world.   The subtle sphere of the Lord's creation, a universe of light and color composed of finer-than-atomic forces, i.e., vibrations of life energy or lifetrons (see *prana*). Every being, every object, every vibration on the material plane has an astral counterpart, for in the astral universe (heaven) is the blueprint of our material universe. At physical death, the soul of man, clothed in an astral body of light, ascends to one of the astral planes, according to merit, to continue his spiritual evolution in the greater freedom of that subtle realm. There he remains for a karmically predetermined time until physical rebirth.

Aum (Om).   The basis of all sounds; universal symbol-word for God. *Aum* of the Vedas became the sacred word *Hum* of the Tibetans; *Amin* of the Moslems; and *Amen* of the Egyptians, Greeks, Romans, Jews, and Christians. *Amen* in Hebrew means *sure, faithful*. *Aum* is the all-pervading sound emanating from the Holy Ghost (Invisible

Cosmic Vibration; God in His aspect of Creator); the "Word" of the Bible; the voice of creation, testifying to the Divine Presence in every atom. *Aum* may be heard through practice of Self-Realization Fellowship methods of meditation.

"These things saith the Amen, the faithful and true witness, the beginning of the creation of God" (Revelation 3:14). "In the beginning was the Word, and the Word was with God, and the Word was God....All things were made by Him [the Word or *Aum*] and without him was not any thing made that was made" (John 1:1,3). See also *Sat-Tat-Aum*.

avatar. From the Sanskrit *avatara*, with roots *ava*, "down," and *tri*, "to pass." Souls who attain union with Spirit and then return to earth to help mankind are called *avatars*, divine incarnations.

avidya. Literally, "non-knowledge," ignorance; the manifestation in man of *maya*, the cosmic delusion *(q.v.)*. Essentially, *avidya* is man's ignorance of his divine nature and of the sole reality: Spirit.

Babaji. See *Mahavatar Babaji*.

Bhagavad Gita. "Song of the Lord." This scripture consists of eighteen chapters from the *Mahabharata* epic. It is chiefly a dialog between the *avatar* Lord Krishna and his disciple Arjuna on the eve of the historic battle of Kurukshetra, about 3000 B.C. The Gita is allegory as well as history, a spiritual treatise on the inner battle between man's good and bad tendencies. Depending on the context, Krishna symbolizes the guru, the soul, or God; Arjuna represents the aspiring devotee. Of this holy scripture Mahatma Gandhi wrote: "Those who will meditate on the Gita will derive fresh joy and new meanings from it every day. There is not a single spiritual tangle which the Gita cannot unravel."

The quotations from the Bhagavad Gita in the text and footnotes of this book are from the translation by Paramahansa Yogananda, which he rendered from the Sanskrit sometimes literally, and sometimes in paraphrase.

Bhagavan Krishna. An *avatar* who lived as a king in India three millenniums before the Christian era. One of the meanings given for the word *Krishna* in the Hindu scriptures is "Omniscient Spirit." Thus, *Krishna*, like *Christ*, is a spiritual title signifying the divine magnitude of the *avatar*—his oneness with God. The title *Bhagavan* means "Lord." In his early life, Krishna lived as a cowherd who enchanted his companions with the music of his flute. In this role Krishna is often considered to represent allegorically the soul playing the flute of meditation to guide all misled thoughts back to the fold of omniscience.

Bhakti Yoga. The spiritual approach to God that stresses all-surrendering love as the principal means for communion and union with God. See *Yoga.*

Brahma-Vishnu-Shiva. Three aspects of God's immanence in creation. They represent that triune function of the Christ Intelligence *(Tat)* that guides Cosmic Nature's activities of creation, preservation, and dissolution. See *Trinity.*

Brahman (Brahma). Absolute Spirit.

breath. "The influx of innumerable cosmic currents into man by way of the breath induces restlessness in his mind," Paramahansa Yogananda wrote. "Thus the breath links him with the fleeting phenomenal worlds. To escape from the sorrows of transitoriness and to enter the blissful realm of Reality, the yogi learns to quiet the breath by scientific meditation."

caste. Caste in its original conception was not a hereditary status, but a classification based on man's natural capacities. In his evolution, man passes through four distinct grades, designated by ancient Hindu sages as *Sudra, Vaisya, Kshatriya,* and *Brahmin.* The *Sudra* is interested primarily in satisfying his bodily needs and desires; the work that best suits his state of development is bodily labor. The *Vaisya* is ambitious for worldly gain as well as for satisfaction of the senses; he has more creative ability than the *Sudra* and seeks occupation as a farmer, a businessman, an artist, or wherever his mental energy finds fulfillment. The *Kshatriya,* having through many lives fulfilled the desires of the *Sudra* and *Vaisya* states, begins to seek the meaning of life; he tries to overcome his bad habits, to control his senses, and to do what is right. *Kshatriyas* by occupation are noble rulers, statesmen, warriors. The *Brahmin* has overcome his lower nature, has a natural affinity for spiritual pursuits, and is God-knowing, able therefore to teach and help liberate others.

causal body. Essentially, man as a soul is a causal-bodied being. His causal body is an idea-matrix for the astral and physical bodies. The causal body is composed of 35 idea elements corresponding to the 19 elements of the astral body plus the 16 basic material elements of the physical body.

causal world. Behind the physical world of matter (atoms, protons, electrons), and the subtle astral world of luminous life energy (lifetrons), is the causal, or ideational, world of thought (thoughtrons). After man evolves sufficiently to transcend the physical and astral universes, he resides in the causal universe. In the consciousness of causal beings, the physical and astral universes are resolved to their thought essence. Whatever physical man can do in imagination, causal man can do in actuality—the only limitation being thought itself. Ultimately, man sheds the last soul covering—his causal body—to unite with omnipresent Spirit, beyond all vibratory realms.

chakras.   In Yoga, the seven occult centers of life and consciousness in the spine and brain, which enliven the physical and astral bodies of man. These centers are referred to as *chakras* ("wheels") because the concentrated energy in each one is like a hub from which radiate rays of life-giving light and energy. In ascending order, these *chakras* are *muladhara* (the coccygeal, at the base of the spine); *svadhisthana* (the sacral, two inches above *muladhara*); *manipura* (the lumbar, opposite the navel); *anahata* (the dorsal, opposite the heart); *vishuddha* (the cervical, at the base of the neck); *ajna* (traditionally located between the eyebrows; in actuality, directly connected by polarity with the medulla; see also *medulla* and *spiritual eye*); and *sahasrara* (in the uppermost part of the cerebrum).

The seven centers are divinely planned exits or "trap doors" through which the soul has descended into the body and through which it must reascend by a process of meditation. By seven successive steps, the soul escapes into Cosmic Consciousness. In its conscious upward passage through the seven opened or "awakened" cerebrospinal centers, the soul travels the highway to the Infinite, the true path by which the soul must retrace its course to reunite with God.

Yoga treatises generally consider only the six lower centers as *chakras*, with *sahasrara* referred to separately as a seventh center. All seven centers, however, are often referred to as lotuses, whose petals open, or turn upward, in spiritual awakening as the life and consciousness travel up the spine.

chela.   Hindi word for "disciple."

chitta.   Intuitive feeling; the aggregate of consciousness, inherent in which is *ahankara* (egoity), *buddhi* (intelligence), and *manas* (mind or sense consciousness).

Christ center.   The *Kutastha* or *ajna chakra* at the point between the eyebrows, directly connected by polarity with the medulla (*q.v.*); center of will and concentration, and of Christ Consciousness (*q.v.*); seat of the spiritual eye (*q.v.*).

Christ Consciousness.   "Christ" or "Christ Consciousness" is the projected consciousness of God immanent in all creation. In Christian scripture it is called the "only begotten son," the only pure reflection in creation of God the Father; in Hindu scripture it is called *Kutastha Chaitanya* or *Tat*, the cosmic intelligence of Spirit everywhere present in creation. It is the universal consciousness, oneness with God, manifested by Jesus, Krishna, and other *avatars*. Great saints and yogis know it as the state of *samadhi* meditation wherein their consciousness has become identified with the intelligence in every particle of creation; they feel the entire universe as their own body. See *Trinity*.

Concentration Technique. The Self-Realization Fellowship Technique of Concentration (also *Hong-Sau* Technique) taught in the *Self-Realization Fellowship Lessons*. This technique helps scientifically to withdraw the attention from all objects of distraction and to place it upon one thing at a time. Thus it is invaluable for meditation, concentration on God. The *Hong-Sau* Technique is an integral part of the science of *Kriya Yoga* (*q.v.*).

consciousness, states of. In mortal consciousness man experiences three states: waking consciousness, sleeping consciousness, and dreaming consciousness. But he does not experience his soul, superconsciousness, and he does not experience God. The Christman does. As mortal man is conscious throughout his body, so the Christ-man is conscious throughout the universe, which he feels as his body. Beyond the state of Christ consciousness is cosmic consciousness, the experience of oneness with God in His absolute consciousness beyond vibratory creation as well as with the Lord's omnipresence manifesting in the phenomenal worlds.

Cosmic Consciousness. The Absolute, beyond creation. Also the *samadhi*-meditation state of oneness with God both beyond and within vibratory creation. See *Trinity*.

cosmic delusion. See *maya*.

cosmic energy. See *prana*.

Cosmic Intelligent Vibration. See *Aum*.

Cosmic Sound. See *Aum*.

dharma. Eternal principles of righteousness that uphold all creation; man's inherent duty to live in harmony with these principles. See also *Sanatan Dharma*.

diksha. Spiritual initiation; from the Sanskrit verb-root *diksh*, to dedicate oneself. See also *disciple* and *Kriya Yoga*.

disciple. A spiritual aspirant who comes to a guru seeking introduction to God, and to this end establishes an eternal spiritual relationship with the guru. In Self-Realization Fellowship, the guru-disciple relationship is established by *diksha*, initiation, in *Kriya Yoga*. See also *guru* and *Kriya Yoga*.

Divine Mother.   The aspect of God that is active in creation; the *shakti*, or power, of the Transcendent Creator. Other terms for this aspect of Divinity are *Aum, Shakti,* Holy Ghost, Cosmic Intelligent Vibration, Nature or *Prakriti.* Also, the personal aspect of God embodying the love and compassionate qualities of a mother.

The Hindu scriptures teach that God is both immanent and transcendent, personal and impersonal. He may be sought as the Absolute; as one of His manifest eternal qualities, such as love, wisdom, bliss, light; in the form of an *ishta* (deity); or as Father, Mother, or Friend.

egoism.   The ego-principle, *ahankara* (lit., "I do"), is the root cause of dualism or the seeming separation between man and his Creator. *Ahankara* brings human beings under the sway of *maya (q.v.),* by which the subject (ego) falsely appears as object; the creatures imagine themselves to be creators. By banishing ego-consciousness, man awakens to his divine identity, his oneness with the Sole Life: God.

elements (five).   The Cosmic Vibration, or *Aum,* structures all physical creation, including man's physical body, through the manifestation of five *tattvas* (elements): earth, water, fire, air, and ether *(q.v.).* These are structural forces, intelligent and vibratory in nature. Without the earth element there would be no state of solid matter; without the water element, no liquid state; without the air element, no gaseous state; without the fire element, no heat; without the ether element, no background on which to produce the cosmic motion picture show. In the body, *prana* (cosmic vibratory energy) enters the medulla and is then divided into the five elemental currents by the action of the five lower *chakras (q.v.),* or centers: the coccygeal (earth), sacral (water), lumbar (fire), dorsal (air), and cervical (ether). The Sanskrit terminology for these elements is *prithivi, ap, tej, prana,* and *akash.*

Encinitas, California.   Encinitas, a seaside city in southern California, is the site of a Self-Realization Fellowship Ashram Center, Retreat, and Hermitage, founded by Paramahansa Yogananda in 1937. The spacious grounds and Hermitage building, which is situated on a bluff overlooking the Pacific Ocean, was a gift to Paramahansaji from Rajarsi Janakananda (q.v.).

Energization Exercises.   Man is surrounded by cosmic energy, much as a fish is surrounded by water. The Energization Exercises, originated by Paramahansa Yogananda and taught in *Self-Realization Fellowship Lessons,* enable man to recharge his body with this cosmic energy, or universal *prana.*

ether. Sanskrit *akash.* Though not considered a factor in present scientific theory on the nature of the material universe, ether has for millenniums been so referred to by India's sages. Paramahansa Yogananda spoke of ether as the background on which God projects the cosmic motion picture of creation. Space gives dimension to objects; ether separates the images. This "background," a creative force that coordinates all spatial vibrations, is a necessary factor when considering the subtler forces — thought and life energy *(prana)* — and the nature of space and the origin of material forces and matter. See *elements.*

gunas. The three attributes of Nature: *tamas, rajas,* and *sattva* — obstruction, activity, and expansion; or, mass, energy, and intelligence. In man the three *gunas* express themselves as ignorance or inertia; activity or struggle; and wisdom.

guru. When a devotee is ready to seek God in earnest, the Lord sends him a guru. Through the wisdom, intelligence, Self-realization, and teachings of such a master, God guides the disciple. By following the master's teachings and discipline, the disciple is able to fulfill his soul's desire for the manna of God-perception. Such a guru, ordained by God to help true seekers in response to their deep soul craving, is not an ordinary teacher: he is a human vehicle whose body, speech, mind, and spirituality God uses as a channel to attract and guide lost souls back to their home of immortality. A guru is a living embodiment of scriptural truth. He is an agent of salvation appointed by God in response to a devotee's demand for release from the bondage of matter. See *master.*

Gurudeva. "Divine teacher," a customary Sanskrit term of respect that is used in addressing and referring to one's spiritual preceptor; sometimes rendered in English as "Master."

Gurus of Self-Realization Fellowship. The Gurus of Self-Realization Fellowship (Yogoda Satsanga Society of India) are Jesus Christ, Bhagavan Krishna, and a line of exalted masters of contemporary times: Mahavatar Babaji, Lahiri Mahasaya, Swami Sri Yukteswar, and Paramahansa Yogananda. To show the harmony and essential unity of the teachings of Jesus Christ and the Yoga precepts of Bhagavan Krishna is an integral part of the SRF dispensation. All of these Gurus, by their sublime teachings and divine instrumentality, contribute to the fulfillment of the Self-Realization Fellowship mission of bringing to all mankind a practical spiritual science of God-realization.

Hatha Yoga. A system of techniques and physical postures *(asanas)* that promotes health and mental calm. See *Yoga.*

Holy Ghost.   See *Aum* and *Trinity*.

intuition.   The all-knowing faculty of the soul, which enables man to experience direct perception of truth without the intermediary of the senses.

ji.   A suffix denoting respect, added to names and titles in India; as, Gandhiji, Paramahansaji, Guruji.

Jnana Yoga.   The path to union with God through transmutation of the discriminative power of the intellect into the omniscient wisdom of the soul.

karma.   Effects of past actions, from this or previous lifetimes; from the Sanskrit *kri*, to do. The equilibrating law of karma, as expounded in the Hindu scriptures, is that of action and reaction, cause and effect, sowing and reaping. In the course of natural righteousness, each man by his thoughts and actions becomes the molder of his destiny. Whatever energies he himself, wisely or unwisely, has set in motion must return to him as their starting point, like a circle inexorably completing itself. An understanding of karma as the law of justice serves to free the human mind from resentment against God and man. A man's karma follows him from incarnation to incarnation until fulfilled or spiritually transcended. See *reincarnation*.

The cumulative actions of human beings within communities, nations, or the world as a whole constitute *mass karma*, which produces local or far-ranging effects according to the degree and preponderance of good or evil. The thoughts and actions of every man, therefore, contribute to the good or ill of this world and all peoples in it.

Karma Yoga.   The path to God through nonattached action and service. By selfless service, by giving the fruits of one's actions to God, and by seeing God as the sole Doer, the devotee becomes free of the ego and experiences God. See *Yoga*.

Krishna.   See *Bhagavan Krishna*.

Krishna Consciousness.   Christ Consciousness; *Kutastha Chaitanya*. See *Christ Consciousness*.

Kriya Yoga.   A sacred spiritual science, originating millenniums ago in India. It includes certain techniques of meditation whose devoted practice leads to realization of God. Paramahansa Yogananda has explained that the Sanskrit root of *kriya* is *kri*, to do, to act and react; the same root is found in the word *karma*, the natural principle of cause and effect. *Kriya Yoga* is thus "union *(yoga)* with the Infinite through a certain action or rite *(kriya)*." *Kriya Yoga* is praised by Krishna in the Bhagavad Gita and by Patanjali in the *Yoga*

Sutras. Revived in this age by Mahavatar Babaji *(q.v.)*, *Kriya Yoga* is the *diksha* (spiritual initiation) bestowed by the Gurus of Self-Realization Fellowship. Since the *mahasamadhi (q.v.)* of Paramahansa Yogananda, *diksha* is conferred through his appointed spiritual representative, the president of Self-Realization Fellowship/Yogoda Satsanga Society of India (or through one appointed by the president). To qualify for *diksha* Self-Realization members must fulfill certain preliminary spiritual requirements. One who has received this *diksha* is a *Kriya Yogi* or *Kriyaban.* See also *guru* and *disciple.*

Lahiri Mahasaya. Lahiri was the family name of Shyama Charan Lahiri (1828–1895). *Mahasaya,* a Sanskrit religious title, means "large-minded." Lahiri Mahasaya was a disciple of Mahavatar Babaji, and the guru of Swami Sri Yukteswar (Paramahansa Yogananda's guru). A Christlike teacher with miraculous powers, he was also a family man with business responsibilities. His mission was to make known a yoga suitable for modern man, in which meditation is balanced by right performance of worldly duties. He has been called a *Yogavatar,* "Incarnation of Yoga." Lahiri Mahasaya was the disciple to whom Babaji revealed the ancient, almost lost science of *Kriya Yoga (q.v.),* instructing him in turn to initiate sincere seekers. Lahiri Mahasaya's life is described in *Autobiography of a Yogi.*

Laya Yoga. This yogic system teaches the absorption of mind in the perception of certain astral sounds, leading to union with God as the cosmic sound of *Aum.* See *Aum* and *Yoga.*

Lessons. See *Self-Realization Fellowship Lessons.*

life force. See *prana.*

lifetrons. See *prana.*

Lynn, James J. (St. Lynn). See *Rajarsi Janakananda.*

mahasamadhi. Sanskrit *maha,* "great," *samadhi.* The last meditation, or conscious communion with God, during which a perfected master merges himself in the cosmic *Aum* and casts off the physical body. A master invariably knows beforehand the time God has appointed for him to leave his bodily residence. See *samadhi.*

Mahavatar Babaji. The deathless *mahavatar* ("great *avatar*") who in 1861 gave *Kriya Yoga (q.v.)* initiation to Lahiri Mahasaya, and thereby restored to the world the ancient technique of salvation. Perennially youthful, he has lived for centuries in the Himalayas, bestowing a constant blessing on the world. His mission has been to assist prophets in carrying out their special dispensations. Many titles signifying his exalted spiritual stature have been given to him, but the *mahavatar* has generally adopted the simple name of Babaji, from the Sanskrit *baba,* "father," and the suffix *ji,* denoting respect. More information about his life and spiritual mission is given in *Autobiography of a Yogi.* See *avatar.*

Mantra Yoga. Divine communion attained through devotional, concentrated repetition of root-word sounds that have a spiritually beneficial vibratory potency. See *Yoga.*

master. One who has achieved self-mastery. Paramahansa Yogananda has pointed out that "the distinguishing qualifications of a master are not physical but spiritual....Proof that one is a master is supplied only by the ability to enter at will the breathless state *(sabikalpa samadhi)* and by the attainment of immutable bliss *(nirbikalpa samadhi)*." See *samadhi.*

Paramahansaji further states: "All scriptures proclaim that the Lord created man in His omnipotent image. Control over the universe appears to be supernatural, but in truth such power is inherent and natural in everyone who attains 'right remembrance' of his divine origin. Men of God-realization ... are devoid of the ego-principle *(ahankara)* and its uprisings of personal desires; the actions of true masters are in effortless conformity with *rita,* natural righteousness. In Emerson's words, 'all great ones become "not virtuous, but Virtue; then is the end of the creation answered, and God is well pleased."'"

maya. The delusory power inherent in the structure of creation, by which the One appears as many. *Maya* is the principle of relativity, inversion, contrast, duality, oppositional states; the "Satan" (lit., in Hebrew, "the adversary") of the Old Testament prophets; and the "devil" whom Christ described picturesquely as a "murderer" and a "liar," because "there is no truth in him" (John 8:44).

Paramahansa Yogananda wrote:

"The Sanskrit word *maya* means 'the measurer'; it is the magical power in creation by which limitations and divisions are apparently present in the Immeasurable and Inseparable. *Maya* is Nature herself—the phenomenal worlds, ever in transitional flux as antithesis to Divine Immutability.

"In God's plan and play *(lila),* the sole function of Satan or *maya* is to attempt to divert man from Spirit to matter, from Reality to unreality. 'The devil sinneth from the beginning. For this purpose the Son of God was manifested, that he might destroy the works of the devil' (I John 3:8). That is, the manifestation of Christ Consciousness, within man's own being, effortlessly destroys the illusions or 'works of the devil.'

"*Maya* is the veil of transitoriness in Nature, the ceaseless becoming of creation; the veil that each man must lift in order to see behind it the Creator, the changeless Immutable, eternal Reality."

meditation. Generally, interiorized concentration with the objective of perceiving God. True meditation, *dhyana,* is conscious realization of God through intuitive perception. It is achieved only after the devotee has attained that fixed concentration whereby he disconnects his attention from the senses and is completely undisturbed by sensory impressions from the outer world. *Dhyana* is the seventh step of Patanjali's Eightfold Path of Yoga, the eighth step being *samadhi,* communion, oneness with God. See *Patanjali.*

medulla. The principal point of entry of life force *(prana)* into the body; seat of the sixth cerebrospinal center, whose function is to receive and direct the incoming flow of cosmic energy. The life force is stored in the seventh center *(sahasrara)* in the topmost part of the brain. From that reservoir it is distributed throughout the body. The subtle center at the medulla is the main switch that controls the entrance, storage, and distribution of the life force.

Mt. Washington. Site of, and, by extension, a frequently used name for the Mother Center and international headquarters of Self-Realization Fellowship in Los Angeles. The 12½-acre estate was acquired in 1925 by Paramahansa Yogananda. He made it a training center for the Self-Realization monastic order, and the administrative center for disseminating worldwide the ancient science of *Kriya Yoga.*

paramahansa. A spiritual title signifying a master *(q.v.).* It may be conferred only by a true guru on a qualified disciple. *Paramahansa* literally means "supreme swan." In the Hindu scriptures, the *hansa* or swan symbolizes spiritual discrimination. Swami Sri Yukteswar bestowed the title on his beloved disciple Yogananda in 1935.

paramguru. Literally, "supreme guru" or "great guru"; the guru of one's guru. To Self-Realizationists (disciples of Paramahansa Yogananda), *paramguru* refers to Sri Yukteswar. To Paramahansaji, it meant Lahiri Mahasaya. Mahavatar Babaji is Paramahansaji's *param-paramguru.*

Patanjali. Ancient exponent of Yoga, whose *Yoga Sutras* outline the principles of the yogic path, dividing it into eight steps: (1) moral proscriptions *(yama),* (2) right observances *(niyama),* (3) meditation posture *(asana),* (4) life-force control *(pranayama),* (5) interiorization of the mind *(pratyahara),* (6) concentration *(dharana),* (7) meditation *(dhyana),* (8) union with God *(samadhi).*

prana. Sparks of intelligent finer-than-atomic energy that constitute life, collectively referred to in Hindu scriptural treatises as *prana,*

which Paramahansa Yogananda has translated as "lifetrons." In
essence, condensed thoughts of God; substance of the astral world
(q.v.) and life principle of the physical cosmos. In the physical
world, there are two kinds of *prana:* (1)the cosmic vibratory energy
that is omnipresent in the universe, structuring and sustaining all
things; (2) the specific *prana* or energy that pervades and sustains
each human body through five currents or functions. *Pran* current
performs the function of crystallization; *Vyan* current, circulation;
Saman current, assimilation; *Udan* current, metabolism; and *Apan*
current, elimination.

pranam.   A form of greeting in India. The hands are pressed, palms
together, with the base of the hands at the heart and the fingertips
touching the forehead. This gesture is actually a modification of the
pranam, literally "complete salutation," from the Sanskrit root
nam, "to salute or bow down," and the prefix *pra,* "completely." A
pranam salutation is the general mode of greeting in India. Before
renunciants and other persons held in high spiritual regard, it may
be accompanied by the spoken word, *"Pranam."*

pranayama.   Conscious control of *prana* (the creative vibration or
energy that activates and sustains life in the body). The yoga science
of *pranayama* is the direct way to consciously disconnect the mind
from the life functions and sensory perceptions that tie man to
body-consciousness. *Pranayama* thus frees man's consciousness to
commune with God. All scientific techniques that bring about
union of soul and Spirit may be classified as yoga, and *pranayama* is
the greatest yogic method for attaining this divine union.

Raja Yoga.   The "royal" or highest path to God-union. It teaches
scientific meditation *(q.v.)* as the ultimate means for realizing God,
and includes the highest essentials from all other forms of Yoga. The
Self-Realization Fellowship *Raja Yoga* teachings outline a way of life
leading to perfect unfoldment in body, mind, and soul, based on the
foundation of *Kriya Yoga (q.v.)* meditation. See *Yoga.*

Rajarsi Janakananda (James J. Lynn).   Beloved disciple of Parama-
hansa Yogananda, and first successor to him as president and spiri-
tual head of Self-Realization Fellowship/Yogoda Satsanga Society of
India until his passing on February 20, 1955. Mr. Lynn first received
Kriya Yoga initiation from Paramahansaji in 1932; his spiritual
advancement was so swift that the Guru lovingly referred to him as
"Saint Lynn," until bestowing on him the monastic title of Rajarsi
Janakananda in 1951.

Ranchi school.   Yogoda Satsanga Vidyalaya, founded by Paramahansa
Yogananda in 1918 when the Maharaja of Kasimbazar gave his sum-

mer palace and twenty-five acres of land in Ranchi, Bihar, for use as a boys' school. The property was permanently acquired while Paramahansaji was in India in 1935–36. More than two thousand children now attend Yogoda schools at Ranchi, from nursery school through college. See *Yogoda Satsanga Society of India.*

reincarnation.   The doctrine, set forth in the Hindu scriptures, that human beings, entangled in a web of unfulfilled material desires, are forced to return again and again to earth until they consciously regain their true status as sons of God: "Him that overcometh will I make a pillar in the temple of my God, and he shall go no more out" (Revelation 3:12).

The early Christian Church accepted the principle of reincarnation, which was expounded by the Gnostics and by numerous Church fathers, including Clement of Alexandria, Origen, and Saint Jerome. The doctrine was first declared a heresy in A.D. 553 by the Second Council of Constantinople. Today many Western thinkers are beginning to adopt the concept of the law of karma (q.v.) and reincarnation, seeing in it a grand and reassuring explanation of life's seeming inequities.

rishis.   Seers, exalted beings who manifest divine wisdom; especially, the illumined sages of ancient India to whom the Vedas were intuitively revealed.

sadhana.   Path of spiritual discipline. The specific instruction and meditation practices prescribed by the guru for his disciples, who by faithfully following them ultimately realize God.

samadhi.   The highest step on the Eightfold Path of Yoga, as outlined by the sage Patanjali *(q.v.)*. *Samadhi* is attained when the meditator, the process of meditation (by which the mind is withdrawn from the senses by interiorization), and the object of meditation (God) become One. Paramahansa Yogananda has explained that "in the initial states of God-communion *(sabikalpa samadhi)* the devotee's consciousness merges in the Cosmic Spirit; his life force is withdrawn from the body, which appears 'dead,' or motionless and rigid. The yogi is fully aware of his bodily condition of suspended animation. As he progresses to higher spiritual states *(nirbikalpa samadhi)*, however, he communes with God without bodily fixation; and in his ordinary waking consciousness, even in the midst of exacting worldly duties." Both states are characterized by oneness with the ever new bliss of Spirit, but the *nirbikalpa* state is experienced by only the most highly advanced masters.

Sanatan Dharma.   Literally, "eternal religion." The name given to the body of Vedic teachings that came to be called Hinduism after the

Greeks designated the people on the banks of the river Indus as *Indoos*, or *Hindus*. See *dharma*.

Satan.   Literally, in Hebrew, "the adversary." Satan is the conscious and independent universal force that keeps everything and everybody deluded with the unspiritual consciousness of finiteness and separateness from God. To accomplish this, Satan uses the weapons of *maya* (cosmic delusion) and *avidya* (individual delusion, ignorance). See *maya*.

Sat-Tat-Aum.   *Sat*, Truth, the Absolute, Bliss; *Tat*, universal intelligence or consciousness; *Aum*, cosmic intelligent creative vibration, word-symbol for God. See *Aum* and *Trinity*.

Self.   Capitalized to denote the *atman* or soul, as distinguished from the ordinary self, which is the personality or ego. The Self is individualized Spirit, whose nature is ever-existing, ever-conscious, ever-new joy. Experience of these divine qualities of the soul's nature is achieved through meditation.

Self-realization.   Paramahansa Yogananda has defined Self-realization as "the knowing—in body, mind, and soul—that we are one with the omnipresence of God; that we do not have to pray that it come to us, that we are not merely near it at all times, but that God's omnipresence is our omnipresence; that we are just as much a part of Him now as we ever will be. All we have to do is improve our knowing."

Self-Realization Fellowship.   The society founded by Paramahansa Yogananda in America in 1920 (and as Yogoda Satsanga Society of India in 1917) for disseminating worldwide, for the aid and benefit of humanity, the spiritual principles and meditation techniques of *Kriya Yoga (q.v.)*. The international headquarters, the Mother Center, is in Los Angeles, California. Paramahansa Yogananda has explained the meaning of the organization's name in this way: "Self-Realization Fellowship signifies fellowship with God through Self-realization, and friendship with all truth-seeking souls." See also "Aims and Ideals of Self-Realization Fellowship," page 449.

Self-Realization Fellowship Lessons.   The teachings of Paramahansa Yogananda, sent to students throughout the world in a series of lessons, available to all earnest truth seekers. These lessons contain the yoga meditation techniques taught by Paramahansa Yogananda, including, for those who qualify, *Kriya Yoga (q.v.)*.

Self-Realization Magazine.   A quarterly journal published by Self-Realization Fellowship, featuring the talks and writings of Paramahansa Yogananda; and containing other spiritual, practical, and informative articles of current interest and lasting value. *Satsangas* (informal spiritual talks) of Sri Daya Mata, president of Self-Realization Fellowship, are also a regular feature.

Shankara, Swami. Sometimes referred to as Adi ("the first") Shankaracharya (Shankara + *acharya*, "teacher"); India's most illustrious philosopher. His date is uncertain; many scholars assign him to the ninth century. He expounded God not as a negative abstraction, but as positive, eternal, omnipresent, ever new Bliss. Shankara reorganized the ancient Swami Order, and founded four great *maths* (monastic centers of spiritual education), whose leaders in apostolic succession bear the title of Jagadguru Sri Shankaracharya. The meaning of *Jagadguru* is "world teacher."

siddha. Literally, "one who is successful." One who has attained Self-realization.

soul. Individualized Spirit. The soul is the true and immortal nature of man, and of all living forms of life; it is cloaked only temporarily in the garments of causal, astral, and physical bodies. The nature of the soul is Spirit: ever-existing, ever-conscious, ever-new Joy.

spiritual eye. The single eye of intuition and omnipresent perception at the Christ *(Kutastha)* center *(ajna chakra)* between the eyebrows. The deeply meditating devotee beholds the spiritual eye as a ring of golden light encircling a sphere of opalescent blue, and at the center, a pentagonal white star. Microcosmically, these forms and colors epitomize, respectively, the vibratory realm of creation (Cosmic Nature, Holy Ghost); the Son or intelligence of God in creation (Christ Consciousness); and the vibrationless Spirit beyond all creation (God the Father).

The spiritual eye is the entryway into the ultimate states of divine consciousness. In deep meditation, as the devotee's consciousness penetrates the spiritual eye, into the three realms epitomized therein, he experiences successively the following states: superconsciousness or the ever new joy of soul-realization, and oneness with God as *Aum (q.v.)* or Holy Ghost; Christ consciousness, oneness with the universal intelligence of God in all creation; and cosmic consciousness, unity with the omnipresence of God that is beyond as well as within vibratory manifestation. See also *consciousness, states of; superconsciousness; Christ Consciousness.*

Explaining a passage from Ezekiel (43:1–2), Paramahansa Yogananda has written: "Through the divine eye in the forehead, ('the east'), the yogi sails his consciousness into omnipresence, hearing the word or *Aum*, the divine sound of 'many waters': the vibrations of light that constitute the sole reality of creation." In Ezekiel's words: "Afterwards he brought me to the gate, even the gate that looketh towards the east; and behold, the glory of the God of Israel came from the way of the east; and his voice was like the noise of many waters; and the earth shined with his glory."

Jesus also spoke of the spiritual eye: "When thine eye is single, thy whole body also is full of light.... Take heed therefore that the light which is in thee be not darkness" (Luke 11:34–35).

Sri. A title of respect. When used before the name of a religious person, it means "holy" or "revered."

Sri Yukteswar, Swami. Swami Sri Yukteswar Giri (1855–1936), India's *Jnanavatar*, "Incarnation of Wisdom"; guru of Paramahansa Yogananda, and *paramguru* of Self-Realization Fellowship *Kriyaban* members. Sri Yukteswarji was a disciple of Lahiri Mahasaya. At the behest of Lahiri Mahasaya's guru, Mahavatar Babaji, he wrote *The Holy Science*, a treatise on the underlying unity of Christian and Hindu scriptures, and trained Paramahansa Yogananda for his spiritual world-mission: the dissemination of *Kriya Yoga (q.v.)*. Paramahansaji has lovingly described Sri Yukteswarji's life in *Autobiography of a Yogi*.

St. Lynn (James J. Lynn). See *Rajarsi Janakananda*.

superconscious mind. The all-knowing power of the soul that perceives truth directly; intuition.

superconsciousness. The pure, intuitive, all-seeing, ever-blissful consciousness of the soul. Sometimes used generally to refer to all the various states of *samadhi (q.v.)* experienced in meditation, but specifically the first state of *samadhi*, wherein one drops ego-consciousness and realizes his self as soul, made in the image of God. Thence follow the higher states of realization: Christ consciousness and cosmic consciousness *(q.v.)*.

swami. A member of India's most ancient monastic order, reorganized in the ninth century by Swami Shankara *(q.v.)*. A swami takes formal vows of celibacy and renunciation of worldly ties and ambitions; he devotes himself to meditation and other spiritual practices, and to service to humanity. There are ten classificatory titles of the venerable Swami Order, as *Giri, Puri, Bharati, Tirtha, Saraswati,* and others. Swami Sri Yukteswar *(q.v.)* and Paramahansa Yogananda belonged to the *Giri* ("mountain") branch.

The Sanskrit word *swami* means "he who is one with the Self *(Swa)*."

Trinity. When Spirit manifests creation, It becomes the Trinity: Father, Son, Holy Ghost, or *Sat, Tat, Aum.* The Father *(Sat)* is God as the Creator existing beyond creation. The Son *(Tat)* is God's omnipresent intelligence existing in creation. The Holy Ghost